Comparative
Criminology

Comparative Criminology

Brunon Holyst
Institute of Crime Problems
Warsaw

LexingtonBooks
D.C. Heath and Company
Lexington, Massachusetts
Toronto

Library of Congress Cataloging in Publication Data

Hołyst, Brunon.
    Comparative criminology.

    Based on the author's Kryminologia na świecie.
    Bibliography: p.
    Includes index.
    1. Crime and criminals.   2. Crime and criminals--
Research.   I. Holyst, Brunon. Kryminologia na
świecie. II. Title.
HV6025.H635   364   81-47713
ISBN 0-669-04726-0   AACR2

Published similtaneously in Canada

Printed in the United States of America

International Standard Book Number: 0-669-04726-0

Library of Congress Catalog Card Number: 81-47713

Contents

Foreword

Brunon Hołyst's book appears at a very critical moment in the evolution of criminology as a science and as a tool of social engineering: in many countries it is the moment of disenchantment and even rejection of scientific research coupled with a temptation to return to the dogmatic responses to crime of an earlier century. And this occurs precisely at the moment when the developing countries of the world have begun to appreciate the cost and perniciousness of criminality and are beginning to turn to scientific criminology for answers: How did we reach this crisis of the developed world and how can we overcome it?

It was, as Hołyst points out, in the years following the devastations of World War II that crime—almost inevitably—increased in many parts of the world, and that the generation of survivors, in the spirit of rebuilding the world, deemed no task too big to be tackled with determination and scientific cunning. Criminological research based largely on the social sciences—but also extending to other disciplines, such as psychology, economics, public administration, and law—experienced a phenomenal growth in many developed countries of the northern belt of the old and new world. Research into the causes of criminality and the effectiveness of the strategies of criminal justice was undertaken and the optimism of the researchers envisaged a world in which, if socioeconomic planning could not solve the crime problem, criminology would.

Yet, after a generation of criminological research, planning, and implementation of research-based policies, the results remained spotty, and a certain disillusionment set in. Optimism was replaced by skepticism as evaluation research began to demonstrate the failure of many crime-prevention programs and, indeed, as evaluation research indicated that the many research methodologies themselves were imperfect and defective. Yet, was not evaluation research subject to the same criticism of imperfection as the research being evaluated by it? It becomes readily apparent that cynicism and nihilism would enter the world of criminology at this point. "Nothing works" became the slogan of the day, and the temptation became great to jettison the optimistic efforts at social engineering which had become the hallmark of the scientific age in criminology, and to return to the retributism of the nineteenth century. Yet, this retributism is not far removed from the harshness and vindictiveness of the eighteenth century (however enlightened it may have been in comparison with still earlier times). And thus we are witnessing, in various parts of the world, an antiscientific and, implicitly, antihumanitarian spirit in criminology, the most visible result of which is the reintroduction of fixed and severe punishments in various penal codes.

In fairness, however, we should note that many scientists in many countries are rejecting such defeatist attitudes and maintaining their spirit of optimism in both nation building and in crime prevention. And why should they not? Positive examples in crime prevention abound. Some of the Middle Eastern countries were able to jump from the biblical age to the jet age in a single generation and still keep their crime rates low. So did highly industrialized Japan, so did some of the socialist countries and indeed, so did countries in all parts of the world. Something does work in the art and practice of crime prevention, whether conceived as part of an overall socioeconomic national planning effort, or as a sectoral effort by itself. Let scientific criminology investigate the criminological successes of this world, so that these become known to all countries, so that no country need repeat the costly mistakes made elsewhere. Let the criminology of optimism and humanism return; let there be a constant effort on the part of all institutions and strategies of criminology to alleviate the expense and suffering which crime all too frequently imposes. I express the wish that Brunon Hołyst's work will make a major contribution toward this end.

G.O.W. Mueller
School of Criminal Justice, Rutgers—The State University, and former chief, United Nations Crime Prevention and Criminal Justice Branch

Preface

Since World War II nearly all countries have experienced increases of crime and other phenomena falling within the sphere of social pathology. Criminality has taken on new, ever more vicious and complicated forms. Suppressing it, particularly by preventing offenses, has become one of the foremost tasks of states and societies.

A precondition for the success of this struggle is the conduct of scientific research on crime and on the means of its suppression. The scientific-technical revolution assigned a new role to empirical studies, the results of which find an application in every walk of life, meeting the daily requirements of organization, management, production, and forecasting. Research is also important for the suppression of social pathology phenomena. There is increasing awareness that evolving a prevention program, the aim of every realistic concept of crime suppression, has to be preceded by detailed acquaintance with the forms, causes, and effects of criminal phenomena; in turn, this acquaintance is the sum of empirical findings concerning the issues of interest.

Every state attaches considerable social status to criminological studies. Irrespective of the traditional efforts by the academic communities, we now have institutes and organizations formed for the purpose of carrying out studies and of inspiring other institutions to do research in this field. Many such bodies operate in highly industrialized countries, where crime has become a serious problem. In the socialist states criminology initially did find it difficult to make headway, though by now the scientific study of crime has come into its own and is recognized in those states as being highly valuable. At present there is not a single state which does not carry out a study to determine the causes of crime prevailing in that state or part of the world and to evolve ways of suppressing it. Taking up the problems of crime prevention and suppression through the United Nations provides a new, global dimension to the efforts of individual countries. This is in part due to the fact that criminality itself often is transitional in character. Narcotics traffic, thefts of works of art, terrorist attacks—all represent the type of crime that transcends national borders. The consequences of criminal activity often concern a number of countries at once, making international cooperation to combat crime feasible.

It has become extremely vital to follow the achievements of criminology throughout the world and to apply results where they may be useful in the context of one's own country. Knowledge of the situation and developments in criminology worldwide is necessary for lecturers on criminology-related disciplines, such as law, psychology, psychiatry, education, sociology, for students of those disciplines, not to mention the practitioners—judges, attorneys, and probation personnel.

Comparative Criminology is a synthetic study presenting the theoretical aspects of criminology (definition, scope, relationship to other disciplines, evaluation of the interpretations made of the etiology of criminal phenomena, research methodology) as well as the practical aspects (evaluation of contemporary crime, new perspectives in crime prevention). The book also discusses the scientific and training activities of criminological centers in various countries and the international organizations concerned with studying crime.

Review and evaluation of the progress achieved by this discipline leads to the conclusion that at present criminology, viewed as a tool of social engineering, is experiencing a fundamental crisis. The outcome of criminological research should find broader practical application in planning and implementing social policy.

The data, information, and materials for this book were obtained by the author through direct contacts with research centers in various countries and through visits made to Poland by criminologists from other countries. Other sources included publications and the results of numerous international congresses, symposia, and other meetings, articles in Polish and foreign professional periodicals concerning the state of research in various countries, and also the sizable collection of materials obtained through the Institute of Crime Problems, Warsaw, through its international contacts.

The available information has not always been entirely satisfactory, as there are gaps in the presentation of research conducted in various countries and regions and gaps in data series. Some of the information may have lost its validity, as data of this type has to be updated constantly; also, new research centers continually arise. Despite these shortcomings, the book provides a general view of the scientific research on crime throughout the world and may prove useful to anyone interested in the issues connected with crime suppression and prevention and with problems of modern criminological theories.

This book is not a literal translation of *Kryminologia na świecie* [Criminology in the world], published in Polish in 1979 by State Scientific Publishers, Warsaw.

The numerous changes which have been introduced also justify the change of title to *Comparative Criminology*. In this edition I devote considerable attention to the theoretical aspects of criminology, also pointing out the specific features of the scope and methods of criminological research in the various parts of the world and in specific countries. The numerous bibliographical notes (largely updated) enable the reader to reach the source materials, in order to delve deeper into any specific issue. More elaborate information is provided in the chapter on criminological research centers in the socialist countries. The issue of crime and criminological research in the socialist countries has become a subject of considerable social and scientific interest in other countries.

The information provided in this volume can be supplemented by readers through following the latest developments in publishing on criminology and associated disciplines.

It is my intention to acquaint the readers of this volume with the state of and trends in criminological research in various countries. The book presents a criminological geography, the knowledge of which is an invaluable aid in drafting programs of preventing and suppressing criminality.

I dedicate this volume to the theoreticians and practitioners who, motivated by the noble ideal of combating social and individual deviations, spare no effort to elevate the quality of life by liberating man from the threat of becoming a victim or an offender.

Acknowledgments

While this volume is the product of one author, the opportunity for its publication and the final form of the book became possible through the efforts of many people of good will who assisted me in various ways. It is my pleasure and honor to thank them most sincerely for their invaluable assistance.

First of all I wish to express my gratitude for the opportunity of publishing this book in English through the renowned house of Lexington Books. For an author writing in Polish this is a major opportunity to have his views presented to a criminological audience outside his native language group. This opportunity came through the good offices of Mr. Mike McCarroll, vice-president and general manager of Lexington Books. I am greatly indebted to him personally.

The world-renowned scholar, Professor G.O.W. Mueller, former chief of the Crime Prevention and Criminal Justice Branch, United Nations, was kind enough to write a foreword to my book, presenting a synthetic picture of criminology as a discipline and as a tool of social engineering. I feel greatly honored by this distinction and offer him my warmest thanks.

The idea of writing this book has met with a favorable reception and support from Professor Denis Szabo, president of the International Society of Criminology and director of the International Center for Comparative Criminology, Montreal; and from Ms. Alice Parizeau, for many years the secretary general of the Center; and further from Professor Ludwik Kos-Rabcewicz-Zubkowski, Department of Criminology, University of Ottawa.

The task of writing the review for the publisher was taken up by Ms. Irene Melup, an outstanding representative of the Crime Prevention and Criminal Justice Branch, United Nations. I owe her a very special debt of gratitude for her valuable comments and a highly positive opinion.

I also wish to express my appreciation to Ms. Marjorie A. Glazer and Ms. Susan J.S. Lasser of Lexington Books for their contribution to this work.

I am much obliged to Mr. Zygmunt Gebethner of the Polish Scientific Publishers, whose friendly efforts supported me in preparing the English version of this book.

To my friends, Mr. Andrzej Konopka, Mr. Bronisław Macieński and Mr. Wojciech Wójcik, especially warm thanks for their valuable assistance in overcoming technical problems.

Last, to my son Robert, a student at the University of Warsaw, my gratitude for emotional involvement at every stage of preparation of this book, and particularly for his good academic record, which provided me with the right atmosphere at home in preparing this book.

1 The Notion and Scope of Criminology

The subject and place of criminology among other disciplines lack a uniform definition; those writing on the subject vary in their definitions of scope and tasks. Also, there is no agreement as to whether criminology is self-standing, or part of a wider discipline, particularly of law, sociology, psychology, or psychiatry. According to William Bonger, the term *criminology* was first used in 1879 by a physician—the French anthropologist P. Topinard. Other sources indicate that the Italian lawyer Raffaele Garofalo, one of the founders of the anthropological school of penal law used this term in his *Criminologia*, published in 1885.[1]

Views questioning the autonomy of criminology as a discipline were still held as late as the 1950s. Such opinions are no longer expressed, though wide disparities continue as to the subject and scope of criminology.

The beginnings of criminology go back to the eighteenth century; to *Dei Delitti e delle Pene*, published by Cesare Beccaria in 1764, and to John Howard's 1777 study of the state of prisons in England and Wales. Presenting in general outline a theory of the causes of criminality, these works noted the need for a humanitarian penal policy and a reform of the penal system. Similar views were to be found in the philosophies of other Renaissance and Enlightenment thinkers.

Yet it was not until the studies carried out by Cesare Lombroso and his disciples Enrico Ferri and Raffaele Garofalo that criminology advanced from the speculative to the scientific stage.[2] Controversies concerning the definition and scope of criminology were particularly marked during the 1950s and 1960s.[3]

The various views as to the notion and scope of criminology can be summarized as belonging to five main schools. The first does not recognize criminology as an autonomous discipline. For instance, in 1911 Edmund Krzymuski held that "the discipline of penal law can be viewed twofold: broadly or more narrowly. *Sensu largo* it encompasses entire criminology, i.e. the system of theoretical research on all issues connected with the offense and penalty and not just on those concerned with the legal relationship developing between the penalising state authority and the offenders. *Sensu stricto* it limits itself exclusively to examining the latter type of issues, and is therefore only the science of legal principles and provisions governing state repressive activities directed against offenders".[4]

1

During the 1950s in Poland there was also a tendency to deny the autonomy of criminology as a discipline. The main accent at the time was on penal law as such. At present such views are of only historical significance.

The second treats criminology as a discipline concerned with offenses in the widest sense, encompassing the causes of criminality, methods of suppressing it, issues of criminal policy, penology, and finally substantive and adjective penal law.

This idea came into its own just at the turn of the century. One of criminology's pioneers, Austrian lawyer Hans Gross (1847–1915), in the introduction to the fourth edition of his *Manual for an Examining Magistrate* (1904), stated that criminology encompasses among other things criminalistic anthropology (in turn divided into criminalistic somatology and objective criminalistic psychology), criminalistic sociology, divided into statistics and social psychology, as well as other disciplines (including criminalistics and subjective criminalistic psychology). To this one should add other disciplines such as criminal policy, penology, and substantive and adjective penal law.[5]

Such a division, difficult to accept in view of its significant methodological errors, had a considerable impact on shaping later criminological ideas even though Gross did not attach much importance to his own classification.

The idea advanced by Gross of pooling all "supplementary disciplines of penal law including the investigative discipline and penology" into a homogenous system of criminology has been reflected by authors in the second half of the twentieth century. For instance, Ernst Seelig, one of Gross's students, divided criminology into two main parts: the study of the phenomenon of offense and the study of combating criminality.[6]

In the first part he included all disciplines concerned with the phenomenon and causes of offenses, that is criminal phenomenology, criminal etiology, criminal biology, and criminal sociology.

The second part covers mainly those fields which are known as criminalistics, plus penology and penitentiaristics.

This classification can be criticized, if only because Seelig erroneously treats criminalistic biology and sociology as separate parts of criminology, next to criminal etiology. In this context it is difficult to determine the coverage of criminal etiology. Further, it would be an error to include criminalistics in criminology, since these sectors are seen as autonomous disciplines.

Various authors have modified Gross's initial ideas. For instance, within criminology, Olof Kinberg distinguished criminal etiology, preventive activities, and offense therapy along with penal policy. Under this approach he included substantive and adjective penal law as part of therapy.[7] Still, the idea of therapy taken straight from medical science cannot explain the complicated functions of the penal law norms system. Another striking feature of this division is the diminished role of penal law which, after all, defines the act that constitutes an offense, that is, defines the subject of criminological studies. The broad interpretation of the scope of criminology is mirrored even in the titles of journals devoted mainly to criminology-related subjects.[8]

The third school, developed by Franz von Liszt (1851–1919), the foremost representative of the sociological direction of penal law, considered criminology as a discipline concerned with the phenomena and causes of criminality, next to criminalistics, penal law, and penal policy within the system of penal law disciplines (gesamte Strafrechtswissenschaft).

In one of his lectures in 1899 Liszt formulated the three prime tasks of penal law disciplines:

1. training personnel for practical crime detection:
   a. in the field of penal law and criminal proceedings (penal law disciplines in the narrow sense);
   b. in practical application of criminalistics;
2. explaining the causes:
   a. of an offense (criminology);
   b. of the penalty (penology);
3. perfecting legislation for better combating criminality.[9]

The views advanced by von Liszt[10] were criticized by Seelig who stressed that pooling penal law disciplines into a single system, encompassing, among other things, both criminology and penal law, could not be upheld from the point of view of theory.[11]

These two schools were similar in their joint treatment of criminology and criminalistics, undoubtedly for historical reasons. Both disciplines, born of the practical need to find out about the causes of the ominous social phenomenon of criminality and to develop effective methods of combating it, came into being almost simultaneously. In the eighteenth century attention was turned to the phenomenon of crime, which generated particular interest in the nineteenth century.

At their inception, neither criminology nor criminalistics had clearly defined scopes for research. These circumstances later reflected heavily on the interrelationship of criminology and criminalistics.

The fourth school is an expression of contemporary tendencies in the development of criminological studies. It approaches criminology jointly with penitentiary issues. These tendencies are particularly marked in the United States.

As defined by Thorsten Sellin in his introduction to a book by Stephan Hurwitz, criminology is understood as the study of offenders and their treatment. The draft statute on the execution of a prison sentence in the Federal Republic of Germany provides for the establishment of a permanent body within the prison warden's office for the purpose of carrying out criminological research (die Enrichtung eines kriminologischen Dienstes). Its task was to carry out continuous research in penitentiaries and analysis of experience gained in the field of prison sentence execution. The draft further suggested the need for cooperation between that body and research bodies in other fields. The statute on execution of imprisonment which came into force on January 1, 1977 made provision for such a research unit under Par. 166 of the statute.[12]

U.S. criminology is a reflection of general American sociological thinking, with a positivist orientation as the most characteristic feature of that discipline.[13] This is evident even from the arrangement and contents of criminology manuals. For instance, Edwin Sutherland devotes a single chapter to the offense, twelve chapters to the offender and sixteen to penology. T. S. Elliot takes three chapters to discuss issues of offenses, eleven to discuss offenders, fifteen to discuss penology. H. E. Barnes and Negly Teeters deal with offenses in five chapters and with offenders in eight chapters, devoting twenty-one chapters to penological issues. R. Cavan concentrates on the issue of offenses in one chapter, offenders in thirteen and penology in twelve. Walter Reckless devotes less than one chapter to offenses, thirteen to offenders and seven to penology.

Some American criminologists take an even broader approach to the subject, including other types of behavior—deviations from the norm rather than offenses—such as prostitution, homosexualism, mental illness, neurosis, or even issues connected with the process of aging. Under this recently popular approach the areas of the criminology and the sociology of deviant behaviors largely overlap and are frequently used interchangeably.

According to Sutherland and D. Cressey, criminology "is the body of knowledge regarding crime as a social phenomenon. It includes within its scope the processes of making laws, of breaking laws, and of reacting toward the breaking of laws."[14] They see this discipline as having three sections:

sociology of law studying the conditions for formulation of penal statutes;

criminal etiology studying the causes of criminality, and

penology—system of penalties connected with suppression of crime.

C. Shaw, H. McKay, E. Burgess, Thorsten Sellin, Edwin Sutherland, Walter Reckless and K. Menninger pioneered the criminological theories that developed in the United States between 1930 and 1960.

The autonomous character of criminology, according to Sellin, is determined by the objective toward which it aims: to explain offensive behavior and the social reaction to it, and to determine the preventive measures required.[15] Criminology, therefore, combines the following four basic disciplines:

psychopathology and psychiatry, sciences applying biological, neurological, psychological, and pathology studies of the offender's personality;

sociology of criminality which deals with the social features of the offender, the social motivations of the act and the genesis of social control mechanisms;

geography or ecology of criminality;

statistics of criminality, including data concerning justice administration, police, penitentiaries.

Clarence R. Jeffery believes that American criminologists devote insufficient attention to studying issues of law and society, and the offenses themselves. He claims that the problem "What is a crime?" historically and logically precedes the stage of studying the offender.

The fifth school approaches criminology narrowly as the study of the causes and manifestations of criminality. It is the approach typical of the European tradition and is currently the predominant direction in the socialist countries. For instance, a manual published in the German Democratic Republic stresses that the problem of the etiology of criminality is the prime sphere of criminological interest.[16]

Leszek Lernell distinguishes between strict and wide definitions of criminology. He considers criminology in the strict sense the "learning about the genetic factor of an offense." Criminology in the wide sense is defined as "learning about the genetic factor of an offense (criminal etiology), learning about the various features and manifestations of criminal acts (criminal phenomenology), and learning about the criminalistic structure and dynamics."[17] This distinction seems unfounded, as it artificially separates questions of etiology and symptomatology which constitute an integral subject of criminological research. The definition further omits problems of preventing criminality, which are also an integral part of the discipline.

This raises the question, which is of more than hypothetical importance, of the scope of criminological studies. The etiologic approach would appear to favor the necessity of having criminological studies encompass the various negative social phenomena which are not recognized as offenses, but which are obviously crime-conducive. One could mention prostitution, drug abuse, dysfunctioning of entire social, economic, and political systems or of individual state institutions, pathology of family and upbringing, and the like.

The need for such a broad scope for criminology further stems from the changeability in the character of offensive behavior and in other pathological types of behavior. Decriminalizing and depenalizing can be applied only to current offenses, while in other cases certain phenomena of social pathology can be classified as offensive behavior.

An interesting presentation of problems in contemporary criminology has ben made by Manuel Lopez-Rey. It starts with the distinction between conventional offenses (against persons, private property, morality, and public order) and unconventional offenses (committed under cover of official or semiofficial positions; against international law and usage; as the sequel to patriotic, political, ideological, revolutionary, and even fanatical religious action; by "intelligence services"; economic and financial frauds; criminal corruption at high levels; illicit trade and exploitation of migrant labor; discriminatory practices; genocide; misrepresentation of products; illicit traffic in persons and drugs). Lopez-Rey states that from the outset criminology has dealt almost exclusively with conventional offenses, though they are only one aspect of the sociopolitical phenomenon of criminality. He is of the opinion that crime is always conditioned by power, development, inequality, human nature, and penal systems. Hence, crime cannot be suppressed but can be decreased by limiting the conditioning factors to a reasonable minimum. Criminology can contribute to it by participating in socioeconomic and political planning. Therefore, criminological curricula should include political science, sociology of law, political sociology, history, human rights theory and practice.[18]

Based on what has been said so far concerning the notion of criminology, I would propose the following definition: *Criminology is a discipline concerned with crime and the offender, with manifestations and causes of criminality and other social pathology phenomena connected with it, and with methods of their elimination.*

Considering the objective of criminology, the prevention of criminality, one can distinguish the following sections of the discipline:

1. *Criminal symptomatology* (phenomenology). This is the section of criminology dealing with with manifest forms of criminality: the dynamics and pattern of criminality, criminalistic geography, ways in which crimes are committed, certain elements of the criminal milieu organization, such as ways of communicating by crime perpetrators, the use of pseudonyms, and the like.

2. *Criminal etiology.* This concentrates on studying the causative factors of criminality; it is a comprehensive and exceptionally important section of criminology. Analysis of causes extends to studies of the offender's personality and is aimed at formulating conclusions concerning the individual factors determining the criminal behavior of the given offender.

The French scholar Jean Pinatel divides criminology into general and clinical, claiming further that it combines several specific disciplines: criminalistic anthropology, criminalistic sociology, criminalistic psychiatry, criminal proceedings, criminalistics, forensic medicine, forensic psychiatry and also the disciplines aimed at preventing criminality such as special education, psychology, penitentiary law, and preventive measures.[19]

With full credit to the practical-service role of clinical criminology it would appear that due to its methods and aims there is no need for establishing an autonomous discipline. After all, the tasks to be performed by clinical criminology fit within the system of existing criminological premises. Problems of clinical criminology can be included as part of criminal etiology and criminological prevention.

The methods applied by clinical criminology are nothing new. Milieu inquiry, general and specialized medical examinations, including neurological or psychiatric, as well as psychological studies, have for years been part and parcel of the classic methods for determining the social factors of the crime and the offender's state of health, along with their significance for the genesis of the act.

The German criminologist Wilhelm Sauer distinguishes theoretical (pure, "reine") and practical (applied, "angewandte") criminology.[20] This distinction is highly artificial.

The field of etiology also covers questions of penal victimology concerning examination of the crime victim and his role in the genesis of the crime. Penal victimology is the newest branch of criminology.[21] For a long time the attention of penal disciplines concentrated on the offense itself (the classic school of penal law) or the person of the offender (the Italian positivist school), while questions connected with the victim were outside the mainstream of interest for both theory and practice. Yet, the structure of crime comprises three prime elements: offender—offense—victim.

Only in the past two decades has attention in the legal literature been turned to the need for studying the victim as a person from the criminological, biological, psychological, and sociological point of view, for organizing an international victimological institute, and for convening international congresses to discuss these issues.[22]

Further, one should point out the criminalistic aspect of examining the victim. The answers obtained in examinations of crime victims are quite significant for proper implementation of penal policy. They also have a great role in the field of criminological and criminalistic prevention.

The object of penal victimology is to carry out detailed studies of the victim's personality in order to better understand the genesis of an offense, to formulate effective principles of prevention, and to create better conditions for detecting crime.

A broader insight into the problems of criminal etiology would require the inclusion of problems concerning the motivational conditions of an offensive act. In this way one would have a comprehensive model of the links constituting a synthesis of the static and dynamic personality features with exogenous factors.

3. *Criminological prevention.*[23] Various authors emphasize that the objective of criminology is to develop the means to prevent criminality. This section of criminology covers a variety of issues connected with the system of education and civic formation, the ideal promoted by culture, the mass media, the effectiveness of sentences, civic self-defense, and so on.

Notes

1. Raffaele Garofalo, *Criminologia* (Naples: 1885). See Criminology, Boston: Little 1914.

2. Hermann Haering, "Der Weg der Kriminologie zur selbständiges Wissenschaft" [The route of criminology to an independent discipline], *Kriminologische Schriftenreihe* 23. 1966

3. Roland Grassberger, "Qu'est-ce que c'est la criminologie?" *Revue de Criminologie et de Police Technique* 1949, no. 1; Manuel López-Rey, "De quelques conceptions fausses dans la criminologie contemporaine" [On certain false concepts in contemporary criminology], *Revue Pénitentiaire et de Droit Pénal* no. 4, 1960.

4. Edmund Krzymuski, "Wykład prawa karnego ze stanowiska nauki i prawa austriackiego" [Lecture on penal law from the point of view of science and Austrian law], Cracow, 1911, p. 77.

5. See Hans Gross, *Handbuch für Untersuchungsrichter als System der Kriminalistik*, 7th ed. [Manual for an examining magistrate as a system of crime detection] (Munich: Hoepler, 1922), p. xiii.

6. See Ernst Seelig, *Lehrbuch der Kriminologie*, 2nd ed. [Textbook of criminology] (Graz: Verlag Jos. A. Kienreich, 1951), p. 11.

7. See Olof Kinberg, *Referat och korreferat til Nordiska Kriminal-stmötat* (Stockholm: 1949), p. 100 (quoted in Stephan Hurwitz, *Criminology* (London: George Allen and Unwin, 1952), p. 14).

8. The most renowned of these publications is *Archiv für Kriminologie* comprising 162 volumes as of December 31, 1979. The first issue of that journal, entitled *Archiv für Kriminal-Antropologie und Kriminalistik* was published in 1898.

9. See Joseph Goldschmidt, "Franz von Liszt," *Archiv für Kriminologie* 1921, no. 2.

10. In order to promote his views von Liszt founded a journal, *Zeitschrift für die gesamte Strafrechtswissenschaft* (78 volumes published by December 31, 1972) which also published articles on criminology.

11. See Ernst Seelig, *Lehrbuch der Kriminologie*, p. 27.

12. "Entwurf eines Gesetzes über den Vollzug der Freiheitsstrafe und der freiheitsentziehenden Massregeln der Besserung und Sicherung—Strafvollzugsgesetz" (St. VollzG) [Draft statute on prison sentence execution and regulations depriving of liberty for betterment and security—penitentiary code]. Wuppertal, 1974, p. 161. "Gesetz über den Vollzug der Freiheitsstrafe und der freiheitsentziehenden Massregeln der Besserung und Sicherung—Strafvollzugsgesetz (St. VollzG) [Statute on prison sentence execution and regulations depriving of liberty for betterment and security—Penitentiary Code], March 16, 1976. "Kriminologische Forschung im Strafvollzug" [Criminological research in penal execution code].

13. See Clarence R. Jeffery, "The Structure of American Criminological Thinking," *Journal of Criminal Law, Criminology and Police Science*, 1956, No. 5.

14. Edwin Sutherland, *Principles of Criminology* (Philadelphia: Lippincott, 1966), p. 1.

15. Quoted in Denis Szabo, *Criminology in the World* (Montreal: Centre International de Criminologie Comparée, 1977).

16. See Erich Buchholtz et al. *Sozialistische Kriminologie* [Socialist criminology] (Berlin: Staatsverlag der DDR, 1971), p. 59.

17. Leszek Lernell, *Zarys kryminologii ogólnej* [Outline of general criminology] (Warsaw: Państwowe Wydawnictwo Naukowe, 1973), pp. 8, 9.

18. Manuel Lopez-Rey, "Criminological Manifesto," *Federal Probation*," September 1975.

19. Jean Pinatel, *La criminologie*, 3rd ed. [Criminology] (Paris: Dalloz, 1975), pp. 3–8.

20. Wilhelm Sauer, *Kriminologie als reine und angewandte Wissenschaft: Ein System der Tatsachenforschung* [Criminology as pure and applied science: A system of facts research] (Berlin: Walter de Gruyter, 1950).

21. Certain penal victimology questions, such as the selection of persons suspected on the basis of alleged relationship or friendship between the perpetrator and the victim are part of criminalistics. For more specific comments on penal victimology see Brunon Hołyst, *Zabójstwo: Studium kryminalistyczne i kryminologiczne* [Homicide: A criminalistic and criminological study] (Warsaw: Ministerstwo Spraw Wewnetrznych, 1970), pp. 71–102.

22. See, for instance, Beniamin Mondelsohn, "La victimologie—science actuelle" [Victimology—current science], *Revue de Droit Pénal et de*

Criminologie 1959, no. 7: Paul Cornil, "Contribution de la 'Victimologie' aux sciences criminologiques" [Contribution of "victimology" to criminological science], *Revue de Droit Pénal et de Criminologie* 1959, no. 7. Other articles on penal victimology were also published in the same issue. Other publications include: Hans von Hentig, *The Criminal and His Victim* (New Haven: Yale University Press, 1948); Fritz R. Paasch, "Grundprobleme der Viktimologie" [Basic problems of victimology], Diss. Münster, 1965; Ezzat A. Fattah, *La victime est-elle coupable?* [The Victim: Is She Guilty?] (Montréal: Les Presses de l'Université, 1971); Hans-Joachim Schneider, *Victimologie: Wissenschaft vom Verbrechensopfer* [Victimology: Science of crime victim] (Tübingen: J. C. B. Mohr (Paul Siebeck) 1975). At the Third International Victimology Symposium in Münster in 1979 Brunon Hołyst submitted a motion to adopt the name "penal victimology," to distinguish this discipline from general victimology which deals with victims of all types of occurences, not just the victims of crime.

23. Leon Radzinowicz has emphasized that issues of prevention constitute an integral part of criminology. See *In Search of Criminology* (London: Heinemann, 1961), p. 168.

2 Criminology: Links with Other Disciplines

Criminality is such a complex social phenomenon that the struggle against it involves a wide range of disciplines. One could cite here the most obvious, namely psychology, sociology, education, medicine, statistics.[1] Still, criminology is a discipline which does not mechanically take over the research methods developed by other disciplines; rather, it creatively adapts such methods to its own requirements. Even further, criminology develops its own methods, such as type-classifying crime forecasting, and it also initiates studies to apply the achievements of various disciplines for deeper understanding of the causes behind criminality, for drafting programs of criminological prevention, and so on. Examples of this include criminological teaching or forensic psychology.

The disciplines to be mentioned here represent a much broader scope than criminology, the latter traditionally being concerned with acts classified by law as offensive.

In keeping with newer trends, the interests of criminological research extend also to certain other negative social phenomena with high criminogenic implications.

For instance, the research range of general psychology extends to questions of the proper course of man's mental processes, their types and classifications, analysis of their structure, elementary processes which can be distinguished within them, and the like.

Developmental psychology deals with the general laws of mental development, the factors determining this development, given phases of development, and so on.

Social psychology concentrates on the processes taking place within human groups, such as the shaping of public opinion and the spread of information within groups.

Physiological psychology studies the conditioning of mental processes by the anatomical-physiological foundations, for example the issue of philogenetic and ontogenetic development of the psyche in connection with the shaping of the nervous system, and the physiological background of various mental processes, such as perception, memory, attention, and emotions.

Psychology finds application in almost every kind of human activity, for example, job psychology, educational, clinical, or scientific psychology. The psychological field of particular significance for criminology is the motivation of a criminal act. Mental etiological factors (motive, impulse) play a fundamental role in the process of deciding on and executing a criminal act.

11

Determining the impulse and motive in the course of the trial exerts an impact on the severity of the sentence.

Finally, in administering the sentence, the individual's adaptation to penitentiary methods and measures must also be based on a close analysis of the convict's motivation.[2]

Contemporary sociology deals with specialized disciplines concerning various aspects of social phenomena and processes. Currently, the ones being studied are: social institutions, home, industry and job, law and justice administration, deviant behavior, social groups, social processes (migration, social advancement or degradation).

General sociology is also far from being a homogenous discipline. It represents, among other things, the theory of social structures and the theory of social development.[3]

Another example could be sociotechniques, formulating ways of implementing the desired social changes on the basis of verifying the outcome of research carried out by the various sections of sociology and other social sciences.[4]

The most important area of criminology is social pathology: the disruption of family life, other aspects of the environment leading to criminal behavior, the negative role of the mass media, the undesirable effects of migration, unemployment, alcoholism, and so forth.[5]

The development of contemporary education is rapid and multidirectional. The growing role of upbringing within the society and the varied forms of formative activities lead to extending the scope of pedagogical studies. Currently education deals with, among other things, the foundations, structure, and aims of upbringing and didactics; autonomous status is also claimed by the theory of moral and esthetic upbringing, and so forth.

From another point of view one can distinguish social and comparative pedagogy, the theory of educational planning and the economics of education.

Considering the various phases of human development one can distinguish the pedagogy of kindergarten, elementary and high school, vocational school, adult education, and the like.

Finally, the different fields of human activity require pedagogical studies. For that reason we find such fields as industrial pedagogy, agricultural, military, and therapeutical pedagogy. One should particularly stress the last-mentioned field, known also as orthopedagogy, dealing with the upbringing and educational efforts directed to children deviating from the norm.

In the field of criminological prevention a significant place is held by methods of reeducational pedagogy. This concerns the exerting of socializing influence on individuals who are ill adjusted to life within the society. The fundamental aim of the efforts made in penitentiary institutions is to achieve the social adjustment of convicts after they serve their sentence.

These issues oscillate on the borderland between pedagogy and social psychology.

The question of social adjustment has been the subject of numerous studies within the United States; there is even a distinct psychological discipline called adjustment psychology.

The medical sciences having particularly strong links with criminology include psychiatry[6], neurology, and endocrinology. Progress made by psychiatry has led to the evolution of many specialized fields, such as forensic psychiatry, social psychiatry (dealing with the role of environment in generating mental disturbances and the question of social readjustment of persons suffering from mental disturbances), juvenile psychiatry, and other fields.

The various pathological symptoms, such as disturbances of perception, attention, thought processes, and emotional life, can become contributing factors to crime. Such symptoms are significant not just from the criminological point of view, but also for the legal classification of the act.

While contemporary psychopathology has greatly aided criminology by focusing attention on the biological sources of criminality, one should also note the reverse feedback through which criminology with its objective methods of studying offensive acts has already contributed and can be expected to contribute further to a more thorough knowledge of intimate illnesses and mental anomalies which so far have not been properly reflected in the classification systems of the pathology of the human psyche.

Neurological diagnosis is being constantly enlarged with numerous supplementary analytic methods, such as the analysis of the cerebrospinal fluid, special methods of X-ray analysis (such as myelography, brain angiography, pneumoencephalography), electroencephalographic analysis, electromyographic analysis and such. In addition to general neurology, children's neurology is now also a distinct field.

Illnesses of the nervous system, such as concussion, postmeningitis states, brain inflammation, degeneration of the nervous system (for instance, in chronic alcoholism), and others, play a considerable role in the etiology of crime.

Endocrinology (study of the endocrine glands) is concerned with the analysis of normal and pathological morphology, and the physiology and biochemistry of endocrine glands. It is closely linked to pharmacology, clinical medicine and veterinary medicine. Irregular (weak or overactive) endocrine glands could have an impact on criminal behavior.

There are also links between criminology and cybernetics. In recent years new opportunities have appeared for applying cybernetics in criminology—for instance, in building prognostic and etiological models.

For criminology the notion of feedback is very useful in changing the traditional views concerning the casual nature of criminality. So far criminology has accepted the linear character of links between various social phenomena and criminality on the lines: factor A (cause)→factor B (effect). On cybernetic grounds such a type of one-way link can no longer be maintained. In accordance with the cybernetic principle of feedback it may so happen (particularly when we are dealing with a multifaceted, complex phenomenon such as criminality), that the effect will in turn influence the cause. Cause and effect will therefore have an interrelationship, described as *feedback*. A classic example of feedback is the relationship of personality and environment which constitutes a dynamic, multfaceted system of relations; we find here the interaction of endogenous and exogenous factors. One should not pass over the degree of linkage between criminology and pharmacy, defined as the group of disciplines encompassing the whole body of knowledge on medications and including applied pharmacy, pharmacognosy, pharmaceutic chemistry, toxicology, and pharmacodynamics. In addition to the conscious application of various toxic substances for the achievement of a criminal objective, such links are reflected in cases of acute poisoning due to the abuse of medications or drugs, particularly by young people, and industrial poisoning due to working conditions (industrial toxicology).

Statistics serves to describe reality. No mathematical methods can represent an objective in themselves. Statistics is a research method in various disciplines, and so it should not be considered in the abstract. In relation to criminology, statistics helps to collect data, describe it and classify it (criminography). The latest example is the application of mathematical statistics for studying the effectiveness of sentence, for optimizing the size of penitentiaries and their personnel, for criminological forecasts, and for evolving theoretical models for explaining criminality.

The closest links connect criminology with substantive and executional penal law, with criminalistics, with procedural law and with crime policy. Substantive penal law points to the main direction of criminological studies by determining which types of acts constitute offenses. Substantive penal law answers the question of where the methods of criminological research should find their main application.[7]

One should also keep in mind here the negative changes in social or economic relations, requiring regulation in penal law; this, obviously, has to be preceded by criminological studies of social phenomena.

The effects of criminological studies enrich our knowledge of criminal phenomena, enabling the penal law discipline to formulate new concepts concerning the actual states of crimes, defining the weight of penalties which better correspond with the severity of the crime, elaborating the general sections of the penal code, and so on.

The days are over when a crime was considered solely from the point of view of violating the rules of penal law, and when a theoretician or practitioner of law was the sole master of the field of antisocial phenomena. At present the exclusivity of the lawyers' point of view on crime and reaction to crime has been considerably eroded. Criminological genetic studies of crime frequently exert an impact on the normative principles of penal law.

Determining the circumstances of a crime, as well as motives and incentives is significant for the sentence itself and further represents a significant prognostic for selecting the right mode of sentence implementation. In this aspect alone it is possible to note the link between criminological functions and the objectives of penal policy implementation.

Penitentiaristics came into being on criminological grounds. It is no surprise, then, that penitentiary practice makes frequent use of the results of criminological research. The two disciplines have very close interrelationships stemming largely from the common final objective of limiting and preventing criminality. Here one notes the connection between criminology and penitentiary law.

Criminology is a descriptive discipline which goes far beyond the strict frames of law. While in the past the subject of studies for criminology was the classic act of crime itself, the contemporary interests of criminology extend further, to social pathology phenomena having an exceptionally high criminogenic potential. As examples one could cite prostitution, car accidents, accidents at work, or the drama of modern life—suicide. All over the world some 1,000 people commit suicide every day and another 10,000 make unsuccessful attempts at it. Even though suicide undoubtedly falls within the research field of criminology, the criminological aspects of this pathological phenomenon still have had no thorough theoretical analysis or preventive directives.

Penitentiary law constitutes a normative discipline, integrally linked with rules and regulations. The penal execution code or penitentiary rules define the convict's position in prison and the mutual relations of prison authorities and the convicts. From this point of view one can distinguish between criminology and penitentiaristics. On the one hand we find an analytical discipline closely linked with psychology, pedagogy, sociology, psychiatry, on the other hand normative discipline. There are also differences in the subject of analysis of the two disciplines. Even though their objectives are similar or even identical, the field of criminology extends to a much wider range of phenomena. It has to study both the causative factors of crime and its symptomatic forms as well as certain issues linked with penal victimology (such as the role of the victim in the genesis of crime). On the other hand, the attention of penitentiaristics focuses on the convict, a person in a special situation which causes the deprivation of needs. Much has been written not just on the convict's psychology but also on the sociology of a prison. This, after all, is a specific milieu, greatly contrasting with the outside world which is the subject of criminological interest. This selected marginal group, extremely dangerous, is separated for a set amount of time from its milieu and subjected to penitentiary efforts requiring application of different therapeutic and educational methods. From the point of view of individual methods of sentence administration, penitentiaristics concerns itself with the circumstances of the crime, motives, relationship of the offender to the victim, and the personality of the offender, and data on these aspects is provided by criminological research.

Criminological studies of recidivism indicating that frequently after serving his sentence the convict returns to crime inspire penitentiary experts to seek optimum conditions for reeducation. The better the system through which the sentence is adminstered, the better are the forecasts for limiting the phenomenon of recidivism and crime in general. There is, therefore, a specific type of feedback between the reeducation process and the reduction in crime.

Criminology and penitentiaristics not only cooperate on initiatives, but actually coordinate their projects. Criminological project findings are fully utilized by penitentiaristics, while observations made concerning the offender in the course of sentence administration are used by criminology as valuable material for numerous analyses, useful particularly in the initial phase of preparatory proceedings. Representatives of prison administration keep the convict under very close scrutiny in order to establish his personality, behavior, and reactions, and the body of information gained in this manner can be very useful in criminological projects.

Another very significant problem requires attention, namely, violence in penal institutions and the participation of criminologists in combating such violence. This concerns both the prisoners' aggressiveness against each other and against prison authorities. In this respect again penitentiaristics should utilize the methods developed by criminology.[8]

Thoughts on the mutual relationship of criminology and criminalistics are still valid, considering the frequent differences of opinion on this subject in various scientific studies.[9] Publications rarely give sufficient attention to the boundaries distinguishing the two, so that one finds considerable discrepancies in the various presentations of the subject and a lack of defined discussion resulting from the adoption of varied and not always correct criteria.

Since criminalistics and criminology have already taken shape as self-standing disciplines, it is necessary, when considering their mutual relationship, to introduce some fundamental criteria, such as the objective, subject, and methods of research and the relationship to other pertinent disciplines.

The objective of criminology is to prevent crime through the removal of general causes. Criminology approaches crime as a social phenomenon. Criminalistics, on the other hand, combats and prevents crimes by uncovering the fact of the crime, discovering its perpetrator, and securing evidence material to criminal justice. The objectives of preventing criminality stem from the prime task of criminalistics, namely the struggle against defined manifestations of criminal activity. This means a significant difference in the approach to crime of criminology and criminalistics. As examples one could cite issues concerning the conditions under which crimes are committed, motives or victimology.

Concerning the conditions of, say, counterfeiting banknotes, criminalistics concerns itself with the techniques of crime in order to establish the group of suspects. A criminologist has to consider, among other things, the ease with which such a crime could be committed and the circumstances conducive to its spread.

Mental etiological factors (inspiration, motive) constitute significant elements of criminological and criminalistic studies, though in different cross-sections.

For a criminologist the important element is to establish the contents and course of the internal mental emotions of the offender; a criminalistics expert studies the motivational process from the point of view of its impact on selecting the method of criminal action and the proper selection of the suspect.

Penal victimology concerns itself with the issues linked with the victim and the victim's role in the genesis of crime.[10] The victim is also the subject of interest for criminalistics. In studying the problem of homicide it can be established that, for instance, getting to know about the life of the victim, the victim's contacts with the outside world, the victim's sources of income—all help or hinder the identification of the suspect.

There is also a different criminological sense to the seven golden questions, generally known in criminalistics: who? what? where? with what? why? in what way? when?

"Why" is answered by criminology with considerations of the general sources of criminal actions and with the objective of eliminating these causes. For criminalistics the answer to the question "why" constitutes a premise for selecting suspects. It is, namely, a question of establishing who or which groups of persons had an interest in committing a given crime.

There are also fundamental differences between criminology and criminalistics in their methods of study. The study methods in these two disciplines are determined by different objectives and differences in the approach to the phenomenon of crime. Criminalistics makes great use of research methods used by the technical and natural sciences. Criminology, on the other hand, is dominated in this respect by methods used in statistical, sociological, and psychological studies.

This is also connected with the relationship of criminology and criminalistics to other disciplines. For instance, criminology has very close links with penal law and with sociology, while criminalistics has closer links with procedural law and a wide range of natural, physical, and chemical sciences.

Despite the existence of a rather clear boundary between these two disciplines one should not forget their overlapping of interests.

Acquaintance with criminology contributes to a more thorough treatment of issues which make up a part of criminalistics and to more effective implementations of its tasks. For instance, one could mention the outcome of criminological studies on the personality of offenders, customs of criminal milieus, and motivational processes of criminal activities, which to a great extent facilitate the establishment of correct investigation methods.

On the other hand criminalistics supplies criminology with much information concerning crime and the criminal. That is why the high proportion of solved crimes enriches the material required for criminological analysis.

The links of criminology with penal procedural law[11] stem from the fact that criminology supplies material concerning the offender.[12] Collecting information as to family relations, welfare, education, occupation, job, record, and when need be obtaining data on character traits of the accused, his personal circumstances and manner of living, is among the important tasks of penal procedure performed largely through actions falling within the scope of criminology and criminalistics.

Particularly characteristic is the relationship among three disciplines—criminology, crime policy, and penal law.[13] Criminology is assigned diagnostic functions, crime policy the role of "therapeutic planning center" and penal law the function of implementing the premises of crime policy.

Notes

1. Leon Radzinowicz points out that studies of criminality have to rely on close bonds with psychiatry, psychology, and sociology. See *In Search of Criminology* (London: Heinemann Books, 1961), p. 181.

2. Elizabeth Mueller-Luckmann, "Psychologie und Strafrecht," *Rechtswissenschaft und Nachbarwissenschaften*, Munich, 1976, vol. 1, pp. 215–230.

3. Jan Szczepański, *Elementarne pojecie socjologii* [Elementary definitions in sociology] (Warsaw: Państwowe Wydawnictwo Naukowe, 1966); Stanislaw Ossowski, *O osobliwościach nauk społecznych* [On peculiarities of the social sciences] (Warsaw: Państwowe Wydawnictwo Naukowe, 1962).

4. Adam Podgórecki, *Zasady socjotechniki* [Rules of sociotechniques] (Warswa: "Wiedza Powszechna," 1966).

5. Stephan Quensel, *Sozialpsychologische Aspekte der Kriminologie: Handlung, Situation, und Persönlichkeit* (Stuttgart: Ferdinand Enke Verlag, 1964).

6. Heinz Leferentz, "Die Stellung der Kriminologie zwischen Jurisprudenz und Psychiatrie," *Studium Generale* 1959, vol. 12.

7. Karl Lackner, "Kriminologie und Strafrecht," *Kriminalbiologische Gegenwartsfragen* (Stuttgart: Ferdinand Enke Verlag, 1964), issue 6; "Die Chancen der Kooperation zwischen Strafrechtswissenschaft und Kriminologie: Probleme und offene Fragen," in *Seminar: Abweichendes Verhalten II: Die Gesellschaftlische Reaktion auf Kriminalität*, ed. Klaus Lüdenssen and Fritz F. Sack (Frankfurt am Main: Verlag Suhrkamp., 1975), pp. 346–385.

8. Brunon Hołyst elaborated on this issue in greater detail in an interview published as "Kryminologia a penitencjarystyka" [Criminology and penitentiaristics], in *Gazeta Penitencjarna* 1981, issue 11/12. This interview was reprinted in *Gazeta Prawnicza* 1981, issue 17.

9. Brunon Hołyst, *Kryminalistyka*, 4th ed. (Warsaw: Państwowe Wydawnictwo Naukowe, 1981); Hermann Haering, "Was erwartet Kriminalistik von der Kriminologie?" *Kriminologische Gegenwartsfragen*, Stuttgart: Ferdinand Enke Verlag, 1974, issue 11, pp. 169–175; Geerds, Friedrich, "Was erwartet die Kriminologie von der Kriminalistik?" *Kriminologische Gegenwartsfragen*, 1974, issue 11, pp. 177–196. Dietrich Rahn, "Kriminologie, Kriminalistik, und Gerichtshilfe," *Kriminologische Gegenwartsfragen*, 1974, issue 11, pp. 191–195.

10. Willem Nagel, "The Notion of Victimology in Criminology," *Excerpta Criminologica*, 1963, no. 3, pp. 145–247.

11. Dragomir Dimitrijevic, "Die wechselseitige Verbundenheit der Kriminologie und des Strafprozesses," *Kriminologische Gegenwartsfragen*, 1976, issue 12.

12. Hans Göppinger, "Angewandte Kriminologie im Strafverfahren," *Kriminologische Gegenwartsfragen*, 1976, issue 12, pp. 56–71.

13. Johannes Andenaes, "Droit pénal, criminologie, et de la politique criminelle," *Revue de Droit Pénal et de Criminologie*, 1962, no. 1; Jacob van Bemelen, "Les rapports de la criminologie et de la politique criminelle," *Revue de Science Criminelle et de Droit Pénal Comparé*, 1963, no. 3; Erwin Frey, "Kriminologie und Kriminalpolitik," *Kriminologische Gegenwartsfragen*, 1958, issue 3; Gerhard O. W. Mueller, "The Function of Criminology in Criminal Justice Administration," *Abstracts on Criminology*, 1969, no. 9, pp. 577–589.

3 An Outline of Criminological Theories

Historical Perspective

Interest in criminality has long been apparent, as evidenced in the earliest sources—Aristotle, Plato, Marcus Aurelius, and, in medieval times, the authors of Catholic doctrines.

A detailed presentation of the ideas passed on from the ancient and medieval world would be superfluous. Suffice it to say that the views of ancient and medieval philosophers on crime and the offender (though frequently varying, depending in part on the level of economic and cultural development represented by the society) are marked by certain common features, corresponding to the views of the day on social phenomena.

Philosophers and lawmakers universally referred to deistic authorities and man's free will; an offensive act was viewed as a violation of religious teachings and state laws by the free though illicit will of man. Such views were held by Aristotle and after him later philosophers, including Thomas à Kempis. The supersititions hidden in scholastic dogma on man's possession by the devil (demonological concepts) further hampered an explanation of the genesis of man's criminal behavior. Human thought of the day was far from the need to investigate the social or other causes of human actions.

The second feature of the old views was the differentiation of human behavior according to social position; this was reflected in the less severe treatment of offenders from the ruling class or even in accepting the acts perpetrated by such persons as morally and legally neutral (such as the killing of a slave by his master).

All the same, even in ancient times attempts were made to discover the link between the physical structure of an individual and his mental and ethical features as well as to explain the genesis of certain crimes through unfavorable economic conditions.

More serious attempts at justifying the social and biological factors influencing human behavior appeared during the Renaissance and the Enlightenment; this was connected with the evolution of social and economic patterns and the progress of the social and natural sciences. Looking at it from the present-day perspective, the value of those attempts at further progress varied considerably, though not for lack of trying. We shall limit ourselves here to some of the more significant ideas which influenced the later development of the social sciences.

Thomas More (1478–1535) attempted to prove that in the countries he knew, criminality was caused by the incorrect pattern of social relations, and the assurance of adequate living conditions for all citizens would free the country of crime against property.[1] More's views had a great impact on the concepts formulated by Tommaso Campanella (1568–1639) and the eighteenth-century French utopians.[2]

Enlightenment was the next stage important for the evolution of criminology.

Charles Montesquieu (1689–1755) in his *Esprit des lois* sets forth the rule that a system of penalties based on wanton cruelty, rather than spreading fear, causes social savagery.

Cesare Beccaria (1738–1794) made particularly great contributions to the progress of criminology. His philosophical work, initially published anonymously, was soon translated into many languages and became immensely popular.[3] This was due not so much to its literary value as its revolutionary, for the times, approach to the problem of penalty. Beccaria was staunchly opposed to cruelty in the carrying out of punishment, advocated the principle of combating criminality, called for formulating laws in such a way as to be clear to all and to act as warnings to potential offenders. Though certain of the ideas promulgated by Beccaria had been formulated earlier (Montesquieu), in view of the wide popularity of his work one has to give him credit for the contribution he made to the history of criminology and recognize him as a forebear of this discipline.

In general the eighteenth century brought with it a great popularity of the thesis that offenses against property are the result of unjust rule, poverty, and the lack of education. This thesis, though formulated in various ways, was promoted by, among others, Voltaire, Morelly, Mably, Meslier, Bentham, Godwin.

Many contemporary etiological–criminological theories contain traces of the views held by eighteenth and nineteenth century philosophers. Classification of such theories according to the main directions taken by criminological thought would be extremely difficult.

Modern theories of crime are based on biology, genetics, psychology, sociology, economics, and anthropology, as well as religion. The four general categories of the theory of crime are sociological, biological, psychological, and sociopsychological.

The sociological theories are the most common. They explain criminogenic conditions created by the social or cultural environment of a given community. Sociological theories are divided into subcultural and structural ones. Structural theories stress, on the one hand, the basic equality of personal needs and abilities, and on the other hand, the essential inequality of opportunities to realize these abilities in socially acceptable ways.

Biological theories take into account genetic inheritance, chromosomal abnormalities, physiological irregularities, and constitutional determinants.

They consider biopsychical factors as predisposing to crime, while re-cognizing also the significance of environmental and sociological impact.

Psychological theories are based on the belief that crime is the outcome of certain personality traits of the criminal. Psychoanalytical theories focus on the assumption that crime is the result of an immature personality.

Sociopsychological theories cover the social learning theories or be-havioral theories. Some of them focus on the learning of criminal behavior and others on the learning of behavior incompatible with criminal conduct.

In the most general terms, there are two orientations, biopsychological and sociological, although the authors of numerous concepts agree on the importance of both sociological and personality factors. The view prevails among scholars that an individual is a bio-psycho-social unit in which biological, psychological, and social elements are interwoven in a dynamic whole. It would, therefore, be difficult, artificial, and arbitrary to strictly separate the biological from the psychological and social factors.

For these reasons the authors of textbooks encounter difficulties in classifying their material. For instance, Hans J. Schneider[4] distinguishes four main directions: criminal-biological; multifactor structures; psychological[5]; and sociological and sociological-psychological.

Gwynn Nettler names two main directions of criminological thought: sociological explanation, which covers subcultural differentiation and struc-tural differentiation; and sociopsychological explanation, which covers sym-bolic interaction and social control concepts.[6]

Many books provide a review and evaluation of the various theories interpreting the causes of criminality.[7] They are good source material, offering a comprehensive comparison of the major theories of crime.

This chapter is concerned both with the "sociological" concepts and with those which, while they recognize the importance of personality,[8] biological, and sociological factors, reveal the multifaceted nature of criminological conditions.

Due to the synthetic nature of the review, the particularly weak or controversial points of the theories presented are only noted.

Early Theories of Biopsychological Orientation

Early theories focused on biological determinants, holding that criminal behavior was inherited or was a manifestation of an evolutionary throwback, or atavism. The biological model of criminality focuses on biological, somatological, and anthropological factors as they influence criminal be-havior. This orientation posits the criminal as biologically different from other humans. Cesare Lombroso's "atavistic criminal," Charles B. Goring's "criminal diathesis" and William Sheldon's somatotypes are examples, although now largely discredited.[9]

Historically, the first work aimed at explaining crime-conducive factors through empirical and scientific analysis was the book by the Italian psychiatrist and anthropologist Cesare Lombroso (1836–1909) *L'Uomo Delinquente* [Criminal Man]. This treatise was the outcome of studying the anatomy (particularly the head) of thousands of criminals. It was published in 1876, though it was preceded by shorter publications. Since 1876 criminology has flowered as a distinct discipline.

Lombroso voiced his belief in the value of empirical studies, writing in the introduction to his book: " . . . one should rather omit the lofty fields of philosophical theories and also the debating of still new facts and rather proceed to direct somatic and mental examination of the criminal man, comparing it with data concerning the normal and insane persons. The fruit of such studies is contained in this book."[10]

On the basis of psychiatric and anthropological examinations, Lombroso concluded that a criminal act is a phenomenon of nature and biology, conditioned by the physical and mental properties of the perpetrator. Certain physical features, particularly those concerning the skull, were ascribed by Lombroso to given categories of criminals. He wrote, "Murderers are marked by the size of the jaw, prominent cheeks, dark and thick hair, sparse stubble, pallor. Violent people–long arms, shortheadedness and relatively broad forehead. Rapists have short arms, narrow foreheads, they frequently have blond hair, anomalies of the nose and sex organs. Among robbers and burglars we rarely find deviations in the size of the head: their hair is thick and stubble sparse. Arsonists weigh less, have long limbs and an abnormal head. Swindlers have prominent jaws and cheeks, are chubby, with pallid faces, often with paresis. Cutthroats have long arms, are relatively tall, frequently black hair, sparse stubble."

Generally speaking, Lombroso claimed that criminals represent anthropologically defined types, and some 40 percent of convicts are criminals by birth. "Criminal man" is an individual retaining atavistic features of prehistoric man and his cruelty as well as moral insanity. Such an individual is destined to become a criminal, since he can not free himself of his inborn properties. Lombroso cited here the example of nature, where such crimes as theft, robbery, killing, sexual offenses were commonplace among animals and even plants.

One should note, in all fairness, that in addition to born criminals Lombroso also recognized habitual criminals, criminals acting on impulse and accidental criminals (pseudocriminals).

Lombroso's ideas were advocated and followed by a number of scholars, physicians, and lawyers, including, in Italy: Garofalo, Marro, and at certain times also Ferri; in Germany: Kurella, Koch, Kraepelin; in France: Bodier, Leturneau; in England Havelock and others. Lombroso's ideas were also advocated in Poland.

Raffaele Garofalo (1851–1934) formulated the theory of "natural" and "artificial" crime and the unchangeability of human nature. Natural crime was linked with violation of one of the two prime feelings: abhorrence of making other people suffer (*pieta*); and respect for the ownership rights of others (*probita*). He shared Lombroso's view on the existence of criminals by birth, having features of "savage" peoples and mental retardation.[11]

A. Marro defined crime as a biological phenomenon, caused by decay of the central nervous system functions.

Certain followers of the anthropological school modified its prime premises, adding new elements borrowed from the sociological-criminal school.

The theories which try to explain the genesis of criminality on the basis of a certain group of various causes are called *eclectic*. For instance, according to Enrico Ferri (1856–1929) the main factors causing criminality are not only the organic system of man and his mental makeup, but also such features and properties as race, age, sex, and also the climate, time of year, time of day, and certain social conditions (density of population, alcoholism, industrialization, economic and political conditions). In support of Lombroso's theory Ferri claimed that one of the criminal types is a criminal by birth, having organic deviations; according to him all human activity is a manifestation of individual properties.[12]

Similar views were held by another representative of eclectic doctrines, Franz von Liszt (1851–1919), accepted as one of the predecessors of criminology. While Lombroso and his followers concentrated exclusively on questions of the etiology of criminality, Liszt revealed the panorama of problems in this discipline; by applying sociological research methods and linking the subject of interest with other disciplines, he laid the foundations for treating criminology as an autonomous discipline.

Resolving the issue of the etiology of criminality was and remains one of the most important problems facing criminology. It may, therefore, be useful to quote Liszt's view: "Crime is a product of the unique properties of the criminal on the one hand and the social relations surrounding the criminal at the time of the act on the other hand."[13] It was this definition of the problem that allowed for extension of the scope for analysis and revealed new, hitherto untouched problems.

Lombroso's work and his views were revealing, yet he had predecessors—the scientists dealing with physionomics, phrenology and cranioscopy; certain of Lombroso's concepts are little more than a development of their thought.

Physionomics is the theory which assumes that the personality of man, his mental properties, and his emotional stance can be defined from his facial features and expressions. In ancient times and during the Renaissance physionomics was practiced as part of astrology or chiromancy and treated as a dark art. In the eighteenth century it was promoted particularly by J. K. Lavater (1741–1801), Swiss writer and theologian and by Ch. Bell (1774–1842), British anatomist, physiologist, and surgeon.

Phrenology is the theory formulated by the Austrian neurologist F. J. Gall (1758–1828) and K. Spurzheim (1776–1832) according to which on the basis of the shape of the human skull, protrusions, indentations, and so forth, it is possible to formulate conclusions concerning a person's mental capacities and psychic properties. Gall believed that the surface of the brain has a special center of given physical and mental functions, with corresponding skull bone protrusions and indentations and that on the basis of these it is possible to diagnose brain diseases and to describe a person's character. Gall's theory gained considerable popularity, but as early as 1802 teaching it in Vienna was prohibited as being contrary to morality and religion. The studies carried out by Gall gave a start to the science of localization of the brain centers governing the activities of given bodily organs. Gall's theories were followed and promoted in the United States by Ch. Caldwell (1772–1853).

The views held by Lombroso were criticized both by the pioneers of the sociological direction in criminology, such as Gabriel Tarde (1843–1904), and by proponents of the biological school. For instance, the British physician Charles Goring, having examined some three thousand recurrent offenders plus a number of students, soldiers, and hospital patients, ascertained that there is no physical type of criminal.[14] One should note, however, that Goring represented the view that crime has a biological and hereditary background, that there are constitutional factors conducive to criminal activities on the part of an individual, and that the criminality of members of one family (parents, children, brothers) is conditioned by heredity.

Critical studies have pointed out that the anthropologists' thesis on the hereditary nature of criminal features is groundless. After all, an individual is the product of society and crime is a historical phenomenon conditioned by economic, social, and political factors. Anthropologists were accused of insuffient regard for the influence of social factors (particularly the social environment) in the etiology of crime.

Recognizing the links between mental and physiological phenomena and the impact of somatic properties on the mental dispositions of a person, the critics warned against overestimating the crime-inducing value of these factors. The problem of chronic criminality could be resolved, but only with the aid of social and political-criminal reforms. The current, highly unsatisfactory state of affairs is due primarily to the present criminalistic policy and not to heredity, constitution, and psychopathy of the criminals.

There was also criticism of the notion of a professional and notorious criminal. The problem of incorrigibility is, just as any other question in penal law, in the final analysis a normative issue. A crime is not exclusively a natural or social occurrence (phenomenon, fact)—it becomes one only when measured by the legal norm, so that anthropological studies can only prove the existence of anthropological types of people, and not types of criminals.

Critics found many inconsistencies and omissions even in the theory itself. First of all, there is absolutely no knowledge as to what is a criterion of a somatic norm; second, the impact of somatic features on mental phenomena is undefined; third, Lombroso failed to explain why only certain people remain in the "state of nature," that is, they are criminals, while others subject themselves to the influence of environment and culture.

Anthropological (biological) concepts returned in the writings of many later authors. For instance, after carrying out elaborate investigations involving over seventeen thousand people including thirteen thousand criminals Ernest Hooton claimed that man's physical imperfections express his mental predispositions.[15] One could also cite the hypothesis advanced by E. Bleurel that a criminal is a man who since birth has suffered from an atrophy of the higher feelings; this hypothesis captured the attention of scholars, becoming the starting point for studies on psychopathy and psychosis.

Seeking the causes of criminality only in biological factors failed to yield the expected reuslts. Along with the progress of psychology, criminology also began to search for a link between the mental properties of man and his somatic features.

Since ancient times there had been attempts at defining the mental properties of people in connection with their somatic features. There is the well-known Hippocrates and Galen division into four types: sanguine, choleric, melancholic, and phlegmatic. Further attempts at classifications were made during the nineteenth and twentieth centuries.

According to Ernst Kretschmer, people represent the following four main physical constitutions: leptosomic (asthenic), athletic, pyknic, and displastic; he linked given mental makeups with these types.[16] Furthermore, there are two extreme forms of mental disturbance: schizophrenia and manic-depressive psychosis; both forms are linked to given personality types: schizophrenia with the asthenic and athletic types, and manic-depressive psychosis with the pyknic type. Certain features of these types were also observed by Kretschmer in psychopaths and healthy individuals (schizothymics and cyclothymics) leading him to the hypothesis that a criminal attitude marks mainly the schizothymics, that it is among them that "born" criminals are to be found. Numerous later studies have shown that linking given psychic features of an individual with a given type of bodily constitution does not always hold.

Studies by Schwab and Saza indicate that the proportion of types in a population of criminals is no larger than the proportion of those types in the general population.[17]

The idea of constitutional types of criminals was developed by William Sheldon.[18] He distinguished three main types: endomorphic (a high degree of internal organ development, including digestions); mesomorphic (a high degree of bone and muscle structure development); and ectomorphic (delicate skin, sensitive nervous system), though also providing for their combination. According to Sheldon the juvenile delinquents he examined usually represented the type dominated by mesomorphy, with a moderate degree of endomorphy and insignificant ectomorphy. Though certain studies have lent support to the Sheldon hypothesis,[19] the idea in general has been evaluated as unfounded.

Progress in medical science turned the attention of scholars to the role of the endocrine glands, and particularly the effects of their faulty functioning, since it has been ascertained that there is an interdependence between them and the nervous system—central and peripheral. Endocrinologists show that disturbances in the functioning of such glands as the pituitary, pineal, thyroid, suprarenal, and pancreas lead to many consequences including mental disturbances. The findings were taken over into criminology. Max Schlapp and Edward Smith as well as Louis Berman claim that disturbances in the functioning of endocrine glands are decisive as crime-conducive factors.[20]

Later studies failed to confirm a significant correlation between the functioning of these glands and criminal activity. With the present state of knowledge on the subject it is only possible to state that the effects of certain disturbances in the functioning of glands can become manifested by such things as aggression, the inability to attain a desired social status, which could have a certain influence on offensive behavior.

In recent years great interest was generated by the discovery in certain persons of one or two additional chromosomes. A cell of a normal male has the X-chromosome inherited from the mother and the Y-chromosome from the father. In certain males showing mental disturbances the discovery was made of an additional Y-chromosome and in rare cases, even two extra Y-chromosomes. It was found that individuals with the additional chromosome are aggressive, antisocial, unstable, emotional, with other similar personality traits.

Some studies have determined that there is a certain link between the atypical set of chromosomes and criminality,[21] but such a set appears so rarely that, even should the hypothesis which was advanced prove true, the practical significance would be almost nil. Further, the test methods and selection of samples in such studies have been criticized so severely that at present there are no grounds for linking the fact of possessing an additional chromosome with criminality.[22] In addition to this, the researchers dealing with this issue overlook a very significant problem: Through what mechanisms could the genetic differences condition the differences in the socially defined behaviors?

Biological concepts concerning criminals link human psychic anomalies with such factors as physique, action of endocrine glands, or the set of chromosomes. Further theories which appeared turned their attention to the experiences of an individual due to mental deficiency or deviation,[23] seeing them as crime-conducive factors. Specifically, studies were made of the impact which mental retardation (oligophreny) has on human behavior. Research was done on the impact of mental illness and other disturbances of the mental equilibrium (psychopathy) and the low level of intellectual capacity on criminality.

There is no agreement among authors as to whether psychopathy is a self-standing crime-conducive factor, if for no other reason than because the very notion of psychopathy is debatable,[24] and psychopathic features manifest themselves in connection with the milieu, environment, or such tendencies as, say, drunkenness.

Hans Eysenck is of the opinion that psychopathy as a factor disturbing the functioning of the conditional reflex system is crime-conducive, since it hampers the adoption of positive patterns (he explains the socially acceptable behavior of man by the "conditioned reflexes" of Pavlovian theory).[25]

Views on the etiology of criminal behavior were influenced considerably by theories relating to the psychoanalytical school. Sigmund Freud, the creator of this school, distinguished three spheres of the human psyche. *Id* is the sphere of inborn, instinctive drives and tendencies which are at the base of all human behavior. Id operates in the subconscious. *Ego* is the conscious personality of man, which it is possible to develop and control. *Superego* (conscience) is the unconscious sphere of internalized norms, prohibitions, and imperatives which are shaped in the socialization process.

There is a direct conflict between id and superego, since id is hedonistic in nature, demanding the immediate satisfaction of drives, while superego represents a brake hindering the full realization of id drives. It, therefore, serves as a sort of internal, subconscious controller of behavior. The spheres of id and superego are rarely in balance, more often in conflict.

Subconscious conflicts lead to feelings of guilt and states of fear. They manifest themselves in the form of substitute behaviors, defusing the subconscious conflicts. In this sense all human behavior, even the strangest, is purposeful and significant. It is a substitute or symbol of the personality elements driven into the subconscious. Psychoanalysis is treated as a system explaining all human behavior, and therefore also criminal behavior.

Scholars dealing with criminality from the psychoanalytical point of view—despite many differences as to the interpretative details—adopt one general assumption: criminal behavior is substitutive in nature, symbolizing the conflicts driven into the subconscious.

For instance, for many authors theft is not a purposeful (in the conscious sense) action for material gain but rather a subconscious attempt to relieve the feeling of guilt through the fact of being penalized.[26] As an additional argument in support of this thesis they cite the fact that certain offenders act carelessly, thoughtlessly, without covering up their traces, as though they desired to be caught and punished.[27]

The views that criminal behavior is compensative in nature and constitutes a way of relieving complexes stem from the psychoanalytical school.[28]

The weak point of the psychoanalytical ideas is that they start with preconceptions concerning hidden mental processes which cannot be proven. Many authors treat the psychoanalytical theories of criminality as downright unscientific.

According to endocrinological, constitutional, chromosome theories and Sheldon's theory, certain individuals have been assigned biological properties by nature which create crime-conducive states and mental processes. The question arises as to the passing on of these traits, something that the theories fail to resolve (they particularly fail to explain whether the ancestors of the criminal, particularly the parents, have also shown these traits and whether they themselves have been criminals).

Attempts have been made by science to carry out the research to answer this question. The studies went in two directions: genealogical (passing on of psychic traits among family members) and gemelliological (comparing common and distinct traits of twins).

An example of the first type of study is the treatise by Charles Goring, who attempted to prove that heredity is significant in the etiology of crime; he developed the notion of "criminalistic diathesis" that is, a certain inherited, familial inclination toward committing crime.[29]

Geneticists and criminologists are critical of the method of genealogical studies, claiming that it is not possible thus to distinguish between inherited traits and traits arising from the environment.

During the 1920s and 1930s the gemelliological method was used for the first time in research on hereditary influences. It consists of multiapproach behavior analysis of uniovular and biovular (conceived by inseminating two different ovums) twins. On this subject, well-known work was carried out by J. Lange, H. Kranz and F. Sumpfl, who found that individuals from the uniovular groups of twins show considerable uniformity in penalization (70 percent correspondence), while from the biovular group the correspondence holds for only 30 percent of the tested pairs.

Such studies are still continuing in many countries, including the Polish Academy of Sciences Anthropology Laboratory in Wrocław. These studies are aimed at explaining to what degree the various processes of human development are influenced by hereditary factors and to what degree by the environment. It was found that among all the pairs of twins of the same sex some 40 percent are uniovular (monozygotic), coming from a single inseminated ovum. Such pairs are the only instance among mankind with identical genetic backgrounds, meaning also identical hereditary predispositions as to physical, physiological, and mental traits. Further findings of these studies could prove useful for criminology.

Cyril Burt[30] and Sheldon and Eleanor Glueck[31] represent the view that human behavior is determined by many factors and it is only the resultant of these factors which may lead a person to perpetrate an offensive act.[32] These factors of both biological and sociological nature have to be uncovered for each case separately. Empirical studies should serve to define the most complete possible list of potential crime-conducive factors which recur most frequently.

A detailed review of all the biological factors playing an important function in the socializing process was presented by Daniel Glaser in his *Handbook of Criminology.*[33]

The Phenomenon of Criminality in Sociological Terms

Even though many of the previously presented biopsychological theories remain valid and for many researchers continue to constitute the foundation for analyzing criminality (particularly the offensive behavior of individuals), currently most criminologists seek the sources of criminality in broadly defined social patterns. The theoretical basis for explanations of this type is provided by the criminological theories arbitrarily known as sociological, though many of them could just as well be described as psychosocial or outright psychological. In view of their popularity and wide application in research practice it would appear justified to devote a little more space to selected sociological theories.

The criterion of selection was primarily the impact of the given theory on the development of criminological concepts and, to a certain extent, its popularity. Chosen for presentation was the anomie theory (the Durkheim and Merton version), Sutherland's theory of differential associations, a few of the better known subculture theories and the recently fashionable labeling theory.[34] The classic Marxist views of criminality, even though they also fit within the sociological school of criminology, will be presented for the sake of clarity along with a description of etiological premises of socialist criminology.

The Anomie Theory

One of the first scholars to consistently approach criminality as a social phenomenon par excellence was the French sociologist Emile Durkheim.

Even though the Durkheim theory is classified as *criminological*, it remains integrally bound to the more general sociological views of that author. It would not be possible to analyze Durkheim's views of criminality without relating them to his concept of a social phenomenon.

Durkheim rejected the views of reductionists, claiming that social phenomena should not be interpreted biologically or psychologically. These are, after all, social facts and as such should be the object of structural-dynamic sociological explanations.[35] Social facts, such as religion, morality, or law have different sources and characteristic features and therefore cannot be reduced to mental experiences of individuals. Social facts are external to an individual's conscience and are subject to their own autonomous laws. They also are not the arithmetic sum of individual consciences. They have their independent existence; a given religious system cannot be characterized by relating it to the mental experiences of its believers.

For Durkheim law is a social fact, and so, therefore, is criminality. Durkheim views criminality as a normal phenomenon, in certain cases even an advantageous one. The "normal" character of criminality is seen not only from the statistical point of view as a phenomenon prevalent in all societies, ancient and contemporary, but also from the functional point of view. According to the French sociologist criminality serves two prime functions.

First, the wavering of individual consciousness from collective consciousness is a precondition for change and progress. Complete uniformity of behavior by members of a given society would mean stagnation, would mean that the society is not developing. Today's offender could be tomorrow's philosopher, claims Durkheim, citing the case of Socrates.

Second, crime can be a factor integrating the society, fostering social bonds. The negative reaction to a criminal act by the whole body of people strengthens the collective consciousness and reveals the boundaries between moral and legal norms.

Durkheim sought the origins of criminality in the social pattern. An individual, according to Durkheim, is never satisfied in his aims. "The more one has, the more one wants, since the prizes gained only stimulate, rather than satisfy, wants".[36] The limits to these individual aspirations can be set only by the external controls of society.

In a properly functioning society the social control causes everyone to understand his own possibilities of advancement and to regulate the aspiration level accordingly. During a time of explosive social change (mainly of economic nature—explosive growth or recession) there is a breakdown of social control so that an individual no longer feels bound in his aspirations by the existing system of norms. This state, described by Durkheim as *anomie*, can hold for larger or smaller groups within the society, but is always connected with explosive social change. The state of anomie, marked by a breakdown of social bonds and the confusion of people as to the behavior norms in force, leads to the revealing of egotistic tendencies, the effect of which is an increase in deviate behaviors, including criminality.

Even though Durkheim correctly pointed to the sources of deviate behaviors in the social structure, the type of division of tasks, the breakdown of the former system of social control and bonds, still (perhaps with the exception of suicide, the author's main concern), this was an excessively general concept. The anomie theory was supplemented and developed by American sociologists, foremost among them Robert K. Merton.[37]

Merton started by refuting certain of Durkheim's claims. According to Durkheim a person is guided by egotistic aspirations which are held in check so long as the system of social control operates effectively. When social control weakens, the unchecked egotistic impulses of man come to the fore with full force. According to Durkheim's theory, man is by his biological nature bad, antisocial—only external forces prevent him from behaving in a manner contrary to social norms. In this theory one could find certain analogies to the psychoanalytical concept of id versus superego. For Merton, both conformist and deviate behavior is the normal manner of adapting to the sociocultural structure, so that deviation in this approach does not necessarily result from a breakdown of social control.

Central to Merton's theory were "culture-defined ends" and "institutionalized means serving their implementation." In a properly functioning society the culture-delineated ends are integrally bonded with the means by which the ends can be attained. Proper functioning of the society could become disturbed by placing excessive emphasis on either the ends or the means.

In the latter situation the previously instrumental actions take on a significance in themselves, abstracted from the end which they were supposed to serve. Such "means without end" are described as ritual.

In the former situation great emphasis is placed on the achievement of culture-sanctioned aims, with little attention to the means by which the aims could be achieved, a "catch-as-catch-can" situation.

American society resembles the first type, since it highly cherishes success (financial worth or something that can be calculated in money terms, such as education), paying little attention to promoting legally acceptable ways of attaining such success. Atrophy of the norms defining the ways of achieving culture aims, combined with a highly egalitarian ideology, leads to situations in which some people realize that their aspirations can not be achieved in a legal manner, and therefore tend to resort to illegal measures.

Merton defines the state of anomie as the breakdown of the culture structure which takes place in a situation of severe dissonance between the culture norms on the one hand and the socially created opportunities for members of the given group to act in accordance with them on the other hand.[38]

There are five types of adaptation to the dysfunction between the culture and the social structure.

One, *conformism*, consists of actions aimed at the achievement of culture-sanctioned aims by legal means. This is most frequent among social groups which have a realistic possibility (financial, professional) to successfully achieve the aim of socioeconomic advancement.

Two, *ritualism*, consists of relinquishing or lowering aspiration to a higher position to such a degree that they no longer cause frustration due to failure. With this method the human adaptation loses sight of the aim to which given actions were supposed to be subordinated, treating the actions as values in themselves.

The first two types of adaptation, obviously, do not lead to deviant behavior. Yet, the next three are of a deviant nature, though different in their degree of social harmfulness.

Three, *innovation*, is the acceptance of culture aims with simultaneous rejection of the prescribed ways for their achievement. According to Merton, this is the most crime-conducive type of adaptation. By this method people do implement the values adopted by their society, but through illegal means. Innovation is particularly probable in those social groups which have relatively limited possibilities for attaining higher social position when acting in accordance with the law. Blocked opportunities for wider advancement (higher earnings, better education, and the like) lead to stresses which can easily turn to seeking new ways to attain the same goals.

Four, *dropping out*, consists of parallel rejection of the aims, toward the achievement of which there are social pressures, and the means which could serve the achievement of those aims. People following this type of adaptation in a way "drop out." This type of adaptation could have some connection with criminality, though the offense in this case would be incidental rather than instrumental in relation to the generally accepted culture aims.

Five, *rebellion*, also consists of rejecting the existing aims and means, at the same time offering a positive program of providing the social system with new ends and new means for attaining them. This means changing both the culture and the social structures, in other words, "playing by new rules." People opting for this type of adaptation are described as reformers, revolutionaries or political criminals (where in a given social system such activity is prohibited).

Theory of Differential Associations

One of the most discussed theories in world criminology was the differential associations theory advanced by Edwin H. Sutherland.

The origins of the Sutherland theory stem from negating the biological and psychoanalytical orientations in criminology and from the positive influence exerted on Sutherland's views by the Chicago school of social psychology (symbolic interactionism) and sociology (ecological studies).

Sutherland totally contradicted the then-dominant criminological orientation which sought the sources of criminality in inherited or inborn human predispositions to act contrary to the law. Also, for Sutherland, a crime was not the effect of some sort of "disturbance" in the form of emotional disorders, subconscious conflicts, or childhood shock. The theory of differential associations assumes that criminal behavior is a normal, learned behavior, and in the process of learning criminal behavior one finds all the mechanisms present in learning any other behavior patterns.

There are two versions of the theory of differential associations,[39] though in order to grasp the difference it is necessary to treat the two versions jointly.

The starting point for the Sutherland theory is differentiated social organization, namely a situation in which a part of the society is organized around the values linked with law observance, and another part around criminal "values." The effect of the differentiated social organization is a culture conflict with respect to legal norms. Criminal culture is defined broadly by Sutherland: Criminal culture is just as obvious as the culture of law observance and much more widespread than is generally believed. It is not limited to slum hoodlums or professional criminals. Prisoners often claim and undoubtedly believe that they are now worse than most people in the outside world. The darkest dealings of businessmen and professional people can be interpreted as in keeping within the letter of the law, though in its logic and effects they could be identical with criminal behavior which leads to imprisonment.

The existence of a culture conflict is a necessary condition for the process of differential associations, or a process through which criminality of an individual takes place. Differential associations mean contact with criminal and noncriminal models of behavior, through which the models are adopted in a learning process.

Learning criminal or noncriminal behavior takes place through interaction with other persons in the process of communication. Such communication could be verbal or nonverbal.

Sutherland attached great importance to direct interactions as the most important source from which people derive their behavior models. He therefore accented the significance of primary groups (family, peer groups, neighbors) due to the closeness and long-lasting nature of contacts between their members. According to Sutherland, the mass media and the other types of groups play a secondary role in the process of assimilating criminal behavior models.

In the course of such interactions people are exposed to patterns which are conducive or nonconducive to law violations. These patterns are contained in the criminal and noncriminal behavior models. Through a surplus of patterns (models) conducive to law violation compared with patterns nonconducive to law violation, a nonconformist attitude towards law is shaped, leading to criminality.

One should note that for Sutherland the "surplus" is not the result solely of a higher quantity of criminal behavior models. Whether a surplus situation will develop depends also on the duration, frequency, and past contacts with given types of models, for instance, frequent though quite superficial contacts with criminal behavior models would not tend to develop such a surplus.

Further, one should keep in mind that the outline of the criminalizing process developed by Sutherland always assumes an interaction of association with criminal and noncriminal behavior models rather than contact exclusively with one type.

The theory of differential associations is classified as a theory of culture transmission. Criminality is treated here as a component of culture and the phenomenon of criminality as a consequence of culture models transmission. It is decidedly sociological in character. The psychological variables which have a key function in other theories play a secondary role in Sutherland's. They can at best serve as the so-called instrumental variables defining the scope of associations with given types of behavior patterns; in themselves, irrespective of the process of adapting criminal behavior models through learning, they are unable to offer an explanation of why a given person chose the path of criminality.

Among contemporary orientations of the learning theory, closest to Sutherland is the theory of social learning advanced by Albert Bandura.[40] He has made a thorough study of learning aggression by modeling and imitating. The theory of social learning distinguishes behavior used in everyday life which is assimilated, but not learned. For instance, a person can assimilate the skills required for certain types of behavior such as aggression, but never apply these skills, viewing them negatively. Proponents of the social learning theory believe, as Freud did, that people learn not only by observing the specific reactions of others, but also by applying the strategy guiding their behavior. They believe that there are three sources of assimilating aggressive behavior: family subculture, and ideas (for instance, transmitted by motion pictures, television, books, and the like).

Aggression is assimilated through observation and perfected through practical reinforcement.

Proponents of the social learning theory attempt to explain both individual aggressive behaviors and collective aggression. The social learning theory gives minimum credit to individual activity and the impact of cognitive processes modifying human behavior, and for that reason has been frequently criticized.

Should it ever turn out that learning criminal behavior models is the effect of noninteraction reinforcing factors, this would not mean that the theory is wrong in its premises, as claimed by Robert Adams.[41] One should only consider the possible narrowing of the scope of its application to interpreting the etiology of criminal behavior.

Numerous social psychologists seek the sources of criminality in disruptions of the socializing process. In most general terms, in social psychology, the socialization of an individual means the process of "becoming" a member of the society, assimilating the norms, behavior models, and systems of values functioning in the society. At the present stage of studies no age limit is set for the completion of this process.

The most important groups in which the socialization process takes place include family, school, peer group, and workmates. The proper course of socialization is determined both by biopsychical factors—type of nervous system, IQ, and other measures, and by environmental factors. Criminological studies devote considerable attention to these.

Disorders of the socialization process could extend to difficulties in identifying with the given sex. David B. Lynn has shown that identification with the male or the female role can lead to many adaptation disturbances. The socialization process further covers the adoption of given attitudes and values concerning one's own person.[42] Heilbrun and Goodstein have conducted various studies showing that an incoherent view of oneself leads to serious perturbations in social behavior. In tests carried out on students, Heilbrun determined significant differences between the type of behavior which the students accepted as socially desirable and acceptable and the types of behavior which they believed as describing themselves.

The process of internalizing social and moral standards is of great significance for proper socialization and adaptation. An interesting attempt at explaining the development of moral character was presented by Jean Piaget, by Lawrence Kohlberg and also by Hartshorne and May. Kohlberg distinguished six stages of an individual's moral development:

Stage 1: Obedience and punishment orientation. Egocentric deference to superior power or prestige, or a trouble-avoiding set. Objective responsibility.

Stage 2: Naively egoistic orientation. Right action is that instrumentally satisfying the self's needs and occasionally those of others. Awareness of relativism of value to each actor's needs and perspective. Naive egalitarianism and orientation to exchange and reciprocity.

Stage 3: Good-boy orientation. Orientation to approval and to pleasing and helping others. Conformity to stereotypical images of majority or natural role behavior, and judgment of intentions.

Stage 4: Authority and social-order maintaining orientation. Orientation to "doing duty" and to showing respect for authority and maintaining the given social order for its own sake. Regard for earned expectations of others.

Stage 5: Contractual legalistic orientation. Recognition of an arbitrary element or starting point in rule of expectations for the sake of agreement. Duty defined in terms of contract, general avoidance of violation of the will or rights of others, and majority will and welfare.

Stage 6: Conscience or principle orientation. Orientation not only to actually ordained social rules but to principles of choice involving appeal to logical universality and consistency. Orientation to conscience as a directing agent and to mutual respect and trust.[43]

While discussing disorders of the socialization process and their link with criminality one cannot pass over the studies on the so-called adaptive delinquency carried out by Richard L. Jenkins. Jenkins distinguished two types of delinquent behavior: "social delinquent behavior" and "antisocial aggressive behavior." Starting in 1941, Jenkins, along with others, carried out numerous studies of juveniles responsible for various types of delinquent behavior. Initially, on the basis of studies carried out in Michigan, he distinguished three clinical groups:

a group of social delinquents, showing the following traits: keeping bad company, banding together in gangs, taking part in gang thefts, skipping school and running away from home;

a group of antisocials attacking people, picking trouble with others, characterized by cruelty, malicious pranks and lack of remorse;

a group of excessively inhibited, shy, apathetic, highly sensitive and submissive individuals.

In recent years Jenkins and Boyer revised this classification, finally adopting the following: cooperative social delinquents, aggressive antisocial delinquents and runaway delinquents. The last group is characterized by running away from home, secret thefts at home, and passive homosexualism.[44]

The very description and classification of delinquent populations can be of great assistance in the therapeutic process and in predicting behavior, though it adds little to the theoretical divagations on the origins of criminality. Only defining the mechanism causing given behavior could contribute to explaining certain criminal behaviors.

Subcultures Theory

The classic concept of criminal subculture was formulated by Frederick Thrasher.[45] In his famous study of juvenile gangs Thrasher related the gang to the idea of social disorganization applied by scientists carrying out research on the territorial spread of criminality in big cities.

The state of social disorganization means a slackening of social bonds and the breakdown of social controls in neighborhoods dominated by certain population groups (ethnic minorities, newly arrived immigrants). This leads to "normative chaos." Individuals living in such neighborhoods lack clearly defined norms delineating their behavior, since the "old" norms are no longer adequate to the new circumstances of the big city, while at the same time the uprooted and atomized communities in the slum neighborhoods lack the capacity to evolve a new system of norms and social controls adequate to such a system. The relative lack of norms increases the probability of behavior conflicting with the law.

Thrasher viewed the formation and functioning of juvenile gangs as a natural consequence of the lack of sufficient social control over the behavior of children (particularly by parents, or in broken families) that, coupled with limited opportunities in slum areas, leads to the formation of autonomous juvenile communities—in other words, subcultures. A subculture represents a "substitute" community, compensating for the shortcomings of the family home, supplying opportunities for fun and excitement which are not available in slum areas by other means.

Contemporary concepts of criminal subcultures include an interesting one formulated by Walter Miller as the result of research which he carried out on life styles of the lower classes.[46]

According to Miller, the formation and operation of juvenile gangs are the result of lower-class culture traditions. Miller defines the lower-class culture as highly independent of middle-class behavior standards. There is great emphasis and recognition of such features as "toughness," "street smartness," "excitement," "autonomy," "troubles" (both making and avoiding trouble). Best-accepted personality models in such a culture are boxers, gangsters, and confidence tricksters. It is clearly oriented toward male social roles. Since families in the lower classes are dominated by women, it is the gang which allows for learning and practicing the social role of a man and of male identification. Gang provides the lower-class adolescents with a feeling of belonging, with a possibility of attaining a higher position by achieving values which, though highly appreciated by the lower-class culture, could be negatively viewed by the middle and upper classes whose behavior standards are reflected in laws.

Albert Cohen also agrees that the existence of delinquent subcultures is characteristic for lower-class adolescents, though he believes that the origins of that phenomenon lie elsewhere.[47]

For Miller the operation and values implemented by gangs represent nothing beyond the general culture of the lower classes, a culture which is largely autonomous.

The staring point for Cohen was the Merton theory and its central assumption that there exists a uniform system of primary aims within the society at large.

According to Cohen, lower-class boys would like to advance materially and attain a higher social position through learning and later through work. Yet, the upbringing received at home greatly hinders their adaptation to the school situation. They have not been properly prepared to give up immediate gratification for the benefit of future success. They have not been sufficiently taught to put reins on their aggressiveness, or the social graces, or respect for property. These differences in upbringing cause lower-class boys to have generally inferior performance compared with middle-class children: they do not learn as well, and they are badly adapted to the school milieu.

The feeling of blocked opportunities for advancement through learning, coupled with aspirations to success in life, leads to frustration and fear, something resolved by the so-called reaction-formation. This means totally reversing the middle-class values and doing everything which is the antithesis of the values promoted by the school.

Gang subculture is, therefore, marked by shortsighted hedonism, and the appreciated values are uselessness, malice, and negativism. In Cohen's view, the formation of gangs is the collective release for adolescents who feel their aspirations blocked.

Synthesis of the Merton and Sutherland theories led to another theory of delinquent subcultures, known as the theory of differential opportunities, formulated by Richard Cloward with Lloyd Ohlin.[48]

Cloward and Ohlin reflect Merton's views on the structural approach to the question of deviation and Sutherland's views on the access to delinquent behavior models at the given level of social structure.

Cloward and Ohlin, unlike Cohen, do not recognize juvenile gang delinquency as an expression of negation of middle-class values. The aim of achieving a higher social position and welfare remains, according to Cloward and Ohlin, a feature of all social classes, and the formation of delinquent subcultures results from the inability to achieve those aims in legal ways. The aim remains the same, it is the means that change.

Access to models of delinquent behavior is not the same for everyone. There is differentiated access both to the legal and to the delinquent means which serve the achievement of culture-sanctioned aims. In this context Cloward and Ohlin distinguish three types of adolescent subcultures.

A typically delinquent subculture will evolve in well-integrated slums where the criminal syndicates operate and where there are various types of adult criminal activities. There the models of delinquent behavior presented by adults will be assimilated by adolescents, with gradual involvement in crime, at first in the form of juvenile gangs, treated as a type of apprenticeship, all the way up to membership in a crime syndicate. Under such circumstances there are illegal opportunities for success, and criminality is treated by adolescents as a normal way of life.

In poorly integrated areas, marked by considerable mobility of its members and general instability (this type is closest to the neighborhoods which, according to Thrasher, have features of social disorganization), there is limited access to delinquent behavior models as presented by adults, so that the behavior models which allow for a higher status would come from peer groups. This will lead to the formation of a conflict subculture, as exemplified by hoodlum gangs geared to fights and vandalism. Such subcultures attach a high value to courage, militancy, and physical prowess, and boys who gain exceptional notoriety in gang fights enjoy great prestige.

The third type of subculture, the so-called drop-out subculture, encompasses those lower-class adolescents who neither have the opportunity for success by legal means nor have they been successful in the two previously mentioned ways of illegal adaptation. This method will also be chosen by the lower-class boys who consciously reject illegal actions as contrary to their moral code. Cloward and Ohlin denote it as a subculture of the "double losers." The drop-out subculture is primarily one of drugs and delinquent activities, limited here mainly to the illegal distribution of narcotics.

Negation of all the former delinquent subculture theories led to David Matza's "drift" theory.[49] According to Matza, there are no basic differences between the delinquent gang adolescents and other young people. It is also incorrect to link the phenomenon of delinquent subcultures only with the lower classes, since the values prevailing in the subcultures are rather similar to those held by the society at large in their leisure time, that is, the desire for pleasure, adventure, thrills, demonstrations of manliness and courage. Therefore, gang norms are not so much a negation as a caricature of certain behavior standards of the rest of society, and the whole problem is that the juvenile delinquents observe these otherwise accepted norms in the wrong situation, as though extending the time of play.

According to Matza the error of all the subculture theories, and to a certain extent even of all the sociological theories of criminality with a positivist orientation, is their excessive determinism. They attempt to explain too many delinquent behaviors. Matza claims that it is not true that membership in a gang in some way obliges one to delinquency or that subculture boys are in a permanent state of war with conventional society. The delinquency of gangs represents for Matza the temporary severance of bonds with an otherwise observed normative system, leading to a "drift" in the direction of delinquency. Defining the phenomenon of juvenile delinquency in the form of a drift is a manifestation of a modified version of determinism, a view that I share.

Matza provides two types of arguments in support of the thesis that delinquency of gang members is neither unavoidable nor is it the only life path for those who have once become involved in delinquent actions.

First, this is contradicted by the so-called growing out of delinquency. According to the more or less deterministic concepts already described, it is not possible to turn back from the criminal path, once chosen. Yet, there is evidence that only a relatively small percentage of juvenile delinquents continue a criminal way of life when they grow up, and even during adolescence boys find it no problem to give up gang membership.

Second, the temporary nature of the break with the rest of society is evident from the fact that gang members are able to distinguish right from wrong and have feelings of remorse. An offense takes place only when the juvenile is able to "rationalize" his improper behavior in such a way that it appears justified.

These rationalizations, described by Sykes and Matza as "techniques of neutralization," can take the following forms:[50]

negating responsibility; an offense has taken place, but the offender is not responsible, such as "I was unable to stop," "I am crazy";

negating harm; an offense has taken place, but nobody suffered, such as "they were insured anyway," "they could afford the loss";

negating the victim; an offense has taken place, but the victim contributed to it himself or deserved it, such as "it's his own fault," "he asked for it";

blaming the blamers; an offense has taken place, but the blame falls on society at large or on the authorities, such as "I had a bad childhood," "everybody is stealing," "the cop provoked me";

claiming higher motivations; an offense has taken place, but it was committed for lofty reasons, such as: "I could not leave my friends without help," "my family was poor."

One should note that in addition to the techniques of neutralization Matza explains gang delinquency also by a "comedy of errors" which stems from the fact that every individual member of the group believes that the other members are more rebellious than he, so he behaves according to expectations having no basis in reality, fearful of losing his position. This explains why a gang as a whole often commits acts which would not be committed by any of its members acting on his own.

Labeling Theory

Presented so far have been theoretical orientations concentrated on the reasons and conditions which cause individuals or certain social groups to violate the law. These theories attempted to answer the question of how a crime situation develops. The presently discussed orientation attempts to explain, first of all, why a person continues in criminality and through what process he arrives at recognizing certain types of behavior as delinquent. This orientation, whose main proponents are Edwin Lemert, Howard Becker, Kai Erickson, and John Kitsuse, is currently having a considerable impact on looking at the issue of criminality and the person of the criminal.[51]

Edwin Lemert is generally recognized as the originator and chief exponent of the labeling theory. The starting point for Lemert might appear paradoxical. He claims that deviant behavior does not require social control nor is it the result of the breakdown of social control. According to Lemert, it is social control itself which is responsible for deviations. In numerous countries, for instance, homosexualism or abortions were once viewed as offenses, subject to penal justice, punishable by often severe sentences. Once depenalized, the types of behavior which previously constituted offenses became completely legal. The reverse is also possible, when legal behavior becomes offensive through changes in the law. This means that the scope and pattern of behavior conflicting with norms is as much influenced by the social reaction to certain types of behavior as by the "bad will" of the offender.

On the basis of these general premises Lemert divides deviant behavior into two categories: primary and secondary deviation.

Primary deviation means for Lemert the mechanisms through which an individual decides to commit an offense. On the question of primary causes of deviation Lemert takes an eclectic approach. He claims that the deviation is caused by a variety of factors: social, culture-related, mental, or physiological, forming lasting or incidental configurations. Uncovering the causes of primary deviation is of secondary importance since the factor which in reality changes the status and mental structure of an individual, making a "normal" person into a deviant is not the fact of theft, alcohol abuse, homosexual relations, or drug abuse, but the labeling process. This causes the given individual to enter the ascribed social role.

Secondary deviation, as defined by proponents of the labeling theory, begins with the moment of social reaction to deviant behavior.

With an offense, the process of secondary deviation begins with the moment of instigating an official proceeding against the offender, reaching the culmination during the penal process. It is then that the given individual is publicly proclaimed an offender, a deviant, someone "queer." Next, serving the sentence, the publicly defined offender is subjected to various external "degrading" acts, such as cutting his hair, special clothes, and the like.

This whole chain of social reaction to deviation causes certain individuals to act in ways expected from the attached labels. A formerly law-abiding boy who, perhaps by accident, was labeled a juvenile delinquent starts to behave as a delinquent because of the labeling. A person abusing alcohol, publicly described as an alcoholic, starts to look upon himself as one to react the way an alcoholic is expected to.

People subjected to the labeling process develop a negative self-image which can have a long-range effect on their future behavior. This orientation directly relates to the interaction orientation in social psychology (G. H. Mead) which particularly accents the phenomena of reflected self and adopting social roles due to given reactions (expectations) of others. Deviation is treated by proponents of the labeling theory as a quasi career, and the process of social degradation is shown as a spiral effect.

In his study which originated the whole orientation Lemert described the following stages of the deviation process: primary deviation; social penalties; successive primary deviation; stiffer penalties and rejection; successive deviation, with a possibility of hostility and resentment which begins to focus on those who penalize; reaching a crisis in the tolerance level expressed in formal action of the society in the form of labeling the deviant; mounting deviant behavior as negative reaction to the labeling and punishment; final acceptance of the deviant social status and attempts at adapting on the basis of the antisocial role.[52]

A person labeled by the society as an offender, alcoholic, homosexual, or mentally ill is rejected by the society. The desire to stop being an outsider and the typical human need to belong causes that the final stage in a deviant career is joining an organized deviant group. Joining an organized deviant group has many consequences for a deviant's career. Compared with individual persons, deviant groups first of all show a greater tendency to rationalize their situation. Next the deviant learns to carry out deviant behavior in such a way as to minimize the troubles stemming from it. All the problems which he encounters in connection with violating the norms have been previously encountered by others. Therefore, there is much greater probability than ever before that the deviant, joining an organized and institutionalized deviant group, is going to continue his former behavior. On the one hand, he learned how to avoid trouble, on the other—the justification for continuing.[53]

The labeling theory can be accused, on the one hand, of many over-simplifications and, on the other hand, of overemphasis. As to the former, there is no difficulty in showing that in many cases individuals systematically violate the law, though their acts are never brought to light, so that the labeling process never takes place. As to the latter, in the majority of cases the fact of social reaction and labeling does prevent individuals from further deviant behavior.

Despite these reservations, the labeling theory caused a marked re-orientation of views and criminological studies from the traditional search for causative factors of criminal behavior to the normative sphere of that issue and the effects which in certain cases can be caused by social reaction to deviant behavior.

The labeling theory has other important practical implications. Its findings should serve as a warning to criminal justice agencies as to the possible negative consequences of processing certain people through the machinery of justice administration. This particularly holds for juveniles whose psyches are still taking shape, so that they are particularly susceptible to adapting to the social roles assigned to them. Overly hasty instigation of proceedings against minors could accelerate the process of degradation rather than prevent it.

Etiological Assumptions in the Criminology of Socialist Countries

Marxist classics did not elaborate much on the subject of criminality, yet on the basis of comments contained in various writings of Marx and Engels the picture of its causes can be seen quite clearly.

Marx and Engels sought the causes of criminality in social conflicts and the contradictions of the capitalist system. Advancing industrialization and the widening gap between classes lead to the formation of the pole of opulence on the one hand, and of poverty on the other. The situation of extreme poverty in which a large part of the working class found itself by the mid-nineteenth century in the highly industrialized West European countries was described by Engels in his *Condition of the Working Class in England*.[54]

The criminogenic character of the capitalist system was also pointed out by Marx. Citing the data of Adolf Quételet concerning the faster growth of criminality than of the population, Marx concluded that the capitalist system itself must be responsible for this state of affairs, since it increases opulence without eliminating poverty. Still, it would be a great oversimplification to reduce the views of Marx and Engels exclusively to economic determinism.[55] Having the Marxist classics concentrate on economic conditions simply exemplified their general theory of social conflict and the contradictions, mainly between the social character of production and the private ownership of the means of production. The antinomics of the capitalist system are reflected in human relationships and the individual psyche. Free competition, fierce struggle for profit, money as the sole and supreme value—all this cannot but reflect on the attitudes, values, and motives of human activity.

Criminality in the existing system was analyzed by William Bonger, one of the first Marxist criminologists, using this more thorough method.

The central term in Bonger's etiological concept is the so-called criminal intention, its formulation, the forces preventing a person from implementing the criminal intention and the circumstances conducive to committing a crime.[56]

Criminal intention, according to Bonger, is the effect of stimulating man's egoistic tendencies by the social system of the bourgeois state. Egoistic tendencies are awakened in the society along with the development of productive forces and the changes taking place in production relations.

During the times of prehistoric primitive communities, or in other words primitive communism, people were guided by altruistic motives. This was due to the fact that the production relations of the day based on simple reproduction made it necessary to integrate the society and act in common for the sake of survival. People were well disposed toward each other, trusting and friendly, giving up their individual interests for the common good. Yet, at the moment when production increases to such a degree that the producer is able to systematically produce more than he needs himself, and the division of labor forces him to exchange the surplus for objects which he is unable to produce himself, man gains the conviction that he no longer has to offer his comrades what they need but can keep his own product and exchange the surplus. It is then that production relations begin to counterpose themselves to man's social instincts, rather than favor them as before.[57]

In this way class distinctions, competition, and private ownership of the means of production cause "individualization" of human aspirations and the increase of egoistic tendencies. The general desire for owning, greed, disregard for other people—characteristic features of capitalist social relations—all this serves as fertile soil for the formulation and implementation of criminal intentions.

Without going into detailed classification of the links between egotism, poverty, and given types of offenses, one should note that the moral climate of capitalism is, according to Bonger, responsible also for the criminality of the bourgeois. While Bonger explains the criminality of the poor mainly by economic pressures, he claims that the criminality of the capitalists results mainly from greed. Although greed, wrote Bonger, constitutes a strong motive in all classes of our present society, it particularly concerns the bourgeois as the result of its position in economic life.[58] Ownership of wealth does not suffice for the capitalists. The desire for even more riches leads them to the path of criminality.

The Bonger concept, in addition to class and structural elements, also notes other factors, making the theory highly eclectic. For instance, Bonger also includes as equally important causes of criminality the lack of culture and education of the lower classes and alcoholism.

There was a characteristic evolution of views on the etiology of crime in

Soviet criminology. In the first stage after the Revolution there were many proponents of the neo-Lombrosian theory. This was probably due to the fact that scholars of the day, applying a literal interpretation of Marxist classics, were of the opinion that since along with the change of the social system the structural reasons for entering the criminal path had disappeared, then the sources of criminality had to be sought in the biological and mental constitution of individuals. The theory of Enrico Ferri also enjoyed great popularity in those days.

The 1930s meant a total dominance of the relict theory, connected with a general regression of Soviet criminology. The relict theory had a number of versions, though in most general terms it boiled down to the view that the sole cause of criminality in the socialist countries is relicts of the past in human minds.

The relict theory in its original, categorical form, is no longer accepted by anyone. Socialist criminologists recognize these factors (relicts of the past) as one of many causes of criminality, applicable to all criminal acts. Taking the Marxist approach that development of a socialist society is not a harmonious process without its upheavals and contradictions, socialist criminologists attempt to uncover the reasons for conflicts of individuals with the society under defined social circumstances.[59]

Soviet criminology is defined as the science of the level dynamics and causes of criminality, methods of studying it and ways and means of preventing it in a socialist society.

Socialist criminology does not accept the biological or biopsychic nature of criminality, as it represents the unacceptability of applying biological notions to the field of social phenomena. This is not to say that socialist criminology fails to consider the personality of the criminal. Rejecting biological factors as causes of criminality, socialist criminology requires, when explaining an individual's behavior, considering his physiological and mental traits as internal conditions interacting with factors from the social milieu.

Soviet criminology differs completely from bourgeois criminology in its approach to personality in that it does not treat the personality as an individual supposedly vested with certain traits or predispositions to criminal acts or as a conglomerate of physiological and mental features treated as "internal causes of criminality" as though proper to a man. Rather, it studies the personality of a member of society living within the society, among people, acting upon nature, society, and people and receiving feedback from them.

Soviet criminologists accent the influence on criminality by social living conditions. The results of natural sciences research, such as genetics research, are not normally used in studying individual criminal behavior.

The need has been suggested for formulating a theory of the causes of crime in a socialist society and the sociopsychological mechanisms transforming those causes in the behavior of offenders.

V. N. Kudriavtsev, an outstanding Soviety criminologist, emphasizes that studies of the reasons behind law violations require analysis from sociological, psychological, philosophical, and general theory of law points of view. Kudriavtsev's findings, that analysis of the reasons behind law violations should take into account all types of behavior contrary to law and not just be limited to offensive behavior, determine the theoretical and research approach to the issue of etiology of offensive attitudes.[60]

Another Soviet author, A.B. Sakharov, points out that in a socialist society crime is linked with certain rules of society's functioning.[61]

V. M. Kogan seeks the causes of crime in the contradictions of the social system; in a socialist society such contradictions are of a nonantagonistic nature.[62]

Soviet literature also touches upon issues of the interrelations between legal and social norms, the process of internalizing social norms and the significance of a sociological definition of social norms when considering issues linked with criminality. Crime is linked with social processes, the functioning of social institutions, changes within social classes, strata, and small social groups.[63]

According to the view of criminologists of the German Democratic Republic, socialist criminology considers the phenomenon of criminality as the feature inherent not in the social condition itself but in the system that exploits the man. In the socialist system criminality is treated as a transitional phenomenon which is either the expression of the factors inherited from the previous system and still inherent in the socialist society, clashing with socialism, or resulting from errors committed while creating a new system.[64]

In Poland a theory of the genetic and dynamic factor of crime was formulated by Leszek Lernell,[65] though segments of this theory were first formulated by other criminologists, notably Stanisław Batawia, Bronisław Wróblewski and Walter Reckless.[66] Lernell states that at the origins of every (or nearly every) criminal behavior we note a position of inequality in which the acting individual finds himself. This position corresponds with the aim to eliminate, cross the threshold, or compensate for the state of inequality. More specifically, it is a question of the tendency to neutralize the negative, for an individual, effects of his unequal position in relation to others. The author explains that inequality constituting the starting position in the view of an individual could concern various spheres: biological, mental, economic, prestige, and the like.

Lernell seeks the genetic factor mainly in the criminal behavior of economic, hoodlum, and unintentional types, which taken together make up the majority of present-day criminality. He does not, however, exclude the possibility of these types of criminal behavior in which the genetic factor does not play a role.

A different Polish criminological theory is advanced by Jerzy Bafia.[67] Starting with the premise that crime is a social phenomenon of a constantly changing nature and that is has its sources both in the social sphere and in the sphere of man's psyche and personality, Bafia concludes that it occurs because of the clash of unfavorable factors in the development of the social milieu, in the personality of individuals, and in presented social attitudes. Appearance of these unfavorable factors leads to a situation conducive to a criminal tendency. Such a setup with factors leading in the criminal direction is called a crime-conducive situation. Bafia explains that a crime-conducive situational setup can be objective (a person does not shape it with premeditation, as in the case of unintentional offenses) or subjective (with premeditated intention of perpetrating an offense).

Adam Podgórecki assumes that in the causative conditioning of criminality the role of the independent variable is played by the socioeconomic system, the dependent variable is the crime, while the intermediary variables are: the standard of living of an offender, his milieu (criminal subculture), criminogenic circumstances directly preceding the crime, and the offender's personality.[68]

One should also point out that Witold Swida, using the example of criminality in Kalisz in the years 1937 and 1952 attempted to determine the impact of a changed socioeconomic system on the scope and type of criminality. Swida found that the 1937 criminals came mainly from social outcasts and professional crime elements as well as from people in poor material circumstances. New types of offenses appeared by 1952, connected with the new social circumstances and committed by reliance on the lack of effective controls.

Leon Tyszkiewicz has made an attempt to classify the criminogenic factors based on his general model of the mechanisms of human actions, which takes into account the following elements: genotype, organism, environment (broken down into natural environment and the social milieu (macrosocial, regional, and microsocial)), personality, external circumstances (current pattern of environmental factors), and internal circumstances (current mental state). This model provides the grounds for dividing the criminogenic factors into somatic, environmental, situational, and mental. Beyond this division remain the complex factors (age, sex, and socioeconomic status) and the manner of living (alcoholism, prostitution, and the like). Tyszkiewicz does not ascribe a general priority significance to any single factor, but rather suggests studying the so-called crime genesis, meaning the process which led the individual to crime. This study should make allowance for all the factors influencing criminality in their inter-relations and changeability.

In my criminology textbooks I have advanced the concept of the criminality syndrome and potential.[69]

One of the most difficult tasks in analyzing the data obtained in empirical criminological studies is to determine the cause-and-effect relationships. The difficulties are compounded when defining the psychosocial determinants of criminal phenomena.

Most manifestations of human behavior have their source not in a single factor or in group of factors, but are rather determined by a practically unlimited complex of equivalent factor sequences.

Social practice, as the sole objective criterion of the value of scientific studies, clearly reveals the dangers of following a "single trail" in interpreting the etiology of crime. The effective value of every single-factor criminological theory has been generally questioned. Criminality cannot be boiled down to a single or even two or three causes. Criminal phenomena are the effect of interaction by a great variety of alternatively convergent determinants, whose nature and combinations can clearly affect one individual differently than another. This means that offenders do not represent a homogenous class of individuals, observing whom a criminologist could easily generalize concerning the causative character.

Figure 3–1 shows the interaction of multicause impacts. Selecting only a few factors "popularly" recognized as crime-conducive and indicating the spider web of interactions leads to a total obliteration of the cause-effect vectors triggered by each factor taken separately.

The factors chosen as examples are shown on three different levels: criminality, the offender, and exogenous factors shaping the criminal behavior trends.

It is easy to see that the classification of factors on one level has little practical value for explaining the value of elements classified on different levels.

The cognitive problem comes down to distinguishing defined configurations of factors which have a particularly important impact on shaping the criminal behavior trends.

When in connection with a given combination of exogenous factors the frequency of offensive behavior for a given individual is significantly higher than for another individual, then such a situation is called *crime-conducive*.

When an individual with a defined combination of endogenous factors violates the law more frequently than an individual who does not have these features, all else being equal, then one describes such an individual as *crime-prone*.

Both a crime-conducive situation and a crime-prone subject are not terms which could be formulated in such a way as to define their designations unequivocally. After studying the scope of phenomena described by these terms it becomes necessary to supplement their coverage with features found not only within their scopes but also within the scope of numerous other terms. The terms defined in such a way take on a context which is too comprehensive to define their designates uniformly. By the same token the context of terms defined in such a manner, in addition to the features indispensable in view of the function of denoting the scope, further contain explicit or at least implicit theses concerning given links, relations between the elements. One does not find here a simple conjunction of features, but instead, a convergence in keeping with given ratios. That is why a body of such features has been named by science a *syndrome* (from Greek *syn*, "with, along with, with the assistance of, along with," and *dromos* "course, track").

The term whose context is defined by a syndrome instead of by a simple combination of features is known as a syndromatic term.

In accordance with what was said above, defining a crime-conducive situation or a crime-prone subject cannot be limited to listing the features connoting those terms, but must also define the relations between those features.

While on syndromatic terms, it has to be considered whether the defined relations, presumed in these terms, are of an absolute or stochastic (conjectural) nature. After all, chemical, physical, or biological syndromes are usually marked by relations which have no exceptions. The syndromes applied by, say, sociology or social psychology are usually stochastic in nature; they only accept correlations of a certain set of features, but not their regular joint appearance or succession. This significantly complicates the possibility of determining whether a given individual or situation is or is not a designate of a given syndromatic notion.

A way out can be found by treating a syndromatic notion as a typological term and by considering individual elements (situations or subjects) from the point of view of how close they come to a given type. An elementary gauge of the difference from the type is the number of features lacking in a given situation or individual in order to meet the syndrome qualities in full.

Each syndromatic notion of a stochastic nature, including crime-conduciveness, always has to be approached as a variable. The crime-conduciveness of a given situation or a given individual can be greater or lesser. Obviously, the largest crime-conduciveness is ascribed to a situation or an individual having all the features specified in defined relations by a given syndrome. Next to a crime-conducivity scale founded only on the number of factors included in the syndrome one could also apply a scale based on the probability of criminal behavior given a set combination of factors.

I propose to name the probability of criminal behavior in a situation having all the features included in the situation syndrome as the *general criminogenic potential* of that syndrome.

The syndrome covering both all the identified situation and subject features could be called the *general criminality potential.*

In addition to the general criminogenic potential there are also sectional potentials. A sectional potential of the given syndrome is the probability of criminal behavior when only certain of the syndrome conditions are met. The number of sectional potentials of a given syndrome is equal to the number of combinations of the factors specified for the syndrome and can be viewed as the gauge of the syndrome complexity.

Let us evaluate, as an example, the following exogenous factors in a juvenile's milieu:

1. parents' alcoholism;
2. family breakup;
3. lack of parental supervision;
4. adverse influence of peer group;
5. negative attitude of school.

These factors are treated as crime-conducive. An assembly of these factors and the interrelations between them forms the general syndrome of the criminogenic situation noted here.

Applying specified statistical methods and techniques, in a properly carried out empirical study one determines the probability of criminal behavior by individuals exposed to given combinations of these factors. A control group is used for verifying the hypothesis concerning the criminogenity of these factors.

Finding, for instance, that the probability that an individual exposed to all the syndrome factors will commit an offense during a specified period of time amounts to 0.36, then this is the general criminogenity potential of the given syndrome.

When, on the other hand, the probability that an individual exposed to only such syndrome factors as, for instance, parental alcoholism and adverse peer group influence, will commit a crime amounts to 0.16, then this is one of the sectional potentials of the syndrome concerned.

The long-range objective of criminological studies is to construct a syndrome having complete explanatory power, namely a syndrome with 1.0 potential. In other words, this would be a syndrome with all the features and relations which, when present in an individual, would make it possible to

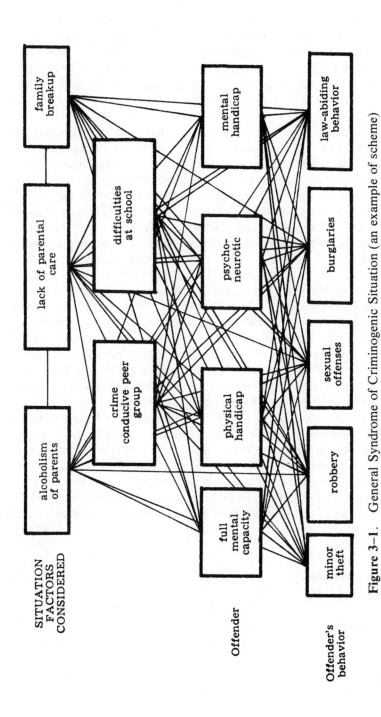

Figure 3–1. General Syndrome of Criminogenic Situation (an example of scheme)

ascertain beyond any doubt that this individual is going to commit an offense in a given span of time. This would amount to an absolute syndrome.

Construction of such a syndrome would be possible only under nearly ideal, artificial laboratory conditions. In view of the limitations on experimenting, criminology only attempts to increase the explanatory power of syndromes relating to real conditions. The explanatory power of present-day criminological syndromes oscillates around 40 to 50 percent.

The criminality syndrome is treated as a diagnostic tool. Yet, when one determines which syndrome elements are susceptible to guidance and which are unguidable, a syndrome can properly direct preventive measures.

Operating with various syndromatic notions, criminology so far has only touched upon the simplest relation of phenomena denoted by syndrome context elements, namely the relation of coexistence. The aim is to have syndromatic notions reflect the pattern of relations among the various components of criminal phenomena in a more detailed way, defining the time sequence of given occurences, the causative relationships among them, depicting the body of various feedbacks in the context of phenomena which are the subject of study. Only then will criminological syndromatic notions deserve to be treated as models of phenomena of full practical significance.

In detailed elaboration of the subject I have presented some of the most significant determinants of criminal behavior. First, I describe certain phenomena and processes of a macrosocial nature, accepted as having a significant link with criminality. These include socioeconomic development and the negative contents of mass culture. Further, I have concentrated on the role of family and school in the genesis of criminal behavior. Dysfunction of these primary cells of the socialization process has been traditionally recognized as crime-conducive. A significant crime-conducive factor can be the wrong job environment, though this question is often passed over in discussions of criminality determinants. Another subject quite frequently brought up in criminological studies is the connection between criminality and the pathology of biopsychic features. Discussion of the main criminal behavior determinants is summed up by presentation of the role played by the victim in certain types of criminality.

The New Criminology

At the beginning of the 1960s, the United States and Britain became the home of a direction known as new, critical, or radical criminology whose proponents[70] analyze criminality on a Marxist or quasi-Marxist platform. The new criminology distances itself from the previous theoretical directions in criminology which to a greater or lesser extent are positivist in nature and are aimed correctionally.[71]

Proponents of this school have questioned the traditional, legal definition of an offense on the premise that what the law reflects is "the will of the ruling class elevated to the dignity of statute," forcing its values, objectives, and behavior models on the exploited classes. This new criminology negates the concensual model of a society based on the notion that there is agreement within the society as a whole as to the prime objectives, norms, and values, and that this is reflected in law. In such a model a "deviant" is an individual differing in behavior from the people at large, with the deviant behavior treated usually as incidental to the external factors acting upon an individual. It is accepted than an individual has negligible or nil influence on his deviant behavior; it remains beyond the individual's control.

The logical follow-up of such a definition of deviation in the practical sphere is the "corrective" or "therapeutic" model. Since the social system is good, the law just and equal for all, and despite the fact that the individual deviates in behavior from allegedly generally recognized standards, the individual requires "resocialization," "reeducation," "treatment," so that he can once again become a regular member of the harmonious and conflict-free society.

Proponents of the new criminology have given back the individual his "free will," questioned by the postivist criminologists. An offensive act is no longer the effect of "external influences" but an act of deliberate choice among alternatives. Theft is not interpreted as the effect of insufficient socialization or the manifestation of subconscious conflicts, but as the conscious act of an individual, a type of rebellion and protest against the injustices of the capitalist system, in which the ostensible equality in the face of law is not accompanied by economic equality and equality in the opportunity for making decisions.

The new criminology speaks of a "criminal social system" rather than of "criminal individuals." That is why the cornerstone of the program proposed by proponents of that school is the total change of the capitalist social system as the main condition for limiting the phenomenon of criminality.

The objection frequently voiced by the radical criminologists against the positivist criminology concerns the latter's ostensible political noninvolvement and the scientifically neutral stance which it tries to adopt. This stance in consequence leads to silent approval (and even "improvement" through suggesting partial reforms of criminal justice or legislation) of the existing, unjust social relations.

Unlike the positivists, the radical criminologists are highly concerned with political issues, and their analysis of deviant phenomena is carried out from Marxist, class positions. The starting point for considerations shifted from the person of the criminal to the legal norms in accordance with which given behavior is defined as criminal (the process of law formation and application and its class context in a wider social and economic context) and the very notion of crime. Proponents of the new criminology have a much broader definition of crime, compared with the positivist criminologists. For instance, Hermann and Julia Schwedinger are willing to accept as an offense certain types of group actions (racism, sexism) or actions carried out by the state (imperialism, economic exploitation, conduct of aggressive wars).[72] In their approach crime should be defined as that which violates basic human rights (right to personal security, racial, sexual, and economic equality, and so on) irrespective of whether these rights find protection in penal code provisions or not.

The new criminology is far from uniform, and its proponents differ even on fundamental issues. Certain of the demands and concepts advanced by the "radicals" are extremely naive, and the center of their theoretical and research interests differs highly from the traditional fields of criminological research (the differences are so great that this school could even be called "political criminology").[73] Despite such objections, the new criminology stream deserves close observation. It could turn out to be quite inventive, particularly in explaining the mechanisms of law creation and application in bourgeois-type states.

Notes

1. Thomas More, *Utopia*, edited with introduction and notes by J. Chuston Collins (Oxford: Clarendon Press, 1904).

2. Tommaso Campanella, *Miasto słońca* [Civitas solis] (Wrocław: Zakł. im. Ossolińskich, 1955).

3. Cesare Beccaria, *Dei Delitti e Delle Pene*. Edition anonymous, no listing of author or publisher, no division into paragraphs. Printed at Livorno in 1764 in the printing shop of poet and abbot Marco Coltellini. The first anonymous English translation appeared, with a foreward, in 1767 under the title *An Essay on Crimes and Punishments* (London: J. Almon) and had a number of printings. In 1880 appeared one of the most outstanding English studies of Beccaria. See James Anderson Farrer, *Crimes and Punishments, Including a New Translation of Beccaria's "Dei Delitti e Delle Pene"* (London: Chatto and Windus).

4. Hans J. Schneider, *Kriminologie, Standpunkte, und Probleme* [Criminology, standpoints and problems] (Berlin: Walter de Gruyter, 1974).

5. Comprehension of psychological theories is greatly helped by knowledge of the general problems connected with the structure and functioning of human mental life. See for instance Paul H. Lindsay and David A. Norman, *Human Information Processing: An Introduction to Psychology* (New York: Academic Press, 1972).

6. Gwynn Nettler, *Explaining Crime* (New York: McGraw-Hill, 1974).

7. Daniel Glaser, ed., *Handbook of Criminology* (Chicago: Rand McNally College Publishing Company, 1974). See also Albert K. Cohen, *Delinquent boys: The Culture of the Gang* (New York: Free Press, 1955).

8. Review and evaluation of contemporary theories of personality is contained in many books on psychology. See, for instance, Calvin S. Hall and Gardner Lindzey, *Theories of Personality* (New York: Wiley, 1970). This publication contains an exceptionally comprehensive review of the subject.

9. *Definitive Bibliography—The Etiology of Criminality: Nonbehavioral Science Perspectives*, U.S. Department of Justice, L.E.A.A., National Institute of Law Enforcement and Criminal Justice, June 1979. This is a compilation of recent literature in the NCJRS collection on biological influences on criminal behavior.

10. The publications of Cesare Lombroso were a subject of wide scientific analysis. See, for instance, Xavier Francotte, *L'anthropologie criminelle* [Criminal anthropology] (Paris: Baillieve et Fils, 1891); Gabriel Tarde, *La criminalité comparéé* [Criminality compared] (Paris: Felix Alcon, 1971); Bernaldo C. De Quiros, *Modern Theories of Criminality* (Boston: Little, Brown & Co., 1911); Hans Kurella, *Cesare Lombroso, A Modern Man of Science* (New York: Rebman Co., 1910); Gina Lombroso-Ferrero, *Criminal Man According to the Classification of Cesare Lombroso* (New York: G. P. Putnam's Sons, 1911).

11. Raffaele Garofalo, *Criminology*, 1st ed. 1885. The excellent English translation completed in 1914 by Robert W. Miller is based largely on the French edition of 1905. See also Francis A. Allen, *The Borderland of Criminal Justice: Essays in Law and Criminology* (Chicago: University of Chicago Press, 1964). Garofalo's criminological ideas are presented in considerable detail there in the essay: "Garofalo's Criminology and Some Modern Problems", pp. 63–90.

12. Enrico Ferri, *Sociologia criminale* [Criminal sociology], 2 vols. (Turin: Bocca, 1929–1930).

13. Franz von Liszt, *Lehrbuch des deutschen Strafrechts* [Handbook of German penal law] (Berlin: Walter de Gruyter, 1927).

14. Charles B. Goring, *The English Convict: A Statistical Study* (London: His Majesty's Stationary Office, 1913).

15. Ernest Hooton, *The American Criminal: An Anthropological Study* (Cambridge: Harvard University Press, 1939).

16. Ernst Kretschmer, *Körperbau und Charakter* [Body build and character] (Berlin: Springer, 1921).

17. George Schwab, "Uber die Beziehungen der körperlichen Konstitution zum Verbrechertyp" [On the link of body build to the type of criminal] in *Monatsschrift für Kriminalbiologie*, 1941, vol. 32.

18. See the following publications by William H. Sheldon, (jointly with S. S. Steven and W. B. Tucker) *The Varieties of Human Physique: An Introduction to Constitutional Psychology* (New York: Harper, 1940); (with S. S. Steven) *The Varieties of Temperament: A Psychology of Constitutional Differences* (New York: Harper, 1942); (with Emil M. Hartl and Eugene McDermott) *Varieties of Delinquent Youth: An Introduction to Constitutional Psychiatry* (New York: Harper, 1949); (with C. W. Dupertuis and Eugene McDermott) *Atlas of Men: A Guide for Somatotyping the Adult Male at All Ages* (New York: Harper, 1954).

19. Sheldon Glueck and Eleanor Glueck, *Physique and Delinquency* (New York: Harper, 1956).

20. Max G. Schlapp and Edward H. Smith, *The New Criminology* (New York: Boni and Liveright, 1928).

21. Marvin D. Casey et al., "Sex chromosome abnormalities in two state hospitals from patients requiring special security," *Nature* 1966, vol. 5.

22. An exhaustive critique of the "chromosome" theory of criminality was carried out by Theodore Sabrin and Justin Miller, "Demonism Revisted: The XYY Chromosomal Anomaly," *Issues in Criminology* 1970, vol. 5.

23. L. S. Garfield and A. E. Bergin, eds., *Handbook of Psychotherapy and Behavior Change: An Empirical Analysis* (New York: Wiley, 1971); *Handbuch der Psychologie in 12 Bänden*, vol. 8, *Klinische Psychologie* (Göttingen: Verlag für Psychologie, C. J. Hogrefe, 1977).

24. Thomas S. Szasz, *The Myth of Mental Illness* (New York: Hoeber-Harper, 1962).

25. Hans J. Eysenck, *Crime and Personality* (London: Methuen, 1964).

26. The feeling of guilt can be the effect of various factors, such as the oedipus (or electra) complex or other delitescent sexual deviations.

27. The psychoanalytical theory of criminality is represented, among others, by Franz Alexander and William Healy, *Roots of Crime* (New York: Knopf, 1935); David Abrahamsen, *Crime and the Human Mind* (New York: Montclair, 1944); Kate Friedlander, *The Psychoanalytical Approach to Juvenile Delinquency* (New York: International Universities Press, 1947).

28. For instance, Alfred Adler seeks the genesis of criminality in the aim of diminishing the inferiority complex.

29. Charles B. Goring, *The English Convict.*

30. Cyril Burt, *The Young Delinquent* (London: D. Appleton, 1925).

31. Sheldon Glueck and Eleanor Glueck, *500 Criminal Careers* (New York: Knopf, 1930) and *Unraveling Juvenile Delinquency* (New York: Commonwealth Fund, 1950).

32. This is the so-called multifactor theory, the most evident example of eclecticism in criminology.

33. A review of the concepts concerning the biological conditioning of aggressive behavior is contained in Kenneth E. Moyer, *The Psychobiology of Aggression* (New York: Harper & Row, 1976).

34. Certain objections are raised by the omission of two well-known theories from this school, the ecological theory and the conflict of cultures theory. They were omitted on purpose, since the presentation of the theory of differential associations, constituting a synthesis of the two previously mentioned theories, should suffice in this respect.

35. Emile Durkheim, *The Rules of Sociological Method,* trans. Sarah A. Solovay and John H. Mueller (Glencoe, Ill.: The Free Press, 1958).

36. Emile Durkheim, *Suicide* (New York: Free Press, 1951), p. 248.

37. Robert K. Merton, "Social Structure and Anomie," American Sociological Review 1938, pp. 672–682, and *Social Theory and Social Structure* (Glencoe, Ill.: The Free Press, 1957), ch. 6.

38. Robert K. Merton, Social Theory and Social Structure, p. 162.

39. Edwin H. Sutherland, *Principles of Criminology*, 3rd ed. (New York: Lippincott, 1939), pp. 4–9; *Principles of Criminology*, 4th ed. (Philadelphia: Lippincott, 1947), pp. 3–9.

40. Albert Bandura, *Aggression: A Social Learning Analysis* (Englewood Cliffs, N.J.: Prentice-Hall, 1973); Albert Bandura, *Principles of Behavior Modification* (New York: Holt, Rinehart and Winston, 1969); Albert Bandura and A. C. Huston, "Identification as a Process of Incidental Learning," *Journal of Abnormal and Social Psychology* 63 (1961): 311–318; Albert Bandura and Richard H. Walters, *Social Learning and Personality Development* (New York: Holt, Rinehart and Winston, 1963); Albert Bandura and Richard H. Walters, *Adolescent Aggression: A Study of the Influence of Child Training Practices and Family Relationships* (New York: Ronald Press, 1959).

41. Robert Adams, "Differential Association and Learning Principles Revisited," *Social Problems* 1973, vol. 20.

42. David B. Lynn, "The Process of Learning Parental and Sex-Role Identification," in *Studies in Adolescence*, ed. R. E. Grinder (New York: 1975), pp. 219–227; also Irving B. Weiner, "Mental Disturbances . . ." ibid. pp. 386–392.

43. Lawrence Kohlberg, "Moral Education in the Schools: A Development View," *Studies in Adolescence* pp. 378–399.

44. Richard L. Jenkins, "Adaptive and Maladaptive Delinquency," *Nervous Child* 11 (1955): 9–11; idem, "Motivation and Frustration in Delinquency," *American Journal of Orthopsychiatry* 27 (1957): 528–537; idem, "The Psychopathic or Antisocial Personality," *Journal of Nervous and Mental Disease* 1960, pp. 318–334; idem, "Types of Delinquent

Behavior and Background Factors," *International Journal of Social Psychiatry* 1968, no. 14, p. 196.

45. Frederick M. Thrasher, *The Gang* (Chicago: University of Chicago Press, 1963).

46. Walter B. Miller, "Lower Class Culture as a Generating Milieu of Gang Delinquency," *Journal of Social Issues* 1958, vol. 14, pp. 5–19.

47. Albert K. Cohen, *Delinquent Boys.*

48. Richard A. Cloward and Lloyd E. Ohlin, *Delinquency and Opportunity: A Theory of Delinquent Gangs* (Glencoe, Ill.: The Free Press, 1960).

49. David Matza, *Delinquency and Drift* (New York: Wiley, 1964).

50. Gresham M. Sykes and David Matza, "Techniques of Neutralization: A Theory of Delinquency," *American Sociological Review* 22 (1957): 554–670.

51. Edwin Lemert, *Social Pathology* (New York: McGraw-Hill, 1951); idem, *Human Deviance, Social Problems, and Social Control* (Englewood Cliffs, N.J.: Prentice-Hall, 1967); Howard S. Becker, *Outsiders: Study in the Sociology of Deviance* (New York: Free Press, 1963); John I. Kitsuse, "Societal Reaction to Deviant Behavior: Problems of Theory and Method," *Social Problems* 9 (1962).

52. Edwin Lemert, *Social Pathology*, p. 77.

53. Howard S. Becker, *Outsiders*, pp. 37–39.

54. Friedrich Engels, *Die Lage der arbeitenden Klasse in England* (Berlin: Dietz, 1947).

55. This is claimed by, among others, George B. Vold. *Theoretical Criminology* (New York: Oxford University Press, 1958), pp. 159–183.

56. William A. Bonger, *Criminality and Economic Conditions* (Boston: Little, Brown, 1961), p. 401.

57. William A. Bonger, *Criminality and Economic Conditions* (Bloomington, London: Indiana University Press, 1969), p. 37, abridged ed. quoted in Ian Taylor, Paul Walton, and Jock Young, *The New Criminology; For a Social Theory of Deviance* (London: Routledge and Kegan Paul, 1973), p. 226.

58. William A. Bonger, *Criminality and Economic Conditions*, 1969, p. 138.

59. Vladimir Zvirbul and Aleksy Shlapochnikov, "O sostoyani y perspektivakh razwitiya sovietskoy criminologee [On the state and perspectives of developing Soviet criminology], *Socyalististisheskaya Zakonnost* 1976, no. 8.

60. Vladimir N. Kudriavtsev, *Przyczyny naruszeń prawa* [Causes behind law violations] Polish translation. (Warsaw: Wydawnictwo Prawnicze, 1978).

61. A. B. Sakharov, "O koncepcji prichin prestupnosti w socialisticheskom obshchestve" [On the concept of causes behind criminality in a socialist state] *Sovetskoe Gosudarstvo i Prawo* 1976, no. 9, pp. 25–35.

62. V. M. Kogan, "Protivorechiya obshchestvennogo razwitiya i prichiny prestupnosti" [Development conflicts and causes of criminality] *Voprosy Borby s Prestupnostu* 1973, no. 19, pp. 3–18.

63. A. M. Yakovlew, "Prestupnost kak socyalno-pravovoye yavleniye (socyalno-psikhologicheskiy aspekt)" [Criminality as a social and legal phenomenon—the social and psychological aspects] *Sovetskoye Gosudarstvo i Prawo* 1978, no. 1, pp. 74–83.

64. Erich Buchholtz et al. *Sozialistische Kriminologie* [Socialist criminology] (Berlin: Staatsverlag der DDR, 1971).

65. Leszek Lernell, *Zarys kryminologii ogólnej* [Outline of general criminology] (Warsaw: Państwowe Wydawnictwo Naukowe, 1973), p. 221 ff.

66. Stanisław Batawia, *Wstęp do nauki o przestepcy: Zagadnienia skłonności przestępczych* [Introduction to the knowledge of the criminal: Issue of criminal inclinations] (Warsaw: Biblioteka Polska w Bydgoszczy, 1931); Bronisław Wróblewski, *Wstęp do polityki kryminalnej* [Introduction to criminal policy] (Wilno: Zawadzki, J., 1922); Walter Reckless, *The Crime Problem* (New York: Appleton-Century-Crofts, 1961).

67. Jerzy Bafia, *Problemy kryminologii (Dialektyka sytuacji kryminogennej)* [Criminological problems: Dialectics of a criminogenic situation] (Warsaw: Wydawnictwo Prawnicze, 1978).

68. Adam Podgórecki, "Etiologia przestępstwa" [Etiology of crime] in *Kryminologia* [Criminology], ed. Witold Swida (Warsaw: Państwowe Wydawnictwo Naukowe, 1977), pp. 203–255.

69. Brunon Hołyst, *Kryminologia* [Criminology] 2nd ed. (Warszawa: Państwowe Wydawnictwo Naukowe, 1979), pp. 234–238.

70. For example, Ian Taylor, Paul Walton, Jock Young, William J. Chambliss.

71. An exhaustive critical analysis of existing deviance theories from a Marxist point of view was carried out by Ian Taylor, Paul Walton, and Jock Young in *The New Criminology*.

72. Hermann Schwedinger and Julia Schwedinger, "Defenders of order or guardians of human right," in *Critical Criminology*, ed. Ian Taylor, Paul Walton, and Jock Young (London: Routledge and Kegan Paul, 1975), pp. 113–147.

73. Raymond Gassin, "De quelques tendances recentes de la criminologie anglaise et nord-américaine" [On certain recent tendencies in English and North American criminology] *Revue de Science Criminelle et de Droit Pénal Comparé* 1977, no. 2, pp. 249–268.

4 Criminological Research Methods

The Aim of Criminological Research

A precondition for research is the definition of a method or set of methods by which defined subjects will be studied. Selection of methods is determined by scientific and other considerations, such as the time and funds available.

From the very outset it is necessary to bear in mind the distinction between the object of research and the research problem. The latter is, in other words, the question to which we seek an answer, while the object of research is the object which our question concerns. The questions, that is, the research problems set by the researcher, can be of a two-fold nature: we can ask about the number of occurrences in which we are interested or the intensity of given traits; these are questions concerning the value of variables characterizing given phenomena or objects; we can also focus our interest on the links between the studied objects, phenomena or traits: questions concerning links could be defined as questions of relation.

Distinguishing between these types of questions is significant, since usually the methods applied to determine the value of variables differ from the methods of studying the relations between them. To answer the question concerning the value of variables it can suffice, for instance, to just add up the answers from the questionnaire. In order to answer the question concerning the relations it is necessary to statistically analyze the correlations between the tested variables. Should the correlation analysis be supported by certain facts concerning the time sequence of events, then it will become possible to formulate hypotheses on cause-and-effect relations.

In taking up research on given phenomena or objects we have to decide whether our aim is to describe a given, single case or to provide a basis for formulating conclusions concerning a whole collection of similar cases, or finally whether our aim is to provide support for a general law or carry out research of more universal nature.

A study of a clearly unique-case nature (a defined, given individual, a given crime) is called a *case study*. When the aim is the widest possible description of a given set, occurrence or case, taking into account numerous variables, when we are seeking an answer to questions concerning both the value of variables and relations, we call it a *monographic study*.

Taking objective as the criterion, one can distinguish diagnostic, explanatory, and prognostic studies.

Diagnostic studies aim at establishing whether certain phenomena in which we are interested occur or how frequently they occur in a given object. Studying criminality in a given area or over a given span of time is a diagnostic study. Such a study could also cover such subjects as testing the intelligence of offenders or studying the ways in which offenses of a given type are committed.

The objective of *explanatory* studies is to uncover the relations among the variables in which we are interested. The fundamental question in studies of this type is the question of causes. Explanatory studies in criminology cover mainly the etiology of crimes.

Prognostic studies are aimed at forecasting future events or forecasting the process of transformation of our object. Forecasts could concern both the structure of crime and the behavior of given individuals.

The presented typology of study patterns is purely analytical. In practice the aims of various studies are linked. Prognostic studies are based, for instance, on explanatory studies. Explanatory studies require the conduct of diagnostic studies. Given projects could include in various degree the different elements of the various types of studies.

It is a general methodological principle that the manner of research (that is, research methods and techniques) should be selected depending on the object and problem of research. The choice of research object and problem should therefore determine the choice of research method or set of methods.

Research methods proper for certain types of problems and objects could be absolutely useless for studying other questions.

The objective of criminological studies is to formulate theoretical generalizations and practical directives concerning the prevention of criminality. In this context several types of general criminological studies can be distinguished:

1. studies of criminal symptomatology (phenomenology);
2. studies of criminal etiology;
3. studies of the aims and functioning of the criminological prevention system.

The scope of application of criminological study findings goes far beyond prosecution, adjudication, and sentence serving. Crime, as a mass phenomenon, touches nearly every walk of contemporary life. Because of this, counteracting the phenomenon cannot be the exclusive domain of prosecution and criminal justice agencies. Preventing criminality and other negative phenomena is the task of society as a whole, of state institution, and individual citizens.

It is therefore necessary to have the findings of criminological studies used widely in evolving social programs of preventing criminality, in drafting legislation, in taking decisions aimed at reducing the scope of crime-conducive factors, and so on.

The scale of problems which combine for the causes and manifest forms of criminality requires the application of numerous study techniques of interdisciplinary nature. The studies of criminal phenomena, rely, therefore, on a variety of research methods and techniques.

Each empirical study is carried out using one of the three following basic methods (*metamethods*); statistics, typology, or case studies. As required, a combination of these methods is frequently used.

Specific research methods and techniques are borrowed, depending on the type of study, from such disciplines as sociology, psychology, psychiatry, biology, physiology, and others.

This schematic presentation shows that the typology method is placed between two extremes: statistics applied only in studying large sets of figures descriptive of groups of crimes and offenders, and a case study covering a unique event. It also shows the necessity of using general methods in applying any type of detailed method. For instance, sociological studies require the use of either statistics or typology of a case study or finally a combination of these.

That is why defined objectives and aims of criminological studies dictate the selection of methods. The very evaluation of criminality dynamics could be, for instance, preceded by statistical analysis. Determining the causes of criminality is not possible without detailed studies of court and prosecution records, the application of psychological tests, milieu interviews, and so forth. In many cases, it becomes necessary to apply several methods jointly, such as statistical analysis, checking court records, and so on. Often statistical analysis of given phenomena suffices for selecting the subject of study.

Methodology could be treated as a specific type of ability to resolve research problems. Every situation is then presented in the form of the following formula:

$$V = f(X, Y)$$

where:

$V =$ gauge of performance or resolution of something to be maximized or minimized;

$f =$ function;

$X =$ aspects of the guidable situation; "decision" (guided) variables;

$Y =$ aspects of the situation (external context of the situation) which cannot be guided under given circumstances.

Resolution of the problem consists of finding such values of decision (guided) variables X which yield the maximum (or minimum) V value.

Formulation of the study problem reduces to a strict definition of the following elements: (1) the person taking the decision (decision maker); (2) objective (result) desired by the decision maker. The objective is defined here as a result of action which represents a positive value for the decision maker. Every problem situation has to have at least two possible results (zero and not-zero), though only one of them can have a positive value; (3) at least two nonidentical effective ways of acting which can lead to the achievement of the desired result. There must be a real difference between the decision maker's choices. When the decision maker can choose between two equally effective or totally ineffective variants, then he can perhaps convince himself that he is facing a problem, though the reality of such a problem becomes entirely subjective, not objective; (4) the state of the decision maker's doubts as to which choice is the best; and (5) the setting or context of the problem. The setting is made up of all factors which can influence the result, and which are not guidable by the decision maker. Problem situations can, obviously, be much more complex than the one described.

In order to place these general methodological constatations in the context of criminology, suffice it to consider the following simple model:

Members of a society are divided into two populations living together, though clearly distinct. One is the criminal population (C), the second the noncriminal population (N). These populations are linked by many functional dependencies, marked by the following features:

one (C) lives off the other (N), undeservedly consuming the products manufactured by the latter; and

transfers (migrations) from one population to the other are frequent.

Assuming that:

C = the set of people who in a given area over a given span of time commit offensive acts,

N = the set of law-abiding people,

W = index of population welfare level,

E = index of educational system effectiveness,

T_1 = index of prevention techniques effectiveness,

T_2 = index of repression techniques effectiveness,

R = index of the force and character of social reaction to actions of criminal justice agencies,

one obtains the following equation:

$$C/N = f(W, E, T_1, T_2, R) + k$$

The ratio of C to N (criminal to noncriminal population) is changeable. Every state authority aims at obtaining a minimum value of this ratio. The objective is formulated in the following way: under given socioeconomic circumstances, with the available forces and means, minimize the ratio of C to N, that is, minimize criminality in the society. This objective is, obviously, a dependent variable, since the value it assumes depends on the values of the other variables in the system. The other variables, called independent variables, cover a variety of controllable and uncontrollable factors.

This function of the objective presents, by way of example, only certain variables determining the size of criminality. The letter "k" denotes the set of functions which were omitted from this model.[1]

Denoting a problem in a mathematical manner does not mean that all the variables in the equation can always be quantified. Thanks, however, to such a denotation, it becomes possible to present the problem in concentrated form and, further, to generalize the selected problem situation.

The order of procedure in making decisions in a problem situation usually presents itself in the following way: selection of objectives; defining its size and value; identification of all possible variables which are linked with achievement of the objective, that is, the right independent variables; determination of links between the independent variables; distinction between the controllable variables (which could constitute a part of the decision maker's strategy) and the uncontrollable variables (classified as either natural states or competitive strategies); definition of the expectations and forecasts as to the uncontrollable variables classified as natural states; determination of whether the forecasts are based on stable or unstable processes; development of a function linking the independent variables with the dependent variable of the objective; definition of permissible limits for the values controllable by the decision maker; selection of those values for the controllable variables, which within the prescribed limits provide the expectation of a result closest to the desired objective.[2]

In the most general terms the task of criminology could be defined here as the performance of the actions presented above in a situation where the objective is defined as minimizing the C to N ratio, or in other words, as achieving the lowest level of criminality possible under given circumstances.

The number of variables which can influence the attainment of that objective is very large. Many of the variables cannot be guided under given circumstances. That is why the first step in scientific research is the definition of a set of possible identified values of independent variables. If, under defined conditions, the variables assume strictly defined values, then one speaks of decision making under conditions of certainty. However, should the variables assume values from a strictly defined collection, though it is not known which of the values will appear under given circumstances, then one speaks of random variables. Resolution of such a problem requires the assignment of probabilities to such values. Meeting this condition allows for making decisions under risk conditions.[3] Links of the variables explanatory to the process of criminal phenomena have a probabilistic rather than determinant character. Determination of any such link requires the application of the probability calculation theory and mathematical statistics methods.

Statistical Methods

These comments are devoted only to the possibilities and ways of applying statistical methods to criminological research.[4] The aim is not to treat this subject from the point of view of a professional statistician, but only to show a few types of criminal statistics applied in studies of criminality, and to present a general outline of the techniques and tools which are used at present. There is also some accent on the historical development of criminal statistics and a warning concerning the dangers facing a researcher who approaches those methods in a purely formal manner.

Before going into detail a few words are necessary concerning the beginnings of scientific application of criminal statistics. This development started in the early decades of the nineteenth century and is linked with the name of the Belgian statistician and professor of astronomy, Adolf Quételet (1796–1874). His most famous writings connected with criminology include *On Man and Development of His Abilities, or, An Attempt at Social Physics, Study on the Propensity to Commit Crime Depending on Age.* Quételet was the first scientist who, by grouping and analyzing comprehensive French and Belgian statitistical data has shown that, just like many other social phenomena, marriage, divorce, suicide, birth, death, or crime, when viewed as mass phenomena, follow certain patterns. By the same token the collection of data assembled as reports of criminal justice agencies became the sole source enabling the discovery of laws governing criminal phenomena, and the sole applicable method was the statistical method. One of the best known of Quételet's observations concerns the relative stability of criminal phenomena. He found that when the prime elements of the social and economic system remain unchanged, the intensity of criminal phenomena show only incidental fluctuations. He expressed this finding in the famous statement describing criminality as a "budget financed by the society with dreadful regularity."

Quételet did not limit himself to assembling numerical collections to show the relative stability of criminality. He also made an attempt to explain this process scientifically. A well-known Dutch criminologist, I. M. van Bemmelen, studying the writings of Quételet, summed up his findings as follows: "The life of man, just as of any other live organism, is subject to given laws of nature. So, when one looks at the society as a whole, then the individual physical, mental, and social traits of society members can be described by given probability functions."

A particular role was played here by the well-known Gauss curve, the so-called standard deviation curve. This type of curve makes it possible to forecast approximately how many offenses of a given type will be uncovered over a given period of time in a given area.

The approach taken by Quételet unveiled considerable vistas of studies of criminality as a mass phenomenon. Yet, limiting oneself to just such a statistical treatment of criminality runs the risk of negating individual psychological factors. The notion of the average man (*homme moyen*) formulated by Quételet was valuable only in studying criminality as a mass phenomenon. In studying a given individual case it lost all meaning. After all, it was no more than, as Quételet himself admitted, pure fiction, a figment of the imagination, the resultant of forces acting in the entire society.

Quételet's disregard of the significance of individual traits of particular people and the extremely deterministic stance which he represented, eliminated the element of will, self-creation, willful shaping of one's fate. The Quételet school influenced the development of criminological thinking up to the time of the first publications by Lombroso, for whom the subject of interest was the individual, including his assemblage of purely individual traits.

Statistical methods came back to the field of criminological studies in the works of the French statistician A. M. Guerry. He took up the analysis of criminality in the various regions of France; applying a cartographic method, he became the forerunner of the criminal etiology school which later developed in Chicago.

Just as in every field of statistical application, criminology also makes a clear distinction between numerical data collected by specially established state institutions and the data gathered by individual researchers. The well-known American sociologist Pitirim Sorokin speaks of "criminal book-keeping" and "highbrow statistics." Criminologist Bowley distinguishes between "administrative statistics" and "scientific statistics." The basic difference between these types of statistics can be described as follows: on the one hand there is a more or less regularly presented body of statistical information covering a certain minimum of data on the operations of criminal justice agencies, and on the other hand, statistical data collected irregularly during individual studies on specific problems, serving to verify a strictly defined criminological hypothesis. As examples one could cite the hypothesis about the link between the family situation of juveniles and their delinquent behavior, between intelligence and criminality, and so on.

The application of given statistical techniques and tools in criminological studies can be discussed in turn, depending on the source of data from whence comes the information used.

These considerations should be preceded by certain terminological clarifications making it possible to clearly distinguish the statistics understood as numerical data obtained from statistical reporting from statistics understood as a self-standing discipline.

Statistical reporting denotes the system of statistical reports drawn up under given regulations and containing numerical data concerning the results attained in various sections of activity, listed in a clearly defined manner, with a subject scope and grouping as prescribed in the various statistical forms. The report data cover strictly prescribed time periods (predetermined) and follow a prescribed report route. The source of data is the information contained in the base documentation of reporting units. Statistical reporting carried out by the criminal justice agencies is called here *criminal statistics*.

Statistics as a discipline is understood as an evolving method of studying objects and phenomena in their mass manifestations and their quantitative or qualitative analysis from the point of view of the discipline of which they are a part. This type of method applied to studies of criminality is called *criminological statistics*.

One generally distinguishes two sectors of statistics: descriptive statistics and mathematical statistics.

Descriptive statistics treats with methods of collecting numerical data and with methods of summary description of these data. The collections of data are described by a system of parameters, of which the most frequently used are averages and measures of dispersion. The generally applied average is the arithmetic average and the most frequent dispersion measure the standard deviation.

The scope of applying the techniques and tools of descriptive statistics in a given field depends on the set of features with which the phenomena in this field are explained. The greater the chance of applying a statistical description, the larger the number of quantitative (measurable) features used in the study. In other words, the scope of applying statistics to a given field depends on the "measurability" of that field.

In criminology this field is clearly limited. The basic criminological variables are, as a rule, ungraduable. One speaks only of the existence of a given trait in an individual or the lack of such a trait. Suffice it to name such variables as the social danger or social harmfulness of an act, demoralization of socialization level of an offender. Until now there has been a lack of methodologically satisfactory scales for measuring these types of variables. In view of the considerable limitations on measurement, the application of statistical description to criminological studies meets with considerable difficulty. These methods are used only in regard to certain variables explaining criminal phenomena, rather than to the criminal phenomena themselves. One calculates, therefore, the average amount of losses per offense, the average age of the offender, the average time for relapse into crime, and so forth. The precondition for wider use of statistical description in criminological studies would be the development of techniques for measuring the basic features of the offense itself, first of all the degree of its social threat.

Statistical description is only the initial phase of statistical research. The main phase is the application of rules for drawing conclusions from data concerning a part of the examined population, selected at random, and extending them to the entire population. Construction of such rules is the task of *mathematical statistics*.[5] Such rules make it possible to generalize the results. Foundations for mathematical statistics are provided by probability calculations, which enable the evaluation of activities and credibility of conclusions concerning the entire studied sample, namely the so-called general population.

There are two prime types of conclusions in mathematical statistics. The first is connected with estimating the magnitude of an unknown population parameter, namely some numerical value synthetically characterizing certain traits of the population. Such a parameter can be, say, the arithmetic average or standard deviation of the tested trait. Precision of the parameter estimate, defined by practical needs, and made on the basis of results obtained from a random selection of a population sample, is obtained on the basis of a function of sample observation, known as the parameter estimator. The problems of estimator construction and testing are the subject of estimation theory.

The second type of statistical conclusion consists of deciding on the basis of sample results whether a supposition advanced as to certain population traits is true or false. Construction of rules for drawing such conclusions is the subject of statistical hypothesis verification theory.

The application of statistical methods for drawing conclusions in criminological studies, just as in the case of every empirical study, requires a strict definition of the general population about whose characteristics one needs to draw conclusions, and a strict definition of the sample, whose results are to form the basis for drawing such conclusions.

The scope of statistical methods application in criminological studies is determined by strictly defined methodological concepts adopted for such a study. For instance, the impact of a given independent variable on the C to N ratio can be determined only under the condition of having observations extend both to the criminal and to the noncriminal population. It is not possible to define the traits determining offensive behavior without a parallel checking of the value of such traits for law-abiding individuals. Fulfilling this condition meets with considerable difficulties in criminology. Criminological analysis is as a rule focused on individuals who are "labeled" in one way or another. These are either suspects, or accused, or sentenced. Within penology the tested population is made up of persons who have served or are serving a given sentence.

After identifying the individuals making up a given population, a definition is made of the traits according to which those individuals will be considered. On the one hand these cover qualitative traits, and on the other hand, quantitative traits. In the former case one adds up the number of persons having this qualitative trait and determines the percentage of the total population which such persons represent. In the latter case the assembly of measurement results is processed in order to obtain such synthetic characteristics as the mean and standard deviation. When the studied population represents a random sample (shown in accordance with one pattern of random selection developed by the theory of sample testing), then one either estimates the unknown magnitudes of such parameters as the percentage, mean, or standard deviation in the population from which the sample was taken, or one verifies the hypothesis formulating the value of parameters in the general population.

This type of procedure is an example of applying statistical methods only to a synthetic description of the collection of numerical results and in itself is, obviously, insufficient for resolving any research problem understood in the previously defined sense. Resolution of a problem requires the determination of links between the variables and ascertainment of to what extent the values of one variable can be explained by the values of another variable. A number of measures have been developed by statistical theory in order to evaluate the force and direction of such a link. As examples one could name here the Pearson linear correlation coefficient, the determination coefficient applied in variance analysis, Spearman and Kendall rank correlation coefficients, or finally the dependence gauges applied in nonparametric statistics (usually based on the χ^2 distribution.[6]

The application of given statistical manipulations can be illustrated by the following example:

Let the study concern persons convicted by court C in the year Y for the offense of stealing public property. An almost classical research move will be the drawing up of a given questionnaire or poll, filled in on the basis of analyzing court records or on the basis of interviews. The questionnaire will contain on one side information about the demographic and vocational traits of the given individual—age, marital status, number of children, education, income, occupation, membership in organizations, and so on. On the other side will be provided a description of the offensive act itself. One of the traits considered is the value of property stolen. After all the questionnaires are filled in, the individuals displaying given combinations of features are added up. Thus one obtains a given number of males and females, young and old, single and married, widowers, childless, people with one child, two children, blue-collar and white-collar workers (or, more specifically, tailors, shoe-makers, lathe operators, miners), and so forth. The results are tabulated. After "processing," one obtains percentages, or structure indices. For gradable traits one occasionally calculates mean values and measures of differentiation (standard deviation). This is used to construct all kinds of correlation tables. One compares, for instance, such traits as occupation, education, income, number of children with a variable such as "value of stolen property." This type of statistical analysis does not allow for an-swering the fundamental question of criminology: why did the individuals concerned under given circumstances decide to take up the given kind of criminal activity? After all, one does not know in which traits they differ significantly from law-abiding individuals.

Effective, from the point of view of practical requirements, application of statistical methods in criminological studies depends strictly on the methodo-logically correct setting up of the control group. Statistics document their cognitive value in analysis of the results of all empirical studies.

Where the subject of analysis covers numerically small populations, such as homicides,, infanticides, or other such rare types of offense in a defined area of a town or a county, 100 percent samples are used.

More often, however, it is necessary to rely on the *representative method*.[7] This is particularly true in cases where studying a 100 percent sample is not possible: for technical reasons, such as an exceptionally large number of certain types of offense; because of the high cost of testing a 100 percent sample; because of the time required for testing a 100 percent sample. Under such circumstances detailed examinations are carried out on a sample which is representative for the unknown whole. Such a result is obtained only when those individuals in a random manner make up a sectional population. The basis for the representative method is probability theory.

According to the classic definition, mathematical probability expresses the ratio of the number of cases favorable to a given occurrence, to the number of all cases, favorable and unfavorable to a given occurrence, under the assumption that all these cases are equally possible.

The representative method yields results in two forms:

1. an estimate, or evaluation of the magnitude of any trait in the entire process;
2. a check, or verification of the statistical hypothesis using a test population.

A properly assembled sample allows for making general statements concerning the entire population from which the sample is drawn.

Interpolation is a specific type of estimation. It consists of determining the missing points in a statistical sequence with known limit values. On the basis of a highly simplified assumption that some value grows proportionally it is possible, for instance, to evaluate criminality in 1967 when data is available concerning criminality in the years 1960–1966 and 1968–1970.

The most frequently used interpolation formulas are the Lagrange and Newton patterns and the finite difference patterns of Newton, Gauss, Stirling, Bessel, and Everett.

Extrapolation is the estimate of certain values outside the measurement limits of a statistical sequence. It is used, for instance, for forecasting criminality, the expected population changes in a country, and so forth.

Observation

Science is based on observation, which means that empirical research starts with observation judgments, purposefully aimed at achieving an answer to some interesting question. Observation thus consists of seeking and finding an answer to certain pre-posed questions.

Criminological observation can focus on individuals or on entire groups, which are observed as nearly as possible under natural conditions.

Participant observation means planned noticing done by an individual who, along with other people, is a participant in the processes observed. In practice, participant observation comes down to the researcher's participation in normal activities of the group. We speak of participant observation when, for instance, the researcher joins a criminal group. Becoming a group member allows for observing "from inside" the mechanisms of the group's activities, structure, customs, values, and norms which are not usually available to an outsider.[8]

While doing participant observation, the researcher should stick to the sidelines of the group and be as "invisible" as possible, remembering that the objective is to study the functioning of the group or individuals.

The prime drawback of participant observation is the difficulty of reconciling the role of observer with the role of group member. A criminal group might require the researcher to participate in criminal activities. The researcher might become emotionally involved, losing the distance required to carry out objective observations.

Participant observation can also be carried out by less than complete participation in group life. The researcher finds a role which does not have to be identical with the roles of other group members. The important consideration is that the role does not alter the manner of behavior adopted by the group. The researcher qua observer limits the field of his observation inasmuch as he is a participant.

Observation is far from a perfect method. Studies of observations show that in keeping with psychological rules, the observer "notices what he wants to notice" and the results of observation are shaped through the personality traits of the observer.[9]

Some of these drawbacks can be overcome by nonparticipant observation: the researcher observes the behavior of people who are members of given groups from an "outside" position, without himself becoming a member of any group.

The most elaborate method of nonparticipant observation is the survey:[10] a multiaspect study of given facts usually by a team, characterizing the interesting milieu in a particular way. The participation of many persons and the team character of the work eliminates the distortions caused by individual observers.

Observers usually keep a log in which they note down observations in keeping with a preadopted pattern. It is useful to note down both the observations themselves and the observer's own interpretations. Observation allows for capturing human behavior in its "natural" state.

At times the point is to test the impact of certain types of stimuli on the behavior of individuals or groups. When the stimuli are produced artificially, (solely for the purpose of testing the behavior of individuals subjected to the study), such a procedure becomes an experiment. For instance, when we take an interest in the constancy of certain attitudes held by an individual, it is possible to create situations which will influence such attitudes for a defined span of time and then test the degree of change. By comparing this individual with others who have not been subjected to such situations (but who do not differ from the tested individual in other respects) we can define the impact of such situations on changing attitudes. The basic prerequisite for the reliability of an experiment is the chance to control all the variables which exert an influence on its results.

In studying social phenomena we do not often meet such situations; an experiment is always incomplete. As much as possible the researcher attempts to control the significant variables, but he cannot control all the elements.

Another problem for the experimenter is that human behavior can change when people know that they are being subjected to an experiment. The methodological problem here is how to establish to what degree (if at all) behavior similar to the experimental situation takes place in "normal life," whether it is determined by the same factors in an identical way.

Questionnaires

Questionnaires are nothing more than a set of written questions or problems, to which we are trying to obtain an answer. The questionnaires used in social surveys could be defined as sets of questions previously drawn to meet the objective of the study.[11] Questionnaires, depending on whether they are to be filled in by the tested persons themselves or by the researcher on the basis of answers persons give, can be divided into inquiry questionnaires and interview questionnaires.

Interview questionnaires are sets of questions drawn up in such a way that much is left up to the interviewer's initiative. We expect the interviewer to adapt the formulation and order of questions to the conditions of the interview, the traits of the person interviewed and the contents of previous answers. We assume that, depending on the course of the interview, the interviewer will supplement the questionnaire with additional clarifying questions, "hammering" at certain groups of issues which the interviewer feels are particularly significant for the problem under study and the particular person.[12]

Interviews, relied on primarily in monographic studies, are usually combined with the technique of observation.

In criminological studies the interview usually takes on the form of a milieu interview. This serves to reveal significant personality traits, particularly socially negative traits difficult to uncover by other methods.

An interview questionnaire, even less definite, in which only the subject and direction of the talk are specified, is called a *free interview plan*: the content of questions is usually left open. Only the person who is to conduct the interview is informed of the central issue of the study, his perception and research intuition are relied upon, in the belief that in the course of the talk the interviewer will reach the significant problems. This technique is used everywhere where it is not possible to obtain information through more formal research techniques which would guarantee a higher degree of comparability.

The use of interview questionnaires makes it possible to obtain in-depth information, making allowance for individual shades of meaning. Their proper use requires a group of properly trained interviewers. This means that the number of people tested by this method can never be very large. Information about a certain person must be comparable with information about others, and information collected by various interviewers must also be comparable. This can only be achieved by standardizing questions and answers. This aim is better served by the *inquiry questionnaire.*

In an inquiry questionnaire (an "inquiry") the variables in which we are interested at a given stage have been fully "translated" into a language of the right questions, and the questions formulated in such a way that their meaning does not require additional commentary from the interviewer, as their very context is in principle sufficient to obtain the proper answer from a cooperative respondent. In other words an inquiry is a questionnaire drawn up in such a way that it can dispense entirely with the intermediary of a third person or, when there is reliance on poll-takers, their functions are limited to faithful and literal transmission of the question, limiting to the absolute minimum their role in interpreting both questions and answers. An inquiry not only allows for standardizing the information collected, but also to a large degree limits, and in many cases eliminates entirely, the distortions introduced to the information by the interviewer.

The drawback of an inquiry is that, because of the standard questions, and more particularly standard answers, it makes it more difficult to obtain in-depth information allowing for an overall view of the studied social phenomenon by presenting many individual elements of similar attitudes, behaviors, and situations. In cases where we need the overall view in depth, much better results are obtained by relying on the interview questionnaire.

In practice the studies of social phenomena are very rarely carried out with the use of completely standardized inquiry questionnaires. Most often space is left for an answer which was not proposed in the questionnaire (questions providing the possibility of answers other than those proposed in the questionnaire are known as "open" questions, in contrast to the "closed" questions in which the respondent has to choose one of the proposed answers). With open questions it is possible to obtain information which goes somewhat deeper.

The use of this type of inquiry tool is particularly desirable considering the great variety of individuals studied. The researcher, in formulating an inquiry, is not able to foresee all possible answers. He then risks not getting at information which can be particularly pertinent to the problem under study.

Drawing up a questionnaire is based on a variety of principles. It is advisable to resort to the assistance of specialists.[13] A poor interview or inquiry questionnaire hinders rather than helps in obtaining information reflecting reality.

Inquiry questionnaires are used most often in polls. Such studies are aimed at obtaining information from many persons over a brief span of time. They can be carried out with the assistance of poll-takers. Sometimes it is possible to reach the selected persons by sending the inquiry questionnaire in the mail, but the effects obtained are as a rule considerably inferior to the results obtained by personal interviews.

Using poll-takers seems particularly helpful when one is carrying out studies on a representative sample, a group of persons or phenomena selected in such a way that the information about them can (in keeping with the rules of induction) be extended to cover the entire studied population and that one can be confident that in studying the selected persons or phenomena one obtains information about all the persons or phenomena in which one is interested. The poll-taker thus has to reach each and every selected person. The assistance of statisticians seems advisable in selecting such a sample.

A necessary condition for selecting the sample is the selection of the variables in which one is interested, namely preparing the "operate" of the drawing. It is only with this information and the use of statistical methods for sample selection can one make the choice (drawing) of individuals who meet the condition of representative value of the entire studied population of persons or phenomena.

Panel surveys, or repeated inquiries, are also a type of inquiry. They consist of conducting an interview or an inquiry with the same person a number of times, at certain time intervals. Mainly used for studying changes taking place over time and changes in attitudes, opinions, habits, and behavior, they allow for studying phenomena connected with the dynamics of certain social processes. They also enable one to define the factors shaping the process of change and the forms of interdependence over time. They form a sound basis for prognostic studies.

Criminology frequently resorts to follow-up studies, fairly similar in character to the panel surveys. They are designed to yield information concerning further life developments of people who have been studied previously. The difference between panel and follow-up studies comes down mainly to a difference in the time interval between studies, which for criminological follow-up studies usually amounts to five years. Using this method of follow-up studies it is possible to obtain much valuable information, used both in drawing up explanatory patterns and in forecasting. The method of follow-up studies is widely applied in various studies carried out by the Polish Academy of Sciences Criminology Section.

One questionnaire version is known as the *sociometric questionnaire*, used in studies to establish the degree and direction in which members of given social groups acts on each other. As a rule it contains questions concerning with whom given members would like to perform given functions. On the basis of information obtained in a sociometric questionnaire it is possible to define group structure, interdependence between subgroups, the rank of members within a group, the degree of group cohesion, and the like.

Sociometric questionnaires are most useful in studies of isolated groups. A criminologist can use them for studies carried out in reformatories, prisons and other places of confinement of isolated groups.

Analysis of the results of sociometric studies allows for identifying the informal group structure and makes it possible to define the informal leaders or other persons influencing the opinions and behavior of group members. It can also provide guidelines as to the desired manipulations in group membership to achieve the optimum for the expected results.

Analysis of sociometric study findings is usually conducted by: the graphic method (sociogram); analysis of figures; matrix analysis; and statistical analysis.[14]

Maximum authenticity of answers in sociometric questionnaires can be achieved when the respondents are informed that as far as possible the results of the study will be taken into account in making decisions concerning the issue analysed.

The main objections to be found in various discussions concerning "questionnaire methods" concern the issue of truthfulness of this type of measures, that is, the correspondence between the collected answers and the real views (opinions) of those who answer. One should consider, first of all, what sort of correspondence is required. An answer given to an interview or inquiry question can be interpreted in two ways: it can be treated as information on how the person sees certain phenomena or as information on how the matters look in reality. The reasons behind false answers can vary:

the person can willfully provide a false answer, fearing social sanctions;

a false answer can be the effect of a badly formulated question; the question can be incomprehensible to the respondent and the proposed answers fail to reflect the respondent's situation; the respondent can select one answer without really having an opinion on the subject;

a false answer can be the effect of faulty observation of reality, even though it is consistent with the subjective feelings of the respondent.

When the answer is to be treated as a source of information concerning an objective state, then the important thing is to eliminate the maximum possible amount of distortion. The question should contain clear formulations, to make certain that they were comprehended in keeping with our intentions. The elimination of the type of distortion due to fear of social reprisal is possible by using anonymous questionnaires. Elimination of distortions caused by erroneous observation of the surrounding reality by the respondent requires that the answer be verified through other information sources. One should also consider whether the person polled has knowledge of the phenomena concerning which we are trying to obtain information. Statements of the polled persons will never quite accord with the course of real events. Elimination of distortions caused by subjective factors is, in principle, impossible.

When the respondent's answer is interesting as a source of information about how he registers the surrounding reality, it will be essential to eliminate the distortions caused by faulty formulation of answers. In this case the subject of analysis will be the honesty of answers. There are no right or wrong answers, there are only honest and dishonest ones.

In criminological studies there are considerable opportunities for cross-checking the answers obtained from interview and inquiry questionnaires with court and prosecution records, police reports, and criminalistic analysis. By comparing the information from various sources it is possible to reconstruct the full course of events.

There are different kinds of questionnaires. The example of inquiry questionnaire used here serves to sound out current public opinion on a given issue, say of social or political nature.[15] A personality study questionnaire would consider longer and shorter time periods, required for a well-rounded study of the individual traits of the person considered against he background of given milieu factors. I will give an example of this type of questionnaire:

Model Questionnaire of a Public Opinion Poll on the Type
of Punishment (extract)

Questions	Answers (underline or fill in)
1. What should in your opinion be the main reason for sentencing criminals to prison terms?	1. to have them separated from society as harmful individuals 2. to reeducate them—turn them into useful members of society 3. to have them suffer for what they did 4. to deter others from committing similar crimes 5. I am of another opinion on this subject (write it out) 6. it is hard to say
2. Some people believe that capital punishment is necessary, many others disagree. In your opinion, should capital punishment be used at all?	1. definitely not 2. rather not 3. rather yes 4. definitely yes 5. it is hard to say
2a. If not, why not (for those who selected answers 1 or 2)?	
2b. If yes, under what circumstances, for which crimes (for those who selected answer 3 or 4)?	
3. In your opinion, under what circumstances could capital punishment be eliminated in your state?	

4. Would you favor, for certain   1. no
    crimes, the reintroduction of   2. yes
    flogging?   3. it is hard to say

4a. If you believe this is advisable,
    then in what cases, and
    against whom?

   Family (biologic and social background);
   A. Father (whether lived with the respondent in childhood; whether he
left the family—if so, how old was the respondent at that time; whether he paid
family support—if he stopped, when; education and vocation; whether he
held a job during respondent's childhood; whether he had any marked
addiction, what kind; financial situation; chronic illnesses and disability;
police record, year and cause of death).
   B. Mother (as under A).
   C. Guardians, if not the same as parents (what was the relation of those
persons to the respondent; education, job; financial situation; types of
community where lived).
   D. Brothers and sisters (how many did the respondents have; order of
birth; whether the respondent was brought up with them; emotional
relationship with them).
   E. Family life (attitude of parents or guardians to the respondent;
whether parents or guardians treated the respondent the same as, better, or
worse than other children in the family; whether the adults had frequent fights
or arguments, whether the respondent was often left untended; whether the
parents (guardians) showed an interest in the respondent; whether the
respondent was treated severely or not; whether the respondent was forced to
earn money; whether the family often changed the place of residence;
whether the respondent was raised partly in a social institution, and if so, since
when, why, for what length of time; which family event made the greatest
impression on the respondent during childhood).
   There is a similarly detailed breakdown in the questionnaire of other
aspects, such as: education history; job history; current job (employment,
human relations, attitude to the job); marriage, children; current family
relations; membership and activity in other social groups and milieus; ways
of spending leisure; personality in own estimation; attitude to own life and its
determinants; motivation for committing offense (offenses); attitude to the
committed offense (offenses); future plans.

Use of Documents

Behavior and views of people can be studied directly. One can also look for records of such behavior in the various existing documents. This type of behavioral study is known as *indirect observation.*

A criminologist, as others who study human behavior, seeks traces of such behavior in memoirs, police questionnaires, statistical documents, the press, court and prosecution records, letters, biographies, monographic source materials and other places, depending on the object of the study and the research problems encountered.

Particularly important in studying human behavior are personal documents. These include, first of all, memoirs, autobiographies, letters, and other documents which mirror the experiences and feelings of their authors.

Analysis of a personal document (just as of any type of human statement) can be carried out with two objectives in mind: a. when we want to find out the real course of events, situations, or processes described by the author of the document and how the author himself really behaved in those situations; b. when we want to find out how the author evaluates the described events, processes, or situations and his own behavior in them.

In the first case the researcher tries to eliminate various distortions and falsehoods. The researcher attempts to trace all the conscious or unconscious selection of facts and to ascertain the facts as they were, irrespective of the degree of distortion. In other words, the researcher attempts to neutralize as much as possible the role of the document's author as the intermediary between the fact and the person.

In the second case the objective of the study is not reality itself but rather its subjective picture, with all the respondent's distortions, falsehoods, and touch-ups. "Classic" writings which used personal documents as a rule applied a thorough quality analysis. They treated the document as a source for formulating hypotheses concerning the mental reality, and the statements therein either as material evidence or illustrative material for the hypothesis.[16]

Personal documents are particularly useful in the second case, when it is a question of describing the reality as seen by the person studied, of describing his attitudes and emotional experiences, and when it is necessary to reach certain internal states of his consciousness. Personal documents make it possible to look at the world through the eyes of others, to see how they see themselves. They are as revealing for emotional experience as observation is for behavior.

Biographic material is particularly helpful in studying the processes by which attitudes, values, and aspirations are shaped. These processes are best studied by reconstructing the psychosocial biography of an individual.

Statistical data and reports, collected by various institutions, can be a valuable source of information about human groups. They enable the researchers to characterize human behavior, on which they focus their attention, from the point of view of the traits, or time in which they are interested.

Using this type of documents one should remember that the data usually differ from those which would have been assembled by the researcher, had he been collecting the information. Also, the fact that the data were collected for the needs of an official institution does not by any means guarantee that they were collected truthfully. The researcher should always consider whether the person (or institution) supplying the information was in a position to give the required information exactly and whether it was interested in supplying truthful information.

Among official documents, criminological researchers frequently use court and prosecution records. They can supply much interesting information concerning offense and the offender. On the other hand, they contain a rather one-sided and incomplete view. Considering a variety of factors, such as lack of sufficient data, gaps in investigation materials in cases discontinued for various reasons, there is no possibility of using a uniform statistical collection.

The study of records often leads to considerable difficulties. In many cases even the most detailed analysis of investigation and trial records does not yield information which would allow for evaluating victims. Often the victim "disappears" from the records; criminal justice agencies—including courts—often fail to devote enough attention to the victim. Analysis of court and prosecution records has to be supplemented with information obtained in other ways.

To obtain more complete information about the victim as well as the application both of punishment and of prevention, it would appear desirable to have prosecution records contain a card listing all the required data about the victim, drawn up from the point of view of criminology and criminalistics.

A good example of studies based on analysis of court records is the book by A. J. Reiss on the link between the lack of social and personal controls of juveniles and their delinquent behavior. The author analyzed the court records of a thousand juvenile delinquency cases.[17] For the purpose of criminological studies it is particularly useful to obtain court records of cases where convictions are obtained.

Analysis of court records is carried out on the basis of a plan containing a list of issues significant for the origins and course of the offense. As an example, here is a list of problems studied in rape cases, where binding convictions were obtained. The selection of this type of crime is not accidental; in many countries this is a very rapidly growing category of crime.

1. Formal data (state, district, case number).
2. Type of rape (individual, more than one person).
3. Number of offenders.
4. Scene of crime (town, country, country lane, park, home).
5. Time of crime (month, day of the week, hour).
6. Was the rape committed or attempted?
7. Was the victim killed or injured?
8. Methods of rape:
   a. circumstances of meeting victim (where?, when?),
   b. way of abducting the victim,
   c. manner of duress (beating, typing hands, terrorizing with a dangerous weapon),
9. Perpetrator:
   a. age,
   b. marital and family status,
   c. education,
   d. vocation,
   e. did he act under the influence of alcohol?
   f. psychological and psychiatric examinations,
   g. previous record or suspicion of similar crimes,
   h. sexual life to date,
   i. milieu (criminal, noncriminal),
   j. relation to the victim (acquaintance, stranger, family).
10. Victim:
    a. age,
    b. marital and family status,
    c. education,
    d. vocation,
    e. was she under the influence of alcohol?
    f. results of psychological and psychiatric examinations,
    g. victim's role in crime genesis (lack of caution, provocation, promiscuity),
    h. family and job milieu.
11. Discovery of the crime of rape:
    a. victim testimony,
    b. testimony of other witnesses,
    c. confidential information,
    d. actions of police patrol,
    e. as part of investigation or trial of another case.
12. Results of medical examination of the suspect.
13. Results of medical examination of the victim.
14. Behavior of the accused (admission, rejection of the accusal).
15. Motivational conditions of the offense.

16. Lower court sentence.
17. Appeal (prosecution, defense).
18. Binding sentence.
19. Sentence motivation (extenuating and aggravating circumstances).
20. Other comments.

Psychological Studies

Tests and other psychological methods are used for revealing in detail a person's mental traits at every stage of his development.

The tests for checking the instrumental mental dispositions (mental tests, as M. Kreutz calls them) serve to measure mental faculties. One example of a test of this type is the Binet-Simon scale for testing a child's level of development. Also, the currently popular Wechsler method (Wechsler Adult Intelligence Scale, Wechsler Intelligence Scale for Children) tests not just the level of mental development—it also allows for drawing conclusions concerning mental disturbances which accompany various illnesses, including organic brain damage. Its verbal scale covers: a vocabulary test, an information test, a comprehension test, a similarities test, a digit test, an arithmetic test. Its performance scale covers: a test of picture arrangement, a test of picture completion, a test of object assembly, a test of block design and a test of digit symbol.

The series of Thurstone tests is also geared to checking various mental abilities. The mental abilities of adults are also checked by tests developed by Meile, Amthauer (vocational aptitude test) and Giese (technical-commercial aptitude test). The checking of fatigue susceptibility and the type of concentration (oscillating or fixed) can be carried out by the Bourdon test of crossing out letters.

To obtain a more specific experimental measurement, particularly of the degree of susceptibility to mental fatigue, the ability to exercise and persevere, one applies the Kraepelin test of constant addition of single-digit numbers.[18]

Both in studies and in psychological practice, particularly in clinical psychology, one finds wide-scale application of various *projective techniques*. These draw conclusions about the personality traits and attitudes of the tested person on the basis of his reactions to certain situations. The verbal techniques include, for example, responding to a word given by the tester or completing a sentence. The person is given a number of unfinished sentences to complete; stress is on the speed of answer. The substance of the answers, as well as the words chosen to supplement other words, yield information concerning the personality traits of the tested person. Akin to this is the method of completing stories, anecdotes, and the like.

Picture techniques present various pictures to the person being tested. The tester asks for a statement concerning each one; personality traits are determined on the basis of analysing the statements obtained.

Psychodramatic techniques are another projection method; they consist of having the person being tested play the role assigned by the tester. The way in which the role is interpreted and the ability to identify with the assigned character provide valuable information concerning the personality of the person being tested.

Among other projective methods are the Rorschach test, the Murray Thematic Apperception Test, the Wartegg test, the sentence completion test of J. M. Sachs and the Elisabeth G. French human understanding test.

1. The Rorschach test (black-grey and color inkblots) is an outstanding projective multiaspect method of personality testing. In the hands of an experienced specialist it allows for an evaluation of both the intellectual level and the type of intelligence as well as the emotional traits and social adaptation of the tested person. It also provides wide opportunities for evaluating the pathological disturbances of personality, from neurosis to mental illness. It also allows for following improvements in mental health.
2. The Murray Thematic Apperception Test (selected photos of situations and persons) allows for measuring the structure of motives on the basis of the author's theories; this is a question of determining the interdependence between needs and the impact of exogenous pressures on shaping those needs.[19]
3. The Wartegg test is a projection personality test through pictures, allowing for multifacet personality analysis. There are a number of methods for interpreting this test.[20]
4. The Sachs sentence completion test allows for uncovering the conflict areas in family relations, relations with other people, sexual life and one's own personality projection.[21]
5. The French human understanding test gauges the needs for affiliating achievements and power.[22]

The methods applied in neuropsychology are highly useful in studying criminals. They are designed for early detection of organic changes in the brain (even very minor changes, often undetectable by clinical methods). Such studies are very important for the etiology of criminality, since there is a generally accepted very close link between the pathology of the brain and the pathology of human behavior. Studies of this type are carried out with the aid of organic tests developed by L. Bender, L. Bentow, F. Graham, and B. Kendall and with the set of methods developed by A. R. Lurii, a prominent Soviet neuropsychologist. In Poland the neuropsychological approach was pioneered by M. Maruszewski.

The need to carry out psychological studies in criminology also extends to studying the emotional aspects of offenders. In view of the role that emotions and feelings play in shaping human personality, the studying of emotions is a widely used method in practical psychology and psychosomatic medicine. It should not be overlooked by forensic and penitentiary psychology.

The subject of studying emotions and feelings is comprehensively treated by R. S. Woodworth and Harold Schlosberg.[23] They concentrated particularly on laboratory experiment techniques, along with the results of studies obtained by this method. They also describe the equipment required for such studies. Such techniques, despite the reservations raised about them in the history of psychology, undoubtedly constitute a vital element in the methodology of modern psychology. Their value stems from the fact that they allow for a high degree of control over the phenomenon which is being studied, making it possible to uncover the exact scientific laws which govern them. Particularly significant in criminology are the studies of physiological manifestations of emotional states. These include: the affective skin conductivity [GSR] and its psychological determinants, such as conductivity changes with physical activity, with mental effort, disturbances in concentration, bodily movements, adaptation, varied emotional states, free associations, under the stress of a given task, and so on.

Significant information can also be obtained concerning other physiological changes under the influence of emotion, such as changes in heart action and blood pressure, respiratory rate, muscular tension, skin temperature, reaction of the pupils, steadiness of motions, and EEG.

Such indicators of emotional activity in various combinations have been used in lie detection. With the assistance of specially built polygraphs it is possible to register a number of physiological indicators simultaneously, such as electrical skin conductivity, respiration, and blood pressure. Their interpretation is not easy and requires specialization, but allows for certainty in determining the truthfulness of the tested subjects.

Quite important for criminology are the personality study methods using questionnaires. For example:

1. The Hathaway and McKinley Minnesota Multiphasic Personality Inventory [MMPI]). It consists of ten clinical scales and three supplementary scales used to adjust the results. The inventory contains the following clinical scales: hypochondria, depression, hysteria, psychopathy, interest in the opposite sex, paranoia, psychasthenia, schizophrenia, hypomania and introversion-extroversion. The resulting psychogram helps to assess certain given personality traits of the subject and pathological deviations from the norm.

2. H. J. Eysenck Personality Inventory. This inventory distinguishes two prime personality dimensions: extroversion-introversion [E scale] and

unbalanced-balanced [N scale]. The notion of introversion and extroversion was taken from Jung. Eysenck characterizes introverts and extroverts. He also made an interesting attempt to explain the etiology of introversion and extroversion on the basis of Pavlovian processes of stimulation and inhibition in the brain core [classic conditioning]. Application of a personality inventory allows for quick orientation as to the degree of the subject's neurosis, and the results of the extroversion scale make it possible to determine the type of neurosis (and eventually psychopathy). The Eysenck inventory is particularly interesting for criminologists, since its author assumes the existence of a positive correlation between extroversion and criminality. He claims that the greater the degree of extroversion, the greater the chance of committing offenses. According to Eysenck, criminals as a group represent extrovert neurotics.[24] The results of studies carried out so far are not conclusive, however.

3. Sixteen Personality Factor Questionnaire of Cattell, Sanders, and Stice. This measures the following personality dimensions: cyclotomy-schizotomy, intelligence, ego strength, dominance-submissiveness, expansiveness, superego strength, resistance to threat, impressionability, suspiciousness, conventionality, rationalism-simplicity, depressive uncertainty of oneself, tendency to radicalism, tendency to conservatism, self sufficiency-reliance on group, self-evaluation, and nervous tension.

4. Buss and Durke, "Feelings and Moods." This is a questionnaire designed to determine the degree of aggressiveness (direct and indirect), enmity, dislike, suspiciousness, verbal malice, feelings of guilt and conflict, negativism, and excitability. The nature of this test makes it useful for studying certain categories of criminals.

5. Gough psychological inventory. This inquiry sheet has numerous questions concerning likes, feelings, worries, and difficulties in life. In addition to determining personality traits it allows for a degree of orientation toward the attitudes of the subject and his sociability.

Examining the State of Health

Studies of physical and mental health represent a valuable source of information on the offender, the victim, and the witnesses. Such studies also yield data for evaluating the etiology of criminality, and indirectly for programming preventive actions.

Examinations of the bodily state are aimed at determining possible disturbance in the most vital organic functions. In addition to an internal examination of the respiratory, circulatory, and digestive tracts they also aim at eliminating disturbances in glandular functions, such as the thyroid and pituitary. Physical examinations also extend to neurological tests aimed at eliminating organic disturbances of the nervous system. The Polish Penal Proceedings Code obliges the accused to submit to external bodily examination and other examinations which do not violate bodily integrity, as long as such examinations are required in assembling evidence. The same code provides for bodily and medical examinations of witnesses, with their consent, again for the purpose of assembling evidence. Medical examination of the victim is also possible, when the penalty to be imposed depends on the victim's state of health.

From the point of view of the penal process, as well as criminology, psychiatric examination plays an important role.[25] Rulings on the offender's insanity or reduced ability to distinguish between right and wrong lead to significant legal and trial consequences. A rational criminal policy would be unthinkable without application of the latest psychological and psychiatric breakthroughs. Only the proper application of results obtained from psychological examination of normal mental processes and psychiatric examination of anomalies in these processes allows for following through with preventive programs.

In view of the significance and the specific character of psychiatric examinations, a considerable role is assigned to information concerning the perpetrator of the offensive act. Such information can be classified in three groups. The first covers all information on the details of the suspect's life and his closest family. This covers both data on the environmental influence on shaping personality and data on hereditary factors. This has diagnostic significance. When the subject has been a· patient of psychiatrists or neurologists, using medical documentation becomes necessary. The second group covers information concerning the circumstances of the act, motives, and method of offensive action. The third group comes from observation of the offender's behavior during investigation and trial, particularly during the early hearing, when certain abnormal features of his personality may become clear.

The conduct of examinations has to be preceded by an exact definition of the objective of the psychiatric examination. Certain texts on forensic psychiatry list a number of issues to be cleared up by the examination. For instance, H. A. Davidson put together sixteen questions, including the clinical psychiatric diagnosis, the level of mental development, the degree of awareness as to the character of the perpetrated act and its negative moral evaluation by society, whether the seriousness of the situation was realized, the ability to premeditate the act, the social threat, the causes of amnesia, such as brain concussion, epileptic fit, or intoxication.[26] Similar issues, put together in ten questions, are raised by J. MacDonald.

Questions concerning the mental state of the offender should be closely linked with the character, circumstances, and motive of the act. There is a certain correlation between the type of mental disturbance, its intensity, and the character of the act. Depressive states predispose to different type of actions than do disturbances marked by increased aggressiveness or a general elevation of the psychomotive drive. Failing to make allowance for the correlation between the ascertained illness and the character plus the circumstances of the act could lead to errors in evaluating sanity.

Supplementary tests are used in an attempt to bring objective criteria to the process of defining the mental state. These include electroencephalo-grams [EEG]. When examining the results of such tests one should keep in mind that there is not always a direct correlation between the EEG results and the clinical state of the subject. It has been noted in specialist publications that a change in EEG notation can be influenced by a variety of factors not due to organic brain damage. For instance, the bioelectric brain activity graph depends among other things, on the biochemical composition of the blood and the concentration of oxygen in the air. In 5–20 percent of the healthy population the EEG is irregular, so that the EEG readout in itself is insufficient for drawing conclusions about the health of the subject. It may even happen that with even serious damage of the central nervous system the EEG can be regular. It is therefore essential to carefully look into the interpretation of the EEG readout and the conclusions drawn on its basis. This becomes particularly important when different groups of experts present varying interpretations of the same EEG readout.

Studying Ways in Which Offenders Communicate

The comprehensive body of criminological studies covers equally the subjective and the objective facets of offenses. Considering this, criminology is interested in penetrating the criminal subculture. The ways in which offenders communicate becomes an issue of considerable theoretical and practical importance, a possible subject of interesting studies.

Studies on this subject cover issues bordering on a number of disciplines; criminology, semiology [semiotics], theory of communication (approached as part of cybernetics and psychology), linguistics and sociolinguistics.

From the criminological point of view most important is the semantic analysis of criminal codes aimed at their decoding. This is significant for crime prevention and will also assist in more effective operation of the prosecution agencies. The task of criminologists is to process in a scientific way the material collected by practitioners having contact with crimes. This material represents random information on gestures, mimicry, specific language, and the like. Criminology has to systematize this varied material, to clasify it in keeping with the terminology applied by other disciplines (in view of the advisability of integrating scientific language), and codifying the data as in the dictionaries of criminal usage. Analysis of writings of this subject shows that so far criminology had closer links with lingusitics than with, for instance, semiotics. This is probably because in the criminal subculture, just as in the entire human culture, language is a special, most privileged system of symbols. The privileged position stems from the fact that language is more communicative than all the other symbol systems.

Since the term "language" is on some occasions applied very broadly, on others in a more limited scope, it becomes necessary to introduce a regulatory definition by which "language" will be used in the sense in which it is the subject of linguistics. One should avoid the term "criminal slang." After all, the system of spoken and written symbols used by criminals contains constitutive features of the general (national) language. The language of criminals is subject to the same grammatical rules as the general language (for instance, in syntax or inflection). Researching the language of criminals enriches general linguistics, while the study of slang does not bear such a general significance.

The language of criminals can also be the subject of sociolinguistics. This, however, would appear to be a matter for future study, to be suggested for the consideration of sociologists with a view to possible application of the research in sociolinguistic analysis of criminal groups. In Poland, for instance, sociolinguistics is completely undeveloped.

In studying the language of criminals, criminology had relied on those results of linguistic studies and on those methods which correspond to the social functions of criminology. In order to facilitate the operation of justice administration it will be important to have such studies of the criminal language which will allow for its decoding, by the same token making this language fully communicative to people outside this rather hermetic group, particularly to prosecution bodies, the police, and so on. Criminology has its closest links with lexicology and lexicography, particularly with linguistic semantics as sections of linguistics.

All the "secret" and "trade" languages, among which one should also include the language of criminals, are marked by lexical distinction (semantic and idiomatic) from the general language. Such distinctions appear particularly easily and extensively in communities which for reasons of their own wish to communicate in a manner in which they will not be understood by others. The motivation of criminal groups in preserving the "secrecy" of their language is obvious, just as the desire of justice administration agencies to decode it is also obvious. The language of criminals undergoes constant change. It is probably the most lexically vital of all the trade languages. The idiom has to change constantly, since the meaning of certain phrases or entire expressions becomes with time comprehensible to others. The changing aspects of the criminal language give urgency to the work on the development of its dictionary.

As was pointed out earlier, for criminologists the semantic analysis will be the most important both in idiom and lexicology. The purpose of such an analysis would be to draw up a lexicon and idiomatic dictionary of the criminal language. This is usually attained by using comparative methods— semantically comparing the general language with the language of criminals. In view of the changeability of the criminal language, such lexicons have to be constantly brought up to date. Comparative (in time) studies of the criminal vernacular in the various languages have not really gotten off the mark, and the diachronic method is applied less frequently than descriptive methods.

There have been recent attempts at a typological-comparative approach in lexicology. Valuable material for such an approach can be provided by dictionaries grouped not alphabetically, but by subject, and this is the most frequently used classification in dictionaries of criminal language.

Under circumstances when the criminals are unable to communicate verbally, or when such communication is difficult (such as in prisons), they resort to other, nonverbal systems of symbols known usually as codes. In analyzing them it would be advisable to rely on the achievements of semiology, the discipline of the systems of nonverbal symbols. The problems of semiology are linked with analyzing the various components of such a system or their interrelations. Analyses of criminal communication (in various aspects) exemplify such problems. One will be the typology of criminal codes in accordance with the terminology used in semiology.

According to this terminology, certain of the criminal codes could be classified as logical codes and as subclasses of paralinguistic codes, such as the "knock on the wall" code or signaling letters of the alphabet in selected panes of a window. Such codes are translatable into the general language, which is significant particularly in the work of prison authorities.

Besides paralinguistic codes people also use other speech-supplementary codes: prosodic, kinesic, and praxemic. The mimicry and gestures of criminals fall in these categories. Another group of codes is represented by social codes, the elements (signs) of which are linked with the structure of the given community. In the criminal community tattoos represent a form of insignia (the function of which is to reflect the organization of the given community and the relationship between the individual and the group), while nicknames (their motivation is a criminological-semiological issue) are the simplest signs of identity.

An example of a problem in which one can distinguish many subordinate problems, is the sense of a communication. Studying whether criminals usually correctly receive communications is significant for criminology, since the sense "assigned" to a communication by its recipient implies his behavior, which often shapes the etiology of criminality.

It would be difficult, well nigh impossible, to provide an exhaustive list of issues bordering on semiology and criminology. Semiology, in English-speaking areas more frequently known as semiotics, is a relatively new and still developing discipline; it is a component of social psychology which, it would appear, could be, similarly to linguistics, psychology, and sociology, useful in analyzing the criminal subculture.

Notes

1. A similar model was presented in a more detailed manner by Alfred Sauvy in "Quelques aspects économiques et démographiques de la criminalité" [Certain economic and demographic aspects of criminality] *Population* 1970, no. 4.

2. This breakdown is discussed in detail by David W. Miller and Martin K. Starr in *Executive Decisions and Operations Research* (Englewood Cliffs, N.J., Prenctice-Hall, 1960).

3. The problems of decision making under conditions of certainty, risk, and uncertainty are treated in detail by Duncan R. Luce and Howard Raiffa, authors of this concept, in *Games and Decisions* (New York: John Wiley, 1957).

4. Oskar, Anderson, *Probleme der Statistichen Methodenlehre in den Sozialwissenschaften* [Problems of statistical methods application in the social sciences] (Würzburg: Phisica-Verlag, 1954); Herbert Basler, *Grundbegriffe der Wahrscheinlichkeitrechnung und Statistische Methodenlehre* [Groundrules for probability calculations and statistical methods application] (Würzburg, Phisica-Verlag, 1971); Heinz Bauer, *Wahrscheinlichkeitstheorie und Grundzüge der Masstheorie* [Probability theory and fundamentals of mass theory] (Berlin: Walter de Gruyter, 1974); Günter Clauss and Heinz Ebner, *Grundlagen der Statistik für Psychologen, Pedagogen, und Soziologen* [Statistical background for psychologists, educators, and sociologists] (Berlin: Volk und Vissen Volkseigener Verlag, 1978); Joy P. Guilford, *Fundamental Statistics in Psychology and Education*, 4th ed. (New York: McGraw-Hill, 1965); Helen M. Wakler, *Statistiche Methoden für Psychologen und Pedagogen* [Statistical Methods for Psychologists and Educators], 7th ed. (Weinheim: J. Beltz, 1954); Karl F. Zimmermann, *Kompendium der Variationsstatistik* [Compendium of deviance statistics] (Berlin: VEB Deutscher Verlag der Wissenschaften, 1959).

5. Marvin E. Wolfgang and H. Smith, "Mathematical Methods in Criminology" *International Social Science Journal* 1966, no. 2.

6. Hans Richter-Altschäffer, *Theorie und Technik der Korelationsanalyse* [Theory and techniques of correlation analysis] (Berlin: Paul Parey, 1932).

7. Hans Kellerer, *Theorie und Technik des Stichprobenverfahrens* [Theory and techniques of random sample use], 3rd. ed. (Munich: Einzelschriften der Deutsche Statistische Gesellschaft 953, 1963).

8. This method was applied in studies of criminal groups by, among others, William F. Whyte, *Street Corner Society* (Chicago: University of Chicago Press, 1943). In Poland, studies of at first thieves' and later burglars' society were carried out by Zbigniew Bożyczko, *Kradzież kieszonkowa i jej sprawca* [Pickpockets: acts and perpetrators] (Warsaw: Wydawnictwo Prawnicze, 1962); idem, *Kradzież z włamaniem i jej sprawca* [Burglary and its perpetrators] (Warsaw: Wydawnictwo Prawnicze, 1970).

9. Claire Sellitz et al., *Research Methods in Social Relations* (New York: Methuen, 1959), pp. 205 ff.

10. Edward G. Bryant, *Statistical Analysis*, 2nd ed. (Englewood Cliffs, N.J.: Prentice-Hall, 1971); Charles Y. Glock, *Survey Research in the Social Sciences* (New York: Russell Sage Foundation, 1967); Mildred Parten, *Surveys, Polls and Samples* (New York: Harper, 1950); Morris Rosenberg, *The Logic of Survey Analysis* (New York: Basic Books, 1968); Frederick F. Stephan and Philip J. McCarthy, *Sampling Opinions: Analysis of Survey Procedure* (New York: John Wiley, 1958).

11. The problem of questionnaires has been comprehensively treated in the literature. See, for instance, Jacques Antoine, *L'opinion: Techniques d'enquetes par sondage* [Inquiry technique by survey] (Paris: Dunod, 1969); Herbert Hyman, *Interviewing in Social Research* (Chicago: University of Chicago Press, 1956); Robert L. Kahn and Charles F. Cannel, *The Dynamics of Interviewing* (New York: John Wiley, 1957); Stanley L. Payne, *The Art of Asking Questions* (Princeton: Princeton University Press, 1951).

12. Stefan Nowak, *Methodology of Sociological Research: General Problems* (Warsaw-Dordrecht-Boston: PWN–Polish Scientific Publishers, 1977).

13. The problem of drawing up a questionnaire for surveys and interviews has been treated in numerous books on the methodology of sociology and other social sciences. See, for instance, Stefan Nowak, *Methodology of Sociological Research*. This book presents the general concept: chapter 1 discusses the social and scientific sources of the research problems in sociology, the object of investigation and the research problem, the various kinds of questions, investigated phenomena as an object of interest in themselves and as a sample of a broader class of phenomena, modes of research with "historical" intention, specifying the research problem and research reconnaissance, choice of research methods and the final operationalization of the research problem and the research assumptions. (pp. 1–42).

14. More specific information on sociometric methods is available in Marie Jahoda, Morton Deutsch, S. W. Cook, eds., *Research Methods in Social Relations* (New York: Dryden Press, 1951).

15. This type of questionnaire was used by the Public Opinion Polling Center of Polish Radio and Television, Warsaw. Text of the questionnaire: Adam Podgórecki, *Prestiz prawa* [Prestige of law] (Warsaw: Ksiazka i Wiedza, 1966).

16. Stefan Nowak, *Metodologia badán socjologicznych* [Methodology of sociological research] (Warsaw: PWN–Polish Scientific Publishers, 1977), pp. 141–142.

17. Albert J. Reiss, Jr., "Delinquency as the failure of personal and social controls," *American Sociological Review* 1951, no. 16, pp. 196–207.

18. Ernst Kretschmer, *Medizinische Psychologie* [Medical Psychology], 13th ed. (Stuttgart: Georg Thieme, 1971).

19. *Biuletyn Psychometryczny* [Psychometric Bulletin] 1968, Komitet Nauk Psychologicznych PAN, vol. 2, p. 216.

20. Ibid, p. 210.

21. Ibid, p. 229.

22. Ibid.

23. Robert S. Woodworth and Harold Schlosberg, *Experimental Psychology*, 2nd ed. (New York: Henry Holt, 1954).

24. Hans J. Eysenck, *Sense and Nonsense in Psychology* (Baltimore: Penguin, 1957).

25. Georges Heuyer, "La methode psychiatrique en criminologie" [Psychiatric method in criminology] *Actes du deuxieme Congrès International de Criminologie*, vol. 3.

26. Henry Davidson, "The Examination of the criminal defendant," *Forensic Psychiatry* (New York: The Ronald Press, 1952), pp. 338–342.

5 A General View of Contemporary Criminality

The Framework for Evaluating Criminality

The universe of human behavior is the most heterogenous collection to be defined in social science categories. In its quest for uncovering the laws of behavior, science abstracts from everything incidental or uniquely individual in that behavior, identifying only the general, essential, and significant moments. After all, every human behavior is intertwined with an infinite number of determinants, of which only certain groups can be intellectually grasped as distinct.

A specific subcollection of this most heterogenous collection is the type of behavior recognized by a given society as offensive. Such types of behavior viewed in their mass are defined as criminality.

Descriptions characterizing general human behavior under set material circumstances are drawn up by conjunction of the findings made by biology, psychology, sociology, and anthropology, which form the general theory of behavior. Evaluation of criminality is carried out in keeping with the findings of criminology, the discipline aiming at developing a general theory of criminal behavior.

A description characterizing criminality in principle comes down to a description of the following issues:

a. the features of criminality determined by the type of social structure;
b. environmental factors differentiating the incidence of criminality in time and space;
c. features of criminal population differentiating criminality in time and space;
d. distinct forms of criminality.

Tying these issues in with situational context, a general pattern characterizing criminality emerges. Within the sphere of social relations there is a fundamental difference between the socialist and nonsocialist systems. Placing criminality in social-system categories becomes an absolute methodological imperative for any proper characterization of that mass phenomenon. After all, social structure is the prime determinant of the individual's "opportunity structure" within the society, and by the same token the determinant of capacity for implementing the individual's aspirations. (See fig. 5–1).

The context of crime analysis				
Level of crime analysis	Type of social system			
	Socialist society		Capitalistic society	
Crime characteristics determined by a type of social structure	highly industrialized	being developed	highly industrialized	being developed
Environmental factors	Ecology: urban environment, rural environment	Economics: Standard of living, Labour conditions	Culture: education, mass media	
Characteristics of criminal population	Demographic characteristics: sex, age, marital status, family conditions		Social and professional characteristics: education, profession, labour conditions	
Particular crime groups	violent	sexual	economic	traffic
	Criminality			

Figure 5-1. Methodological Bases for Crime Research

This chapter is devoted to presenting certain general features of criminal phenomena in the industrialized countries, the character of criminality in the socialist countries and the general outlines of criminality in the developing countries.

Criminality in the Highly Industrialized Countries

In view of the ever more rapid changes in the sphere of technology and thorough changes in customs, the range of interests of western criminologists has been undergoing significant transformations in recent years. Despite the inflexibility of legal institutions, numerous attempts are made at piecemeal adaptation of the social system to the new situations. The explosive growth of criminality is becoming treated as a symptom of far-advanced moral degradation which, without encountering the right social preventive reactions, could lead to the downfall of western civilization.[1]

In various writings by western criminologists the amount of criminality is estimated on the basis of the number of persons held in prisons. This index varies quite significantly from country to country. The clearly leading position in this respect is held by the United States. Are the forms of American criminality clearly distinct from those observed in Western Europe? It would be difficult to give a precise answer here, since in recent years the model of American criminality is being ever more precisely copied in Western Europe. In the United States one can, however, much more clearly observe the phenomena of broadly defined social pathology.

Faced with a feeling of insecurity, the society allots ever more resources to strengthening police forces, courts, and penitentiary administration. All these measures are taken to intensify the struggle with street crime, robbery, homicides, and organized crime.[2]

It is well known that the forms of crime shift along with changes in social life. Even the classic, from the point of view of motive, criminal behavior takes on new forms.

Among the forms of criminality which have lately come into being in the United States and Western Europe and are increasing steadily are the following:

a. crime as business on a national or multinational scale, organized crime, white-collar crime, corruption;
b. crime directed against works of art and other cultural treasures;
c. criminality linked with alcohol and drug abuse;
d. acts of physical violence by persons against other persons;
e. violent acts of multinational and international significance.

It is obvious that these do not exhaust all the issues raised by the complex problem of criminality in the differentiated capitalist world. One should stress, for instance, the weighty problem of juvenile delinquency. Analysis of the listed issues does allow, however, for covering the main changes in the forms and scope of criminality in the western countries.

Criminality as business, now occupying the foremost spot in criminological research, is studied in order to establish, as clearly as possible, the interlinks between certain types of criminal activity in economic life. It is just this type of criminality which for many western countries is becoming a particularly important problem, often of supranational importance. It is becoming ever more difficult to distinguish between professional criminals and persons committing crime while officially occupied as businessmen, industrialists, or finance managers. Such persons commit crimes in connection with their otherwise legal activities. Sociological and criminological literature describes this type of crime as white-collar crime.[3] It is estimated that the economic and social effects of "crime as business" are much greater than the effects of traditional individual violent acts committed by individuals on other individuals or of crimes against property (private and state).

Seeking a proper descripton of "crime as business," criminology almost universally accepts this as a heterogenous group of criminal acts having the folloiwng traits (or at least some of them): they are committed primarily for economic benefit and are centered mainly in industry and trade; the basis for action is provided by formal agreements between the parties organizing the business-type criminal activity; these actions establish an organization in the sense of a definite order or system; the agreements provide for the application or abuse of legal business or industrial techniques; the persons who participate in the agreement and who commit this type of crime often occupy a prominent social position and occasionally also wield political power.

The economic effects of "crime as business" often reach beyond the borders of a single country or even a group of countries. The crime takes on supranational aspects. The illegal or at least economically harmful behavior of multinational corporations gives rise to many complicated problems; there is evidence that such organizations aim at maximizing profit, with no consideration given to the social and political conditions of the states in which they operate. An example of this mode of operating is "transfer pricing" through which the main branch of the corporation sets higher export prices in order to obtain export bonuses, while the foreign subsidiary sets lower export prices for the mother company, in order to lower the import charges, or the other way around.

Significant concern is also raised in western countries by the criminal economic pressure applied by businessmen and managers on the very functioning of justice administration.

Next to organized "crime as business," is the increasing criminality directed against works of art and other cultural treasures.

For quite some time there has been a decrease in the respect shown for the esthetic and cultural appeal of works of art. At present one finds an increasingly commercial approach to a work of art; it is judged primarily from the point of view of its material value. In recent years the theft of works of art has been growing on a major scale; international gangs are often perpetrators of such crimes.

In addition to illegal exports, art treasures are also seriously threatened by simple vandalism, destruction of art treasures and historical monuments for religious or political motives, and occasional thefts committed by tourists as "souvenir collectors." Other factors facilitating the theft of art treasures include the steady growth of art prices, transport facilities, and mass tourism.

While "crime as business" and crimes against works of art fall clearly within the criminologist's range of interests, the phenomena of social pathology are analyzed by them mainly as "criminogenic feedstock" on the basis of which traditional criminality clearly intensifies. The phenomena of social pathology in many countries have now reached unheard-of dimensions. There is a steady growth in prostitution, vagrancy, number of suicides, alcoholism, and drug abuse.

Besides "crime as business," criminality in the field of art treasures, and criminality due to social pathology, there is also the full range of traditional criminality—murders, armed robbery, and rape. The increase in these types of crimes has been so rapid in many western countries that one could describe it as a distinct qualitative phenomenon. Certain criminologists seek the causes of this phenomenon in increasing unemployment, growing discrimination toward ethnic groups, and mounting handicaps in opportunities to attain approved social status by legal means. The increased criminal behavior based on violence is treated as the most evident symptom of the crisis of social policies in the capitalist countries. Individuals who see the paths of social advancement and achievement being steadily blocked for them come to the conclusion that legal methods are ineffective, so they resort to violence as an alternative solution. This leads to the appearance of subcultures where open aggression is viewed as justifiable. The spread of such subcultures is particularly dangerous for adolescents.

Within criminality connected with the use of violence western criminologists distinguish criminality based on so-called moral violence. One of its forms is the hijacking of planes. The hijacking technique consists of forcing the crew, usually the pilot himself, by threat, to change the plane's destination. When met with refusal, the hijackers threaten to kill the pilot.

One of the most detestable forms of criminality which is on the increase in western countries is the kidnapping of minors for ransom. The crime itself is not new, but the scale of the phenomenon and the techniques used are without precedent.

A completely new phenomenon is the kidnapping of prominent persons, in particular diplomats and politicians. Here threat, pressure, or blackmail can be applied not just to selected individuals, but also to various government authorities and political organizations. Threatening to exterminate a diplomat, the kidnappers demand either the payment of a set ransom (when the purpose of the kidnapping is to obtain monetary resources) or freeing specified persons from detention (when the kidnapping is done by a terrorist organization with set political aims).[4]

Both the hijacking of planes and the kidnapping of diplomats are classified in certain analyses of criminality as terrorism. A precise definition of this term encounters considerable difficulties. Attempts have been made to classify terrorist acts according to the three following types:

> as acts of individuals (for instance, an individual's behavior in an airliner in flight, regardless of whether the motive is profit or the act of a psychopath);

> similar acts committed by a group of individuals;

> acts similar to those described above, yet committed not for a private motive but for a cause in which the individual or group of perpetrators is involved.

The developed countries (the United States, France, Canada, Italy, Japan, the Federal Republic of Germany) are plagued by organized crime, a specific combination of violent and premeditated subtle forms of actions. This can be illustrated by a brief description of the tendencies, growth, and pattern of criminality in selected highly industrialized countries.

In the United States a number of agencies assemble data concerning criminality and other phenomena in the sphere of social pathology. A majority of the programs are the responsibility of the Federal Bureau of Investigation or the National Criminal Justice Information and Statistics Service (NCJISS). However, some of the programs are operated by the Drug Enforcement Administration (DEA), the National Institute on Drug Abuse (NIDA), the Administrative Office of the United States Courts (U.S. Courts), and the Federal Prison System (FPS). The Census Bureau, the National Council on Crime and Delinquency (NCCD), and the Institute for Law and Social Research (INSLAW) operate some programs for the

NCJISS. One program is run for the National Institute for Juvenile Justice and Delinquency Prevention (NIJJDP) by the National Center for Juvenile Justice (NCJJ). Although the National Center for Health Statistics (NCHS) Mortality Statistics is not a criminal statistics program, it does provide important national data on homicide.[5]

Such coverage means the availability of multilevel sources of information on crime. Within agency statistics one finds: Uniform Crime Reports, Juvenile Court Statistics, National Prisoner Statistics, and Uniform Parole Reports. Criminal Justice Record Statistics compile: Computerized Criminal History, Offender Based Transaction Statistics, State Judicial Corrections Information System, and Prosecutor's Management Information System. The Specialized and Limited Programs cover: Homicide (Mortality) Statistics, Addict Reporting Program, Drug Awareness Warning Network, and Client Oriented Data Acquisition Program. Federal Criminal Statistics encompass the following types of sources: DEA Defendant Statistics, Federal Defendant Statistics, Automated Inmate Information System, and Federal Supervision Statistics.

The Uniform Crime Reporting Program uses seven crime categories to establish a "crime index" in order to measure the trend and distribution of crime in the United States. Crime index offenses include murder and nonnegligent manslaughter, forcible rape, robbery, aggravated assault, burglary, and larceny-theft. The "Total Crime Index" is a simple sum of the index offenses. In 1960 the total crime index came to 3,384,200; in 1965, 4,739,400; in 1970, 8,098,000; in 1975, 11,256,600; in 1976, 11,304,800; in 1977, 10,935,800. The largest single item is property crime—for instance, in 1970, 7,359,200; in 1975, 10,230,300; in 1976, 10,318,200; in 1977, 9,926,300. Between 1960 and 1977 the largest number of murders and nonnegligent manslaughters, no less than 20,710, were noted in 1974. The highest coefficient of 9.8 per 100,000 population was also noted in 1974. Every year about a million cars are stolen.[6]

The scope of the most serious crimes is illustrated by the FBI crime clock, drawn up for 1967—every minute there was a crime with the use of violence; every 43 minutes a murder; every 19 minutes a rape; every 2.5 minutes a robbery; every 48 seconds a car theft; every 20 seconds a larceny.

Many crimes cannot be reached by statistics; they are known as the dark number. Such crimes do not come to the attention of the police either because of the drop of public confidence in police ability to uncover crime, so that it abstains from reporting the crimes or, as in case of rapes, because of the victims' fear of publicly revealing their ordeal.

Data have shown that in the first half of 1980 New York suffered the worst period in its history. The number of the most serious crimes committed exceeded the national average by 60 percent, which moved this metropolis up to second place, following St. Louis, on the list of most dangerous cities in the

United States. New York headed the national list in the number of burglaries. It also broke the murder record (1,818 cases in 1980).[7]

White-collar crime presents a very serious problem. Criminals committing this type of offense come from the regular community and usually have links with leading politicians and bankers. In their operations they observe two rules: first, never start at anything less than a million; second, the larger the scale the lesser the danger of discovery. According to Gilbert Geis the number of those crimes is unknown and cannot even be estimated with any degree of probability. Various financial estimates of the cost of such crimes have been made. It is possible that the overall costs of white-collar crimes exceed $100 billion annually.[8] It was on the basis of just such data that U.S. Congressman John Conyers, chairman of the subcommittee on crime stated during congressional debates that he views white-collar crime as the most serious, all-permeating, insidious problem of present-day America.[9]

In 1969 a special group of scholars established by a Presidential Commission informed the nation that Americans have become a people disposed to violent actions and reactions to the actions of others.

Not until the assassination of President John F. Kennedy in 1963 did gun control become a major issue. A count of magazine articles dealing with gun control from 1935 to 1977 indicates that coverage was nonexistent from 1941–43 through 1953–55. The proposed tightening of the administration of the Federal Firearms Act of 1938 created a small swell of attention cresting at five articles in 1957–59. The rate then fell to an average of one article per year from 1959–61 through 1962–63, before surging to twelve articles per year over the next four years (1963–67). Interest climbed sharply over the next two years and peaked at forty-seven articles in 1968–69; the time of the passage of the Gun Control Act of 1968. Subsequent coverage remained stable at about ten articles per year until 1975–77 when legislative activity on handgun control pushed coverage to about thirty articles per year.[10]

The attempt on the life of President Ronald Reagan in March 1981 again brought the issue of firearms control to the fore. A public opinion poll conducted jointly by ABC and the *Washington Post* indicated that 65 percent of the public were in favor of controlling the firearms in private hands. At the same time 80 percent of the public doubted the effectiveness of such controls, stating that this method will not check the wave of killings.

Illegal drug traffic and the connected drug abuse is the next major social problem faced in the United States. The scale of organized crime in this field can be perceived from the fact that in August 1972 police in the United States arrested 57 gang members operating under the name of Eternal Brotherhood of Love and believed to represent one of the largest criminal groups on earth dealing in drug trafficking. Recently published statistical data show that 30 million Americans use marijuana and nearly 400,000 use heroin, while more than 80,000 (mostly young) people are undergoing federal government sponsored treatment for drug abuse.

It is understandable that the growth of these types of criminality in the United States are at the center of public attention and are part of the classic repertoire of election oratory. The concern about these issues is evident from the establishment in 1965 by President Lyndon Johnson of the President's Commission on Law Enforcement and Administration of Justice for drawing up recommendations on how to limit crime and improve the effectiveness of criminal justice.

The commission began by investigating four major fields: police, courts, functioning of correctional institutions, and the evaluation of crime. Its field of interest later extended to juvenile delinquency, narcotics and drug abuse, and drunkenness. In this way the commission's attention focused on issues encompassing criminology, criminalistics, sociology and psychiatry, police organization, technical facilities, and even salaries.

In 1967 the commission published a comprehensive 340-page report on various aspects of crime in the United States.[11] It provides a valuable source of information on current problems of criminality in general.

The most serious problem faced in the United States in this field concerns organized crime, the extent of which is difficult to gauge and which has roots extending back to Prohibition days.

Criminological literature provides various definitions of organized crime. Applying economic criteria it is called big business; from the sociological point of view the participants in organized crime have been called "an autonomous social class"; finally a criminologic view allows for advancing the view that organized crime represents an extensive conspiracy hindering the effective operation of criminal justice.

The core of organized crime, according to the presidential commission's report, is made up of twenty four groups having the character of criminal cartels. The most influential of these operate in the states of New York, New Jersey, Illinois, Florida, Louisiana, Nevada, Michigan, and Rhode Island. Each of the twenty four groups is known as a "family," with membership ranging between 20 and 700. Most cities have only a single "family," though New York has no less than five. The main objective of a "family" is to maximize profit and to protect members from the criminal justice system. The hierarchic structure of the "families" is reminiscent of the structure set up by the mafia operating in Sicily for more than a century.

The "family" is headed by a *boss* who has a deputy, the *underboss*. The counsellor (*consigliere*) of the boss also holds important status. This office is usually held by an older gangster, experienced in "the trade," one who still enjoys respect in his milieu, but who is gradually withdrawing from active "business." The highest body governing the twenty four "families" is a commission made up of bosses of the most influential "families."

First place among all criminal cartels operating in the United States is certainly held by La Cosa Nostra, previously known as the Mafia. J. Edgar Hoover testified before a congressional commission in 1966: "La Cosa Nostra is the largest criminal organization of the underworld, marked by strict discipline. It commits every type of crime on earth. . . . It has its own laws and its own justice system as well as extensive international dealings."

The major feature of organized crime is its extensive nationwide and even international scope. The difficulty in identifying "family" members stems from the fact that they try to hide among the regular society, setting up the right front allowing them to infiltrate various social groups, milieus, and the society in localities where they settle.

In the light of recently assembled data on the functioning of criminal syndicates one notes a new style of recruiting. In the past syndicate members came mostly from criminal milieus, while at present, as required by their mode of operation, they aim for various types of specialists, such as lawyers, administrators, and accountants, who have a chance to reach and corrupt highly placed officials in the administration, police, and so on.

The gangs protect their members from justice. Usually they are secured by a "fix," a go-between with influence in police circles.

Crime in the United States is a subject of extensive interest as more than just a domestic problem of that country. In certain European countries (the Federal Republic of Germany, the United Kingdom, France) one notes the "americanizing" of criminal methods, bringing in its wake the need for getting to know these methods, if they are to be counteracted.

In Canada crime is particularly rampant in the big cities, such as Montreal and Toronto. Between 1970 and 1974, the number of offenses against the Canadian Criminal Code rose by 30.9 percent and the crime rate (number of offenses per 100,000 inhabitants) increased by 24.7 percent in 1974. Violent crimes accounted for 8.7 percent of all crime during 1974. A total of 126,053 murders, attempted murders, manslaughters, rapes, other sexual offenses, woundings, assaults, and robberies were reported—7 percent over 1973 and 23.1 percent higher than in 1970. Property crimes comprised 65 percent of all offenses against the Canadian Criminal Code in 1974. A total of 946,793 offenses of breaking and entering, motor vehicle and other thefts, handling of stolen goods, and fraud were reported in Canada during 1974—13.6 percent higher than in 1973 and 26.5 percent higher than in 1970. The property crime rate was 11.8 percent higher than in 1973 and 20.5 percent higher than in 1970. There were 174,325 persons charged with property offenses: 123,174 adults and 51,151 juveniles. In addition, 40,812 juvenile offenders were dealt with informally. The clearance rate for all property crimes was 21.7 percent. An examination of the dark figure by a victimization survey reveals a striking contrast between the overall crime rate and the crime rate reported to the police. On an average, the reported crimes amount to only a fifth of the crimes actually committed. It should be noted that Canada has endured terrorist activities in the province of Quebec.[12]

In Japan, the statistical data concerning all types of offenses in the country have been gathered by police since 1886. Other statistics are provided by public prosecution, correctional administration, and probation and parole data issued by the Ministry of Justice, judicial data compiled under the direction of the Supreme Court, annual white papers on the police published by the National Police Agency, and annual white papers on crime prepared by the Ministry of Justice Research and Training Institute.

In Japan, national and average personal incomes have risen since 1955 and the crime rate has fallen steadily during the same period. The incidence of serious crimes like homicide, bodily injury, rape, and robbery as well as less dangerous offenses like theft is far lower in Japan than in most nations, showing that Japanese advanced industrial society exists without a simultaneous increase in crime. During the last twenty five years crime decreased in Japan by approximately 50 percent.

In explaining the causes of this phenomenon, William Clifford attributes the Japanese success in curbing and controlling crime to several factors:

1. a homogeneous, socially cohesive society which maintains a degree of orderliness and control unheard of in Western society;
2. the ability of the Japanese to retain effective small grouping; and
3. the interlinking of social obligations and dependence imposed on each individual which in turn produces enormous internal pressures to avoid deviant behavior. The end result is that the average Japanese has a strong moral commitment to lawful behavior and, in effect, acts as his own internal policeman.[13]

The general trends in crime since World War II show that the peak rate occurred in 1948, with 1,603,265 Penal Code offenses (in 1946 there were 1,387,080) and decreased to 1,344,482 in 1953. The trend began to increase in 1954 and culminated in 1964 with a total of 1,609,741 Penal Code offenses. The following two years showed a slight decrease; then began a third period of acceleration with a peak of 1,932,401 in 1970. From 1971 onward the rate decreased steadily to 1,671,947 in 1974. Since then, there has been a slight increase to 1,776,801 offenses in 1978.

The rate of clearance by the police was 68.6 percent in 1978 (known Penal Code offenses). The annual clearance rate during the past ten years varied between 68 percent and 71 percent of offenses known to the police. The figure of 1,219,578 in 1978 represented an increase of 59,502 over the previous year and the number of offenders investigated by police increased to 843,295 in 1978 (21,077 more than in 1977).

A high degree of industrialization and affluence have had an impact on social changes which, in turn, caused the emergence of new trends in crime. In 1978 the Japanese police investigated 29,680 cases of stimulant drug law violation involving 17,740 persons, twenty times more than in 1969. Also in 1978, 1,247 persons were investigated on suspicion of having committed offenses relating to other drugs (including narcotics and marijuana). It has been observed lately that young persons are using marijuana with ever greater frequency.

A serious development of domestic terrorism has been a series of time-bomb attacks against major Japanese corporations: in 1974 there were twenty three bomb attacks and attempted bombings; in 1975 eight members of an extremist group were apprehended. The arrested terrorists formed the core of the "East Asia Anti-Japan Armed Front" including the three subgroups: "Wolf," "Fang of the Earth," and "Scorpion."

The increase in international terrorist criminal activity did not bypass Japan. In 1977, an ultraleftist group, the "Japan Red Army," hijacked a Japanese plane from Dacca, taking many hostages and compelling the Japanese government to release nine dangerous offenders from prison (some of them had committed homicide). In 1978 there were many violent actions, in particular by the ultraleftist groups demonstrating against the opening of the new Tokyo International Airport at Narita.

Juvenile criminality in Japan shows a significantly increasing rate over a period of several years. It should be noted that the average age of juvenile offenders has steadily declined; in 1978, 66.2 percent of all delinquent acts were committed by juveniles between fourteen and sixteen years old. Illicit use of stimulant drugs and organic solvents is increasing among juveniles; female delinquency is also increasing and more girls run away from home than boys; juvenile delinquents more often come from middle class families; delinquent acts are often perpetrated in a quest for "fun" or "thrills." A police survey of Japan published in January 1981 informs us that 42 percent of all crimes committed in 1980 were cases of juvenile delinquency. The number of youths charged in 1980 was 149,500. There was an increase of 16.8 percent in youth offenses, compared to 1979.

The ratio for female offenders steadily increased for several years, while for male offenders it has dropped (by 15 percent in the years 1966–1977). In 1978, 19 percent of all nontraffic penal code offenses were committed by females (1.6 per 1,000 females) in the population fourteen years old and over. Females most frequently commit infanticide (91.2 percent of all offenders), theft (27.6 percent), assisting suicides (26.1 percent) and homicides of parents and grandparents (20 percent).

Racketeer groups defined by the Japanese police as antisocial organizations commit various violent crimes. According to police records there are about 2,500 gangster groups with 108,000 members. Racketeer groups have close ties based on hierarchical obedience patterned on medieval structures and resting on adherence by members to fictitious blood relationships. During 1978 racketeers committed 26.9 percent of all homicides, 26.8 percent of violent crimes, 28.5 percent of bodily injury crimes, 50.9 percent of extortion offenses and 52.1 percent of stimulant drugs law violations. They perpetrated 179 out of 233 crimes with the use of firearms. As regards recidivism, the Ministry of Justice Research and Training Institute published a study report based on a randomly selected sample of 500,000 offenders convicted in the past thirty one years. The findings show that 12.5 percent of all first offenders who were sentenced to punishment or released from prison in 1975 had committed a new offense within three years (24.1 percent in 1956). The rate was higher for persons granted suspension of execution of sentence under probationary supervision than those released from prison. Only 9.1 percent were multiple recidivists with five or more convictions; they constituted 28.8 percent of all the convictions received by the whole sample.

Police records show that 34.3 percent of all persons investigated in 1975 for nontraffic penal code offenses were prior offenders; they committed 48.6 percent of homicides and 49.5 percent of rapes. In 1974 too, 29.3 percent of all adult offenders investigated by police were previous offenders—of these, 24 percent were multiple recidivists with five or more prior convictions; 63.7 percent of all persons adjudged guilty in 1974 after first instance trial (excluding summary proceedings) on charges of nontraffic penal code offenses had been convicted before.

In the United Kingdom indictable crimes have shown a considerable increase in recent years; for instance in England and Wales in 1950 there were 461,435 registered cases, and in 1960 this was up to 743,713 cases.[14] The total number of convictions in 1969 came to 1,606,728, for acts representing various degrees of social threat. This included one million people convicted of traffic offenses and 250,000 of nonpayment of the radio registration tax.

In 1975 the number of convictions came to 1,988,679, an increase of nearly a quarter since 1969. There was a particularly large increase of convictions for indictable crimes, from 304,070 to 402,481, up nearly a third; convictions for homicides were up (from 239 to 369) as were robbery convictions (2,526 to 3,458).[15] Convictions for indictable crimes continued upward, to 415,500 in 1976 and 428,700 in 1977.[16]

Compared with 1945, London criminality was 80 percent higher in 1966. During five months of 1969 there was a 24 percent increase in London crime as compared with the situation one year previous, with a 31 percent increase in homicides.[17]

Criminals in Britain ever more frequently resort to the threat of kidnapping. In 1971 there were no less than forty three child kidnappings. The epidemic of threats is a menace to the British public and, obviously, to the British police, unable to secure personal protection for everyone who could be of potential interest to kidnappers.[18]

Next to robberies directed against banks, jewelry stores, and money transport (for instance, the famous train robbery), car theft is also becoming a serious problem.

The crime situation appears particularly menancing, considering that the detection rate is inversely proportional to the number of offenders. In 1938 the detection rate was 50.1 percent, in 1958, 45.6 percent, in 1960, 44.4 percent and in 1964 only 39.6 percent. This is due, despite the strengthening of police forces, to higher population density, greater value of property concentration in given areas, and an increase in the number of motor vehicles.

British opinion blames the growth of crime on the glorifying of criminals in films and on television and on the corruption scandals in certain police units. Sociologists point to yet another source: lesser authority of the law and excessive liberalism with respect to the mass media.

A specific problem which considerably shakes the social order is the bloody fighting in Northern Ireland and, since July 1981, also the wave of violent disorders in many towns, accompanied by looting and burning of stores.

Analysis of police statistics in the Federal Republic of Germany shows that in 1978 the country recorded a total of 3,380,516 indictable offenses (excluding traffic offenses and offenses against state security). Compared with 1977 this figure is 2.8 percent higher. The index of crimes per 100,000 population (as of June 30, 1978) came to 5,514 and was 3 percent higher than the year before.[19]

In 1979 there was a further 4.5 percent increase in crime, with a total of 3,533,802 indictable offenses; the crime index increased to 5,761.[20]

The highest crime indexes are noted in large cities of over 500,000 population. This holds particularly true for such crimes as thefts, robberies, sexual offenses, bankruptcies, narcotics offenses, homosexualism, insolvency, and white slavery. Offenses of this kind are primarily the domain of large cities.

A large number of crimes was committed with the use or the threat of using firearms: in 1978 there were 13,370 such crimes (13,381 the year before). Firearms were involved in the major proportion of homicides, bodily injuries, offenses against private liberty, robberies, the taking of hostages, and kidnappings for blackmail.

The sources used in analyzing these data make it possible to determine the trends in crime between 1974 and 1978. A particularly high increase was noted in the illegal narcotics traffic (73.7 percent), simple thefts (30.5 percent), bodily injuries (22.6 percent), resisting state authority and acts directed against the public order (28.0 percent), indictable offenses against private liberty, including the taking of hostages (18.2 percent), robberies (14.1 percent). One notes the increase in the percentage of juveniles and minors in the total number of suspects: the share of juveniles between fourteen and eighteen years of age went up from 13.5 percent in 1974 to 15.4 percent in 1978; the share of children correspondingly rose from 6.2 percent to 7.7 percent. The noted increase in juvenile delinquency centered mainly on thefts and street thefts, but also extended to homicides, often sex killings.

These trends continued unchanged, as shown by 1979 data. One should add that police statistics also indicate an increase in murders and homicides committed by women.

Terrorism is a dangerous West German phenomenon. Since the turn of the sixties terrorist bullets and bombs were responsible for the death of 30 people, the maiming of 100, while another 110 people were victims of other types of attempts. By May 1980 the courts convicted 242 terrorists and their supporters. Terrorist attacks are directed mainly against representatives of the state (particularly justice administration personnel), against banks and large companies, and also against persons prominent in the political and economic life of the country. In the face of growing terrorism numerous conferences have been organized in West Germany on the fundamental problems of domestic security. Significant changes have been made in penal legislation to counter this phenomenon.[21] The bibliography on the subject of *Terrorismus und Gewalt* (Terrorism and Force) by February 1978 registered over 1,500 titles of monographs and various types of articles.

West Germany is also faced with a rapid growth of drug-connected crimes (Rauschgiftkriminalität) since the early 1970s. In 1953 it had 1,535 suspects, 1,256 in 1958, 786 in 1962, 1,226 in 1967, 16,188 in 1970, 22,607 in 1972 (after the passage of new legislation—Betaeubungsmittelgesetz of January 10, 1972), 35,876 in 1977, 39,962 in 1978, and 47,258 in 1979. The share of juveniles between the ages of fourteen and eighteen came to: 10.4 percent in 1977, 9.4 percent in 1978 and 8.4 percent in 1979.[22]

Criminality in France is marked by a progressing trend. In 1959 the total number of registered offenses came to 829,898, 912,072 in 1963, 1,250,000 in 1969 and 1,823,953 in 1976.

In 1969 there were 803 cases of murder (including 219 in Paris, 125 in Lille, and 27 in Marseilles). This number includes 46 murders committed by gangs.[23] Juveniles (aged under 21) shared in every type of crime. While in 1959 juveniles accounted for 5.8 percent of all crimes, by 1969 their share was already up to 20 percent.[24]

In 1969 the number of thefts rose by 16 percent, and armed robberies went up by no less than 97 percent.[25] Between 1964 and 1976 the number of burglaries increased more than 200 percent; by 1976 there were over 204,000 burglaries, with only 20 percent of the offenders apprehended and brought to trial.

In connection with growing criminality *Paris Match* of May 16, 1979 wrote:

> In the field of crime, theft, robbery, violence, fraud, and smuggling France finds itself expanding greatly. Offenders are to be found everywhere, even in the best society, not only in criminal milieus, as in the past. The barrier between criminals and respected citizens is crumbling. The perpetrator of numerous thefts, assaults, and a killing turned out to be a respected teacher. Record-breaking thieves turn out to be the sons of a businessman and store owner. A person apprehended for robbing an old man after slashing his throat with a knife admits to 4 thefts, 10 assaults and 43 burglaries over the course of the previous 14 months. He worked with a friend. One is 13, the other 17. In the south of France a man was held for robbing a villa. Asked why he did it, the man said that he was married recently and he needed a refrigerator, washing machine, TV set and some furniture—he did not care for buying it, waiting, making payments; he needed all that immediately; these are things without which there can be no happiness.

Between 1967 and 1976 the overall number of crimes and misdemeanors doubled. Yet, the number of armed assaults went up fivefold: from 685 to 3,506. There was an even more drastic rise in crimes involving ransom; this sort of crime increased twenty times, from 63 to 1,359.

Since 1971 the growth of crime has been faster than the growth of population. Along with declared criminality one finds force and violence permeating social relations. These phenomena can be observed in every walk of social life, with greatest prevalence in the large cities. Violence and force are not limited to public life, extending also to private life, responsible for havoc there. The second highest cause of death for juveniles, next to road accidents, is suicide; drug abuse is also on the rise among adolsecents.

Open or disguised manifestations of force and violence give rise to a general feeling of insecurity. A report drafted under the guidance of Alain Peyrefitte says: "Over 80 percent of the French people now acutely feel the mounting violence and force. . . . Most people believe that over the next few years the situation will deteriorate even further."[26]

In Italy there has been a steady increase of criminality for many years. Statistics for 1965 registered 402,741 offensive acts, 625,669 such acts for 1978.[27] There was a particularly sharp increase in the number of the most serious crimes, such as homicides, armed robbery of banks, post offices, business premises, daring thefts (for instance, in museums).

There is a steady high level of offenses against property. In 1978 there were 106,385 such cases (including 17,220 robberies), and a further 167,110 economic crimes (including 163,862 unsecured checks).

American-style crimes (serious theft, bank robberies, large store robberies) occurred mainly in Milan and in the other large cities in the northern part of the country; these were committed usually by members of organized gangs.

In the southern part of Italy crime in certain cases is linked with local traditions; for example, Calabria, Sicily, and Sardinia are plagued by murders "defending honor." Further, Sardinia has the more modern forms of criminal activities, such as demanding ransom for those kidnapped. The plague of banditry there takes on a form and scale which is beyond control.

Wolf Middendorff has put together a classification scale of terrorist acts, distinguishing eight categories.[28] These are individual, group, committed on orders of the commanders attempts directed against life, bombings, arson, kidnapping, plane hijacking, bank robbery. Each one of those forms and categories has had its examples in Italy. In September 1977 Calabria alone was the site of seven kidnappings. The kidnapping epidemic gradually extended to the entire country, with political motives often behind the acts. This holds particularly true of kidnappings, killings, and maiming of politicians and criminal justice personnel. Such an escalation of terrorist attacks is alarming both to Italians and to the world at large. Italian legislation established an entire system of antiterrorist measures, though it would appear that the preventive impact of that system is almost nonexistent.

Juveniles are responsible for a considerable proportion of the offenses committed in Italy. Among the 469,105 suspects in 1978 there were no less than 11,386 juveniles under 18 (more than 24 percent).

Italy's parliament has passed a new law directed against organized crime. The law, in two parts, provides for increased penalties for various crimes. Under the new law offenders may be sentenced to as much as twenty years at hard labor; for kidnapping the maximum sentence may go as high as twenty five years at hard labor.[29]

In Sweden the total number of offenses reported to the police in 1964 came to 336,435, increasing by 1970 to 532,431. In 1977 there were a total of 759,407 offenses indictable under the penal code and other statutes.[30]

The number of people prosecuted increased from 450,742 in 1972 to 515,506 in 1974, a jump of 14 percent in just two years. The increase was particularly marked in cases against offenders responsible for homicides (from 54 to 83), robberies (from 361 to 456) and offenses against public safety (from 278 to 306) and against public order (from 66,758 to 78,418).[31]

The high number of armed assaults on police personnel led the Swedish authorities to adopt sterner rules against the illegal possession of arms. The very fact of owning a firearm by the offender at the moment when the offense was being committed constitutes an aggravating circumstance, regardless of whether the weapon was used in action or not. Most firearms used as tools of crime came from army weaponry registers. Every year there are between 200 and 300 cases in Sweden of military firearms theft; a fifth of that represents machine pistols, used ever more frequently in criminal acts.[32]

There was an increasing number of violations of the illegal narcotics traffic laws: in 1977 there were 20,753 such cases, compared with 19,047 in 1975. The law against driving while intoxicated is also regularly violated; in 1977 there were 20,753 such cases.

Switzerland's crime rate has climbed in parallel with the general population growth. Through the 1950s the number of convictions increased 15.3 percent while the population growth was 15.9 percent. Since 1963 there was even a slight regression in crime, followed by stabilization.

Switzerland does not compile federal police statistics; such statistics are available only in some of the cantons. Analysis of crime can, therefore, be carried out only on the basis of court statistics. Between 1974 and 1977 there were some 50,000 convictions per year, on the basis of all federal statutes, with convictions of juveniles accounting for only 7 percent. Convictions are dominated by offenses connected with road traffic, followed by offenses against property and against life and bodily integrity.[33]

There seems to be a considerable amount of white-collar crime; in this respect the dark figure is probably sizeable. This is due to the fact that Switzerland serves as an international finance and business center. Such suspicions were confirmed by research carried out by M. B. Clinard and others.[34]

A disquieting development is the frequency of bombings: between 1968 and 1978 there were 251 such acts, killing a total of 45 persons. In June 1980 the anarchist movement organized mass demonstrations, during which shops were demolished and there were scuffles with the police.

Drug abuse and its incident criminality has also become a problem. Convictions based on the federal statute concerning stupefying drugs oscillate around 2,000.

Compared with other western countries, Switzerland's lower rate of juvenile delinquency is ascribed to such factors as the low percentage of employment among married women (29 percent), a good school system with high standards, and mass participation in sports.[35]

Switzerland has eighty-nine penitentiary institutions with an average total of 18,000 inmates. It is estimated that between 30 and 40 percent of the inmates are held due to alcoholic intoxication.[36]

One of the most trying social problems of Spain after that country's return to democracy is the skyrocketing rate of criminality. Municipal, regional, and peace courts in 1977 convicted 149,959 people (134,284 people in 1976).[37] Between 1966 and 1977 the number of thefts increased fivefold.

Juveniles under twenty-one years of age represent a large share of the offenders.[38] Official statistics show that the crime threat is greatest in the big cities, particularly in the peripheral neighborhoods, plagued by numerous juvenile gangs. Lack of security is generally felt.[39]

The earliest data on criminal statistics in Austria were published during the reign of Maria Theresa in 1775 in the "Status elaboratum." Since 1848 regular statistical data are available on the activities of police, courts and on the crime index.[40] Current Austrian police statistics cover offenses indictable by law and registered by the police and the gendarmerie. In 1978, 313,233 such acts were registered (including 39,025 road traffic offenses). The crime index per 100,000 people, including road traffic offenses came to 4,166, and excluding such offenses 3,647. Compared with 1977 the total number of offenses increased 3.2 percent, and compared with 1976, 2.7 percent. Data for 1979 show a further 5.4 percent increase in crimes, particularly offenses against life and bodily integrity (9.5 percent) and morals (5.0 percent).

A particularly unfavorable development is the steadily climbing number of robberies: from 250 in 1953 to 937 by 1977. According to Christian Mayerhofer[41] such crimes are committed mostly by young males resident in large urban centers and also by foreigners (the latter, mainly Yugoslavs, shared in 15 percent of offenses committed in 1977). The victims are usually pedestrians and strangers to the criminal.

Between 1971 and 1977 there was a nearly fourfold increase in the number of armed robberies, mostly directed against banks or post offices. In 1977 there were 115 armed robberies (representing more than 12 percent of all robberies).

Terrorism is also a dangerous phenomenon to be found in Austria, with acts directed against foreigners and arson of department stores. Between 1973 and 1979 such actions resulted in the kidnapping of 75 people as hostages and the killing of 3 people.

Authorities are disquieted by the growing drug abuse. In 1978 there were 807 cases of traffic in stupefying drugs (an increase of 47.8 percent over the previous year) and 2,881 other acts aimed at the use of such drugs (an increase of 38.7 percent).

As shown by studies conducted by Roland Grassberger, there is an explosive increase of crimes directed against property.[42] Interpol data show that Austria has become a center for smuggling stolen cars.[43]

Criminality in The Netherlands is rising. The total number of crimes known to the police amounted to 265,732 in 1970; 453,178 in 1975; and 622,390 in 1979. The greatest share represented crimes against property (189,469 in 1970; 345,710 in 1975; 436,824 in 1979), showing an increase between 1970 and 1979 of about 130 percent. Road traffic offenses also increased in the same period by more than 90 percent (36,774 in 1970, 70,183 in 1979). The crimes against life and person increased from 11,305 in 1970 to 12,027 in 1975 and to 18,235 in 1979. Crime against public order and public authorities also increased: 3,568 in 1970; 4,274 in 1975 and 6,298 in 1979. Sexual offenses dropped from 8,312 in 1970 to 7,905 in 1979.

In the same period the number of crimes cleared up amounted to: 109,241 in 1970; 149,579 in 1975 and 199,573 in 1979, showing a decrease from 41 per 100 crimes known to the police in 1970 to 32 in 1979.

The number of finally sentenced individuals also increased, from 45,303 in 1970 (41,066 men, 4,237 women) to 68,299 in 1978 (63,928 men, 4,371 women) with an index per 100,000 inhabitants of 347 in 1970 and 490 in 1978.[44]

Crime in the Republic of South Africa has reached terrifying proportions.[45] Crimes against persons in the year 1972–1973 constituted 22 percent of the total. A large number of crimes are being committed under the influence of alcohol (29 percent). The absolute figures for the year 1974–1975 went as follows: murder 8,543, manslaughter 9,016, infanticide 128, bodily injury 151,444. During a single year that country has more murders than England and Wales combined in fifty years (1900–1949).

The largest number of crimes are being committed by persons between twenty five and thirty four years of age (in the years 1969–1970 such persons were responsible for 146,729 crimes, or 32.4 percent of the total), even though they represent only 14 percent of the population. The next highest group covers people between the ages of eighteen and twenty four who committed 142,529 crimes or 31.5 percent of the total. Offenders between thirty five an forty four years of age were responsible for 78,547 crimes or 17.3 percent.

Between July 1, 1976 and June 30, 1977 the Republic of South Africa registered 1,052,697 crimes and misdemeanors. As of June 30, 1977 prisons of that country held 99,208 inmates (of whom 15,916 were under arrest). During that single year there were 7,478 murders (excluding infanticide),

3,872 acts of manslaughter, 110,733 burglaries, 44,141 robberies, 36,900 car thefts and 2,186 cases of firearm thefts.

In 1976 there were 61 capital punishment executions (2 whites, 8 Coloreds and 51 blacks).[46]

Criminality in the Socialist Countries

The description of criminality, with presentation of its main qualitative and quantitiative features requires specific placement of the examined phenomena in a given socioeconomic system. This is not to say automatically that every system develops its own specific forms of criminality. A certain sphere of criminal phenomena continues to be common to every social system. Socialism, revolutionizing the old social structure in the sphere of being, at the same time inherits given consciousness patterns which have been shaped over many centuries. Radical changes in the sphere of production relationships do, however, lead to the evolution of a distinct system of socialist morality. As time passes there is a steady decrease in those forms of crime which occurred on the soil of social inequality. The very structure of the socialist system practically hampers the spread of those criminal phenomena which are bred by the contradictions present in the developed capitalist countries.

The building of a new system, including a new system of people's state authority, always leads to revolutionary transformations in national consciousness. It forces the abandoning of various biases and prejudices, the reevaluating of many traditional patterns of thought. Still, the system of power and the system of applicable law has to function from the moment when the state of the new type is established. For that reason many such states in the early years of their existence continue to widely apply old institutions, vested with a new class meaning. The prosecution and criminal justice bodies, using many forms of the former legal system, fill these forms with a new socialist substance.

Changes in the structure and dynamics of criminal phenomena in the countries building a socialist system also follow specific rules. Space does not allow for an exhaustive presentation of all the problems of crime in each one of these countries. The specific problems of crime will best be illustrated by using the example of a single country, Poland in this case, covering the period following World War II.[47]

There will be some additional comments on criminality in Bulgaria, Czechoslovakia, the German Democratic Republic, and Hungary in those same years.

The years following World War II can be divided into five distinct time periods.[48]

The first spans 1944 through 1948. During this period the country was being rapidly rebuilt from the ravages of the war, at the same time establishing and consolidating the structure of people's authority, including prosecution and criminal justice institutions. No significant changes were made in the legal acts in force since the pre-World War II days. The legislative system changed through the issuing of new legislative acts amending former statutes or limiting the scope of their application. These new regulations were aimed at combating the crimes which were particularly dangerous for the new system, considering the still numerous armed attempts against the people's authority.

The second period covered the years 1949 through 1955. This was the time of laying the foundations of socialism in Poland, as mapped out in the Six-Year-Plan. More fundamental reforms were then made in the statutes and criminal justice institutions of pre-World War II vintage. Reforms were implemented in the structure and system of operation of the courts and prosecution bodies. General penal courts were given broader competences, along with the elimination of certain special courts. The Special Commission for Combating Economic Abuse and Pestilence was disolved and limitations were placed on the authority of military penal courts in cases of offenses committed by civilians.

Specific statutes were still being adopted in the field of substantive penal law, as required by justice administration. For instance, it became necessary to increase the protection of public property, of freedom of conscience and beliefs, to step up the combating of speculation, of currency crimes, and the like.

The third period covered the years 1956 to 1970. This was the time of the great codifications. New codes of civil law (substantive and procedural) and of penal law (substantive, procedural and executory) were drafted and later adopted by the Sejm, the Polish parliament.

The fourth period began in 1970 and continued to mid-1980. The three new penal codes drafted and adopted in the previous period came into force in early 1970. This was a development of fundamental significance for the entire legal process as well as for the practice of combating and preventing criminality.

The fifth period began in August 1980, when actions of the working class, which was dissatisfied with the forms in which the system was being implemented, led to very significant social and political changes. This started a new stage in the development of the socialist state which, along with planned growth, is able to correspondingly shape the various spheres of social life, and as part of that, to exert its impact on criminality.

There is no doubt of the influence which the social changes exerted on the legislation and practice of justice administration. In February 1981 numerous actions were taken to improve the effectiveness of the struggle against crime, to limit the consumption of alcohol, to increase the scope of protecting the rights and the personal security of the citizens. Efforts began to implement the program of improving and bringing up to date the methods applied by prosecution and criminal justice bodies. These institutions were faced with the task of significantly improving social discipline and law observance in the country.

Out of the entire catalogue of crime in Poland, a synthetic analysis will be made of acts representing a very high degree of social menace and of the acts with the highest incidence.

The number of registered homicides in Poland between 1962 and 1979 oscillated around 500 cases per year. For instance, in 1979 there was a total of 498 homicides. The following year, 1980, brought a considerable increase of more than 18 percent to 589 such acts (index per 100,000 population of 1.6).

The incidence of homicides measured as the number of such offenses per size of population is very similar in urban and rural areas. There are differences in the direction of change in the incidence of that offense: in towns the number of homicides is on the increase, while in the countryside it is dropping.

This offense category is dominated by acts committed due to conflicts in the family, with the neighbors, concerning property, jealousy, and revenge. The rapid increase in 1980 was accounted for mainly by homicides connected with robbery or for sexual motives. Forecasts for the next few years are unfavorable. The unstable social and economic situation of the country leads to the violation of customs and moral norms, gives rise to conflicts and manifestations of aggression, aiding the activities of criminal and hooligan elements operating with ruthlessness.

In analyzing offenses which cause bodily injury one should distinguish two periods: 1964–69, when the courts applied the penal code of 1932, and the second period starting with enforcement of the new penal code (1970). In view of the changes in the principle of registration, the numerical data concerning bodily injury for the years 1964–1969 are not comparable with the post-1970 data. Since 1970 the number of offenses leading to bodily injury varies only slightly: in 1980 it amounted to 9,556 and in the preceding year 9,422 (index per 100,000 people of 27.0). There is also a steady number of indictable assaults and battery: in 1980 there were 3,840 such offenses, in the preceding year 3,876 (index per 100,000 population of about 10.8).

As to rapes [Art. 168 of the Penal Code] in the years 1965 through 1969 the average annual number of such offenses came to 1,886 and average annual growth equaled 128 such offenses or 7 percent of the average. In the years 1970 through 1973 the rate of increase accelerated to an average of 163 offenses per year. A significant difference was noted starting in 1974, when the number of recorded rapes came to 1,996 and was 25.7 percent lower than the theoretical figure of 2,644 which would result from extrapolating the growth trend of the years 1970 through 1973. In 1976 and the following years there was a further drop in offenses of this type: in 1980 there were 1,576 rapes, compared with 1,578 the preceding year (index of 4.5 per 100,000).

The number of robberies increased between 1962 and 1973 by an average of nearly 400 cases per year. Analyzing the number of cases one concludes that the trend was clearly unfavorable. For instance, by 1976, the level of this type of offense increased 66 percent compared with the 1962–1965 level. Such a significant quantitative jump has to be recognized as a qualitative change. The number of robberies in the years 1966 through 1969 remained almost constant. The average for that period came to 4,327 cases, a nearly 60 percent rise compared with the average for the previous period. The average annual deviation from the average came to some 87 cases, or merely 2 percent of the average annual number of robberies.

A qualitative jump took place in 1969, when the number of registered robberies came to 5,888, meaning 1,561 cases more than the 1965–1968 average. The number of robberies in 1969 was 36 percent higher than the 1965–1968 level. In 1970, the first year of the new Penal Code, there was a slight (7 percent) drop in the number of robberies.

1971 brought a further increase in comparison with the previous two years. The absolute growth in the number of robberies in 1971 compared with 1970 amounted to 1,281 cases, equivalent to 23 percent.

In the next two years (1972 and 1973) the number of robberies came close to the 1969–1970 level (an average of 5,919 cases) and in the years 1974–1975 dropped decidedly below that level (an average of 5,254 cases), a decrease of 11 percent. This decreasing trend continued also in 1976 when there were 4,906 robberies. In recent years this trend continued, though one should note that 1980 brought 5,149 cases of robbery thefts, robbery, and robbery extortion when the preceding year saw 4,570 such cases (an increase of 12.7 percent). This can be ascribed to the factors noted in the discussion of homicides.

Changes in cases of burglaries of public premises and burglaries of private property are discussed separately.

Between 1962 and 1972 the number of public premise burglaries increased every year by an average of 1,640 cases, equivalent to 7.9 percent of the annual average, the latter amounting to 20,783 cases. In the years 1973–1974 there was a drop to the 1969 level, and in 1975 another increase (by 15 percent compared with the 1973–1974 average).

This trend accelerated further in 1976. The number of burglaries was 4 percent higher than during the preceding year. In the years 1979–1980 this trend was checked; the number of burglaries of public premises continued on the same level (over 31,000 cases, or an index of 89 per 100,000).

Change in burglaries of private property were basically similar to those observed for public property burglaries, though the increase in private property burglaries in 1977 was faster (6 percent) than of public premise burglaries (2 percent). An increase in this type of burglaries was noted also in 1980: the number of registered crimes came to 39,235, compared with 36,803 the previous year.

Starting with 1970 there has been a systematic and steady drop in thefts of private property. In 1970 the number of such cases came to 92,677. Since 1976, with oscillations in individual years, there was a steady decrease. In 1980 there were 63,400 such thefts, compared with 63,733 the preceding year.

In public property misappropriation there has also been a steady drop since 1966: in 1980 there were 48,682 such cases (index of 137.5 per 100,000), compared with 51,052 cases the year before (index of 144.2 per 100,000).

The synthetic analysis of the main (measured by the degree of menace or incidence) categories of offenses points to a varied course of changes between 1962 and 1980. In summarizing one should note that in certain categories of serious crimes an improvement was noted. This does not, however, hold for homicides, robberies, and burglaries.

During the first six months of 1981 the number of registered crimes did not increase, compared with the corresponding period of the previous year (about 160,000 crimes). The same refers to the crime index which was at the same level as the year before, amounting to 448 per 100,000 inhabitants.

In Bulgaria there has been a steady drop in the crime rate, though not in all crime categories. There are increases in certain serious crimes against life and bodily integrity, morals, and road traffic offenses.

There has been increasing incidence of crimes connected with the spread of drug abuse, particularly among juveniles. A great majority of crimes is committed by young people under the age of 30.

The causes of criminality are ascribed to errors in the upbringing of adolescents, a parasitic style of living, low social consciousness of certain groups, and alcoholism.

Reviewing the present state and changes in criminality in Czechoslovakia one notes visible signs of a slowdown in the former unfavorable trend and a clear drop in the number of crimes in certain categories.

Up to 1971 criminality in Czechoslovakia was marked by a steadily higher crime rate which started its upward climb in the early 1960s. This trend held, with varying intensity, for all types of crimes, all groups of offenders and over the entire territory of the country.

Available statistical data on crime make it possible to bring together time series back to 1952 which was the year of developing and strengthening of the new penal law. Up to 1959 the Czech parts of the country applied the Austrian penal law of 1852, while Slovakia applied the Hungarian penal law of 1878.

Changes in criminality since 1952 can be briefly characterized as follows: sizable criminality during the 1950s with a slowly decreasing trend, the biggest drop coming in 1960. During the 1960s there was an upward trend with minor deviations. A clear deviation from the trend and an upward jump occurred around 1970, with symptoms of a more stable situation and a drop in the crime rate in the years 1972–1973 and 1974–1975.

The positive trends in the contemporary development of Czechoslovak society provide conditions for further reinforcement of socialist social relations and the limitation of crime.[49]

Crime in the German Democratic Republic has undergone significant changes both in the scale of the problem and its manifestations. The strongest and fastest drop in criminality took place during the first fifteen years of democratic changes in the country; this was the time when professional and organized crime was eliminated. From the very outset a serious problem for the newly established state was the foreign-inspired and organized action counterrevolutionary crimes (sabotage).

The decreasing trend appeared in the early 1960s, though with considerable oscillations from year to year. Certain crime categories took on relatively stable forms and magnitude; more than half represented acts against property, with half of that crimes against public property. A relatively large position was held by thefts from retail stores. Serious crimes, particularly robbery-connected homicides were relatively rare.

The crime curve in the GDR shows that the scientific and technical revolution does not have to bring in its wake an explosion of crime. On the contrary, the consistent application of scientific and technical advances in the service of mankind allows for studying and applying countermeasures to antisocial forms of behavior.[50] An expression of this is the finding that in the years 1960–1969 the average annual number of criminal acts amounted to 132,741 (an index of 776 per 100,000), in the years 1970–1979 dropping to 124,802 (the index dropping to 739 per 100,000).[51]

Analysis of statistical data for 1978 shows that the most common group of offenses in the GDR is the theft of private property (32,303), followed by theft of public property (25,214), bodily injury (11,807), borrowing car without owner's permission for joyriding (6,917). Other offenses are less prevalent: homicide, 145 (an index of 1 per 100,000), robbery and extortion,

831 (index 5 per 100,000). One notes the relatively large number of sex crimes involving children and adolescents. Even though it has dropped in recent years, in 1978 there were 1,308 such crimes against children and 272 against adolescents.[52]

Crime in Hungary shows a slight growth trend. In 1965 Hungary registered a total of 121,961 cases and in 1978 126,907 cases, while in 1980 prosecution authorities registered 130,440 indictable acts, uncovering 77,000 offenders.

Recent comparative studies indicate that in the number of homicides Hungary holds the fourth place in Europe, the index of homicides amounting to 5.3 per 100,000 people. Statistics for 1976 registered 200 cases of homicides and 300 attempted homicides.[53]

The statistical data concerning criminality in Yugoslavia have been compiled from court statistics. In the years 1970–1972 Yugoslavia recorded about 300,000 crimes annually, 208,103 in 1973, 305,994 in 1974, 298,191 in 1975 and 294,798 in 1976. This gives a crime index of 1,459 per 100,000 for the 1970–1972 period and 1,406 for 1973, 1,433 for 1974, 1,393 for 1975, 1,380 for 1976. This drop in crime incidence was accompanied by an increasing rate of convictions, amounting to: 1970: 495; 1971: 482; 1972: 496; 1973: 444; 1974: 515; 1975: 562; 1976: 552. The rise in convictions was largely accounted for by more effective trial proceedings.

Significant changes were noted in the pattern of Yugoslav criminality in the years 1965 through 1976. The share of crimes against persons dropped markedly by the mid-1970s. In 1965 this crime category accounted for 24.9 percent of convictions, in 1970 for 25.9 percent and in 1976 for 18.9 percent. Between 80 and 85 percent of these crimes represented assaults. Persons convicted for homicide constituted 2.2 percent of this crime category in 1965 (628 persons); 2.4 percent in 1966 (703 persons); 2.3 percent in 1967 (634 persons); 2.4 percent in 1968 (648 persons); 2.6 percent in 1969 (720 persons); and 2.6 percent in 1970 (685 persons).

The data for the following four years list only the number of persons accused of such crimes. For the years 1971–1972 there was an average of 862 such accused persons each year, 786 persons in 1973, 821 persons in 1974, 746 persons in 1975.

The convictions for rape were as follows: 358 persons in 1967, 407 persons in 1968, and 369 persons in 1969,—0.3 percent, 0.4 percent and 0.3 percent respectively of the total number of convictions.

On robbery, statistics for the years 1967–1969 list 179, 280, and 252 convictions respectively.

A growth trend was noted in crimes against property. This type of crime accounted for some 18.5 percent of all convictions in 1970, growing to about

25 percent of all convictions by 1976. Similarly, there was an upward trend in crime against the national economy: between 1971 and 1976 the number of convictions in this category was up from 6.4 percent to 7.1 percent. Latest data available on crimes against the national economy show that 1980 brought more than 50,000 charges and 35,000 convictions in this category, a 30 percent rise compared with 1979. The total bill for the damages to the national economy is estimated at 760 million dinars (about $25 million). Theft of social property was the most common category, with more than 8,000 accused. More than 5,000 persons were charged with making out uncovered checks, a new item on the list of ordinary offenses. One sees frequent cases of abusing power for personal gain; the accused here include mostly managers and staffs of financial institutions and directors of various types of enterprises.

The increase in the number of cases connected with usurpation of public property can reflect both a general upward trend in economic crimes and a higher effectiveness of crime detection.

Criminality in the Developing Countries

The nature and specific features of criminality in the developing countries have been the subject of a very small number of criminological studies. This is mainly due to the shortage of specific data illustrating the overall problem of criminality in those countries. For that reason the significance of changes due to the changeover to rapid economic and social development has been amply stressed only in sociological and anthropological studies. Attention is turned there to the breakdown of the very foundations of traditional society, to the need for adaptation of both individuals and entire social groups to the new life-style, to a different way of thinking. The changes occur in every sphere of human activity. In societies with a primitive agricultural background the traditional order breaks down under pressure of modern production techniques. There is an evident erosion of the former social and family patterns. The value systems linked with religious beliefs lose their sociotechnical attraction when set against the model of an industrial consumer society, the model thriving on constant change of technical processes and the resulting permanent modification of consumer tastes. For many countries the precondition for entering the age of rapid development is the change in their approach to the domestic cultural heritage. Obviously, under such conditions conflicts concerning norms and values are unavoidable, at least temporarily. Such conflicts, as shown by criminological research, are often the roots of psychosocial maladaptation and the resultant deviant and criminal behavior.

Research on criminality in the developing countries is carried out mainly in the context of a lack of demographic balance in those countries, the rapid social changes, and the inability to adapt to the new conditions.

Better standards of hygiene and medical care, coupled with the prevention of famine, have significantly cut down the rate of infant mortality. This leads to very rapid population growth in the developing countries. A higher number of people goes along with modifications in the demographic patterns. A consequence of the changing age structure is the clear change in the conditions of social equilibrium within the tribal communities. So far these social structures have remained relatively stable. Customs rooted in bans and taboos acted as guardians of order and a historically proven determinant, defined by such factors as sex or age, of social structure within the community. Within the record of cultural heritage passed on by word of mouth, all the main social roles in politics, religion, economy, upbringing, and sanctions rested until recently almost exclusively with the tribal elders, the true and unique depository of traditions and customs. Now people under twenty make up more than half of the population in the developing countries. It is this new demographic pattern, the growing share of young people, which causes cracks in the "gerontocracy" regime of the old tribal structures, in entire national economies and in the general traditions of the value systems.

The centuries-old information barrier between western civilization and the countries until recently viewed as backward is being rapidly torn down, with the mass media responsible for the inroads. The picture of "rich societies" projected selectively by these media acts as a commercial which turns the attention of viewers to only the most spectacular features. It is the young people who are the most vulnerable to this "demonstration effect."

Higher levels of education make possible a more critical evaluation of the information coming in from the industrial countries concerning new ideological trends and different models of consumption. New aspirations appear, impossible to implement under the old tribal spiritual leadership. There is rejection of both the former personal authority and a considerable part of its ensuing culture. Next to the generational conflict manifesting itself in this way, the rapid population growth, particularly in the economically most backward regions, leads to serious economic problems. The classic, cultivation-oriented type of rural economy continues to retain its autarchic character based on home consumption of the harvested crops. The primitive agricultural technology prevents higher yields and the adaptation of food production to the steadily growing demand.

The resulting lack of prospects for the future forces a large segment of the population to quit the villages in search of means for survival. The migration is directed mainly to the large plantations and the mines. The growing migration waves carry with them chiefly the young, the most rebellious and dynamic individuals. This process becomes the cause of advanced social disintegration in its rural starting point and greatly disturbs the course of collective life at its arrival point—the city, the industrial zone, the plantation.

The countryside becomes largely depleted of its active and most productive element. One encounters a secondary, postmigration demographic disequilibrium. Women and old people represent a relatively higher share in the rural community. On the one hand the disproportion of sexes is taking on pathological forms, on the other hand the elders as upholders of law and order are losing their prestige to the migrants who represent increasingly higher earned wealth. The traditional system of social controls is undermined.

The job situation and social conditions in the target areas are completely unsuited to absorb such large contingents of immigrants. The unnatural change in the proportion of sexes due to the large increase in the number of men present in the area leads to the rapid spread of prostitution and the ensuing forms of crime.

Immigrants from the countryside encounter a totally different style of life, quite alien to them. Separated from their clan, uprooted from the homogenous family circle, in effect deprived of the structures guaranteeing them moral and emotional balance, they move into a highly varied environment. In this environment the varied customs and traditions of the many ethnic groups are compressed within the mold of obligation and character of job as known in the industrialized western countries. This breeds frequent conflicts between the various value systems. They are both the symptom and a new source of mental and social maladjustment. They make the immigrants feel completely deserted and act as "criminogenic fodder."

The fundamental social problem faced by the developing countries is the relatively harmonious transfer from the heritage of the past to progress defined in contemporary terms. Acceptance of economic development carries with it the great risk of weakening the functional efficiency of numerous institutions required for guiding social development. The accelerated growth of urban populations is only in a small degree due to local birth rates; it stems mainly from the intensive rural migration. That is why the developing countries speak not of intensive urbanization but rather of the extensive type of urban growth. This growth is simply the resultant of forces with which the cities attract newcomers and the forces with which the countryside pushes out its migrants due to its stagnation and lack of prospects. The countryside is unable to withstand the demographic pressures. For many members of tribal communities escape to the cities is the only way of breaking the bonds of tribal customs. Decisions to migrate are taken by, for instance, the barren and divorced women held in contempt by their tribes, the young in conflict with their parents or those who refuse to accept the spouse selected for them by the elders.

For the developing countries the city becomes the symbol of modern times and the new way of life. For some it is only a transitory stage, a momentary attempt to grasp the new life which, when they return to the countryside, will allow them to attain higher prestige in the traditional community. Others migrate for a clearly defined, utilitarian purpose. The goal could be, for instance, to obtain the means required for buying the first wife or paying off the family debts. For the majority the main motive of moving to the metropolis is the availability of such urban facilities as public services, municipal facilities, opportunities for education, and attractive options for recreation.

All these factors are behind the great domestic and even international migrations. These population shifts to the cities give rise to a myriad of social problems. Population growth increases much faster than the growth of economic potential, expansion of industry, development of public services, and particularly the development of new housing. In effect this type of "urbanization" brings with it unemployment and the sprouting of new shantytowns around the cities.

In addition to these obviously pathological aspects city life leads to fundamental evolution of the traditional family roles and patterns. It weakens various social pressures and allows a state of apparent freedom for the individual to do as he or she pleases. Yet the new arrival becomes quickly lost in the new moral categories and the new social and economic conditions. This situation gives rise to frequent conflicts between individuals and among various cultural groups. This state, common to every society undergoing rapid changes, leads to the appearance of new and the increase of old forms of offensive behavior, among both adults and juveniles. Studying these phenomena allows for an evaluation of the degree of social degradation.[54]

Economic conditions and the very character of the urban life-style are conducive to a changeover from the model of the large, multigeneration family, to the model of an "atomized" family. Still, this change is too rapid, leading in consequence to a marked weakening of family stability. Ever more frequently one meets with divorce, separation, informal cohabitation. Children become the first victims of this type of social change. The disappearance of prohibitions, which formed the foundation of tribal up-bringing, and breakdown of the classic model of a large family which guaranteed intensive emotional links, brings about a situation where in numerous families the children remain without sufficient supervision and care, and are deprived of the right emotional atmosphere. Such a situation provides a fertile soil for breeding juvenile delinquency.

Where economic development is both rapid and spontaneous, failing to respect the nature of the so-called backward social structures, one meets with real "culture genocide" accompanied by much social pathology. An explosion in criminality is one of the most evident symptoms.[55]

Determining the magnitude of criminality in the developing countries is extremely difficult. Statistics, often subject to sizeable error, fragmentary, and incomplete make it possible to note only the most basic outlines of antisocial behavior.

Urbanization, industrialization, universal schooling, improvement of health standards, higher material welfare—all these act as agents of progress, though their excessively rapid introduction disturbs the balance and stability of the traditional social communities. The clash of two cultures—the "western" and the "primitive," unleashes a whole pack of criminogenic factors. There is wide agreement among criminologists concerning the evident intensification of criminal behavior in the developing countries.

The nature of criminality in the developing countries manifests itself, on the one hand, in the need to penalize certain types of traditional behavior and, on the other hand, in reacting to the type of crime common to industrial societies.

On the former plane there is an overlap of numerous and highly varied types of crime. On the one hand there are offenses linked with magic, withcraft, or charlatanry. Poisonings, laying a curse, commerce in human blood and bones, the killings of witches, ritual rapes, are a few examples of this type of crime. It is common chiefly to rural communities.

On the other hand there is mounting crime stemming from situations breeding conflicts between different value systems. This is mainly the problem of the proliferation of confidence tricks, appropriation of public property, bouncing checks, corruption. These types of offenses have their roots in the conflict of values and culture customs, the contrasts of city and tribal life. Individuals living in the cities have various obligations toward the members of their clan. Unable to repay them they are strongly tempted to meet their needs in an illegal manner. Against such a background one sees the proliferation of contemporary crime forms. One meets with an epidemic of robberies, organized crime, narcotics traffic.

On the second plane, the one defined by penal law, two types of crime overlap: one is the criminality defined by modern, codified penal legislation, the other is behavior classified as offensive by old common law. Introduction of penal codes has turned into offenses many types of acts which formerly were classified as normal. In this context one could cite polygamy, dowry demands, witch trials, abortions, infanticide, and similar acts.

In the Third World countries there are some three billion people deprived of all property, harnessed to the exploiting mechanism only by their manual labor. The living conditions of these people are deteriorating. They illustrate the law which still holds in that world, of absolute pauperization of the masses.

On the Sahara and its perimeters just a decade or so ago about four-fifths of the population was made up of nomads. Industrialization of the oil-bearing desert areas has brought drastic changes. By now some two-thirds of the Saharan population lives in shantytowns erected near the oil wells and gas pipelines. In these oil-rich centers the number of slum dwellings grows by some 20 percent every year.

Children there are in a particularly difficult predicament. One UNICEF report put it this way: "Frequently a child is so starved as to be in stupor, having to share food, clothing, shelter and all else with eight, ten, a dozen or more people. . . . The barracks furnishings are as a rule the most primitive."

Under such socioeconomic conditions, the increase of criminality is also a feature of the developing countries.[56]

The Ivory Coast, thanks to its urbanization, industrialization, and migration, experienced a drop in the traditional offenses which stemmed mainly from family and tribal solidarity and from the cult of dead spirits, with a parallel rise (mainly in the cities) of frauds, thefts, and misappropriation of state funds. There is increasing traffic in drugs (hashish), manslaughter, injuries, and organized crime. Two-thirds of all offenses are committed by immigrants from other African countries.[57]

In the Malagasy Republic the most serious problem is the growing number of cattle thefts and deliberately set forest fires for the purpose of obtaining soil for growing rice. There is also mounting usury and vagrancy.

In Senegal urbanization and western patterns of life take and increasing toll of local traditions. This is reflected in the numbers of morally endangered minors, which could reflect on the incidence of juvenile delinquency. This is particularly true of Dakar, the capital.

In Algeria there has been an increase in juvenile delinquency. Dominant urban forms are frauds and the sale of stolen goods in towns, minor thefts and offenses of public morality in the countryside. The outflow of population from the rural areas to the cities, urbanization preceding the development of industry, population growth, and industrialization of formerly agricultural areas are the conditions which transformed the living conditions in Algeria, leading to psychological shocks and acting as sources of conflicts and crime.

Crime statistics in many developing countries of Africa reflect only the structure of criminal justice institutions and their efficiency. This was the conclusion reached in a study conducted in 1959 by the International Children's Center. The study was held in Madagascar, the Cameroon, and the Ivory Coast and showed that the number of juveniles who come in contact with criminal justice institutions cannot serve as a reliable gauge for statistical analysis of criminality, since this number is only a segment of a much larger and unknown general number of juvenile delinquents.[58]

On the basis of a study conducted in Abidjan, M. A. Boni, president of the Ivory Coast Supreme Court, classified crime in Africa into four groups:

1. specifically African criminality, to be found mainly in the most backward African communities, in which the dominant role is played by witchcraft, charlatanry and magic;
2. circumstantial criminality resulting from the need to possess a given object at a specific moment;
3. utilitarian criminality, which encompasses the majority of crimes;
4. perverse criminality as the type of crime defined as a new phenomenon in Africa; it includes burglaries committed by organized groups, robberies, and similar crimes.

Even though this classification is far from precise, it does provide an illustration of the type of criminality common in the African countries.

A few examples can be added of crime in the countries of Asia,[59] highly differentiated in their levels of development.

In Bangladesh the crime rate has been climbing since the second half of the 1960s. Such crimes as homicide, robbery, and dacoity (a specific type of robbery known in the Far East) have presented and continue to present a serious threat to the life of the people. Following the war of independence large quantities of firearms found their way into the hands of juveniles and minors. Using these firearms groups of young men have robbed banks, shops, and private houses. In recent years there has been a mounting wave of crime against the economic interests of the country (smuggling, black marketeering, counterfeiting invoices, violation of customs regulations, hiding produce, speculation).

Crime in Hong Kong started on its rapid upward trend in 1949, in connection with the influx of refugees from China. After a brief spell of stability, during the 1960s the crime rate again rose sharply, this time including much armed robbery. Since 1974 there has been an increase of juvenile delinquency (by those under the age of sixteen). Crimes connected with narcotics present a serious problem. Gangsters are much in evidence (criminal activities of the Triades). These organized, professional criminals carry out robberies, thefts, trade in narcotics, operate illegal gambling casinos, and run prostitution chains. Arrests of the leaders of these organizations in recent years have to a certain extent checked the operations of organized crime.

Criminality in Indonesia has had varying tendencies in recent years. The increase, noted until 1972, slowed down somewhat. There is still a steady climb of juvenile delinquency, though the proportion of such acts to the total number of offenses is fairly insignificant (some 3 percent). There has also been an increase in robberies, sexual offenses, kidnapping, frauds, white collar crimes, and road traffic offenses.

Criminal youth gangs became a problem during the 1960s. These groups, often fighting among each other, engage in blackmail, robberies, selling "protection" to shop and company owners, organizing of gambling houses. Every year there is an increase in the number of persons arrested for narcotics trade and in the number of deaths caused by narcotic overdoses. The growing corruption of state officials led to the 1971 passage of the Law of Repressing Corruption.

Iran has in recent years undergone political upheavals which could also reflect on the state and character of its criminality, although the available evidence is insufficient to formulate any hypothesis. Some years ago, on the basis of incomplete statistical data, a slight upward trend in juvenile delinquency was noted. Since the passage of the Arms Act in 1972 there has been a drop in the illegal possession of firearms. Drug addiction and drug smuggling presented serious problems, despite the 1955 ban on growing poppy.

In Malaysia the number of serious crimes increased by 45 percent between 1973 and 1975 (particularly robberies: 1,568 cases in 1973, 2,422 cases in 1974, 3,378 cases in 1975). There was an equally rapid growth of thefts and homicides. Juvenile delinquency jumped markedly (partly due to narcotics). An undetermined number of gangs operate in the country: they are believed responsible for most of the violent crimes—homicides, injuries, extortion, kidnapping.

In Nepal there has been a rise in juvenile delinquency, linked with drugs, prostitution, and gang warfare. In 1973 a prohibition was placed on the growing of hashish and its derivatives, since the production and smuggling of these drugs were up sharply, particularly since the mass influx of hippies from all over the world.

In Pakistan the crime rate has not changed significantly over the past few years. Still, the number of violent crimes has been high for a long time, particularly in the countryside, in tribal areas. This holds particularly for homicides, injuries, thefts, robberies, and dacoity. Firearms are frequently used, there is even illegal production of arms. Juvenile delinquency is also on the rise, mainly in urban areas. Recently attention was turned to offenses against the economic interests of the state (smuggling, tax evasion, currency dealings).

There was a considerable amount of crime in the Philippines before martial law was proclaimed in that country in September 1972. After that time the number of offenses reported to the police went down; the number of homicides in 1973 was half that of the preceding year. There was also a drop in other crimes, including drug traffic, smuggling, and kidnapping for ransom.

In Singapore crimes against persons (rapes, kidnapping) have been on the increase since 1971. An upward trend is also noted in juvenile delinquency of persons under 21 and in drug-connected offenses. In 1973 only 10 persons were arrested for the use of heroin. In 1974, 110 persons and in 1975 no less than 2,263 persons were charged with the same offense. Singapore, as Hong Kong, also has criminal organizations of Triades. In recent years this tiny state has introduced strict environmental legislation, namely the Environment Public Health Act, Water Pollution Control and Drainage Act, and the Prohibition on Smoking in Certain Places Act.

The total number of crimes in Sri Lanka increased by 103 percent between 1960 and 1970, with a 146 percent rise in crimes against property and a 45 percent rise in crimes against persons. During the 1970s there were no significant changes in the situation. The index of serious crimes per 100,000 population increased from 331.6 in 1970 to 400.0 by 1973. Juvenile delinquency also increased. Urbanization brought with it crimes connected with organized prostitution and gambling, as well as illegal production and commerce in alcohol and narcotics. There is also mounting white collar crime (smuggling, illegal curreny dealings, counterfeiting invoices, speculation, bribery).

Since 1962 there has been a steady growth in serious crimes committed in Thailand. A good portion of them is accounted for by criminal youth gangs. A considerable number of crimes involve firearms.

According to a government report published in August 1980 certain serious crimes, such as homicides and robbery are on the wane in South Korea.[60] There was a small increase in sex crimes, bodily injury, and certain other offenses. In contrast to the world trend of increasing narcotics-connected crimes, South Korea does not face this problem. Nevertheless, juvenile delinquency was up 153 percent over the 1969–1978 decade, with recidivism ever more frequent. Offenses connected with abuse of authority take on the form of fraud and can be connected with such acts as the sale of property, offering opportunities for foreign employment, and tax evasion.

In the Republic of India crime has been climbing for the past twenty-five years.[61] In 1957 there were 603,505 registered offenses indictable under the penal code (154.7 per 100,000 population); a decade later this number was up to 881,981 (172.5 per 100,000), while twenty years later, in 1977, it was no less than 1,267,004 (an index of 202.5). Over those twenty years the number of offenses punishable under the penal code went up by 110 percent. The increase was accounted for mainly by violent crimes, namely homicides, up 76.4 percent; dacoity, up 126.6 percent; robbery, up 206.8 percent; burglaries, up 49.4 percent; and thefts, up 85.2 percent.

These data exclude acts punishable under special or local laws; the number of such offenses is considerably higher: in 1967 there were 2,663,267 cases and 2,699,061 in 1977.

In 1977 the number of people arrested for Indian Penal Code offenses came to 1,538,515, and for other offenses, 2,826,118.

There was also a large increase in the number of offenses against the Arms Act and in the cases of offenses committed with the use of arms.

There was also an increase in juvenile delinquency and in the number of offenses committed by women. By 1975 female crime was up 46 percent over the 1971 level. The index of penal code offenses per 100,000 women went up from 6.18 in 1971 to 8.32 in 1975.

The latest data on crime in India published in January 1981 by the Bureau of Police Research and Development indicate a further increase, including white collar crime.

The examples cited above indicate that in many of the developing countries in Asia the crime menace is considerable both in terms of the large scale of the crime phenomenon and in terms of the forms of crime (violence, the use of weapons). One also notes the increase in juvenile delinquency and female crime. For many of the countries in that area organized crime and narcotics are a serious problem.

Latin America in recent years has become the site of terrifying growth in political violence, both in urban and in rural areas. This is the effect of a lack of political stability in the area and of the political immaturity of the populations and, some observers claim, the effect of interference by foreign intelligence services.

The presence and activity of terrorist groups is doubly harmful: believing that the end justifies the means they fail to consider the number of victims of their terrorist acts; the society cannot achieve balanced development when threatened with violence.

Another significant aspect of criminality in Latin America is the operation of undereground paramilitary organizations dedicated to the persecution of criminals and killing or maiming them. These include the Death Squads, White Hand, and similar groups. As the reason for their own criminal activity they cite the low effectiveness and inability of the formal criminal justice institutions to combat crime. Considering their techniques and mode of operation they are suspected of having links with the police in the cities where they operate.

Latin America has further been the site of genocide of entire local ethnic groups or of their inhuman exploitation. Such groups are threatened with total extinction. Their soil and reservations are reduced through the progress of civilization.

The number of road traffic offenses has grown excessively. The reasons behind this were the increase in car output, the ease with which they could be purchased, and the abuse of alcohol and narcotics.

Latin American countries are part of the international narcotics trade network. This is facilitated by the high mobility of criminals, suspectibility to corruption, operation of contact points in air and sea ports, participation of foreign criminals and financing with foreign capital. Furthermore, legislation in the area is uncoordinated.

Commerce in firearms has also become a significant problem. Many persons deal in arms, outfitting the "private armies" of this region. The customers are recruited among revolutionary groups or organizations, guerrillas and private citizens; all of them violate legal restrictions and create situations which could lead to unknown consequences. The different laws applicable in the various Latin American countries are a boon to such trade. Certain countries strictly control and severely punish the sale and ownership of arms; other countries, where crime of violence are not a major problem, have liberal rules allowing the free sale of firearms.[62]

In recent years smuggling has also become a more common type of offense. Along with industrial development, the Third World countries institute policies to protect their local industries, which in turn leads to the rise of smuggling. Offenses of this type are a hindrance to economic and social progress.

A disquieting phenomenon in this region is the sale of medicines produced in the laboratories of developed countries, but the sale of which is prohibited in their countries of origin. The harmful effects of such trade are kept quiet for the purpose of making high profits. In the same way, the use of children (or adults) for experimental purposes in introducing new pharmaceutical products, the circulation of which has not been permitted in the producer's country, represents a particularly serious problem, particularly where those persons or the parents of the children have not been informed of the nature of this experiment and the risks involved. In addition, there are examples of the violation of elementary human rights, such as forcing the use of birth control measures or broadly applying sterilization without the patient's permission and without medical justification

In Latin America, offenses against the environment are common. One manifestation is the pollution generated as a negative side effect of badly planned industrialization. Many of the large cities in the area suffer because of pollution, growing to an extent exceeding all permissible limits. Legal rules in this field are uncoordinated and frequently insufficient to protect the health of the citizens. Offenses against the environment also include the illegal cutting down of large forest areas.

Typical of this region are the offenses committed by the multinational corporations, one frequent offense being the payment of high bribes to top state officials. There is rampant corruption, and white collar crime is frequently exempt from any punishment, to the detriment of the national economies.

Organized criminal groups most frequently engage in illegal narcotics trade, white slave trade, car thefts, and organization of prostitution chains.

Latin American countries have a specific type of crime connected with archeological excavations: the smuggling of historical objects from illegal excavations. The objects are sent either to American or European museums or to rich private collectors.

Notes

1. Paul Cornil, "Criminalité et déviance: Essai de politique criminelle," *Revue de Science Criminelle et de Droit Pénal Comparé* 1970, no. 2, p. 290.

2. Paul Cornil, "Criminalité et déviance," p. 295.

3. The term *white-collar crime* was first used in literature by Edwin H. Sutherland. See *White-Collar Crime* (New York: Holt, Rinehart and Winston, 1949) and "White-Collar Criminality," *American Sociological Review* 1940, no. 2. Other writings on the subject include: Earl E. R. Quinney, "The Study of White-Collar Crime: Toward a Reorientation in Theory and Practice," *Journal of Criminal Law, Criminology, and Police Science* 1964, no. 2; Zigfried Zbinden, "Zur aktuellen Wirtschaftskriminalität," *Kriminalistik* 1971, no. 3; L. Léon Cappuyns, "Les infractions économiques," *Revue de Droit Pénal et de Criminologie* 1960, no. 3; "Spezialisten für White-Collar Verbrechen," *Die Exekutive* 1961, no.1.

4. In recent years international criminological and criminalistics literature has devoted much attention to kidnapping. See, for example Wolf

Middendorff, "Geiselnahme und Kidnapping," *Kriminalistik* 1972, no. 12; Günther Bauer, "Die Einführungskriminalität," *Die Polizei* 1972, no. 12; idem, "Geiselnahme aus Gewinnsucht," *Archiv für Kriminologie* 1972, no. 3–4.

5. Roland Chilton, "Criminal Statistics in the United States," *Journal of Criminal Law and Criminology* 71 (1980): 56–67. See also Ronald H. Beattie, "Sources of Statistics on Crime and Corrections," *American Statistical Association Journal* 1959, no. 54, pp. 582–592; Harry Alpert, "National Series in State Judicial Criminal Statistics," *Journal of Criminal Law and Criminology* 39 (1948): 181–188.

6. Timothy J. Flanagan, Michael J. Hindelang, and Michael R. Gottfredson, eds., *Sourcebook of Criminal Justice Statistics 1979*, U.S. Law Enforcement Assistance Administration, National Criminal Justice Information and Statistics Service (Washington, D.C.: U.S Government Printing Office, 1980), p. 402.

7. *Time* magazine, March 25, 1981.

8. Gilbert Geis, "Przestepczość białych kołnierzyków w Stanach Zjednoczonych Ameryki Północnej" [White-collar crime in the United States]. An article written especially for publications of the Institute of Crime Problems in Poland, *Przestępczość na świecie*, Warsaw, 1980, vol. 14.

9. U.S. House of Representatives, Subcommittee on Crime: Hearings on White-Collar Crime (Washington, D.C.: Government Printing Office, 1979), p. 1.

10. A count of articles under the heading "Firearms—Laws and Regulations" was made for each issue of the *Readers' Guide to Periodical Literature* from 1937 to 1977. See also Tom W. Smith, "The 75% Solution: An Analysis of the Structure of Attitudes on Gun Control, 1959–1977," *Journal of Criminal Law and Criminology* 71 (1980): 300.

11. *The Challenge of Crime in a Free Society*. A Report by the President's Commission on Law Enforcement and Administration of Justice, Washington, D.C., 1967.

12. Hans J. Schneider, "Crime and Criminal Policy in Some Western European and North American Countries," *International Review of Criminal Policy* 1979, no. 35, p. 55.

13. William Clifford, *Crime Control in Japan* (Lexington, Mass.: Lexington Books, 1976).

14. *Criminal Statistics England and Wales 1960: Statistics relating to crime and criminal proceedings for the year 1960* (London: Her Majesty's Stationery Office, 1961), p. viii.

15. *Annual Abstract of Statistics 1976* (London: Her Majesty's Stationery Office, 1976), Table 80: *Justice and Crime.*

16. *Annual Abstract of Statistics 1979* (London: Her Majesty's Stationery Office, 1979), p. 102.

17. "L'explosion criminelle britannique," *Revue Internationale de Criminologie et de Police Technique* 1978, no. 1.

18. David Norman, "Les menaces d'enlèvements—un grave problème," *Revue Internationale de Criminologie et de Police Technique* 1980, no. 2.

19. Presse und Informationsamt der Bundesregierung, Bulletin No. 60/S, 545, 1979. Polizeiliche Kriminalstatistik für das Jahr 1978.

20. Uwe Doermann, "Polizeiliche Kriminalstatistik 1979," *Kriminalistik* 1980, no. 10, pp. 431–436.

21. Rudolf Rupprecht, "Entwickelt sich in der Bundesrepublik ein rechtsextremistischer Terrorismus?" *Kriminalistik* 1979, no. 9, pp. 285–290.

22. Manfred Hammes, "Rauschgiftkriminalität. Präventive und repressive Aktivitäten in den Bundesländen," *Kriminalistik* 1980, no. 9, p. 2 (Kriminalistik-Dokumentation).

23. "Report on the Activities of the French National Police," 1969. *International Criminal Police Review* 1970, no. 238.

24. "Die Kriminalstatistik in Frankreich," *Internationale Kriminal-polizeiliche Revue* 1965, no. 188.

25. *Annuaire Statistique de la France 1976* (Paris: Institut National de Statistique d'Etudes Economiques, 1976), ch. 12, table 3.

26. *Réponses à la violence.* Rapport du Comité présidé par Alain Peyrefitte, Paris 1977. La Documentation Française.

27. *Compendio Statistico Italiano 1980* (Rome: Istituto Centrale do Statistica).

28. Wolf Middendorff, "The Personality of the Terrorist," *International Summaries* 3, 1979, p. 91.

29. Council of Europe: Legal Notes, *International Criminal Police Review*, February 1976, no. 295, p. 54.

30. *Statistik Arsbok för Sverige* (Stockholm: Liber Distributiun, 1978).

31. *Statistik Arsbok 1976* (Stockholm: Liber Distributiun, 1976), table 351.

32. Alvar Nelson, "La politique criminelle en Suède, 1965–1979," *Nordisk Tiddsskrift for Kriminalvidenskal* [Revue nordique de Science criminelle] 1980, no. 3.

33. *Statistisches Jahrbuch der Schweiz 1979* (Basel: Bundesamt für Statistik. Birkhauser Verlag), p. 523.

34. Marshall B. Clinard, *Cities With Little Crime: The Case of Switzerland* (London: Cambridge University Press, 1978), p. 154.

35. Paul Noll, "Das Land mit der geringsten Kriminalität," *Neue Züricher Zeitung*, April 4, 1979.

36. Erwin Meier, "Blicke in die Gefängniswelt," *Baustein* 1980, no. 6, p. 1.

37. *Espana Anuario Estadistico 1980* (Madrid: Instituto Nacional de Estadistica).

38. Adolfo S. Gomez, "La délinquance juvenile en Espagne et son evolution," *Revue Internationale de Police Criminelle*, January 1980, no. 334, pp. 16–27.

39. "Espagne: forte hausse de la criminalité," *Revue Internationale de Criminologie et de Police Technique* 1979, no. 3.

40. "Historische Kriminologie in Oesterreich," *Kriminalistik* 1980, no. 5, p. 226.

41. Christian Mayerhofer, "Die Raubkriminalität in Oesterreich," *Oesterreichische Juristen Zeitung* 1979, issue 9, pp. 231–239.

42. "Wirtschaftswunder und Kriminalität," *Die Exekutive* 1961, no. 1.

43. "Schmuggel mit gestohlenen Autos blüht," *Die Exekutive* 1968, no. 5.

44. "Justice and Prisons." Reprinted from the *Statistical Yearbook of the Netherlands* (The Hague: Central Bureau of Statistics, 1980).

45. *South African Journal of Criminal Law and Criminology*, 1977, no.1.

46. *South African Journal of Criminal Law and Criminology*, 1978, no. 3.

47. Brunon Hołyst, *Przestepczość w Polsce* [Criminality in Poland] (Warsaw: Wydawnictwo Prawnicze, 1977); Maria Jarosz, ed., *Wybrane zagadnienia patologii społecznej* [Selected issues in social pathology] (Warsaw: Central Statistical Office, 1975); Jerzy Jasiński, ed., *Zagadnienia przestepczości w Polsce* [Issues on criminality in Poland] (Warsaw: Wydawnictwo Prawnicze, 1975); Jerzy Jasiński and Edward Syzduł, *Materiały statystyczne* [Statistical materials] (Warsaw: Zakład Kryminologii PAN, 1969); Jerzy Jasiński and Edward Syzduł, "Przestepczość w latach 1954–1958 w świetle statystyki milicyjnej" [Criminality 1954–1958 in the light of police statistics] *Archiwum Kryminologii* 1960, vol. 1; Marian Lipka, *Zjawiska patologii społecznej wśród młodziezy* [Social pathology phenomena among youths] (Warsaw: State Scientific Publishers, 1974).

48. Andrzej Murzynowski and Józef Rezler, *Wymiar sprawiedliwości w Polsce w latach 1944–1970: Ustawodawstwo, organizacja, działalność* [Criminal justice in Poland 1944–1970: Legislation, organization, activity] (Warsaw: Warsaw University Publications, 1972), pp. 18 ff.

49. Zdenek Karabec, "Struktura i dynamika przestepczości w Czechosłowackiej Republice Socjalistycznej" [Structure and changes in criminality in the Czechoslovak socialist republic] *Przestepczość na Swiecie*, Institute of Crime Problems Publishers, Warsaw, 1975, no. 2/4, pp. 65–90.

50. Report on the GDR Delegation to the Fifth UN Congress on the Prevention of Crime and the Treatment of Offenders, Geneva, 1975.

51. "On some aspects of crime prevention in the German Democratic Republic" (materials provided by the GDR delegation to the Sixth UN Congress on the Prevention of Crime and the Treatment of Offenders, Caracas, 1980).

52. *Statistisches Jahrbuch der DDR 1979* (Berlin: Staatische Zentralverwaltung für Statistik, 1979), pp. 380–381.

53. Leon Korinek, "Die Kriminalitätsentwicklung in Ungarn," *Archiv für Kriminologie* 1979, no. 5–6, vol. 164, p. 173.

54. Georges Balandier, "Le contexte socio-culturel et le coût social du progrès," *Tiers Monde*, Paris PUF 1956, p. 302.

55. Yves Brillon, "Développement économique et criminalité en Afrique Occidentale," *Revue Internationale de Criminologie et de Police Technique* 1973, no. 1.

56. Research on criminality in African countries is conducted by, among others, the Scandinavian Institute of African Studies organized at Uppsala in 1962. See the publications of this institute: Ralph Tanner, *Three studies in East African criminology* (Uppsala, 1970); idem, *Homicide in Uganda 1964* (Uppsala, 1970); idem, *The witch murders in Sukumaland: A sociological commentary* (Uppsala, 1970); Lynn Panx, *Alcohol in Colonial Africa* (Helsinki, 1975). Published by the Finnish Foundation for Alcohol Studies in collaboration with the Scandinavian Institute of African Studies.

57. Jean Pinatel, "La criminalité dans le monde," *Revue de Science Criminelle et de Droit Pénal Comparé* 1971, no. 2.

58. Yves Brillon, "La délinquance juvénile en Afrique noire: une augmentation réelle en voie de régression apparente," *Revue Internationale de Criminologie et de Police Technique* 1980, no. 2.

59. *International Review of Criminal Policy* 1979, no. 35, United Nations, New York, 1980.

60. Sixth United Nations Congress on the Prevention of Crime and the Treatment of Offenders, August 1980. Ministry of Justice, Republic of Korea.

61. Sixth United Nations Congress on the Prevention of Crime and the Treatment of Offenders. India—Country Paper. Ministry of Social Welfare, Government of India.

62. Jorge A. Castro Montero, "Crime trends and crime prevention strategies in Latin American countries," *International Review of Criminal Policy*, United Nations 1979, no. 35; idem, *Problems y Necesidades de la Politica Criminal en America Latina*, Latin American Institute for the Prevention of Crime and the Treatment of Offenders (ILANUD San José) 1976, pp. 13,14.

6 The Costs of Crime

The issue of the costs of crime[1] has been gaining in importance for quite some time. This issue was the main point on the agenda of the 1975 Fifth United Nations Congress on the Prevention of Crime and the Treatment of Offenders in Geneva.

Despite its significance, the issue of the negative consequences of crime has not yet been studied in depth. Criminological textbooks deal with traditional subjects, such as criminal symptomatology and etiology, treating the problem of the costs of crime as incidental.

Abstractions from the theoretical aspects, the negative consequences of crime should be considered in the context of social policy. Criminal justice is, or in any case should be, an element of social justice.

Criminal actions generate a variety of effects. Some are of an economic nature, quantifiable in money terms. Those measurable in money are comparable in time and space: one could speak of the measurable consequences of crime, say, in 1980 in country X versus country Y. Others, what we may call the social consequences of crime, produce a climate conducive to further manifestations of social pathology or depreciate the values accepted in a given society. The social consequences of crime are defined as those negative repercussions which do not directly concern an individual but instead disturb social life and consist of destroying the sort of values which cannot be calculated in money terms.

Classification of the negative consequences of crime into economic and social cannot be absolute or even clear-cut: the economic consequences of crime also represent a negative social consequence.

In order to analyze the problem it is also necessary to distinguish between direct costs, such as the loss of material property by the victim, and indirect costs. For instance, large-scale thefts of public property in the socialist countries could lead to hampering the production process or the rate of housing construction. In the western countries some companies go bankrupt because of embezzlement or theft. In France, a recent wave of private home burglaries has forced a number of insurance companies into bankruptcy.

One could also classify the costs of crime on a macro or micro scale. In the former case the entire society or defined social strata will bear the losses; in the latter case the losses will be the concern of individual citizens. This differentiates the social magnitude of the losses incurred.

One should also keep in mind that the dark number of the losses incurred is considerably higher than the dark number of offenses really committed.

141

The consequences measurable in money terms, comparable in various time segments, can be described by the economic term of loss or cost.

Loss is the financial and accounting measure of the diminution of property. Here one can speak of losses caused by criminal actions. As an example one could use the theft of public or private property, which always causes a diminution of property owned by a legal or physical entity. The appearance of shortfalls in public property, such as a shortfall in the quantity of stocks, is of the same nature. Serious consequences are caused by inefficiency, superfluous or improper use of substantial means by an economic unit. One could also apply the term *loss* to denote the lack of justly expected profit. Under such a definition a loss would mean the criminal destruction of raw materials originally destined for resale. The loss incurred through the destruction will cover two items: the cost of purchasing, bringing in and storing the raw material (cost to the company) and the loss of justly expected profit (the markup, which the company was to earn by resale of the stored quantities).

It has been pointed out that a part of the offenses against property consists exclusively of transferring given economic values from one unit to another, so that the value available to society at large remains unchanged. Still, since after the transfer the goods in question are actually at the disposal of an unauthorized body, the situation is obviously undesirable from the social point of view. The value by which the property of the authorized unit was decreased cannot be treated as anything but a loss.

One cannot, however, accept as a complete loss the compensation paid under various insurance schemes, such as car insurance. After all, these are expenditures borne by institutions established for this very purpose; the payments are generated from the insurance premiums paid.

Cost is the outlay of human labor, direct and contained in objects, expended for the purpose of attaining given ends. Combating crime, preventive measures, detecting, prosecuting, and penalizing generate certain expenditures borne by society. They are usually allocated in the state budget. *Fixed* costs, such as those connected with employing the police, attorneys, judges, and auxiliary personnel vary little and remain the same irrespective of the actual magnitude and form of crime. *Variable* costs are highly influenced by the type and scale of criminal activities; they are of a different nature in economic crimes from traditional crimes. In economic crimes a part of the variable cost is due to the hiring of experts, assembling documents and records, and so on. In traditional crimes the variable costs include police actions, such as arrival on the scene of crime, securing clues, laboratory analysis, and the like. The economic effects occur on two planes: the macro- and the micro-economic. The macro scale concerns the economic consequences of criminal or other activities on a national scale, such as the expenditures for prison overheads. On the micro scale, the negative consequences could be felt, for instance, by the victim's family.

Section Five of the UN Congress devoted to the cost of crime adopted draft motions and recommendations for UN member states in this respect. The draft covered such issues as: taking into account the principle of profitability of operations of criminal justice institutions, taking up interdisciplinary research on the economic and social costs of criminality, integration of crime policy plans with general national plans, conduct of actions to acquaint the general public with the economic harm caused by crime, conduct of research on finding ways for the just redistribution of the negative consequences of crime.

Before the problems of crime costs were taken up by a United Nations Congress, they were the subject of numerous symposia and meetings.

In 1972 Poland hosted a regional seminar of Central European countries devoted to rationalizing the activities of criminal justice systems, including the cost of crime. This seminar was organized by the Crime Research Center of the Ministry of Justice in Warsaw and the International Comparative Criminology Center in Montreal.

Certain countries have undertaken attempts to estimate the costs of crime. As an illustration, the overall costs of crime in the United States in 1974 amounted to $88.6 billion, compared with $51 billion in 1970. By 1978 the expenditure for criminal justice activities alone amounted to $24.1 billion of which $13.1 billion was spent on police protection, $3.1 billion on the judicial branch, $1.5 billion on legal services and prosecution, $0.5 billion on public defense, $5.5 billion on corrections and $438 million on other matters concerned with criminal justice.[2] Overall, the cost to the United States from stolen cash and property was staggering; the total losses during a three-year period, as determined by data from a crime survey, amounted to roughly $1.2 billion, or an average of about $400 million each year. Not every unlawful entry ended in theft; in 15 percent of the offenses committed between 1973 and 1975 there was not property loss. When they did end in theft the median value of the loss was $60.[3]

Other countries also register increases in the cost of crime. In Canada fraud connected with purchases of farm land in the northern provinces cost the state treasury $30 million.[4] In Italy the annual loss just from capital flight abroad (tax evasion) is estimated at $5 billion. France incurs tremendous losses caused by tax evasion and, recently, a spate of robberies. That country's 1969 private expenditures on combating crime amounted to 780.3 million ,rancs or some 34 percent of the overall sum of public spending for this purpose. The spending by the gendarmerie on combating crime is estimated at some 2 billion francs, police spending at some 2.5 billion francs and the Justice Department at around 1 billion francs. In 1968, insurance companies paid around 112 million francs as theft insurance compensation, not including car theft. No estimates have been made of the costs of hiring civilian guards and private detectives by the various companies, offices, and individuals. The large department stores and supermarkets claim theft losses equaling 15 percent of their cash flow; in 1970 this was equivalent to 250 million francs. The total domestic trade losses, calculated at just 5 percent of the turnover, amounted to some 1 billion francs. Human life, obviously, is not included in the calculations of crime costs. Each year criminals kill some three hundred people in France.[5]

Analyzing the Belgian budget for the years 1950 through 1967, J. Zeegers presented data on the cost to the state of crime supression.[6] Between 1950 and 1967 the real expenditures per capita increased as follows: gendarmerie by 69 percent; municipal police by 77 percent; criminal police by 90 percent; judiciary by 88 percent; Justice Department by 117 percent.

The countries of northern Europe have been spending between 0.5 and 1.0 percent of their gross national product on upholding the legal order. Expenditure is the highest in Finland and the lowest in Norway. Spending on research concerned with criminality accounts for between 0.03 and 0.11 percent of the overall spending on the legal order, the highest being in Norway and the lowest in Finland, with Denmark spending 0.06 percent. In Sweden the present total cost for the administration of criminal justice is estimated to be around $1 million, corresponding to 2.1 percent of the national budget for 1980–81. The police take almost 60 percent and the Prison and Probation Service nearly 20 percent, mainly because of the constantly climbing personnel costs. The costs to be carried by individuals, corporations, and society at large for losses by crime cannot be easily estimated, nor can the suffering of crime victims be accurately measured.[7]

In Finland and Norway upholding the legal order costs an average of $1 thousand for each offense registered by the police, in Denmark around $600 and in Sweden around $500.

In Japan, which had somewhat of a drop in the crime rate in recent years, the losses caused in 1972 by thefts, frauds, and robberies exceeded $300 million. Crime suppression costs were some $2.3 billion per year, equivalent to 3.8 percent of the state budget and 0.8 percent of gross national product (with 82.7 percent of the sum taken up by spending on the police). In the last decade Japanese spending on crime suppression quadrupled.

The Fifth UN Congress on crime prevention determined that UN member countries spend between 2 and 16 percent of their budgets on crime suppression, with the less well off countries spending more. The data from the developing countries such as Jamaica, Ecuador, and Mexico indicate that spending on crime suppression takes up a large part of their budgets and GNP. As is evident from the UN Congress materials, the quantitative data fail to reflect the real cost of crime, which is in reality much higher than that listed in statistical tables.

In my report to the UN Congress, I cited estimates concerning the cost of crime in Poland.[8] The losses of public and private property due to crime in 1973 amounted to some $98 million (at $1 = 20 zlotys); spending on the functioning of the Supreme Court, the Justice Department, and prosecution bodies connected with penal cases, could be roughly estimated at some $80 million per year.

One should keep in mind that the costs of crime calculated by various state institutions and research organizations cover only the crimes which have been detected. In reality the costs of crime are much higher and bear a direct relation to the magnitude of total criminality detected and undetected, both. The fact that a given crime was actually committed but has not come to the attention of prosecution bodies in no way changes the fact that the crime has led to real losses.

The problem of calculating crime costs is particularly difficult partly because an interdisciplinary approach is needed. The cost issue calls for examination by criminology, penology, criminal policy, economics, sociology, social psychology, statistics, and other disciplines.

Under the Polish system now in force one can fully gauge and compare the losses caused by crime directed against state property and economic interests. These encompass theft of public property (Penal Code Articles 134, 199–202), shortages in that property (Article 218, Par. 2) and indictable mismanagement (Art. 217). Losses due to such offenses detected and confirmed under investigation are summarized in table 6–1.

Losses caused by theft of public property in an impudent manner or through burglary or with the use of firearms in 1973 amounted to some 133,700 zlotys. Losses to the detriment of individuals due to theft or fraud committed in various ways amounted to some 372,800 zlotys. It should be noted that the registered losses and the losses uncovered in preparatory proceedings discontinued for various reasons represent a negligible percentage of the national income. The Polish national income for 1973 amounted to 1,062 billion zlotys, while all the measurable losses due to crimes against the public sector and individuals were 1.96 billion zlotys.

Table 6–1

Losses Due to Crimes Directed against Public Property: Poland, 1970–1975

(*thousand zlotys*)

Losses	1970	1971	1972	1973	1974	1975
Total	567,999	546,500	626,000	680,800	645,492	712,003
theft	367,400	385,800	439,000	462,800	572,037	519,158
shortages	147,000	125,700	130,000	141,000	185,259	148,895
mismanagement	53,500	35,000	57,000	77,000	88,196	43,950

Source: Brunon Hołyst, "Economic and Social Effects of Crime in Poland" (materials provided by the Polish delegation to the Fifth UN Congress on the Prevention of Crime and the Treatment of Offenders, Warsaw, 1975), pp. 43–47.

Crimes against life and health should be viewed as leading not only to physical but economic consequences—for example, educational costs incurred by the family for a victim of crime.

The social consequences connected with the existence, detection, and punishment of offenders, could be presented in a variety of ways, though nonquantifiable in money terms. The main groups of social consequences could be classified as follows:

1. Any tardiness in detecting, prosecuting, and punishing offenders violates the canons of law and social order. Such neglect represents a significant criminogenic circumstance, encouraging potential offenders to commit acts which are prohibited but profitable to them primarily in the material sense. The speed of punishment and the belief in unavoidability of punishment serve as great detriments to crime.

2. Procrastination and slowness of criminal justice both in penal and in civil law is conducive to disturbing the faith in social law order, providing an undeserved boon (actual, not legal) to persons violating the law, enabling them thus to reap various material and personal benefits.

3. Slow turning of the wheels of justice is also conducive to financial losses, difficult to calculate, though easy to perceive logically. Estimates made in Poland indicate that time losses in that country due to errors and other incorrect proceedings during preparatory investigations each year total some half-a-million hours of prosecution personnel time and 700,000 hours for people subpoenaed to investigations and other preparatory proceedings. A flagrant example is the hearing of witnesses. Rough calculations indicate that some 2.6 million people in Poland are called each year as witnesses during the various stages of investigation. Assuming that half of them are employees of the public sector, 1.3 million workdays are lost in this way. In terms of full-time employees this is equivalent to the absence of 3,500 employees and, paid or unpaid, but definitely undone work valued at 120 million zlotys in terms of wages.

The same holds true for civil cases. Problems of increasing the efficiency of criminal justice and reducing the social losses caused by penal procedures were addressed in 1974 by the Polish Supreme Court and Bar Association. The recommendations formulated by this study were:

calling in individuals as witnesses should be limited, where possible, to the preparatory, pretrial stage of proceedings;

during the trial more use should be made of previously recorded testimony, to be read in the courtroom;

the widest possible use should be made of evidence in documentary form, particularly in cases concerned with economic offenses, accidents, and the like, especially in cases where such documents exist or are specifically drafted (such as protocols of on-site investigations and expert opinions);

organizational improvements were also required.

4. Convicted persons who commit an offense in a state of alcoholic or narcotic intoxication are usually treated in special medical facilities. Both the medical care and the required medication in such cases are given free of charge. In many cases, even persons who are not arrested must be provided with special financial assistance for their period of medical detoxication, when their earning capacity is severely impaired.

5. A distinct and very significant issue is connected with the social and economic consequences of imprisonment. These costs include the spending on the upkeep, maintenance, and renovation of prisons, as well as salaries of prison personnel and the costs of food and medical care for the prisoners. There are also losses due to the detention of healthy ablebodied unemployed people or the employment of convicts who are often highly trained people, in jobs where those qualifications are not used (this is particularly true for economic offenders). In estimating the social and economic costs of imprisonment one cannot avoid the issue of recidivism due to the demoralizing influence of the prison environment. A high crime relapse rate means that the funds spent on keeping that group of convicts in prison did not yield the expected effects; this is an economic loss.

The social and economic costs of imprisonment further include the expense to society of supporting the convict's family at at least a subsistence level. Because of the imprisonment of a family member, the family economic situation usually deteriorates sharply. Since it would not be correct to burden the family with the consequences of the convict's actions, the social system of the state in such cases provides the family, particularly the children, with various benefits aimed at upholding a decent living standard, such as school scholarships, monetary grants or product donations, free enrollment of children in summer or health camps, kindergartens, or neighborhood social centers. The expense to society is quite considerable, though often impossible to gauge accurately.

In recent years many countries have gradually limited imprisonment, as being excessively costly compared with the rehabilitative effects, instead using other forms of punishment such as fines or probation. A judiciously applied system of fines can often successfully replace a prison sentence. This holds particularly true for countries with relatively high living standards. Studies indicate that a fine can be just as painful to the offender and serve a deterrent role as well as a short-term prison sentence, without negative consequences.

Many countries, including Poland, have so far paid insufficient attention to the social and economic consequences of imprisonment. In such countries imprisonment is still treated as the main form of penal repression, and the number of convictions to prison (without provision for suspension) remains high there, even though the penal codes usually provide for a whole range of other forms of punishment. Studies concerned with the true social and economic costs of imprisonment compared with the effectiveness of this form of punishment could bring changes in existing penal policies. I would recommend that such studies be undertaken as soon as possible, on the widest possible scale.

Security is one of the prime human needs. Criminal activities violate this need; fear of criminal violation of life, health, or property, can lead to negative changes in the human psyche and can reduce the scope of human actions (such as staying indoors after dark for fear of street violence).

Leszek Lernell has justly pointed out that the issue of security, the personal feeling of security, elimination of the crime threat, should be considered as part of the quality of life. Security, after all, is one of the fundamental human needs which, unsatisfied, leads to dire consequences for the individual psyche.[9]

The feeling of security is difficult to gauge in view of the subjective nature of this term; reducing it to financial categories gives rise to ethical doubts. One should note, however, that treatment of human life in economic categories is not equivalent to discounting other human qualities. The point is only to register the harm done by crime on every plane. A complete register of the losses caused by crime in the social and economic sphere is a condition for evolving a program of actions aimed at combating and preventing crime, and including those as part of economic development plans.

Exhausting the complex issue of the social consequences of crime is a very difficult task; therefore this discussion will be limited to only a few selected additional aspects. For instance, the costs of economic offenses should not be viewed exclusively as direct losses. Organized criminals responsible for premeditated appropriation of public property may, before they act or during their action, execute many moves aimed at preventing discovery of the crime and connection of the crime with them. They may create an atmosphere of chaos in the plant conducive to the appearance of stock shortages, mismanagement, destruction of property through the application of improper technical methods, and so on. The economic costs of such actions go far beyond the losses resulting directly from the appropriation of property of a given value.

It is absolutely impossible to gauge the social consequences stemming from offenses against public property through corruption of personnel. The organized theft of public property often continues over long periods, leading to a feeling or impunity among the offenders.

Criminality among state functionaries weakens social confidence in state institutions, leading to a widespread belief that such institutions in general guide themselves in their activities by principles which have little to do with morality, that criminal methods of acting are a universal phenomenon.

No data is available to evaluate the effectiveness of preventive measures such as the ratio between financial outlays on such measures and the losses which would be incurred, were the crimes which were prevented to take place.

The use and abuse of alcoholic beverages is responsible for many offensive acts. Studies have shown that many road accidents occur in connection with or against the background of the use and abuse of alcohol by the offender or the victim. The same holds true for accidents at work or on the way to and from work. This leads to direct expenses, such as the need to haul away the wrecked cars, the provision of first aid, and long-term medical treatment, and indirect expenses, such as the loss of services provided by the damaged vehicles.

Considering the costs of crime one should keep in mind that a portion of road and work accidents are in reality offenses and the huge economic and social costs they cause have to be counted against the costs of crime.

The same holds true for environmental pollution, for trade in pharmaceuticals which have not been sufficiently tested, or trade in foodstuffs containing substances harmful to human health. Some of these are also offenses and the negative consequences of such acts must also be treated as costs of crime.

Terrorism gives rise to new issues in the consequences of crime. The economic costs of terrorist acts are immense and probably beyond calculation. For instance, the costs of hijacking and destroying a single civil aircraft go into the millions, for the aircraft alone. One can only roughly guess at the other material losses of states and individuals and at the costs borne by individuals and states which try to prevent other terrorist acts. Yet it is the social consequences of terrorism which are really impossible to calculate. The psychological burden of a terrorist threat weighs most heavily on only certain categories of individuals (high state officials, industrialists, diplomats, members of their families), though it frequently also affects random persons (plane passengers, bank customers) and, indirectly, their relatives. The feeling of insecurity disturbs the smooth course of activity of state and social institutions, lowering the quality and standard of living, changing social attitudes and customs. Misdemeanors also lead to various social and financial consequences, as criminal acts do.

The suppression and prevention of criminality requires considerable resources. National development plans should make provisions for these items. In order to spend the earmarked amounts in a purposeful, economically warranted manner, it is necessary to assemble a considerable amount of data concerning the costs of crime. A variety of models are used to determine the numerical values of the costs of crime. One could cite here the model developed by the French Ministry of Justice or the U.S. Offender Based Transaction System (OBTS). No model is available for the interrelations among the various consequences of criminal activities.

Having criminal justice and prosecution authorities give more consideration to economic categories, introduction of the notion of profitability could lead to a shift to the secondary position of the tasks faced by those institutions, even when their execution would not be profitable.

In summary, one could conclude that both criminal actions and their broadly defined consequences can be reduced through the reasonable application of legal, organizational, and sociotechnical measures, with certain possibilities for reducing the costs of crime inherent also in lowering the spending on legal proceedings.

To round out the picture one should point out the view that crime leads not just to losses but also to benefits. For instance, the transfer of property through theft can be socially justified when the property passes from someone very rich to poor, economically underprivileged people, leading to an improvement of their lot. Such spontaneous transfers can produce not only anarchy and social disturbances but even become egotistical, antisocial tendencies and could be abused for purposes leading to significant social and economic losses. Some also maintain that corruption can become the driving force to stimulate economic initiative. Clearly this view should also be rejected. As a negative social phenomenon corruption in effect also leads to immense economic losses, undermining the legally established manner of regulating economic activity. There is some paradox in this opinion regarding the possibility of involving a broad spectrum of the society in suppressing crime (police, courts, penitentiary institutions, companies producing security devices, researchers, and the like). In this sense again it is claimed that criminality is a socially advantageous phenomenon. There is no doubt that it is an economic loss to employ the talents, training, and efforts of such a large number of people for ends which bring no economic gain, while the financial resources could be spent on further advancement of economic life. To sum up, the "gains" from crime are rather illusory, while the losses—we should particularly emphasize this—are real and severe, both for the society at large and for individuals.

Notes

1. The term *costs of crime* serves as an abbreviated denotation of the complex of negative consequences caused by criminal phenomena.

2. Timothy J. Flanagan, Michael J. Hindelang, and Michael R. Gottfredson, eds., *Sourcebook of Criminal Justice Statistics 1980*. U.S. Law Enforcement Assistance Administration. National Criminal Justice Information and Statistics Service (Washington D.C.: U.S. Government Printing Office, 1981), p. 5.

3. *The Cost of Negligence: Losses from Preventable Household Burglaries*. A National Crime Survey Report: U.S. Department of Justice. Law Enforcement Assistance Administration, Washington D.C. 1979, p. 6.

4. Denis Szabo, ed., *Le coût de l'administration de la justice et de la criminalité* (Ottawa: Information Canada, 1971).

5. Jacques Léauté, "Au moins cinq milliards pour la prévention et la répression," *Revue Internationale de Criminologie et de Police Technique* 1970, no. 4.

6. André Jacquemin, "L'allocation des resources privées et publiques dans la lutte contre la délinquance" (Paper presented at a seminar in Poland in 1972).

7. Alvar Nelson, "Crime and Responses to Crime." Sixth UN Congress on the Prevention of Crime and the Treatment of Offenders, p. 18.

8. Brunon Hołyst, "Economic and Social Effects of Crime in Poland" (materials provided by the Polish delegation to the Fifth UN Congress on the Prevention of Crime and the Treatment of Offenders, Warsaw, 1975), pp. 43–47.

9. Leszek Lernell of Poland was chairman of Section 5 at the Fifth UN Congress on the Prevention of Crime and the Treatment of Offenders, Geneva, 1975.

7

Development of Criminological Research Institutions in Highly Industrialized Countries

The United States has a particularly elaborate network of criminological research and study facilities.[1,2] This can be attributed to the high rate of criminality in that country.

Criminality in the United States can be viewed as a specific type of experimental material on etiology and symptomatology. It is no accident that numerous U.S. sociologists limit their field of interest exclusively to social pathology or that numerous federal and state institutions, academic and unaffiliated institutes as well as civic organizations concentrate their activities on problems of criminality.

Much attention has been devoted in the United States to obtaining current data on criminal justice. Recognizing the value of this information, the National Clearinghouse for Criminal Justice Systems was established in 1976, to promote and facilitate the transfer of proven criminal justice information systems. In support of this purpose, the clearinghouse has automated the information available from the previous surveys to create a computerized index which is continually updated to reflect the current status of operational systems throughout the country.[3]

According to W. P. Holtzman, Director of the Systems Development Division, Bureau of Justice Statistics, the first Law Enforcement Assistance Administration (LEAA) Directory of Automated Criminal Justice Information Systems was published in 1972. It contains information on criminal justice information systems in 153 jurisdictions, mostly in state government and in cities of over 250,000 population. The next directory, published in 1976, contained over five hundred separately defined systems in 278 jurisdictions of state and local government; coverage was extended to include cities and counties of 100,000 or greater population.[4] A new Directory of Automated Criminal Justice Information Systems was published in 1980.

More than a hundred U.S. institutions are concerned with the study of criminality. Some of the leading institutions include:

American Academy of Forensic Sciences, established in 1948, conducts training and research.

American Academy of Political and Social Sciences, established in 1889, conducts research.

American Association of Criminology, established in 1953. The association carries out research projects aimed at developing criminology as a distinct academic discipline, advancing studies on penology and exchanging views and information with foreign and international criminological organizations.

American Bar Association, Section of Criminal Justice, conducts research; the association sponsors numerous monographs in the fields of criminology and criminal justice.

American Correctional Association, established in 1870, and concerned mainly with research. Its aim is to bring the personnel of all American juvenile correctional institutions within the ACA framework. One form of ACA activity is to conduct experiments on new forms of probation. ACA also offers advisory services to correctional and penal institutions.

American Institute for Research, established in 1946; examines various aspects of law enforcement and the criminal justice system such as evaluation of programs and studies of delinquency, manpower and training, administration of criminal justice.

American Judicature Society, established in 1913; the field of activity covers courts, juvenile justice, evaluation. The society aims to promote the effective administration of justice through research studies, program planning and evaluation of the judicial administration.

American Justice Institute, founded in 1959. It was originally known as the Institute for the Study of Crime and Delinquency. The aims of this institute cover the study and practical improvement of criminal justice and the prevention of crime. The institute employs specialists in such fields as sociology, psychology, public administration, criminology and criminalistics. AJI carries out law and information systems analysis and conducts public opinion polls.

American Society of Criminology, founded in 1941. It conducts research and coordinates training offered by criminological institutions. The annual congresses result in numerous publications devoted to current problems of criminality. For instance, volume 4, on the topic of crime prevention and social control (ed. R. L. Akers and E. Sagarin, New York, 1974) was divided into three sections: crime prevention and deterrence; the police, and criminal justice and the courts. This book is strongly recommended.

Behavioral Law Center, founded in 1974; the center conducts research on the relationships between the law and behavior, in particular on behavior modification and its legal and ethical implications, and product safety as related to human factors.

Behavioral Research Institute, founded in 1973. Its research centers on the causes of crime and delinquency, the evaluation of prevention and treatment programs, diversion programs and two national longtitudinal surveys on hidden delinquency among American adolescents aged 11–17 and on the relationship between delinquency and drug use among adolescents.

Bureau of Social Sciences Research, Inc., established in 1950; the bureau does survey research, data analysis, and criminal justice manpower planning research. Recent studies include projects on prosecutorial decision making, the use of social science data, research and development planning in crime victimization.

California Council on Criminal Justice, founded in 1967. Its tasks cover the collection of statistical data on car thefts and drafting a prevention program. Under council auspices research is done into civic expectations concerning the police, the courts, and correctional institutions. The council aims to cover the state with a network of forensic laboratories. Further, it is developing a new program to create a system of coordinating the activities of federal, state, and local correctional institutions. It publishes annual reports on its activities and maps out annual plans for the activities of criminal justice institutions in the State of California.

California Crime Technological Research Foundation, established in 1967 as a state and federal government agency. Its main task is to set up a uniform system of crime statistics, standardizing the systems of police and court registration. Its further aim is to develop a court information system.

California Youth Authority was organized in 1941. It is one of the larger government organizations comprehensively involved in youth problems. The CYA has a staff of three thousand researchers and five hundred technical employees. It carries out research consisting chiefly of defining various therapeutical systems in the various detention institutions, evaluating the effectiveness of modifying warranty pledges and probation forms, drug abuse among adolescents, classification of criminals and drawing up forecasts.

Center for the Administration of Criminal Justice, founded in 1967; activities cover research and demonstration programs for improving the criminal justice system.

Center for Applied Social Research, founded in 1972 at Northeastern University in Boston. It carries out research on such problems as the significance of racial prejudices in death sentences and their execution.

Center for Criminal Justice at the Boston University School of Law was established in 1969; its main activity is research. Its efforts led to drafting a code of prisoners' rights and obligations and a model for prosecuting cases in juvenile courts.

Center for Criminal Justice, founded in 1969 under Harvard University auspices, conducts studies and evaluations on selected aspects of the criminal justice system focusing on policy issues in juvenile justice, court practice, and criminal sanctions.

Center for the Study of Crime and Delinquency, established in 1972 in Ohio. The center, operating under academic status, conducts research on: follow-up studies of adult criminals serving prison sentences or with suspended sentences; biomedical studies of female criminals with socio-pathological symptoms; therapeutical programs for imprisoned socio-paths; evaluation of the impact of criminal labeling on male juveniles; evaluation of the effectiveness of the therapeutic program for juvenile delinquents placed in the Training Institution of Central Ohio; new systems for diagnosing and classifying criminals, comparing the effectiveness of various probational forms.

Center for the Study of Crime, Delinquency and Corrections, established in 1961 as part of the Southern Illinois University. In addition to teaching, the center also conducts research on the effectiveness of new rehabilitation systems.

Center for the Study of Law and Society, established in 1961 as part of the University of California. The center focuses on social attitudes concerning law, the law-making process, and legal practice.

Center for Studies of Crime and Delinquency, established in 1968 as part of the National Institute of Mental Health. Its main interests cover the process of labeling and proceeding with persons requiring care of the institute, evolving forms of proceeding with criminals, new forms of therapy, studying law and mental health related issues, including the system of juvenile justice. The center also conducts studies of aggressive behavior.

Center for Studies in Criminology and Criminal Law, founded in 1966 under University of Pennsylvania sponsorship, is involved in research and training in the study of crime and delinquency with an inter-disciplinary approach based on sociology, law, psychiatry, and related disciplines.

Center for Studies in Criminal Justice at the University of Chicago Law School, sponsored in 1965 by the Ford Foundation. The main tasks of the center cover studies of the criminal justice system, etiology and prevention of criminality, and training in the field of criminal law.

Research projects focus on: penitentiary issues, including the evolution of penal measures, the Swedish system of punishment, penal measures applicable to dangerous recidivists, gangs in prisons, capital punishment; a draft uniform penal code for the State of Illinois, studying criminal offenses, such as homicides in Chicago and abortions in New York.

Center for Women Policy Studies, founded in 1972, engages in formulating model innovative programs for female offenders, studying family violence and national policy issues affecting women.

Chicago Law Enforcement Study Group, founded in 1970; the scope of this group covers empirical research, development of strategies for change, public education on criminal and juvenile justice issues, and community crime prevention.

Committee on Research on Law Enforcement and Criminal Justice, founded in 1975; the committee conducts studies on areas of concern to public policymakers or to professionals in the field of criminal justice, law enforcement, and courts, as well as evaluation studies.

Correctional Association of New York, active since 1844 as an independent organization. The association evolves new correctional programs and offers advisory services to institutions dealing with rehabilitation.

Council of State Governments, founded in 1933; its purpose is dissemination of information and research reports concerning the overall criminal justice system.

Criminal Justice Center (John Jay College of Criminal Justice), founded in 1975; activities cover education, training, research, and evaluation, as well as publishing in the field of police, courts, correctional institutions, juvenile justice, community crime prevention, advanced technology, security.

Criminal Law Education and Research Center, founded in 1959 at New York University. In addition to studying criminological problems, the center also deals with legal-penal issues, the penal process, comparative law, and comparative criminology. It also carries out comparative studies, including international comparative studies of police activities, international comparative studies of legislation on narcotics, and comparative studies on violence.

Delaware Agency to Reduce Crime, active since 1968 as a government agency studying robberies, burglaries, diversion shortening the time elapsed between arrest and sentencing, and similar matters.

Florida State University Criminology Department, established in 1952, conducts research, holds the annual Southern Conference on Corrections.

Division of Information Systems—Statistical Analysis and Reports Branch, Administration Office of the U.S. Courts, Washington, D.C., active since 1940 in collecting and processing statistical data on court cases and on defendants. Its tasks further include methods of coding and classifying court cases and collecting information on persons under the federal system of probation.

Division of Research, Planning and Development of the Ohio Youth Commission, established in 1973. It is charged with setting up and running a computerized information system for studying criminality and with coordinating the activities of information services in other agencies.

Federal Judicial Center, founded in 1968 as a government agency charged with research and training in court administration. Its scope also includes reorganizing the structure of federal courts and evolving more advanced methods of collecting and retrieving court statistical data. The center developed and is installing a program for computerizing federal court verdicts and Supreme Court rulings. The cost of computerizing amounted to over $360 million.

Forensic Sciences Foundation, Inc., founded in 1969; its activities include conducting studies, analyses, evaluations and tests of forensic procedures, developing and carrying out educational and training programs, promoting public education, doing research in forensic science-related areas, organizing seminars.

Georgia Department of Offender Rehabilitation, Research Division is an interdisciplinary state-operated research organization. The division employs specialists in sociology, economics, psychology, law, and rehabilitation. Projects center on problems of guiding behavior changes.

Illinois Academy of Criminology, established in 1950, is a forum for exchanging views by persons dealing professionally with criminology and by others interested in this discipline.

Illinois Department of Corrections, Division of Research and Long Range Planning was founded by the state in 1970, to carry out research connected with developing a correctional information system; each year it publishes a report on its activities.

Institute for Advanced Studies in Justice at the American University Law School was founded in 1970 as an institution with academic status. Employing specialists in sociology, psychology, economics, pathology, and law, the institute carries out research on such problems as juvenile

drug abuse, political terrorism and political criminality, and on rehabilitation measures.

Institute for Community Development at Michigan State University,
founded in 1958 performs research, consulting and training in the field of
police, courts, and juvenile justice.

*Institute of Contemporary Corrections and the Behavioral Sciences at
Sam Houston State University* was organized in 1965. In addition to
regular training, scientists connected with the institute organize professional training courses for working justice personnel, offer consultations and technical assistance to justice institutions, and develop training
programs in criminology and rehabilitation. Institute staff represents a
comprehensive cross-section of specialists, including sociologists, psychologists, clinical psychologists, psychiatrists, criminologists, lawyers,
mathematicians, and statisticians. The various projects carried out by the
institute include: evaluating the applicability of psychological tests in
correctional institutions; studying college students' attitutes to justice and
the court process; descriptive analysis of Texas antidrug laws violations;
testing college students' attitudes on the disproportions in penalties and
the traffic in arms among Texas convicts.

*Institute of Criminal Justice and Criminology at the University of
Maryland* was founded in 1969. The institute is one of the leading U.S.
centers of criminological training and studies.

*Institute of Law, Psychiatry, and Criminology at the George
Washington University School of Law* was founded in 1965. The
institute staff includes specialists on sociology, criminology, psychology,
psychiatry, and law. Interests of the institute focus on criminal responsibility of the mentally ill and mentally handicapped. Research is
also carried out on the rules for determining qualification of mental states
in offenses, legal protection of the mentally handicapped, and juvenile
delinquency.

Institute for Court Management, founded in 1970, engages in training
court personnel and in research relating to justice system agencies.

Institute of Criminal Law and Procedure, founded in 1965. The institute
is part of the Georgetown University Law Center; it conducts interdisciplinary research directed toward empirical analysis of the criminal
justice process and ways of improving it. Studies are directed to the role
of the police, attorneys, judges, and correctional officials; the topics cover
the right to counsel, prosecution and defense functions, criminal law
reform and victims in the criminal justice system, pre-trial release, plea
bargaining, police discretion in drug cases, employment of ex-convicts.

Institute of Judicial Administration at New York University School of Law, founded in 1952, conducts studies of structure, operation, and manpower in courts; offers training programs for appellate and trial judges and for court administrations; coordinates efforts of bar associations and judicial councils.

Institute for Law and Social Research (INSLAW), founded in 1973; the institute develops systems and procedures supporting both criminal justice administration and research, and the transmission of such systems and procedures to criminal justice agencies.

Institute for Research in Public Safety, Indiana University, established in 1970. Its staff specializes in the following problems: justice administration system; analysis of legal systems; social psychology; organized crime.

Massachusetts Correctional Association, established in 1940 in Boston. The association deals with problems of administrative structures in justice, provision of legal assistance and postpenitentiary assistance for former convicts, development of new convicts classification systems, and organization of conferences and symposia.

Midwest Research Institute, founded in 1944. The institute has carried out research for criminal justice agencies since 1968 (police, courts, corrections, juvenile justice, community crime prevention, advanced technology, information systems training, evaluation). Studies concern various problems of criminal justice such as standards and goals, crime against the elderly, training, and crime laboratory planning.

Minnesota Department of Corrections, Research, and Information Systems, formed in 1960 as a research agency for the state.

National Association of Attorneys General—Committee on the Office of Attorney General, founded in 1968. Research on courts, corrections, juvenile justice, prosecution and organized crime, with results offered exclusively to offices of Attorneys General.

National Center for State Courts, founded in 1971. The objective of the center is to aid the courts in improving all areas of judicial administration through basic research and consulting services.

National Council on Crime and Delinquency, Hackensack, N.J. This council relies on the cooperation of some 60,000 social workers and justice administration employees. It was founded in 1907 as a civic organization, changing its scope of operation in 1921. The council is made up of the following sections: research; training; information; library; juvenile; social education.

The council's objective is to prevent juvenile delinquency and drug abuse, deinstitutionalize the status of offenders, and define the costs of criminality. The council serves as an advisory coordinating body: it publishes bibliographies, guides and indexes, including an index of U.S. and Canadian projects of criminological research institutes, and a guide for juvenile judges.

An autonomous section of the council is the Research Center, established in 1966. The center has a staff of specialists in psychology, clinical psychology, psychiatry, criminology, and rehabilitation as well as such subsidiary disciplines as statistics and computer programming. Its research fields cover such topics as the decision process concerning suspension and probation, methods of classifying offenses, evaluation of juvenile correctional institutions and the effectiveness of existing ways of preventing juvenile delinquency.

An NCCD initiative led to the creation of a central data bank which collects materials needed both for research and for practical crime prevention. The assembled data made it possible to form: a professional library, constantly updated with the latest publications, including foreign books; a bibliographic index of publications not available in its own library; an index with synopses of articles published in periodicals; indexes of current research projects.

Operation of the data bank led to wider dissemination of project findings among people practically involved in crime prevention.

National Institute of Corrections, founded in 1974; created by the U.S. Congress within the Federal Bureau of Prisons. Its goal is to improve the correctional process at federal, state, and local levels. The institute carries out research and evaluation, and sponsors projects in policy formulation and execution, providing training, technical assistance, and clearinghouse services.

The National Institute of Law Enforcement and Criminal Justice, created in 1968 in Washington, is the research, development, and evaluation center of the Law Enforcement Assistance Administration. The institute has been entrusted by the Congress with the following tasks: identifying the areas in which new knowledge is needed to improve the workings of the criminal justice system; sponsoring the studies of major unsolved problems of criminal justice and criminal behavior; using the research findings to design and test promising new approaches in criminal justice; evaluating current criminal justice practices; developing new tools for criminal justice research and evaluation; promoting scientific and technological advance; transmitting key research and evaluation findings to criminal justice administrators across the country; helping the Law Enforcement Assistance Administration to develop large-scale programs for prevention of crime and improvement of criminal justice.

The institute is divided into four branches; Office of Research Programs, Office of Program Evaluation, Office of Research and Evaluation Methods, Office of Development, Testing, and Dissemination. These offices are responsible to the Office of the Director, the tasks of which cover management, planning, and setting priorities.

The Office of Research Programs works through five divisions: Police Division, Adjudication Division, Corrections Division, Community Crime Prevention Division, Center for the Study of Crime Correlates and Determinants of Criminal Behavior. The task of the Office of Program Evaluation is providing information on the effectiveness and efficiency of criminal justice and crime prevention programs. The most important task of the Office of Research an Evaluation Methods is measuring the impact of programs intended to deter crime and developing new performance measures for criminal justice agencies. The Office of Development, Testing, and Dissemination identifies the information, validates it through applied research and conveys it to the appropriate audiences, and promotes the transfer of knowledge gained through solid practical experience.

Office of Crime Analysis, District of Columbia Government, was established in 1969 for the purpose of organizing a general system of statistical information on criminality, polling public opinion on subjects of criminal justice, and putting together statistical reports on activities of justice bodies.

The Pennsylvania Association on Probation, Parole and Correction was established in 1921. It is an association of criminal justice personnel, primarily prison and correctional institution wardens, as well as specialists on probation. It does research on ways of improving the forms of suspending sentences and granting parole.

The Rand Corporation was founded in 1948 as a private research body with the objective of studying selected areas of the criminal justice system (police, courts, corrections, evaluations, community crime prevention, advanced technology).

School of Criminal Justice at Rutgers, the State University of New Jersey, besides training, has a research center which conducts studies of all aspects of the criminal justice system to increase knowledge and to provide data for improving the system.

School of Criminal Justice, State University of New York at Albany was established in 1966. In addition to training, the school is also involved with research projects on various aspects of criminology.

School of Criminology, University of California, was organized in Berkeley in 1950. It carries out research and training.

Social Science Research Center was established in 1945 within the Social Sciences Department of the University of Puerto Rico. Center research tied directly to criminology includes studying the links between violence and the social structure in Puerto Rico, studying poverty and its consequences in the Puerto Rican society and studying juvenile delinquency.

Southeastern Correctional and Criminological Research Center was established in 1968 by the Florida State University. This represents an interdisciplinary facility, with projects such as: evolution of a uniform system of statistical information on criminality; studying the situation of prisoners' families; new ways of reeducating incorrigible criminals; work under supervision as a form of rehabilitation.

Stanford Research Institute was founded in 1946. Institute projects of criminological character include: problems of houses of detention for boys; organized crime; review and evaluation of programs to combat recidivism; costs of crime and the prevention of crime; drug abuse and its prevention by local justice agencies.

Texas Department of Corrections, Research and Development Division, established in 1971. Projects undertaken by the division include: evolving a program of drug addiction therapy; analysing the Texas antialcohol program; evaluating special therapeutic groups.

Division publications are concerned with such topics as statistical data on female crime, homicides, sexual offenses, analysis of the drug market and characteristic of first-time offenders.

Vera Institute of Justice, New York, was established in 1961. Its task is to find solutions for the practical problems facing the justice and prosecution bodies of New York City. Institute research is geared to such practical issues as: reform of the New York justice system and its various institutions; change in the bail system; attempts to change temporary arrest for obligatory subpoenas; combat of alcoholism and drug abuse and provision of assistance to addicted persons; development of diversion for settling misdemeanors; reform of the penal procedure; postpenitentiary assistance and treatment of drug addicts.

University of California Youth Study Center was founded in 1958. Many books on fundamental criminological problems were published under the center's auspices including: *Community Organization of Delinquency Control, Positional Authority and Delinquent Behavior, Use of Authority in Treatment of Deviant Youth, Anomie, Population Characteristics and Juvenile Delinquency.*

In addition to the institutions listed here, several smaller bodies active in the United States also do some research on criminological issues:

Addiction Research and Treatment Correction Evaluation Team, organized in 1968 by the Columbia University School of Social Work. Within the 23-person team eight carry out research on drug addiction and rehabilitation.

Americans for Effective Law Enforcement, Inc., founded in 1966, provides research assistance in civil liability of law enforcement agencies (police, courts, attorneys) and administrators.

Association for the Psychiatric Treatment of Offenders (APTO) organized in 1950 in New York. This is a pioneering group devoted to the therapy and reeducation of offenders.

Battele Law and Justice Study Center, founded in 1971, conducts basic and action-oriented research programs relating to the problems of crime and justice (community crime prevention, white-collar and sophisticated crime issues, consumer protection, police, courts evaluation).

Crime and Justice Foundation, organized in 1878; its field of activity includes research, promotion, and implementation of standards for criminal justice systems (juvenile justice, community crime prevention, courts, corrections, evaluation).

Institute for the Reduction of Crime (IRC), founded in 1977; its goal is to help schools maintain safe and secure school environments through assistance programs, research, and publications.

John Howard Association, founded in 1901; conducts surveys, research, consultation, public education, technical assistance, program evaluations and planning for criminal justice systems at the state and local levels.

Market Opinion Research, founded in 1941; it is a survey research and consulting organization conducting evaluation studies and planning on attitudes toward crime and criminal justice system. MOP also evaluates the results of programs to reduce specific types of crime.

National Fire Prevention and Control Administration, founded in 1974; engages in fire and arson research, collects statistical data on fires.

National Institute of Judicial Dynamics, founded in 1968; activities cover research, surveys, studies, and training projects concerning judicial and correctional problems. Studies include, among others, the impact of alcohol-related offenses.

National Legal Aid and Defender Association (NLADA), founded in 1911; the Defender Division of the association is involved in, among other things, research, standards and goals, technical assistance and evaluation relating to courts and defense services.

Police Foundation, formed in 1970 by the Ford Foundation; it fosters innovation and improvement in police functions through experimentation, evaluation, and research, with the assistance of publications.

Program on Criminal Justice and the Elderly, founded in 1976; its purpose is to conduct research on victimization of the elderly and on victim compensation and restitution programs affecting the elderly; in addition, it disseminates information on new developments in criminal justice relating to the elderly.

Public Administration Service, founded in 1933; conducts research and takes other actions to improve governmental operations. PAS also provides technical assistance and consultancy services for the criminal justice system.

Roscoe Pound–American Trial Lawyers Foundation, formed in 1956; its activities include continuous research on specific subjects relating to courts, corrections, juvenile justice, and law.

Western Behavioral Sciences Institute, founded in 1959; it deals with evaluation and community crime prevention (preventing violent crimes in convenience stores, including robbery vulnerability screening, employee training programs, management planning assistance).

The United States is exceptionally well endowed with criminological publications in periodical form. The publications include:

American Criminal Law Review, quarterly, 1971 (formerly *American Criminal Law Quarterly*), published by the American Bar Association, Section on Criminal Justice, Chicago. Each issue is devoted to a single legal topic and contains news notes on ABA.

American Journal of Corrections, bi-monthly since 1920, American Correctional Association, College Park, Md. This journal deals with the problems of corrections (halfway houses, staff-inmate cooperation, jail management, juvenile correction).

American Journal of Criminal Law, tri-annually since 1972, University of Texas School of Law, Austin. Carries articles on such topics as conspiracy law in theory and practice, prosecutorial discretion, public dissemination of arrest records, and notes on current developments in criminal law.

California Youth Authority, quarterly since 1948, California Youth Authority, Sacramento. The quarterly is devoted to the problems of juvenile delinquency and corrections. Among the topics presented: how schools contribute to delinquency, treatment of the serious offender, and student volunteers in correctional institutions.

Corrective and Social Psychiatry and Journal of Behavior Technology Methods and Therapy (formerly *Corrective and Social Psychology: Journal of Applied Behavior Therapy*), quarterly since 1955, Martin Psychiatric Research Foundations, Inc., Olathe, Kansas. The articles in this journal concern the effects of rehabilitative programs on inmate attitudes, empathy training with inmates and staff, and the psychological-social impact of incarceration.

Corrections Compendium, monthly, Lincoln, Neb. This monthly covers federal and state legislation concerning correction practices and programs in this field.

Corrections Digest, bi-weekly since 1969, Washington Crime News Services, Annandale. Contains information on the Law Enforcement Assistance Administration and on research in the field of corrections.

Corrections Magazine, quarterly since 1974, Criminal Justice Publications, New York. Concerns America's prison system, surveys of the prison population, probation and parole officers.

Correctional Research, annually since 1952, Crime and Justice Foundation, Boston. Reviews literature in the field of corrections, with bibliographies concerning parole, prison administration and industries, rehabilitative alternatives, and similar topics.

Counterforce: The Monthly Magazine in Terrorism, monthly since 1977, Dallas. The articles treat the protection of vulnerable persons and companies from the threat of terrorism; description of latest terrorist actions is also provided.

Crime Control Digest, weekly since 1967, Washington Crime News Services, Annandale. This weekly provides information about the activities of the Law Enforcement Assistance Administration. It also contains reports on court cases concerning police practices and personnel.

Crime and Delinquency, quarterly since 1955, National Council on Crime and Delinquency, Hackensack. This publication deals with the effectiveness of law enforcement, juvenile and criminal courts, correctional institutions, criminal justice programs. The original research, analysis, and commentary on all aspects of criminal justice are presented in articles.

Crime Prevention Review, quarterly since 1973, Attorney General's Office, Los Angeles. This is a professional periodical covering a variety of topics related to crime prevention.

Crime and Social Justice, semi-annually since 1974, Crime and Social Justice, Berkeley. This publication covers such topics as a leftist view of street crime, the class nature of the urban police, crime in Chinatown; it also offers book reviews.

Criminal Justice and Behavior, quarterly since 1974, Sage Publications, Inc., Beverly Hills. Articles present original research, theoretical aspects, innovative programs and practices; the subject matter also covers prediction of dangerous behavior, delinquency causation, the self-esteem and violence of prison guards, and inmate interpersonal relationship skills.

Criminal Defense, bi-monthly since 1973, National College of Criminal Defense, University of Houston, Houston. This journal presents articles of general interest to criminal defense lawyers and public defenders as well as book reviews.

Criminal Justice Quarterly, quarterly since 1973, Division of Criminal Justice, Princeton. This quarterly is devoted to crime control issues and their legal consequences for law enforcement officers in New Jersey.

Criminal Justice Review, semi-annually since 1976 (formerly *Georgia Journal of Corrections*), Georgia State University, Atlanta. Articles on trends, problems and research of the U.S. criminal justice system: law enforcement, courts, juvenile justice, corrections, education, planning, interrelationships among the various components of this system.

Criminal Law Bulletin, bi-monthly since 1970, Warren, Gorham, and Lamont, Inc., Boston. This journal presents the decisions of the U.S. Supreme Court, federal courts and state courts. It also carries abstracts of recent publications, book reviews, articles on a variety of issues, such as halfway houses in adult corrections, prisoner rights, parole theory, and attorney-client privelege.

Criminal Law Commentator, bi-monthly since 1973, Federal Legal Publications, Inc., New York. Contains notes and briefs on significant issues and developments in criminal law.

Criminology: An Interdisciplinary Journal, quarterly since 1970 (formerly *Criminologica*), Sage Publications, Inc., Beverly Hills. This is the official journal of the American Society of Criminology. The scholarly articles deal with different subjects from the psychological, sociological, and legal points of view. Topics include behavioral approaches to the treatment of offenders, drug addicts, poverty, female homicide victims, and the inhibiting effects of imprisonment on rehabilitation.

Drug Enforcement, quarterly since 1973 (formerly *B.N.D.D. Bulletin*), U.S. Drug Enforcement Administration, Washington. The quarterly contains information about production, transportation, processing, and distribution of illicit drugs, news on international law enforcement agreements to reduce production and smuggling, surveillance measures and prosecution of offenders.

Economist Crime Digest, bi-monthly since 1974, National District Attorneys' Association, Washington. Journal devoted to the problems of economic crime, from antitrust and used-car fraud to price-fixing and welfare fraud. The operating techniques and fraudulent economic schemes practices in the United States are briefly described.

Enforcement Journal, quarterly since 1962, National Police Officers Association of America, Inc., Louisville. The articles cover such topics as community crime prevention, forensics, judicial procedures, anti-terrorist techniques, and computer applications to law enforcement.

Federal Probation, quarterly since 1936. Administrative Office of the United States Courts, Washington. Articles deal with theoretical, philosophical, and practical aspects of prevention and corrections concerning juvenile delinquents and adult offenders.

FBI Law Enforcement Bulletin, monthly since 1945, Washington. Articles present such issues as police cooperation and coordination, police reserves, white-collar crime, bank fraud and embezzlement, and railroad crime.

Fingerprint and Identification Magazine, monthly since 1919, American Institute of Applied Science, Syracuse. This journal covers such topics as the exchange of identification-related information and techniques among law enforcement personnel, identification and finger-print technicians, public and private security and safety officials.

Fire and Arson Investigator, monthly, International Association of Arson Investigators, Marlboro, Ma. Articles are devoted to fire prevention and, in particular, to the causes and prevention of arson and the control of arson.

Identification News, monthly since 1960, International Association for Identification, Utica. Articles describe the latest techniques, equipment, materials and scientific discoveries in the field of identification.

International Annals of Criminology (Annales Internationales de Criminologie) semi-annually, Center for Study in Criminology and Criminal Law, Philadelphia. Articles on every aspect of criminology. Recent topics have included crime prevention, clinical and therapeutical treatment of offenders, criminal justice system clients, staff education, statistical information, and notes on pertinent legislation.

International Journal of Comparative and Applied Criminal Justice, semi-annually since 1977, Carolina Academic Press, Durham. The content of articles concerns the administration of criminal justice around the world and the theoretical as well as the practical implications of justice administration.

International Journal of Criminology and Penology, quarterly since 1973, Academic Press, New York. Articles present a global cross-cultural and comparative perspective of theory and practice in the field of criminology and penology.

International Journal of Offender Therapy and Comparative Criminology, tri-annually since 1957, Association for the Psychiatric Treatment of Offenders. This journal deals with offenders' therapy and correction, including such topics as general system theory in psychotherapy, forensic psychiatry, predicting criminal behavior, and the treatment of psychopathic juveniles.

Issues in Criminology, semi-annually since 1965, University of California, School of Criminology, Berkeley. A scholarly journal edited by graduate students. Features such topics as social class and crime, crime control in a western society, community corrections, and drug laws.

Jail Administration Digest, monthly since 1978, Washington Crime News Service, Annandale. Contains programs and projects concerning corrections and jail administration, jail policies and standards, and handling of special prisoners.

Journal of Community Correctional Centers, semi-annually, Community Correction and Research Center, Inc., Baton Rouge. Articles deal with the origins, dynamics, treatment, cost of crime, psychotherapy in criminal rehabilitation, community-based treatment, halfway houses, and community correctional centers.

Journal of Correctional Education, quarterly since 1949, Correctional Educational Association, Houston. This publication contains information on the activities of the Correctional Education Association, and some articles about educational and vocational problems in prisons.

Journal of Criminal Justice, quarterly since 1973, Academy of Criminal Justice Sciences, John Jay College of Criminal Justice, New York. This quarterly presents analytic methodologies and new disciplines applied to criminal justice problems and such topics as factors influencing crime on campuses, youth attitudes toward the police, the effects of increased security on prison violence, and alternatives to the conventional procedure of investigating crimes.

Journal of Criminal Law and Criminology, quarterly since 1973, The Williams and Wilkins Co., Baltimore. Journal divided into four sections: criminal law, criminology, research notes and book reviews. Articles deal with issues of major interest in criminal justice at the theoretical and operational levels.

Journal of Forensic Sciences, quarterly since 1955, American Society for Testing and Materials, Philadelphia. This quarterly features original investigations and scholarly inquiries in the various forensic science disciplines: forensic pathology, psychiatry, toxicology, immunology, jurisprudence, and criminalistics.

Journal of Juvenile and Family Courts, quarterly since 1949 (formerly *Juvenile Justice and Juvenile Court Judges Journal*), National Council of Juvenile and Family Court Judges, Reno. Articles deal with theoretical and practical issues in the field of juvenile and family courts, treatment and control of juvenile delinquency, general administration of juvenile justice in the United States. The journal also provides a review of the latest legislative developments.

Journal of Legal Studies, semi-annually since 1972, the University of Chicago School of Law. Articles concerning crime and administration of criminal law, addressed to criminal defense lawyers and prosecutors.

Journal of Police Science and Administration, quarterly since 1973, International Association of Chiefs of Police, Inc., Gaithersburg. Scholarly articles of this journal deal with the problems of terrorism, police-community relations, training, investigation and prosecution of the crime of rape; also, new developments in forensic sciences and criminalistics.

Journal of Research in Crime and Delinquency, semi-annually since 1964, National Council on Crime and Delinquency, Hackensack. Articles present the outcome of research projects in criminology and juvenile justice. Topics cover juvenile diversion, recidivism, arrest release decisions, and development of a parolee classification system.

Judicature, montly (bi-monthly in June–July and December–January) since 1966, American Judicature Society, Chicago. The content focuses on research studies, evaluation of judicial administration and program planning.

Justice System Journal: A Management Review, tri-annually since 1972, Institute for Court Management, Denver. Articles treat issues related to the justice system, with its historical, political, social, and legal implications. This journal presents original research and empirical reports for justice system managers.

Juvenile Justice Digest, bi-monthly since 1973, Washington Crime News Service, Annandale. This periodical carries information on juvenile delinquency and the corresponding parts of the criminal justice system. The problems of societal factors affecting the development of children are also discussed.

Juvenile Law Digest, monthly since 1978 (formerly *Juvenile Court Digest*), National Council of Juvenile and Family Court Judges, Reno. This publication carries articles dealing with the administration of juvenile justice and the protection of the rights of juveniles. The topics concern, among other things, the right to a speedy trial, custody, adoption, child support, and truancy.

Law and Contemporary Problems, quarterly, Duke University Press, Durham. Contains scholarly articles discussing legal issues. Each issue focuses on a single topic, such as the American Indian and the law, police practices, and criminal process in the seventies.

Law and Computer Technology, quarterly since 1960, World Peace Through Law Center, Washington. This quarterly provides information about current activities in the field of computer technology, law and legal institutes, the relation of computer technology to justice administration, and similar topics.

Law Enforcement Communications, bi-monthly since 1974, New York. Contains information on the use of communications hardware and software in the field of law enforcement. The issues discussed include surveillance an emergency communications systems and the use of audiovisual technology as a training tool in law enforcement.

Law and Order, monthly since 1953, Law and Order Subscription Department, New York. This monthly includes such topics as one-officer car patrols, driver training for police and mounted patrol duty; also book and training film reviews.

Law and Society Review, quarterly since 1966, the Law and Society Association, Denver. Articles contain such issues as legal services programs, juveniles and the courts, and legal assistance for the poor. The journal is aimed at supporting research and teaching of the political, social, and economic aspects of the law.

National Journal of Criminal Defense: semi-annually since 1975, National College of Criminal Defense Lawyers and Public Defenders, Houston. Contains professional information of interest to criminal defense lawyers and public defenders.

New England Journal on Prison Law, semi-annually since 1974, Boston. This journal examines the application of substantive and procedural law within prison systems in the light of constitutional guarantees. It acts as a national forum for the discussion of historical developments, present trends and future prospects regarding prison-related legal issues.

Offender Rehabilitation, quarterly since 1977, Hawthorne Press, New York. Carries articles about interdisciplinary approaches to the reintegration of ex-offenders into society (diversion programs, prerelease centers, halfway houses).

Police Chief, monthly since 1934, International Association of Chiefs of Police, Inc., Gaithersburg. Articles concern training, professional recognition, organized crime.

Police Magazine, bi-monthly since 1978, Criminal Justice Publications, Inc., New York. This journal deals with such issues as trends in crime, child abuse, the use of deadly force, high speed chases, and gambling.

The Prison Journal, semi-annually since 1921, The Pennsylvania Prison Society, Philadelphia. Articles deal with current problems of criminology and penology.

Prison Law Monitor, monthly since 1978, Prison Law Monitor, Washington. This monthly contains a thorough analysis of the prison law. All federal and state reported decisions on prisoners' rights and most of the unreported decisions are presented in written briefs.

Probation and Parole, annually since 1969, New York Probation and

Parole Association, New York. Articles present the issues of capital punishment, juvenile justice, classification of adult probationers, and manpower and recruitment problems in probation and parole.

The Prosecutor, bi-monthly since 1965 (formerly *Journal of the N.D.A.A.*), National District Attorneys Association, Chicago. Information on events sponsored by teh NDAA, reports on NDAA grant projects and programs. Problems of the evolution of the prosecutorial function in America, litigation support, evidence in computer cases and other issues are discussed.

Rutgers Journal of Computers and the Law, semi-annually since 1972, Rutgers Law School, Newark. Articles on computer applications in the legal system: computer-aided legal analysis, computer programs and subject matter, patentability and electronic fund transfer systems. A classified bibliography of this journal covers: computer usuage in law practice, government use and regulation, sales and service, and computer science developments of potential significance to the legal profession.

Search and Seizure, monthly since 1973, Quinlan Publishing Co., Inc., Boston. Reports of court decisions and related cases involving search, seizure and stop-and-frisk practices. Topics cover fingerprinting, open field search, search of a handbag, and the like.

Security Management, monthly since 1974 (formerly *Industrial Security*), American Society for Industrial Security, Washington. Subjects of interest to industrial and retail security personnel such as retail security, industrial espionage, access and entry control, and present the information on technological developments in this field.

Security Systems Digest, bi-weekly since 1970, Washington Crime News Services, Annandale. Various topics of international interest to commercial and industrial security personnel; also, information on new developments in security products.

Security World, monthly since 1963, Security World Publishing Co., Inc., Los Angeles. This monthly is of interest to security organizations and security management executives; it discusses such topics as computer crime, security and equipment technology, airport and subway security, and credit card fraud.

Trial, bi-monthly since 1965, Association of Trial Lawyers of America, Washington. Problems of victims' rights, the invasion of privacy and breach of confidence, videotapes in the courtroom, speedy trial, and similar matters.

Victimology: an International Journal, quarterly since 1976, Visage

Press, Inc., Washington. Focuses on victimization research, including theories, methodologies, concepts, and practices. Articles discuss such issues as victim compensation, the recidivist victim of violent crime, the rape victim, the victimization of the American Indian, and child and spouse abuse.

In Canada, the development of academic interest in criminology is relatively recent.

The first school of criminology, still active, was established at the University of Montreal in 1960. It was followed by criminology centers at the University of Toronto in 1963 and at the University of Ottawa in 1967. The University of Alberta established the first program of criminology in 1972.

Two autonomous research centers work closely with the Montreal School of Criminology. They are the Montreal-based International Center for Comparative Criminology and the Research Group on Juvenile Maladjustment. The school carries out applied and basic research, each year receiving a number of grants for research and implementation of forensic criminology methods. Publications deal with a wide range of topics on criminology, penitentiary issues, sociology, psychology, and research methods. In addition to project monographs, the school publishes the *Acta Criminologica*, an annual devoted to studies on antisocial behavior. An editor's note in volume 1 (1968) indicates that the publication takes a complex, interdisciplinary approach to criminology, dealing with bio-psycho-cultural issues. The treatises published in *Acta Criminologica* are aimed at integrating theoretical research into a theoretical synthesis, studying criminal phenomena and applying scientific knowledge in criminal justice administration. The school also has a documentation center, a computer, and an audio-visual facility, facilitating teaching and practical experiments.[5]

The objective of the International Center for Comparative Criminology is to train specialists and to organize regional scientific symposia in various parts of the world; it is led by Denis Szabo, who deserves great credit for developing comparative studies. Alice Parizeau is the author of numerous criminological publications.[6] Research carried out at the center is of considerable theoretical and practical significance; its interest is focused on issues concerning the social reactions to deviant behavior, varying preventive methods in accordance with individual needs, use of spare time, and juvenile delinquency. Publications deal with various issues in penal law, comparative criminology, criminological theory and practice, sociocultural systems in the etiology of criminality, protective policy of the society, crisis of the justice administration system, costs of crime, and terrorism.[7]

Ottawa University Department of Criminology, founded by Tadeusz Grygier in 1967, represents Canada's first college of applied criminology. It trains specialized personnel for the federal and provincial prison authorities; research findings of that department had a profound impact on Canadian legislation on prisons and juvenile correctional institutions. Grygier drafted the basic legal pattern for the treatment of juveniles, which differs fundamentally from U.S. patterns and is more akin to Polish legislation (in 1976 the Collection of Social Defense Principles written by Grygier was published in Warsaw by the Institute of Crime Problems). The new federal draft is founded on the same principles.

The Social Protection Code and its introduction represent a distinctive model of criminal justice. This new model code is unlike any other penal code in that it rejects the concepts of guilt and punishment. It is not restricted to any given country; it is a model for any civilized country to follow. The code has its roots as much in philosophy and science as in jurisprudence, and some of its concepts are closer to the civil than to the criminal law.[8]

The University of Toronto established a Center of Criminology in 1963, which also deals with problems of criminal policy. Since 1971 the center has published the "Canadian Studies in Criminology" series, in addition to numerous monographs, devoted for instance, to the additional Y chromosome and deviant behavior, social attitudes to police and criminality in Toronto, crime prevention, and bibliographies.

Simon Frazer University, in British Columbia, established a Department of Criminology in 1975, which offers undergraduate-level criminological training.

Institut Philippe Pinel de Montréal, formed in 1968, conducts research and publishes writings on the treatment of offenders.

The McGill Clinic in Forensic Psychiatry, McGill University, Montreal, organized in 1955, focuses on problems of homicides and habitual criminals. It serves as a research center and treatment facility for prisoners with mental anomalies.

Criminological research is also carried out by the Department of the Solicitor General. The department supervises the Royal Canadian Mounted Police, federal detention services and the National Parole Board. Its research section focuses on criminality controls, development of the criminal justice system, problems of diversion, female criminality, victimization of people in Canada, prevention of crime by the police, the deterrent role of the death sentence, and the like.

Prevention of crime is a high-priority subject in Canada. In 1977 the Canadian Criminological Association became the Canadian Association for the Prevention of Crime. The history of the social crime-prevention movement dates back to 1919. CAPC efforts are sponsored by the Governor General of Canada; it has branches in most of the provinces. Twice a year it holds congresses devoted to crime prevention. The Association regularly publishes its findings in the *Canadian Journal of Criminology*.

The Canadian prison system has recently come under severe criticism by specialists and laymen, partly because of the high prisoner population. In 1978 Canada had 21,000 prisoners in detention, out of a total population of 22 million. The old prison buildings are deemed inadequate for the contemporary functions of the prison system, and the training of prison personnel leaves much to be desired. Prisoners' rights are frequently violated. In view of this a special group was formed for controling the observance of prisoners' rights; the chairman of that group reports directly to the Solicitor General.

Canada has long shown a tendency to wide-scale application of parole.[9] As early as 1898, Parliament adopted the Ticket of Leave Act, which allowed for early parole of prisoners for the purpose of social rehabilitation. In 1916 specific parole rules were adopted for Ontario, and in 1948 for British Columbia. Since 1898 members of the Salvation Army have been actively working in programs of effective social rehabilitation of paroled prisoners. Since 1905 the federal Department of Justice has had a special service to supervise implementation of the Ticket of Leave Act. Various civic associations have also been working toward the same end, including the John Howard Society of Saskatchewan, the Elizabeth Fry Society and the Société d'Orientation et de Réhabilitation Sociale of Québec.

In 1959 Parliament enacted the formation of a National Parole Board, empowered with very broad prerogatives: it has discretionary power to grant or recall parole. Every convict sentenced to a term of no less than two years in federal prison has to serve at least nine months, and those convicted for terms of three years or more, a third of their sentence, in order to become eligible for parole. Prisoners serving sentences of up to two years in provincial houses of detention have to serve at least a third of their sentence. Rulings of the board are final and cannot be appealed. If a prisoner's petition for parole is rejected, the board reconsiders the petition after two years.

Parole is an extrajudicial decision concerning mainly the manner of serving the sentence. The objective of the progressive program is the quickest possible social readaptation of the prisoner. Each individual program comprehensively considers the prognosis of the prisoner's behavior under new circumstances. In 1964 a new procedure was introduced, giving prisoners much better chances of obtaining parole.

A paroled prisoner has to observe specific requirements, such as residing in a given territory which he cannot leave without the consent of his probation supervisor. Alcoholics and drug addicts must eliminate or reduce their habit and they are not allowed to congregate in specified places, such as on streets and squares which are notorious as meeting places of criminal elements, and are not allowed to leave home at night.

Statistical data show that these provisions find increasing practical application. For instance, in 1972 parole was granted to 8,210 prisoners in federal prisons and 12,528 held in provincial institutions of detentions. These figures increased in the following years.

Consideration of criminal justice economy (keeping one prisoner in prison costs about $25,000 per year and on parole $2,600 per year) make it imperative to experiment further with limiting the application of imprisonment.

The National Parole Board consists of three to nine members nominated by the Governor General for a period of ten years. The board relies on consultations by criminology professors and other specialists, and has its own specialized staff for conducting scientific research and follow-up studies. It works closely with the Provincial Probation Services and with private agencies; for instance Quebec has a Committee for the Orientation and Preparation for Employment, while British Columbia has special social centers.

The Planning and Reseach Branch, Ministry of Correctional Service, Province of Ontario, was organized in 1968. Its research covers problems of rehabilitating juvenile delinquents and individual prognostics.

The Staff Training and Development Center was formed by the same ministry in 1961 for training qualified personnel in criminological issues.

A great role in developing criminology as a discipline in Canada has been played by the following scientific or trade groups:

The Canadian Corrections Association, founded in February 1956; the first issue of the *Canadian Journal of Corrections* appeared in 1958 and in 1959 the first Research Conference on Delinquency and Criminology was held. In 1961 the *Journal* inaugurated a continuing section, "Current Correctional and Criminological Research." It serves as a practical source of information on criminological research and theories; in addition to articles, the *Journal* reviews writings and films on criminal subjects.

The John Howard Society of Saskatchewan, formed in 1958, publishes annual reports and regular newsletters.

The Société de Criminologie du Québec is a forum for various views on criminal justice administration in the province of Québec. Its headquarters are in the Montreal School of Criminology; it brings together judges, lawyers, police functionaries, prison authorities, criminologists, and psychologists. L'association Professionelle des Criminologues du Québec is made up of scholars specialized in criminology.

Certain government departments have bureaus of criminological consultation. Among the provincial departments, British Columbia has focused mainly on family studies and young offenders, their correctional treatment and community integration. In Alberta new interest in corrections led to the Alberta penology study in 1968. In the Maritime Provinces no research activities are reported by government departments; however, a study has been undertaken by an outside consultant in New Brunswick and Prince Edward Island involving the reorganization and development of correctional services.[10]

Criminological issues are also a subject of interest for other institutes, whose scope goes beyond questions of social pathology, for example the Centre de Recherches en Relations Humaines de Montréal established by Mailloux in 1950, and the Institut de Psychologie of the Université de Montréal, also organized by Mailloux in 1942. The Forensic Clinic of the Toronto Psychiatric Hospital, although it tends to concentrate its research on sexual deviation and sexual offenses, also concerns itself with studying intrafamily relations, pattern formation, group therapy and the sociology of deviance.

Traditions of French criminology[11] date back to the mid-nineteenth century, the time of activity in the criminological field by two prominent sociologists—Gabriel Tarde and Emile Durkheim. The latter dealt also in problems of criminality.[12] The impact of those two French pioneers on contemporary criminology and the sociology of deviation is quite clear, particularly the ideas advanced by Durkheim which, thanks to American research on deviant behavior, have become one of the cornerstones of this discipline.

A compendium done by the Comité de Coordination des Recherches Criminologiques indicates the existence of thirty-four training centers and twenty-two research facilities with a criminological interest.[13] There are also research facilities dealing primarily with other problems, but touching upon criminology,[14] for instance, a group of studies on social functions, the general sociology laboratories, such as the Bourdieu and Touraine centers, and the laboratory of the College de France.

Among these centers, which vary greatly in their significance in criminological research, a special place is held by the Training and Research Center in Vaucresson formed in 1951 by the Direction de l'Education Surveillée of the Ministère de la Justice.

The second most important center is the Penal and Criminological Studies Service, formed in 1969 within the Directorate of Criminal Affairs and Probation on CNRS (Centre National de la Recherche Scientifique) initiative.

Among the Paris facilities there are the National Center of Penitentiary Studies and Research; the Criminal Sociology Laboratory of the University of Paris II; the two CNRS laboratories: the research unit on criminal sociology and the criminological research center; the Paris Institute of Criminology which does both training and research; and the French Association of Criminology which holds annual criminological congresses.

Among the many provincial university institutes and Centre National de la Recherche Scientifique (CNRS) units are: the Lacassagne Institute of Lyon; Research Service for Safeguarding Childhood in the Basque country of Bayonne; the Center of Criminal Sciences in Pau, linked with the Pau University and the Adour region; the Institute of Penal Sciences and Criminology of the University of Aix-en-Provence; the Center of Studies on Objective Methods in the Humanities at Toulouse.

Criminological research, up to now dominated by biopsychology and law, is increasingly coming under the influence of sociology. Clear boundaries between the disciplines are disappearing.

Clinical teams, such as the Lyon group, are gladly joining ranks with the sociologists, the latter now taking psychological analysis seriously. Nevertheless, the general picture of criminological research in France shows considerable variety, ranging from the most classical concepts of certain medical teams, to the radical tendencies of Foucault and his disciples. In methodology also there is a range from fundamental research to complicated, specialized studies, such as those carried out by the Service d'Etudes Pénales et Criminologiques (SEPC).

The same kind of variety exists in the sphere of criminological theories.

The Jean Pinatel theory of criminal personality is too well known to be repeated here. It has, however, been supplemented in recent years through integration with the vision of a "criminogenic society" (*La Societé criminogène*, 1971), which the author verified through empirical studies of a population of juvenile delinquents in the Basque country research center at Bayonne.

The other end of the doctrinal spectrum is represented by the Foucault ideas, which exerted a profound impact on French criminology (numerous books, notably *Surveiller et Punir* [Supervise and punish], 1975. The writings of Foucault can be considered as representative of modern criminology, although he refers to various orientations, from Marxism and anarchism through left-wing Christianity.

The comprehensive network of training and research facilities and the multifaceted approach of certain centers to criminology as a discipline cannot conceal the weak spots of French criminology. As Verin points out, these are mainly the unequal distribution of funds among the various centers and the discrepancies between criminology and the official criminal policies.

Higher budgets are allotted to the Paris centers (particularly the three facilities of the Justice Ministry). Thus there is relatively little development of criminological training in other parts of the country and, in consequence, there is a shortage of funds for research by the various university centers; low status for criminology as a discipline (relatively little time devoted to teaching criminology at the universities); a lack of correspondence between research and training (the Vaucresson center being a notable exception); a lack of interest in teaching shown by criminological researchers. Universities are being refused funds to establish structural units, which could modify the division of professors' time between teaching and scientific research. There is an imbalance between theory and practice. Theoretical structures are insufficiently grounded in empirical studies and remain suspended in a vacuum. The leading research teams are subordinated to the Ministry of Justice, which tends to steer research toward detailed issues which reflect current needs.

French criminology still fails to get its due recognition from the French authorities. The authorities are often wary of its findings. While penal law is accepted as a noble and realistic discipline, criminology is considered marginal, its scientific character questioned, so that is ends up being treated as the domain of ideologists and oppositionists.

In the day-to-day practice of criminal justice this discipline also fails to enjoy the same status as it does in other countries. For instance, the Penal Procedure Code of 1958 provides for checking the suspect's personality, but fails to establish a specialized panel of experts which would carry out criminological tests, relying instead solely on ad hoc nominations of individuals by the Ministry of Justice (usually retired policemen), thus failing to utilize the possibility of individualizing the penalty.

There is no question of the significance which new trends represent for criminology, by revising many existing concepts and methods of action. Still, it would be useful to have modern criminology rid itself of certain demands which detract from its value. An attempt of this type was made by Jean Pinatel, one of the participants in the Eighteenth Criminological Congress at Aix-en-Provence in October 1979 on the "labeling theory and criminological reality."

This necessary "cleaning up" fosters efforts to define the relationship between criminology and criminal policy. It was started in 1975 on the initiative of Marc Ancel and the Center of Criminal Policy Studies. Only after a precise distinction between scientific analysis on the one hand and, on the other, dilemmas of moral, political, or philosophical nature, which determine the drafting and application of penal systems, will it be possible to strive for objectivity in criminology, which is not to say resignation from a given point of view.

Finally, after ridding modern theories of elements contrary to the spirit of science, and with a strictly defined scope of criminology and criminal policy, it will be possible to unify criminology. Many criminologists are striving toward this objective—Jacques Sélosse, director of the Vaucresson center, Jean Pinatel, and others.

Despite the many shortcomings in its structure, French criminology has shown a great deal of vitality, guaranteeing it successful development in the future.

A review of criminological projects in France is contained in an interesting study by Jean Pinatel and Jean-Paul Sabatier.[15]

French criminology has focused a great deal of attention on evaluating criminality and developing preventive methods.[16] However, just as in other countries, juvenile delinquency has become a major problem in France. Numerous studies have been devoted to this subject.[17]

The individual types of crimes have also been the subject of French criminological research.[18]

In recent years there has been an explosive growth of facilities devoted to studying problems of criminality, a phenomenon linked with an increased incidence of criminality. The number of criminological projects and publications also increased significantly[19] and the activities of some facilities, such as Vaucresson, have gained international renown. The institutional base of French criminology is quite sizeable, numerically, compared with other European countries.

This general evaluation of the state and prospects of French criminology, conducted mainly on the basis of Jacques Verin's article, can now be followed by a survey of the research activities of selected research centers.

Among the criminological facilities operating in France a special place must be accorded to the Coordinating Committee of Criminological Research, established by the Ministry of Justice in 1968.

The main tasks of the committee include drawing up inventories of the resources required for conducting research, organizing the exchange of information concerning the research being carried out in France, inspiring and supporting new research directions, drafting and evaluating training programs in criminology, and organizing the training of criminal justice practitioners. The committee also organizes foreign contacts, scientific exchanges, criminological congresses and symposia. There are five working groups, one for each type of activity; for example, the committee sponsored a project on the criminality of foreigners in France. Since 1972 the committee has annually awarded the Gabriel Tarde prize for best publications in the field of criminology.

The Ministry of Justice also has a Service for Penal and Criminological Studies. Between 1970 and 1979 this research facility of the Ministry, led by Philippe Robert, carried out more than twenty empirical research projects. Among these are the problem of social controls over criminality or the costs of crime. There are numerous publications concerning project findings.[20]

The National Center of Penitentiary Studies and Research (CNERP), founded by the Ministry of Justice in 1964, deals with evaluating the effectiveness of existing penal measures and studies of new rehabilitation methods. The center carried out, among others, two major long-range projects. The first concerned the conditions of relapse into crime of persons freed following the serving of their sentences; it covered all persons released from prison in the years 1960 through 1962. The second project concerned probation. It covered a sample of 1,500 persons. This project was aimed, first of all, at identifying the categories of criminals to whom this measure could be applied with a great chance of success. The main objective of studying recidivism was the identification of factors determining this development and designing a model of "diagnostic function." The center published the collective "Studies of Prison Population," which described the results of research carried out by the center in penal institutions.

International recognition was gained by the Center of Training and Research on Supervised Education (Centre de Formation et de Recherche de l'Education Surveillée) in Vaucresson.

In keeping with its designation, the center carries out two types of activities: teaching in the form of permanent training of juvenile judges, and research. The center conducted the following long-range research projects:

1. Studying the phenomenon of juvenile social maladjustment. Under this general heading the following specific projects were carried out:
    a. a national study of juvenile delinquency which covered 1,000 juvenile delinquents—boys aged 16–17. This multifacet socio-psychological study was designed to identify the various etiologically and behavioristically uniform groups among the juveniles in order to attain a higher degree of success and individualization in the application of preventive and rehabilitation measures;
    b. a study of juvenile drug abuse aimed at determining the scope of this phenomenon, its intensity and accompanying factors;
    c. a study of the psychological features of criminal populations and the use of the results obtained from personality tests. The main objective of this study was to emphasize the diagnostic nature of the personality tests used for studying delinquent juveniles, including the du Village and Rorschach tests and also the DPI Grygier test;
    d. the evolution of juvenile delinquency between 1825 and 1968; this historical study was aimed at evaluating the changes in the structure and dynamics of juvenile delinquency and the evolution of legislation concerning such delinquency.
2. Study of the methods of procedure to be applied in rehabilitation efforts. Two specific projects were implemented:
    a. a study of maladjusted and delinquent juveniles and ways of reeducating them; this study encompassed, among other things, maladjusted girls and girls who committed offenses. Self-evaluation of maladjusted juveniles was also carried out;
    b. evaluation of the results obtained through psychotherapy of juveniles during supervised education.

3. Study of the rehabilitation effects, covering two problem areas:
   a. a study of the effectiveness of reeducational measures applied in institutions under the directorate of supervised education; it encompassed a sample of 2,747 persons; the study aimed at identifying the link between applied educational measures and the degree of readaptation;
   b. a study of the later life of persons to whom penal and reeducational measures were applied; it encompassed former inmates of correctional institutions, former prisoners, and persons on probation. The objective of this study was to determine reactions to the various reeducational measures applied by the courts.
4. Studies with general institutional implications; these covered a variety of research programs often ranging outside the bounds of narrowly defined criminology. Two such programs were implemented:
   a. school maladjustment and social maladjustment; difficulties in school and social adaptation of students in the first year of high school; the objective of this study was to identify the sociopsychological conditions of school failures and the link between failure in school and other forms of maladjustment;
   b. a study of the links betwen socioeconomic development levels and criminality; this project was carried out with the assistance of scientists from Poland, Yugoslavia, and Hungary.

Further, the Vaucresson center carries out studies on the methods of training educational personnel and juvenile judges and studies on the sociology of law. Project findings of the center are published in *Annales de Vaucresson, Le Droit de l'Enfance et de la Famille,* and *Marginalités.*

The Criminology Institute formed in 1910 in the Faculty of Law, Economics, and Social Sciences of the University of Paris, in addition to its educational activities, also carries out extensive research. The research section of the institute studied four basic projects:

1. The character of the jury. This study, which encompassed six hundred assessors, aimed at determining to what degree the composition of juries corresponds to composition of the population in the Paris region. An attempt was made to determine the expectations held by assessors toward the professional judges, toward themselves, and toward the activities of the jury.
2. The opportunity for preventive action in new towns. This concerned towns built from scratch, which did not inherit the errors of urban development committed in the past.
3. Contemporary forms of vagrancy.

4. The structure and character of criminality in France, with particular consideration to the structure and forms of the more serious intentional crimes in individual departments.

Institute of Penal Sciences and Criminology in Aix-en-Provence, formed in 1958, also conducts training and research. "Criminality in Aix-en-Provence" is one of its more significant projects. Studies cover statistical data (court and police) from the years 1960 to 1970; their objective is to define the scope, structure, dynamics, and forms of criminality in Aix in the light of the population changes taking place in that town. The data was compared with similar national data. The institute also organizes criminological symposia and colloquia.

The Institute of Criminological Sciences of Bordeaux was organized in 1942 by the Law Faculty of Bordeaux University and for many years concentrated almost exlusively on teaching. In recent years the institute has taken up research activities. In 1972 it started an interesting legal-economic project on the costs of juvenile justice in the Gironde Department. This study was designed to identify all costs, with division by the institutions involved, incurred from the moment of obtaining information about an offense up to the final decision.

Alexandre Lacassagne Institute (formerly the University Institute of Forensic Medicine and Clinical Criminology) was established in Lyon in 1972. It operates within a hospital center, conducting both research and training. The institute has an interdisciplinary staff: physicians, biologists, psychiatrists, and psychologists, supplemented by lawyers, sociologists, and economists.

The research interests of the institute center on such topics as: penitentiary issues, alcoholism, and drug addiction. Interesting projects concern suicides and the causes and social complications of abortions. The institute publishes the *Bulletin de médecine légale et de toxicologie médicale*, and co-edits *Instantanés criminologiques*.

The Research Center of Juvenile Delinquency was formed in 1970 by the Medical-Psychological Center of Bois-Maison, conducting observations and examination of boys aged 14–18 remanded there by juvenile judges. The juvenile delinquents studied in the center are either in the most derelict category or have obvious psychopathic or psychotic disorders. The first series included seventy patients, the second thirty. The center publishes reports on the results of its research.

The Psychiatric Clinic of Toulouse University carries out studies of criminological nature, mostly victimological problems, particularly the notion of a secret victim and initial reactivity. The objective is to define the mechanisms leading to criminal actions and their link with the psychological traits of the victim as well as the conditions of crimes committed under situations of stress, such as infanticide. Another field in which the clinic specializes covers pharmacological treatment of character irregularities and aggressive behavior. The clinic also makes attempts to apply pharmacological therapy in a penitentiary milieu.

The Institute of Comparative Law, of the University of Paris, carries out criminological research, the results of which are published in the "Revue de Science Criminelle et de Droit Pénal Comparé."

The Criminology Institute of the Lille University II is involved, among other things, in problems of customs offenses.

The Criminal Sociology Laboratory of Paris University II has carried out a study of criminals benefiting from suspension of sentence and parole.

The subjects of criminological studies carried out by French research institutions and the subject of numerous national and international congresses represent a comprehensive range. They encompass not only a variety of very specific issues, but also the criminological concepts of contemporary epistemology, such as confrontation of the general theory of penal liability with data obtained by criminology, the limits of repression in penal law, and the future of penology.

The aims of the Family Liaison and Action Committee of the national association "Drogue et jeunesse" (Drugs and Youth) are to bring together parents whose children take drugs, with a view to helping them, and to encourage the exchange of information among the medical profession, psychologists, educators, social workers, and other groups or individuals affected by the problem.

Since 1976 the association has launched a monthly journal, *Drugstop*, which is intended to provide reviews and magazines with reference material providing detailed information likely to be of interest to various sectors of the public.

The "operational teams for suppressing traffic in women and children", an association recognized as acting in the public interest, since 1974 has published a quarterly entitled *Esclavage, Document Social* (Slavery, a Social Document). It contains a summary of the association's endeavors to fight prostitution and to rehabilitate prostitutes.

Criminological research in the United Kingdom[21] is carried out primarily by academic institutions.

One of the more famous academic centers is the Institute of Criminology, established in 1959 at Cambridge University, and headed for many years by Leon Radzinowicz. The institute carries out scientific research and develops research programs jointly with other institutions. It also publishes a series called Cropwood Conference Proceedings; the conferences are sponsored by the Cropwood Trust and bring together academic experts and other specialists with criminological experience to discuss specific issues in penal policy, criminology, and law enforcement. To date the series includes:

1. *Psychopathic Offenders*, ed. D. J. West, 1968;
2. *The Residential Treatment of Disturbed and Delinquent Boys*, ed. R. F. Sparks and R. G. Hood, 1968;
3. *Community Homes and the Approved School System*, ed. R. G. Hood and R. F. Sparks, 1969;
4. *Criminological Implications of Chromosome Abnormalities*, ed. D. J. West, 1969;
5. *The Security Industry in the United Kingdom*, ed. Paul Wiles and F. H. McClintock, 1972;
6. *Parole, Its Implications for the Criminal Justice and Penal Systems*, ed. D. A. Thomas, 1973;
7. *The British Jury System*, ed. Nigel Walker with the assistance of Annette Pearson, 1974;
8. *Control Without Custody?* ed. J. F. S. King with the assistance of Warren Young, 1975;
9. *Penal Policy-making in England*, ed. Nigel Walker with the assistance of Henri Giller, 1976;
10. *Problems of Drug Abuse in Britain*, ed. D. J. West, 1977;
11. *Pressures and Changes in the Probation Service*, ed. J. F. S. King, 1978.

Staff members of the institute have published a number of valuable books, the most renowned being: F. H. McClintock, *Crime in England and Wales;* D. J. West, *Present Conduct and Future Delinquency and Murder Followed by Suicide*; K. Hawkins, *Parole*. The institute publishes "The Cambridge Studies in Criminology," and organizes courses in criminology; the curriculum includes 150 hours of lectures, ninety seminars and field projects. The lectures are devoted to such issues as: methodology of criminological research, psychological and psychiatric aspects of criminality, sociology of crime, fundamental problems of penal law and penal procedure, effectiveness of punishment, and crime prevention.

The Institute of Advanced Legal Studies was formed in 1947 by the University of London. Its activities include research on law and organization of postgraduate training. It also conducts criminological research and sociological-legal studies, publishes bibliographies, and indexes foreign periodicals as well as legal monographs.

The Department of Law, University of Keele was formed in 1967 as a research and training facility. Leading research projects have included polling public opinion concerning the criminal propensities of immigrants and studying the decision-making process of judges.

Similar research and training facilities have been organized in the universities at Edinburgh, Manchester, Sheffield, Birmingham, and Bristol. They have addressed such issues as rehabilitation and reeducation of criminals, economic aspects of crime, sexual offenses, diversion concerning juvenile delinquents, judicial decisions, and crime deterrent and preventive measures.

The Home Office Research Unit was formed in 1957 in London; by now it is one of Britain's leading crime analysis centers. Among its most significant projects are studies on criminals sentenced to prison, typological studies of recidivists and first-time offenders, and probation and post-penitentiary therapy of drug addicts. The unit has engaged the cooperation of the most outstanding British criminologists, including Herman Mannheim and Wilkins. A number of monographs have been published mainly on forecasting criminality and issues connected with probation.

The British Academy of Forensic Sciences, an autonomous research unit, was organized by the Department of Forensic Medicine in London. Since October 1960 it has published a quarterly, *Medicine, Science and Law*, of interest to criminologists. Foreign correspondents of the academy represent a total of fourteen countries.

The Institute for the Study and Treatment of Delinquency was formed in 1931. Under its auspices there is a "scientific discussion group on criminological issues," bringing together representatives of all the relevant disciplines.[22] The institute publishes the *British Journal of Criminology* (formerly the *British Journal of Delinquency*).

The Howard League for Penal Reform was formed in 1921 from the merger of the Howard Association for Penal Reform, established in 1866 and the League for Penal Reform, established in 1907. A nonprofit organization, it presents proposals for changes in the penitentiary system, shaping public opinion views on punishment, penal measures, the effectiveness of punishment, humanitarian methods of implementing sentences. Its publications include the *Howard Journal of Penology* and monographs: H. J. Klare, *Changing Concepts in Crime and Its Treatment*; and L. Bloom-Cooper, *The Hanging Question—Essays on the Death Penalty*. It has the status of a UN consultative organ.

The Association for the Psychiatric Treatment of Offenders (APTO) was established in 1950. The association does research, and publishes the *International Journal of Offender Therapy and Comparative Criminology*. Its monographs include the "Offender Therapy Series" and *Drug-taking Girls in England*.

Criminological research is also carried out in some prison-connected facilities, such as at Wormwood Scrubs and Wakefield for men and at Holloway for women.[23]

In the Federal Republic of Germany criminological research is mainly the domain of university-based institutes, departments, and seminars on criminology. Leading among them are:

University of Tübingen Criminology Institute (Institut für Kriminologie), established in 1962, conducts interdisciplinary empirical research, such as projects concerned with the factors which decide criminality and the possibility of socially rehabilitating juvenile delinquents. Publications have included a study of life imprisonment sentences; this study took into account the criminological, penal law, victimological, psychiatric, and psychological aspects.[24] A joint study with the Anthropology and Genetics Institute was concerned with chromosome changes in young adults. Other criminological studies were concerned with the homeless and with adolescent and juvenile thieves. Hans Göppinger, the director, has several interesting publications to his credit, including *Strafe und Verbrechen* [Penalties and Offenses], 1965, *Arzt und Recht* [Physician and the Law], 1966, Kriminologie, *Eine Einführung* [Criminology, An Introduction], 1971.

The Frankfurt University Criminology Institute (Institut für Kriminologie) was founded in 1964 by Friedrich Geerds; it is concerned with criminology, criminological teaching, criminalistics, and criminal policy. Dissertations by institute scholars are concerned with various offenses viewed in their legal and criminological context: robbery, extortion, exploiting prostitution, poaching, tax evasion, bogus bankruptcy, disseminating pornography, embezzlement, "mass" crimes, and others. The institute's periodical is *Kriminalwissenschaftliche Abhandlungen*.

The Freiburg University Criminology and Penology Institute (Institut für Kriminologie und Strafvollzugsunde) was founded by E. Wolf in 1930. The Institute has carried out and published numerous studies on the family and juvenile delinquency. Current research is concerned with reforming the system of serving sentences, particularly with prison labor, free time in penal institutions, proceeding with prisoners, open and semi-open institutions, prison newspapers, cooperation between prisoners and the prison administration, and prisoner classification. A study has been completed on bank robberies in the Federal Republic of Germany, including such topics as the personality of the offenders and the sentences. One of the studies concerned "Boycott and the Penal Law." Research was undertaken on crime indexes and international crime statistics. The institute publishes periodical series: *Kriminologie: Abhandlungen über adwegiges Sozialverhalten* (since 1964), and *Beiträge zur Strafvollzugswissenschaft* (since 1967).

The Heidelberg University Criminology Institute (Institut für Kriminologie) was formed in 1962; it carries out research on various aspects of criminology and on execution of punishment. Recent studies concern psychiatric-criminological forecasting, credibility of witness testimony, arson committed by adolescents and juveniles, training and psychotherapy of convicts, self-induced injuries of prisoners, preventive arrests of sexual offenders, the harm that can come to children as a result of interrogation concerning sexual crimes, and road traffic offenses. Sociological and criminological surveys have been carried out in the section of Heidelberg populated by antisocial groups. Since 1965 the institute has published the so-called Heidelberg Documentation, covering all German-language criminological literature.

Munich University Criminology and Juvenile Law Institute (Institut für Kriminologie und Jugendrecht) was founded by P. Bockelmann in 1963. It has conducted an analysis of the Bavarian penal institutions, including a study conducted thorough interviews with twelve murderers serving sentences in increased-rigor prisons.

The Saar University Criminological Institute (Kriminologisches Institut) at Saarbrücken was founded by Ernst Seelig in 1953; it is concerned with juvenile delinquency and juvenile punishment, particularly with indefinite sentences.

The Giessen University Criminology Institute (Institut für Kriminologie) studies the procedures applied to juvenile prisoners and forecasting their future behavior. This has lead to a follow-up study of one hundred formerly diagnosed prisoners one year following their release from prison.

The Göttingen University Penology and Criminology Department (Lehrstuhl für Penologie und Kriminologie Universität Göttingen) carries out research on such topics as recidivism of released prisoners and persons on probation, prisoner rehabilitation methods, the significance of correspondence and visits for long-term prisoners, temporary arrest and its impact on suspects, and bank robberies. Highly significant are the studies which attempt to determine the magnitude of the "dark number." A study was conducted in Göttingen, a city of about 130,000, in January and February 1974, in an attempt to ascertain the "dark number" for certain types of offenses committed in 1973, and to establish why various offenses were not reported to the authorities.[25]

The Kiel University Criminological Seminar (Kriminologisches Seminar) was formed in 1957 by H. Mayer. The subject of study covers the etiology and the combating of crime, as well as the problem of executing prison sentences and other penalties, particularly the link between the length of stay in a penal institution and the social rehabilitation of juvenile delinquents. Such a study was completed in 1977 in the port and border town of Flensburg. The seminar publishes the "Kriminologische Forschungen" series. K. Hellmer has published the following monographs: *Der Gewohn-*

heitsverbrecher und die Eicherrungsverwahrung 1934–1945 (1961) and *Kriminalitätsatlas der BRD und Westberlins* (1972).

The Münster University Criminology Department (Fakultät für Kriminologie) was established in 1971. At present it is concerned mainly with the impact of the mass media on criminality and the problem of dangerous recidivists. H. J. Schneider has published a well-received monograph: "Viktimologie: Wissenschaft vom Verbrechensopfer" (1975).

The Münster University Penal Sciences Institute (Institut für Kriminalwissenschaft) was founded by P. Peters in 1955. In addition to penal law, substantive, procedural and executory law, the institute also carries out research on criminological problems, especially methods of combating white-collar crime.

The Penal Sciences Institute of the Cologne University (Kriminalwissenschaftliches Institut) was founded in 1923 by G. Bohn. Its scope of interest extends to penal, substantive, procedural, and executory law as well as to criminology.

Mainz University carries out regular criminological studies on such subjects as: revalidating the Glueck forecast table for research carried out in Germany; cheating in gambling; murders of taxi drivers; real estate agents' offenses; waiters' offenses; white-collar offenses; offenses connected with orders for the West German army (Bundeswehr).

The Criminological Seminar of Bonn University (Kriminologisches Seminar) was founded in 1943 by H. von Weber. It carries out criminological research using case study methods. It publishes a periodical, the *Kriminologische Untersuchungen*.

The Penal Law and Criminology Seminar of Hamburg University (Seminar für Strafrecht und Kriminologie) was formed in 1969. An abridged German index lists, under the same address, a Seminar für Strafrecht und Kriminalpolitik formed in 1920. Studies are concerned with forecasting juvenile (14 to 17 years of age) delinquency, the contents of crime films on television and an institutional analysis of the Hamburg prison.

Criminological research is also carried out by the academic centers for sociology and for forensic psychiatry and psychology.

The Biefeld University sociology faculty has completed a study of the various aspects of and conditions for rehabilitation. Studies are underway on delinquency and other deviant behavior of adolescents. Future plans call for a study of the social situation of persons released from prison. Research has centered on such issues as: school as an instrument of social control; police as an instrument of social control; drug addiction as a theoretical and practical problem for social psychology, social medicine, and on the job.

The Social Sciences Research Center (Sozialwissenschaftliches Forschungszentrum) of the Erlangen-Nurenberg University has completed a study of the impact of the family and environmental factors on juvenile delinquency. These studies are part of an elaborate project under the temporary heading: "The impact of family situation on the individual, his links with society and on the next generation." Another study carried out as part of the same project concerns the obstacles to the development of social behavior. Part of it includes the examination of on-the-job behavior of juveniles released from prison.

The Sociology and Social Anthropology Institute (Institut für Soziologie und Soziologische Antropologies) of the Erlanger-Nurenberg University is studying the role of the probation officer in the probation process.

The Sociology Institute (Institut für Soziologie) in Freiburg has completed a study on store thefts in that town.

The Sociology Chair (Lehrstuhl für Soziologie) in the Historical, Social, and Political Department of Regensburg University has carried out a study of the structure and changes of crime in one of the Cologne neighborhoods and another study has been instituted on the homeless in that town.

The Psychological Institute (Psychologisches Institut) was established in 1922 at the Hamburg University. It concentrates on such issues as: personality correlation of perpetrators of various types of crime; the factors leading to self-accusation; migrant worker crime; danger of various crime forms in social perception; psychological theories of crime.

The Sexual Studies Institute (Institut für Sexualforschung) of the Hamburg University carries out studies of sex offenders and researches sexual life in prisons.

The Forensic and Social Psychiatry Institute (Institut für Gerichtliche Psychologie und Psychiatrie) of the Saarbrücken University is involved in a research project entitled "The Psychological-Biological Follow-up Studies of Sex Offenders." It also studies the effectiveness of obligatory education of children with antisocial attitudes, and carries out criminological studies on juvenile sex offenders as well as on the conditions and effects of set-duration punishment of juveniles.

At the Child and Youth Psychiatric Clinic (Klinik für Kinder- und Jugendpsychiatrie) of the Saarbrücken University studies have been carried out on the drug addiction of juveniles and the inborn propensity to crime of male juvenile offenders. Plans call for studying the significance of conflicts resulting from the violation of the self-respect of the handicapped as causes of criminal deviations of juveniles.

The Psychiatric Clinic of the Tübingen University analyzes the possibility of forecasting the behavior of children and juveniles who have committed offenses, studies juvenile killers and carries out research on children—the victims of "indecent" acts.

This review of the general directions which West Germany academic centers follow in criminological studies shows that the "clinical" criminology, dominant in the past and championed mainly by psychiatrists, is increasingly giving way to crime sociology. The share represented by psychology in criminological studies is rather marginal.

The leading nonacademic criminological facilities are the Max Planck Institute and the Federal Crime Office.

The Max Planck Institute of Foreign and International Penal Law in Freiburg was formed in 1938; it represents West Germany's sole research facility on comparative penal law and criminology. The Criminological Research Unit (Forschungsgruppe Kriminologie), headed by the renowned criminologist Günther Kaiser, was formed in 1970. It contains the largest German-language collection of criminological literature, covering some 20,000 volumes and some 160 periodicals. This unit concerns itself with the issue of criminality and crime control (Gesamtspektrum von Verbrechen und Verbrechenskontrolle[26]). Unit projects have been devoted to such fields as crime statistics, social forms of deviant behavior control, diversion methods of resolving penal cases, decriminalization and penitentiaristics. Projects are planned on police activities, prosecution activities, treatment of offenders, crime structure, the dark number of crimes, road traffic offenses, and rapes. Projects were completed in 1978 on the effectiveness of psychotherapy of young offenders before trial, the prosecution of economic crimes in West Germany and the place of fines in the system of penal measures. Other research topics have included "Homicide and its Prosecution" and "Prosecutors in the Process of Social Control."

Institute publications comprise the series on penal law (Zeitschrift für die gesamte Strafrechtswissenschaft), comparative studies of penal law (Rechtsvergleichende Untersuchungen zur gesamten Strafrechtswissenschaft), translations of the texts of foreign penal codes (Übersetzungen ausserdeutscher Strafgesetzbücher), current penal law regulations in other countries (Ausländisches Strafrecht der Gegenwart) and *Kriminologisches Journal*.

The Federal Crime Office (Bundeskriminalamt), in Wiesbaden, in its Criminalistics Institute (Kriminalistischen Institut des Bundeskriminalamt) retains a research team comprising lawyers, criminologists, criminalistics experts, a psychologist, and economic experts. The team is charged with critical studies of the theory and practice of combating crime; it also arranges for a comprehensive exchange of information between the representatives of research disciplines significant for the police and the practice of criminal police. One of the projects was, "Police and Juvenile Delinquency." The findings of the numerous criminological projects find practical application by the police.[27]

Criminological research is also carried out in the Federal Republic of Germany by certain other state institutions. These include some of the Land (state) ministries of domestic affairs and of justice, police departments in the larger cities and the police schools of Baden-Württemberg and Schleswig-

Holstein, the Crime Research Office (Forschungen Kriminalamt) in Hesse, the Federal Statistical Office (Federalamt für Statistik) in Wiesbaden, the German Youth Institute (Deutsche Jugend Institut) in Munich (criminological research concerning juveniles) and the Academy of Basic Criminological Research (Akademie für Grundsätzlichen Forschungen der Kriminologie) in Kassel which concerns itself with the etiology and prevention of juvenile delinquency and of robberies.

The Lower Saxony Ministry of Justice has organized a special working group for criminological studies (Planung und Forschung). Its objective is to draft programs of crime prevention, to work out the modalities of cooperation between the criminal justice bodies and the special services in training unemployed young people, studying the systems of punishment execution, and the like.[28]

The Federal Republic of Germany has the following main criminological organizations and societies:

The German Criminological Society (Deutsche Kriminologische Gesselschaft) in Frankfurt am Main. Established in 1960, it is concerned with the empirical—from the point of view of the natural and social sciences—study of criminality, its prevention and suppression. It publishes its own periodical, *Kriminologische Schriftenreihe.* The society carried out a survey in which it asked the readers of *Kriminalistik* to answer the query (the respondent listed only his or her occupation, sex and age) as to what punishment should be meted out to an offender who committed the following crime: killing a person for profit, committing an offense against morals with a minor, robbing a bank and killing the cashier, mugging a man and taking his briefcase, attacking a girl and raping her, breaking into a house and stealing a radio, while intoxicated causing a serious road accident with injury and running away from the scene, stealing a car and crashing it, setting fire to his neighbor's farm. (The whole list consisted of twenty-five items.)

The German Association for Juvenile Justice and Court Assistance (Deutsche Vereinigung für Jugendgerichte und Gerichtshilfe), founded in 1927 in Hamburg and reconstituted in 1952, concerns itself exclusively with juvenile delinquency issues.

Criminal Biology Society (Kriminalbiologische Gesellschaft) is an international organization, most active, however, in West Germany and Austria, formed for the purpose of studying the endogenous factors in criminal behavior. It publishes the periodical *Monatsschrift für Kriminalpsychologie.*

Since 1965 the Federal Republic of Germany has instituted a federal-level program of crime prevention. The objective of this program is to increase general social awareness of the crime menace. In this connection police bodies have undertaken the publication of some 20–25 million leaflets monthly, providing a statistical illustration of crime intensity and advice on possible preventive actions, and initiating media campaigns, such as "The Criminal Police Advises."

Since 1970 there have also been specific actions aimed at emphasizing a single selected prevention-connected topic concerning a given type of crime, such as thefts and house burglaries, drug abuse, and economic crimes.

The Federal Republic of Germany has 100 consulting offices which provide free advice to citizens concerning the available technical means for protecting property and information on building security requirements (for architects).

Youth counselors (Jugendbeamte) retain permanent contacts with young people. Their objective is to defuse problems before they reach the conflict stage. The German Federation of Child Protection (Deutscher Kinder-schutzbund) and the Youth Protection Association (Aktion Jugendschutz) have as their objective the protection of young people from crime.

Specially trained police personnel, the so-called contact persons (Kon-taktbereichsbeamte) are charged with regular contacts with the general population.

The "Weisser Ring," an association of private individuals, aims at supporting the efforts of state authorities in the field of crime prevention.

Based on the Scandinavian model, the Federal Republic of Germany has also established a Crime Prevention Council with the participation of the police, criminal justice bodies, youth services, state institutions and private individuals.[29]

Institutions active in the field of criminology also include the General Criminology Society (Gesellschaft für die gesamte Kriminologie), the Crime Prevention Society (Gesellschaft für vorbeugende Verbrechens-bekämp-fung), the German Society for Studying Sexual Problems (Deutsche Gesellschaft für Sexualforschung), the German Forensic and Social Med-icine Society (Deutsche Gesellschaft für Gerichtliche und Soziale Medizin).

Criminological studies also play a significant role in the Federal Republic of Germany in shaping the rules of penal legislation. One should also note here the application of foreign experiences in this field, especially the Swedish.[30]

Swedish crime policy has had a significant impact on the reform of penal law in the Federal Republic of Germany, since its inception in 1950 up to the new final draft of the penal code in 1975 and the penal execution code in 1976. One could not find a better example to illustrate the value of comparing law for the reform of penal law. The Parliament, the Ministry of Justice, and the West German theoreticians of penal law have studied the Swedish experience, in which a breakthrough was achieved in 1934 by Karl Schlyter, then Minister of Justice, with his famous slogan, "Depopulate prisons."

The main credit for promoting Swedish legal ideas in the Federal Republic of Germany must go to Gerhard Simson who translated and provided explanatory notes to the Swedish Penal Procedure Code of 1948 and the Penal Code of 1962, thus popularizing various articles and papers on Swedish crime policy.

In viewing imprisonment as "ultimo ratio," the German reformer went a step further even than his Swedish colleagues, establishing the principle of priority of fines in offenses punishable with imprisonment of up to six months, including intoxicated drivers. In view of this West Germany had an even sharper drop than Sweden in the number of short-term prison sentences. The total number of prisoners in the Federal Republic of Germany since introduction in 1969 of the preference for fines dropped from 46,000 to 37,000, even though the ovreall number of convictions was up 12 percent, from 618,000 to 700,000.

The 1976 Penal Execution Law in the Federal Republic of Germany in the section concerning individual prevention was patterned after the Swedish 1974 code. Just as the Swedish law required the adaptation of prisoners to life in society, the avoidance of the harmful effects of serving the sentence, and sufficiently early preparation for release, so does the West German law list as the objective of the penalty the preparation of prisoners for a socially responsible life free of crime, requires the prisoner to balance life in prison against his general life conditions and to avoid the harmful effects of imprisonment. The accent is on preparing for the release and assistance in the process of rejoining society. Cooperation between the prison and the employment office and social assistance bodies is achieved through informal contacts. Even though this was one of the main points of the reform, so far the pay for prison labor has not been brought up to par with the pay of free labor; at the end of 1980 this pay equaled 5 percent of the pay of a free laborer. A gradual increase in this pay is planned.

One should emphasize that imprisonment is applied to only 8 to 10 percent of convicts and monetary fines to 85 percent. Sentences are suspended for 65 percent of those convicted to prison terms. Decriminalization will continue to advance, though one should also keep in mind the requirements of general crime prevention and public security.

A number of periodicals have already been mentioned in connection with the various research organizations. Other publications include: *Monatschrift für Kriminologie und Strafrechtsreform*, *Kriminologisches Journal*, *Archiv für Kriminologie*, *Kriminalistik*. The findings of criminological studies are also publihsed in such police periodicals as *Polizei* and *Die Neue Polizei*.

Italy is a country with exceptionally rich criminological traditions dating back to the mid-eighteenth century.[31] It was the home of Cesare Beccaria, the father of the classical school of criminology, whose views exerted a major

impact on the theory and practice of justice administration throughout
Europe. A hundred years later Italy was again the site of another criminological direction—the positivist school started by Cesare Lombroso.
The impact of this school on criminological theories and on the directions
and methods of criminological research is felt to the present day, even though
the fundamental theses advanced by Lombroso have been disproved by contemporary criminology.

The anthropological theory of criminality has for many years been a
major influence on the development of Italian criminology. While world
criminology has long since shifted to the sociological school, Italian
criminology could not shake off anthropological-biological ideas, bringing a
stagnation to the discipline. By now Italian criminology has overcome this,
although the impact of biological theories is still much in evidence in that
country.[32]

The Institute of Anthropological Criminology (Istituto di Antropologia
Criminale) of Genoa University, formed in 1966, carries out its activities
largely from this point of view. It conducts research and training in criminal
anthropology, clinical criminology, forensic medicine, psychology, psychoanalysis, and psychiatry. Projects cover such topics as drug abuse, deviant
behavior, shoplifting, and recidivism. The institute publishes monographs in
the series "Aspetti criminologici e medico-legali della pericolosita."

Interesting activities are being conducted by the International Criminological Center for Advice to Interested Countries and the Training of Experts
in the Prevention and Treatment of Antisocial Behavior, established in 1971.
The center is devoted to the development of the most effective therapeutical
and preventive methods and to training specialist practitioners of criminology, penology, psychology, and pedagogy. The center publishes its findings
in the form of monographs.

In addition to the two aforementioned institutions, criminological studies
and research are also carried out by a number of academic and independent
institutions, mostly with a sociological profile. These include the National
Center for Social Prevention and Defense (Centro Nazionale di Prevenzione
e Difesa Sociale), established at Milan in 1948. It carries out research and
publishes monographs, largely on topics related to criminal justice administration reforms.

The Penitentiary Studies Center (Centro Studi Penitenziari) was established at Rome in 1936. Its research findings have been published since
1950 in the periodical *Rassegna di Studi Penitenziari*. In the years 1930–
1943 there was a penitentiary periodical, *Rivista di Diritto Penitenziario*,
while one of the earliest serious penitentiary periodicals was *Rivista di
Discipline Carcerari.*[33]

The School of Penal Law and Criminology (Scuola di Spezializzazione in

Diritto Penale e Criminologia) was formed in 1911 as part of the Law Department of the University of Rome. It concentrates on training.

The Penal Law Institute (Istituto di Diritto Penale) is one of the oldest facilities, dating to 1870, operating as part of the University of Rome. It is concerned with research and training in the field of criminology; its studies are devoted to such topics as recidivism, the cultural and social factors in deviant and criminal behavior, and compensation for crime victims.

The International Center of Sociological, Penal, and Penitentiary Studies (Centro Internazionale di Ricerche e Studi Sociologici, Penali e Penitenziari) was founded in Messina on April 2, 1977. Among its founders were the University of Messina, the Administration of the Messina Province, the Town Council, the Chamber of Commerce, and the Tourist Office of the Province. By a presidential decree of December 5, 1978, the center became a legal entity. Its fundamental purpose is to study, using various social disciplines, the different forms of criminality which threaten civil and democratic liberties and present a menace to the stability of various state institutions. The sociological, penal, and penitentiary aspects are examined to obtain a complete picture of criminality.

By statute the center is obliged to contribute to the professional training of national and international specialists in these diverse disciplines. The Messina Center has been growing at a fast pace. It already hosted four international seminars devoted to violence in penal institutions, psychopathy, juvenile vandalism, and the criminogenic aspects of culture. It also has a number of valuable publications to its credit.[34] Such successes were largely possible through the efforts of Gaetano Livrea, Giacomo Barletta, Domenico Cucchiara, and Aldo Grassi.

The National Institute for the Scientific Study of Prisoners (Istituto Nazionale Osservazione Scientifica del Detenuto) was formed in 1954 at Rome; it concentrates on research on this subject.

The Regional Center for Preventing Criminality (Centro Regionale di Profilassi della Criminalità) was established in 1965 at Cagliari (Sardinia). The center carries out psychopharmacological studies, particularly of aggression. It publishes the periodical *Rivista Sarda di Criminologia*.

The Social Assistants Training Center (Centro di Educazione Professionale per Assistenti Sociali) was established in Rome in 1946, with collegiate status. It should be explained that the institution of social assistants is connected with the Italian system of juvenile reeducation, carried out by an elaborate network of reeducation centers. Every appellate court has its own center, run by a director, with observation facilities, methodological-psycho-pedagogical sections, educational sections, semi-open centers, reformatory and penal facilities, special schools, workshops, and social court services. The latter are staffed by professionally trained social assistants, who supervise the juveniles on liberty, carry out milieu checks, keep in contact with the family environment, and carry out other duties, as specified by the courts.[35] The Rome center trains such assistants and publishes its own periodical, *Centro Sociale*, and the *International Review of Community Development*.

The Italian Criminological Society (Societa Italiana di Criminologia) was established in 1957, with headquarters at Rome. It carries out empirical research and publishes the periodical *Rassegna di Criminologia*.

Austria[36] is, next to Italy, one of the foremost countries to treat criminology as a subject of academic interest.[37] As early as 1912 the Law Department of Graz University formed the Institute of Criminological Disciplines (Kriminologisches Universitätsinstitut), led by Hans Gross. After World War II its name was changed to the Criminology Institute (Universitätsinstitut für Kriminologie der Universität Graz). Its curriculum covers penal law, criminal psychology, anthropology, criminology, criminalistics, and crime statistics.

The characteristic feature of Austrian criminology is its close bond with criminalistics. According to certain views criminology comprises such disciplines as criminalistics, substantive and adjective penal law, criminal policy, penology and penitentiaristics—in other words, the totality of penal law disciplines. The idea of such a broad interpretation of criminology was first advanced in the early days of the twentieth century. Gross, in the foreword to the fourth edition (1904) of his *Handbook for an Examining Magistrate*, presented such a wide scope of the term *criminology*. This view exerted a certain undesirable effect on later criminological theories. The trend pioneered by Gross to bring together all the specialized disciplines, including investigation, into a closed system of criminology can still be found in the writings of certain contemporary authors. For instance, Ernst Seelig adopts a system of criminology with a very elaborate scope of interest.[38]

The Penal Law and Criminology Institute of the University of Vienna (Institut für Strafrecht und Kriminologie) was organized in 1923. Since 1946 the institute has been publishing the periodical *Kriminologische Abhandlungen Neue Folge*. Many valuable works have been published by Roland Grassberger, including: *Die Brandlegungskriminalität* (1928), *Gewerbs und Berufsverbrechertum in dem Vereinigten Staaten* (1932), and *Die Psychologie des Strafvergahrens* (1950).

The Austrian Penal Law and Criminology Society (Oesterreichische Gesellschaft für Strafrecht und Kriminologie) was established in 1952. It represents a forum for discussion between theoreticians and practitioners.

The beginnings of criminology in The Netherlands, going to the closing years of the nineteeth century, are closely linked to the development of sociology. It is accepted by historians of the subject that S. R. Steinmetz, the first professor of sociology, also initiated criminological studies in the Netherlands.[39] The history of criminology is also linked with the name of another prominent sociologist, William A. Bonger, the author of many pioneering works, foremost being *Criminality and Economic Conditions* (1916), *Religion and Crime* (1913), and *Race and Crime* (1934).[40]

In the Netherlands there are three academic criminological institutes and one facility of the Ministry of Justice.

The Criminology Institute of the University of Utrecht (Criminologisch Instituut, Universiteit van Utrecht), established in 1934, is linked with the Law Department and works hand in hand with the Psychiatric Observation Clinic organized in 1949 by the Ministry of Justice on the initiative of P. H. Baan, professor of forensic psychiatry. The observations encompassing some two-thirds of offense suspects and about half of all the prisoners, are carried out in part for the purpose of establishing the chance for parole.

The Criminology Institute of the University of Leiden (Criminologisch Instituut Universiteit van Leiden) was formed in 1936 as the Institute of Penal Law and Criminology. It is financed mainly by the Modderman Foundation and by the university. Its research concerns problems of certain types of sex offenses (such as exhibitionism), suicide, the impact of criminological research on shaping court legislation and practice, and fraud. The institute publishes *Abstracts on Criminology and Penology* and *Abstracts on Police Science.*

The Criminology Institute of the University of Groningen (Criminologisch Instituut van de Rijksuniversiteit de Groningen), formed in 1952, is also financed by private foundations. Its studies encompass numerous problems connected with individual prognosis, the social and psychological effects of imprisonment, alcoholism, parole, road traffic offenses, and juvenile delinquency.

Criminology is also a subject offered at the University of Amsterdam in the Law and Social-Political Sciences Departments and also at the Municipal University in Amsterdam.

The Scientific Research and Documentation Center of the Ministry of Justice is administered by the directors of four ministry departments: prisons, rehabilitation, youth protection, and legal. Its objective is to keep close contact between the ministry and the academic centers, particularly on penal law and criminology. The center publishes the bi-monthly *Documentatieblad* and organizes annual national conferences for studying exceptionally important problems.

The Central Advisory Council (Centrale Raad van Advies) was formed in the Ministry of Justice in 1953. It comprises forty members: judges, prosecutors, professors of criminology, penal law, forensic psychiatry, psychology, and other specialists connected with criminal justice. The council conducts its activities through three sections: Prison Administration and Treatment of Offenders, Probation, and Post-penitentiary Care. The council mainly takes up projects ordered by the Minister of Justice, though it can also initiate action where it deems it necessary.

The most significant periodical in the Netherlands concerned with this field is the more-than-seventy-year-old *Tijdschrift voor Strafrecht*, which publishes mainly articles on penal law. Criminological issues are taken up principally in the bimonthly *Nederlands Tijdschrift voor Criminologie*.

In Belgium most criminological research and training in the field is concentrated in university centers.[41] These include:

The Sociology of Law and Justice Center, Sociology Institute of Brussels Free University (Centre de Sociologie du Droit et de la Justice, Institut de Sociologie de l'Université Libre de Bruxelles), established in 1964.

School of Criminology, University of Liège (Ecole de Criminologie, Université de Liège), established in 1947.

"Léon Cornil" School of Criminological Disciplines (Ecole de Science Criminologique "Léon Cornil") established in Brussels in 1935.

School of Criminology (School voor Criminologie) established in Ghent in 1938.

Criminology Research Unit of the University of Louvain (Unité de Recherches en Criminologie de l'Ecole de Criminologie, Université de Louvain) established in 1967, thirty-nine years after the foundation of the school of criminology. It publishes the periodical *Cahiers de Criminologie et de Pathologie Sociale*.

The René Marq Study Center (Centre d'Etude René Marq) was organized in 1938 by a group of professors from the University of Brussels Law Department. Various sections of the center are devoted to the advancement of various criminological disciplines.

Academic centers are also responsible for significant contributions to general criminology, such as E. de Greef, *Introduction à la criminologie* (1946); J. Constant, *Eléments de criminologie* (1949); E. Yamarellos and Georges Kellens, *Le crime et la criminologie* (1970); to clinical criminology: C. Debuyst et al.: *La criminologie clinique—Orientations actuelles* (1968); to sociology: P. Legros and J. Estenne, *Sociologie du droit et de la justice: Actes du colloque international de Bruxelles* (1969). The periodical *Revue de l'Institut de Sociologie* publishes numerous articles treating various topics connected with social pathology.

The significance of the juvenile delinquency issue has been formally recognized through the formation in 1957 of a special research facility, the Center for Juvenile Delinquency Studies (Centre d'Etude de la Delinquance Juvenile).[42] This facility brings together specialists in sociology, psychology, education, and law. It works closely with the Ministry of Justice and the academic centers. In addition to studying the patterns and changes in juvenile delinquency, the activities of youth supervisory committees, and preventive methods, the center drafts the major legislation concerning juveniles and organizes training courses for judges, probation officers, physicians, teachers, social workers, and others. The statute of April 8, 1965, opened new prospects for the center. Its highly regarded publications concern such issues as juvenile delinquency in Belgium between 1939 and 1957, the sociocultural determinants of juvenile delinquency, and spare time and the role of the school in shaping the moral attitudes of children.[43]

The center has published many valuable monographs, the most notable being Ch. Vassert's study of the "provos" (a neologism coined from the word "provocateur" the word is used to describe rebellious youths). It also offers interesting publications presenting the fruits of scientific conferences.[44] Many publications concern juvenile delinquency directly; these are as a rule presentations of research findings by the center.[45]

The Criminological Center of Studies on Crimes against Humanity (Studiecentrum voor Kriminologie en Gerechtelijke Geneeskinde) at Sint Niklass Waas is financed privately. Its scope of interest covers issues of genocide, war crimes, crimes against humanity and against peace. In 1970 the center published monographs on electroencephalographic examinations of criminals, on the Klinefelter syndrome, and on other chromosomal anomalies.

The Belgian Criminological Society (Société Belge de Criminologie) is a meeting ground for discussing the various currents in Belgian criminology.[46]

In recent years criminological research on the treatment of convicts was intensified in Belgium; such studies have been organized by the so-called university attachés, nominated by the Minister of Justice upon the recommendation of university authorities. In a selected penitentiary the study is conducted as a rule by a team comprising four specialists: a sociologist, a psychologist, a psychiatrist, and a criminologist.

The interests of Belgian criminologists also extend to changes in crime patterns, to the appearance of new forms of crime, such as thefts in the large department stores, the growing number of hold-ups, and to the conditions conducive to these types of crime. The increase in vagrancy also led to a study of this social phenomenon.[47]

Georges Kellens, a leading exponent of Belgian criminology, has devoted two publications to economic crimes.[48] A bibliography of writings by Belgian authors is contained in E. Cosyns-Verhagen, *Criminologie*, Brussels, 1974.

The *Revue de Droit Pénal et de Criminologie*, published under the auspices of the Ministry of Justice, serves to voice the views of the Union Belge et Luxembourgeoise de Droit Pénal, established in 1907 and directed by A. Prins (1907–1920), J. Servais (1920–1934), Léon Cornil (1934–1950), Jules Simon (1950–1952) and P. E. Trousse (1975–1978). Much credit for the renown of this publication must go also to Raymond de Ryckere, Henri Jaspar, Simon Sasserath, Séverin-Carlos Versele, Jules Gillard, and Jules Simon.

Belgium is well known for its traditions in penitentiary anthropology. In 1907 L. Vervaeck organized a penitentiary anthropology workshop. During the 1960s the central penitentiary selection facility was formed at Saint-Gilles; it is devoted to examining difficult cases which cause problems in diagnosis and selection.

The oldest research facility in Japan is the Training Institute for Correctional Personnel, established in 1890. The institute is concerned mainly with offering courses on criminology, sociology, psychology, penology, administrative law, administration of correctional institutions, and the history of these institutions. It publishes the *Bulletin of Correctional Research.*

Still, the beginnings of Japanese criminology are usually traced back to no earlier than 1913, the year in which the Japanese Association of Criminology came into being as part of the Criminal Psychology Department, University of Tokyo. The association conducts research on psychology, sociology, psychiatry, penal laws, and forensic medicine. Since 1935 the association has been publishing the *Acta Criminologicae et Medicine Legalis Japonica.*

At present the most important role in designing and executing criminological research is played by the Research and Training Institute of the Ministry of Justice, established in 1958. It has a Criminological Research Department, which concentrates its attention on such topics as the patterns and changes in crime, juvenile delinquency, recidivism, parole, readaptation processes of offenders released from prison, and the like. It publishes the *Bulletin of the Criminological Research Department.* Statistical data on crime have been published since 1960 in the form of special reports (since 1963 in an abridged form in English).

The University of Tokyo also has a Research Institute of Forensic Medicine and an Electroencephalographic Research Institute. The research of Japanese scientists centers on the following issues:

differences between homozygous and heterozygous twins;

the criminal career of habitual offenders, analyzed by a method developed in 1951 by Shufu Yoshimasu, based on comparing three indicators: the age of committing the first offense, the types of offenses committed and the time elapsed between the dates of given offenses;

the characteristics of the given crime groups: sexual crimes, offenses by women and girls, habitual fraud and other;

juvenile delinquency. This was described in an interesting study by Ishikawa conducted in 1966 concerning the lack of symmetry in the mental and physical development of adolescents and the immaturity of personality leading to primitive and impulsive reactions and to a lack of self-control;

criminality of the mentally ill;

drug addiction and crime;

biological mechanisms contributing to offensive activities.[49]

Studies in psychology, sociology, teaching, and forensic psychiatry are also carried out by the Japanese Association of Criminal Psychology, established in 1963. The results of its research are published in the *Japanese Journal of Criminal Psychology*.

The foundations for criminology in Switzerland were laid by the professors of penal law who exhibited a criminological manner of analysis and who in effect provided the impulses for criminological studies, namely Carl Stoos, father of the Swiss penal code, Ernst Hafter, commentator and originator of crime policy, disciple of Franz von Liszt, and Hans Schultz, professor of penal law at the University of Bern. The lawyers, penitentiary experts, psychologists, and representatives of associated disciplines interested in criminology rely on foreign achievements in this field. Despite the frequent resort to foreign publications, especially West German and American, and the importance attached to French criminology, Switzerland has to seek its own solutions which would take into account its own experiences in the field of penal law, the differences in the political, social and economic institutions, the differences in legislation (twenty-six control statutes on penal procedure) and the differences in crime statistics.

The opinions expressed at the tenth Association Internationale de Droit Pénal (AIDP) Congress on the comparative method in criminology support the reservations voiced in Switzerland concerning even a partial reception of foreign criminology.

University research is not carried out in a coordinated manner; as a rule it is conducted by the lecturers in penal law and their postgraduate students. Since 1971 there has been regular publication of the *Der Schweizerische Strafvollzug* (Swiss Penitentiary Law) series, edited by Stratenwerth. The *Schweizerische Zeitschrift für Strafrecht—Revue Penale Suisse*, founded by Carl Stoos, has been published regularly since 1888. This periodical publishes articles on substantive and procedural penal law, criminology, and penitentiaristics.

The financial outlays on criminological research are insufficient. Various federal administration agencies carry out their own criminological research or sponsor private projects.[50]

The following Swiss organizations specialize in criminological topics.

Swiss Criminological Association (Schweizerische Gesellschaft für Kriminologie) was founded on June 6, 1953. Its objectives are set out in the statute:

> The Association aims at studying the causes as well as the biological, psychological and social manifestations of criminality for the purpose of developing legislation and institutions for prevention and the therapy of offenders. It develops activities without preference for any set scientific doctrine and guarantees the complete scientific autonomy of its members. It works closely with the organizations and associations which have similar objectives.

One could claim that criminology is the science concerned with the phenomenon of criminality. All the same, Swiss scientists emphasize the description of the forms of crime and the personality of the offender, while others accent criminal justice in penal cases.[51]

The Swiss Criminalistic Society (Schweizerische Kriminalistische Gesellschaft), established in 1942 following the adoption of the Swiss Penal Code, represents a broad range both as to its membership and as to the variety of topics taken up at the annual conferences and training sessions. However, it does not carry out criminological research, and its reports are concerned mainly with penal law subjects, rarely with criminology.

The Swiss Union for Penal Affairs, Penitentiaries and Supervision (Der Schweizerische Verein für Straf-Gefängeniswesen und Schuzaufsicht) has a range of interests covering problems of serving out sentences and alternative measures and discussion of these issues in their practical aspects. It organizes annual meetings and professional conferences where papers are presented. The papers and discussions are then published in "Der Strafvollzug in der Schweiz" quarterly.

Swiss Working Group on Criminology (Schweizerischen Arbeitsgruppe für Kriminologie), formed in 1972 as a private organization, brings together specialists on penal law, psychiatry, psychology, and sentence execution. It has sponsored a number of events devoted exclusively to criminological issues. Its *Kriminologische Bulletin*, published biannually, publishes papers presented at seminars and information on activities in the field of criminology in Switzerland and in other countries. Since 1974 the Swiss Working Group organized international symposia and seminars on delinquency and school, new perspectives in criminology, criminological problems of the police, possibilities of criminological research in Switzerland, alternatives to short prison sentences, connections between minimal brain dysfunction and delinquency, the functioning of the penal system, stigmatization by the penal process and confinement in prison, male and female delinquency, and mentally abnormal and drug-addicted offenders. The subject of the seminar in 1983 will be the battered child.

There are other Swiss facilities concerned with criminological issues. Since the early 1970s studies have been conducted in Switzerland concerning penal sanctions, particularly imprisonment. Execution of prison sentences or alternative measures is founded in a system of multiple norms, the variety of which presents a serious obstacle to research. Study findings have not so far exerted any measurable effect on the revision of penal law. This leads to justifiable demands that criminological research should not be carried out in a sociopolitical vacuum, considering that criminology is a social science with implication for changes in legislation, sentencing, sentence execution, and crime prevention. One must treat as outdated the views of certain authors counterposing the humanitarian character of penal law to natural methods of criminology.

In addition to these institutions, criminological issues are also handled by the Criminological Institute of the University of Zurich (Kriminologisches Institut der Universität Zurich), formed in 1958. The institute has carried out numerous projects concerned with offenses specific to the era of prosperity: victimology, car thefts, road accidents caused by intoxicated drivers, economic crimes, and the like.

The socially sponsored Criminological Action Committee (Comité d'Action Criminologique) publishes the periodical *Revue Internationale de Criminologie et de Police Technique* which is prominent in the development of criminological theory and the promotion of empirical study findings. C. Moretti is the editor-in-chief.

The University of Lausanne concerns itself both with criminalistics and with criminology. As early as 1902 R. Reiss (1875–1929) organized the Criminalistics Institute (Institut de Police Scientifique) which by 1909 was granted academic status. In 1959 it extended the scope of its activities to include criminological issues. Its current designation is the Criminalistics and Criminology Institute (Institut de Police Scientifique et de Criminologie).

The Forensic Medicine Institute of the University of Geneva (Institut de Médecine Légale de l'Université de Genève) was formed in 1961. Next to the analysis of problems linked to forensic medicine, toxicology, serology, and pathology, it also carries out research in criminology and penitentiaristics; it has handled such problems as the image of the prisoner to the prison staff and the role of closed facilities in shaping the social attitudes of juvenile delinquents.

The Higher School of Economic and Social Sciences at St. Gall in 1971 organized a Study Group on Penitentiary Reform (Groupement de Travail pour le Réforme Pénitentiare à l'Ecole des Hautes Etudes Economiques et Sociales de St. Gall). Their study projects are concerned mainly with models for rehabilitating offenders through work, education, and recreation in penal institutions.

The most prominent center of criminological research in Australia is the Australian Institute of Criminology, established in 1971 at Canberra. Its prime objective is to carry out criminological studies, to promote the findings of such studies and to organize seminars and training courses.

The Research Division formed in 1974 has carried out studies concerning penal policy, supervision of persons released on probation, life imprisonment, and bringing uniformity to crime statistics. Some of the projects taken up in the years 1972–1975 concerned issues of current interest for given states: juvenile delinquency in Victoria and South Australia, the effectiveness of rehabilitating girls in closed reformatory centers as well as the history of prisons in western Australia, and the implementation of crime prevention programs in Victoria.

The Training Division attempts to link theory and practice in criminal justice and to elevate the level of criminological training. Between 1973 and 1975 the institute organized fourteen training sessions, covering a broad spectrum of topics from crime prevention to the participation of women in criminal justice administration. Much attention was devoted to the economic and social consequences of crime and the problems of victimology.

In 1975 the institute published the first issue of its quarterly newsletter and an information bulletin listing the latest publications and studies. It also published a monographic series of occasional papers on selected criminological issues. Annual reports are published.

Coordination of criminological research and disbursement of special funds is achieved through the Criminology Research Council, which is also under institute administration.[52]

The University of Melbourne organized a Criminology Department in 1951. Its research concentrates on juvenile delinquency, road traffic accidents, and measuring crime.

The Sydney University Law School has had an Institute of Criminology since 1965. The institute is charged with issues of penal law and forensic psychiatry; it has published a number of seminar reports, including: "Drug Abuse" (1968), "Sexual Offences against Females," (1969), and "Social Defense" (1971). Institute papers are published in the quarterly *Proceedings of the Institute of Criminology, University of Sydney*.

Selected issues in criminology, psychology, and psychiatry are handled through the Institute of Mental Health Research and Postgraduate Training in Victoria.

The Australian and New Zealand Society of Criminology, established in 1962, devotes much attention to research and the organization of training.

The society publishes *The Australian and New Zealand Journal of Criminology*.

Criminological research findings are often published in the *Australian Police Journal* which has been appearing regularly since 1946.

The most important center of criminological research in Spain is the University of Madrid Institute of Criminology (Instituto de Criminologia de la Universidad Complutense de Madrid) formed in 1964. Its studies are concerned with criminology, criminalistics, penology, penal law, and psychiatry.

Close links with forensic medicine, toxicology, and criminalistics are a feature of the research program followed by the University of Barcelona Institute of Criminology (Instituto de Criminologia), formed in 1955. Projects are devoted to such topics as the criminal vernacular and the social factors determining crime in the cities.

The University of Valencia Institute of Criminology (Instituto de Criminologia), organized in 1968, is concerned with problems in criminology and penal law.

The National Institute of Legal Studies (Instituto Nacional de Estudios Juridicos), established in 1944, has a wider scope; it is the publisher of *Annuario del Derecho Penal y Ciencias Penales*.

Juvenile delinquency issues interest a special research facility of the Ministry of Justice (Consejo Superior de Proteccion de Menores, Ministerio de Justicia), formed in 1969. It publishes the *Revista de la Obra de Proteccion de Menores*.

During the 1970s, Spanish criminology has made great strides, producing numerous monographs and valuable empirical studies, including books containing an evaluation of criminality,[53] theoretical abstracts,[54] books on juvenile delinquency[55] and recidivism.[56]

For more than twenty years criminology in Israel has been actively represented by the Institute of Criminology, of the Hebrew University in Jerusalem. This institute, formed in 1959, is interdisciplinary in its approach to issues. Its staff includes lawyers, psychologists, psychiatrists, forensic medicine specialists, and sociologists. Research covers a variety of issues in victimology, the attitude of offenders to their victims, children as victims, and compensating victims for their losses. Institute publications similarly cover a wide ground; for example, *Law in the Computer Age* (1971), *Drug Abuse in Israel* (1971), *Chromosomal Aberration and Penal Liability Issues* (1968), *Amnesty in Israel* (1963), *Road Accidents in Israel* (1962), *Penal Reform in Israel* (1963), *Crime Causes and Prevention in the Developing Countries*

(1963), *The Role of Education in Preventing Juvenile Delinquency* (1962) and *Crime Statistics in Israel* (1962).

Great contributions to the development of victimology have been made by I. Drapkin. He sponsored the organization of the First International Symposium on Victimology, which was held in Jerusalem on September 2–3, 1973. He is also the author of several books on criminology.

The Institute of Criminology and Criminal Law was organized at the University of Tel Aviv in 1970, which publishes the *Israel Quarterly of Criminology, Criminal Law, and Police Science.* Institute projects cover topics in the field of penitentiaristics (typology of prison populations), psychiatry and criminology (schizophrenia, drug addiction), as well as penal law and criminology (white-collar crime). Much attention is also devoted to the problem of violent crimes.

The beginnings of criminology in Greece date back to the 1920s. The Institute of Criminal Sciences was organized in 1926 at the University of Thessaloniki. The projects undertaken are closely linked to penal law and penology. One of its more interesting projects covered air piracy.

The Criminological Research Center was formed in Athens in 1959. Its studies are concerned with the sociological aspects of crime. It publishes monographs and bibliographies of works on penal sciences in Greece since 1830.

Criminological research in Turkey[57] is concentrated at the Institute of Criminal Law and Criminology, Faculty of Law, at the University of Istanbul. Since 1943 its studies have been concerned with the impact of industrialization and urbanization on criminality, drug addiction, juvenile delinquency, and reform of the penal system.

Crime in the Republic of South Africa has recently attained terrifying proportions. Suffice it to note that in the years 1974–1975 this state of 22 million people was the scene of 8,543 murders, 9,016 homicides and 151,444 cases of bodily injury. In just one year the number of murders in South Africa equaled the number of murders committed in England and Wales in the span of half a century (1900–1949).[58]

This led to intensive criminological efforts, starting in the early 1970s when the National Institute for Crime Prevention and Rehabilitation of Offenders was organized in Cape Town. It carried out research concerning such problems as drug abuse, psychopathy, shoplifting and violence. Since 1973 the institute has been publishing the periodical *Crime, Punishment and Correction.*

The Pretoria-based Institute for Sociological, Demographic, and Criminological Research of the Human Sciences Research Council has completed a number of research projects since its formation in 1969. Study topics included crime statistics in South Africa, etiology of serious crime, and drug abuse among juveniles.

Notes

1. Thorsten Sellin, "United States of America," UNESCO Report 1957, pp. 138–154.

2. Marvin E. Wolfgang, Robert M. Figlio, and Terence P. Thornberry, *Criminology Index, Research and Theory in Criminology in the United States, 1945–1972* (New York: Elsevier Scientific Publishing Co., 1975); Gerhard O. W. Mueller, *Crime, Law and the Scholars* (Seattle: University of Washington Press, 1969); Walter C. Reckless, *American Criminology: New Directions* (New York: Appleton-Century-Crofts, 1973).

3. U.S. Department of Justice, *1980 Directory of Automated Criminal Justice Information Systems* (Washington, 1980). "Introduction," p. 1.

4. Ibid., Foreword by W. P. Holtzman.

5. Document 100B, Ecole de Criminologie (Montréal: Université de Montréal, 1976); Document 120A, Publications de l'Ecole de Criminologie (Montréal: Université de Montréal, 1977). *Acta Criminologica* (Montréal: Les Presses de l'Université de Montréal), vol. 1, 1968.

6. Rapport Annuel du Directeur du Centre 1975–1976. (Montréal: Centre International de Criminologie Comparée, 1976).

7. Publications of the International Centre for Comparative Criminology 1969–1975 (Montreal: University of Montreal, 1975). A more comprehensive list of criminological publications in Canada is contained in the publication prepared in collaboration with the Office of the Attorney General of Canada. See *Criminologie canadienne, bibliographie commentée.*

8. Tadeusz Grygier, *Social Protection Code: A New Model of Criminal Justice.* The American Series on Foreign Penal Codes 22, London 1977, "Preface," pp. xv, xviii.

9. Alice Parizeau and Denis Szabo, *The Canadian Criminal Justice System* (Toronto: Lexington Books, 1977).

10. J. W. Mohr, "Research into Crime and Its Treatment in Canada," in *Crime and Its Treatment in Canada,* ed. William T. McGrath (Toronto: Macmillan Company of Canada, 1976), pp. 565, 566.

11. Jean Pinatel, "France," in UNESCO Report 1957, pp. 88–99.

12. There is some historical significance to the collective book analyzing criminality in France in the seventeenth and eighteenth centuries. See A. Abbiateci, F. Billacois, and Y. Bongert, *Crimes et Criminalité en France, 17ᵉ–18ᵉ siècles.* [Crimes and Criminality in France in the 17th and 18th

centuries] (Paris: Armand Colin, 1971), and M. Levade, et al., *La délinquance des jeunes en France (1825–1968)* [Juvenile delinquency in France (1825–1968)] (Vaucresson: Centre de formation et de recherche de l'Education Surveillée, 1972).

13. *Criminologie en France (Unités d'enseignement, centres de recherches, recherches en cours, centres de documentations)* [Criminology in France: task units, research centers, empirical centers, documentation centers] (Paris: Comité de Coordination des Recherches Criminologiques, Ministère de la Justice, 1978).

14. Jacques Verin, "La criminologie aujourd'hui: l'exemple de la France" [Criminology today: The French example] *Revue Internationale de Criminologie et de Police Technique* 1980, vol. 33, no. 3, pp. 243–250.

15. Jean Pinatel, "A survey of criminological research in France," in *Collected Studies in Criminological Research.* European Committee on Crime Problems, *Current Trends in Criminological Research* 1979, vol. 6, pp. 149–181; See also Jean-Paul Sabatier, *Criminologie en France* [Criminology in France] (Paris: Comité de Coordination des Recherches Criminologiques, 1975).

16. Jean Pinatel, *La Société criminogène* [Criminogenic society] (Paris: Calmann-Levy, 1971); Marie-Therese Mazerol, *Evolution et devenir du criminel* [Evolution and state of the criminal] (Mayenne: Le Marabout, 1977).

17. Roger Benjamin, *Délinquance juvenile et société anomique* [Juvenile Delinquency and the anomic society] (Paris: Editions du Centre National de la Recherche Scientifique, 1971); Michel Henry and Guy Laurent *Les adolescents criminels et la justice* (Vaucresson: Centre de Formation et de Recherche de l'Education Surveillée, 1974). Josse Breuvart, Andrée Algan, and Jacques Selosse, *Que deviennent-ils? Etude comparative des niveaux d'integration social d'une population de mineurs du justice* [Where are they going?—a comparative study of the levels of social integration of a population of legal minors] (Paris: Centre de Formation et de Recherche de l'Education Surveillée, 1974).

18. Two research programs should be mentioned here: L. Deltaglia, *Les Enfants maltraités: Depistage et intervention social* [Mistreated children: Social detection and intervention] (Paris: 1976); and Catherine Ballé, *La Ménace en language de violence* [Danger in the language of violence] (Paris: Editions du Centre National de la Recherche Scientifique 1976).

19. "Réponses à la violence: Les recommandations du Comité d'etudes sur la violence, la criminalité et la délinquance," par Alain Peyrefitte [Response to violence: Report of the presidential commission] *Revue Internationale de Criminologie et de Police Technique* no. 2, pp. 169–178, no. 3, pp. 302–309, 1978.

20. Jean C. Weinberger, Patrick Jakubowicz, and Philippe Robert,

Société et perceptions des comportements déviants incriminés: Déviance et contrôle sociale [Society and perception of criminal deviant behavior: Deviance and social control] (Paris: Service d'Etudes Pénales et Criminologiques, 1977); Philippe Robert and Claude Faugeron *La Justice et son public: Les representations sociales du système penal* [Geneva: Masson, 1978); Philippe Robert and Bernard Laffargue, *L'Image de la justice criminelle dans le société: Le Système pénal vu par ses clients* [The image of criminal justice in society: The penal system as seen by its recipients] (Paris: Service d'Etudes Pénals et Criminologiques, 1977); Philippe Robert, Thibault Lambert, and Claude Faugeron, Image du viol collectif et reconstruction d'objet [Image of collective violence and reconstruction of the object] Genève: Médecine et Hygiène, 1976; Philippe Robert and Thierny Godefroy, Le Coût du crime en France ou l'économie poursuivant le crime [Cost of crime in France or the economics of prosecuting crime] Genève: Médecine et Hygiène, 1978; Pierre Lascoumes, Prévention et contrôle social. Les contradictions du travail Social. /Prevention and Social Controls/. Genève: Médecine et Hygiène, 1977.

21. Herman Mannheim, "United Kingdom," UNESCO 1957 Report, pp. 116–137.

22. Herman Mannheim, "Development of Penal Law and Criminology in Post-War England," *The Journal of Criminal Law, Criminology and Police Science* 1961, no. 6.

23. Nigel Walker, *Crime and Punishment in Britain: The Penal System in Theory, Law and Practice* (Edinburgh: Edinburgh University Press, 1971); John E. Hall Williams, *The English Penal System in Transition* (London: Butterworth, 1970).

24. Bernd R. Wulf, *Kriminelle Karrieren von "Lebenslänglichen": Beitrage zur empirischen Kriminologie* [Criminal careers of "lifers": Examples for empirical criminology], Brochure 5 (Munich: Minerva Publikation, 1979); Hans Göppinger, *Kriminologie* [Criminology], 3rd ed. (Munich: C. H. Beck'sche Verlagsbuchhandlung, 1976) (1st ed. published 1970).

25. Hans Dieter Schwind, *Dunkelforschung in Göttingen 1973/74* [Research on the "dark number" in Goettingen 1973/74] (Wiesbaden: Bundeskriminalamt, 1975).

26. Günther Kaiser, ed., *Empirische Kriminologie: Ein Jahrzehend kriminologischer Forschung am Max-Planck-Institut Freiburg: Bestandaufnahme und Ausblick* [Empirical criminology: A decade of criminological research at the Max Planck Institute, Freiburg: Achievements and Prospects] (Freiburg: Forschungsgruppe Kriminologie, 1980); Günther Kaiser, "Tasks and Activities of the Criminological Research Unit at the Max Planck Institute," *Acta Criminologica Japonica* 1975, vol. 41, pp. 221–227; Edwin H. Johnson, "Comparative and Applied Criminology at the Max

Planck Institute in Freiburg," *Journal of Comparative and Applied Criminal Justice* 1979, pp. 131–141; George Wilson, *Socio-Legal Research in Germany*. A report to the SSRC Committee on Social Science and the Law of the Social Research Council, London, 1980, pp. 9, 25, 74, 91.

27. Edwin Kube, "Kriminalistisch-kriminologische Forschung des BKA" [Criminalistics-Criminological research of the BKA], *Kriminalistik* 1980, no. 11, pp. 471–474.

28. "Kriminologische Forschung bei der Justiz in Niedersachsen [Criminological research with justice in Lower Saxony], *Kriminalistik* 1979, no. 1, p. 28.

29. Gernot Steinhilper, "La prévention en République Fédérale d'Allemagne" [Prevention in the Federal Republic of Germany], *Revue Internationale de Police Criminelle*, February 1979, no. 325, pp. 34–37.

30. Hans H. Jescheck, "Der Einfluss der neueren schwedischen Kriminalpolitik auf die deutsche Strafrechtsreform" [Impact of the new Swedish crime policy on the reform of the German penal law], *Zeitschrift für die gesamte Strafrechtswissenschaft* 1978, fasc. 3, vol. 90, pp. 777–803.

31. Carlo Erra, "Italy," UNESCO Report 1957, pp. 100–106.

32. Renata Treves, *Giustizia e giudici nella societa italiana* [Justice and judges in Italian society] (Bari: Laterza, 1972); Franco Ferracuti, Criminological Research in Italy. Report presented at the seventh Conference of Directors of Criminological Research Institutes. Council of Europe, Strasbourg 1969.

33. Jerzy Sliwowski, "Projekt reformy penitencjarnej we Włoszech" [Draft penitentiary reform in Italy], *Przeglad Penitencjarny* 1966, no. 4, pp. 42–61.

34. *La Violenza nelle sue implicazioni penitenziarie* [Violence in its penitentiary implications] (Messina: Centro Internationale di Richerche e Studi Sociologici, Penali e Penitenziari, 1978); *Lo psicopatico delinquente* [The psychopathic offender] (Milan: Istituto di Scienze Giurdiche, Economiche, Politiche e Sociali Della Università di Messina, 1980).

35. Henryka Cybulska-Veillard, "Przestępczość nieletnich i jej zwalczanie we Włoszech" [Juvenile delinquency and its suppression in Italy], *Nowe Prawo*, 1961, nos. 7–8.

36. Leon Radzinowicz, *In Search of Criminology* (London: Heineman, 1961), p. 19.

37. Roland Grassberger, "Austria," UNESCO Report 1957, pp. 59–68.

38. Ernst Seelig, *Lehrbuch der Kriminologie* [Handbook of criminology], 2nd ed., (Graz: Verlag Jos. A Kienreich, 1951), p. 11.

39. Leon Radzinowicz, *In Search of Criminology*, p. 99.

40. Bonger himself points out that A. Alterino (1858–1916) was the first

professor of criminal anthropology in the Netherlands. See *An Introduction to Criminology* (London: Methuen, 1936), p. 60.

41. Paul Cornil and Rolland Grosemans, "Belgium," UNESCO Report 1957, pp. 69–81.

42. Colette Somerhausen, *Les comités de protection de la jeunesse: Approche sociologique d'une institution nouvelle* [Committees of juvenile protection] (Brussels: Centre d'Etude de la Délinquance Juvénile, 1976).

43. Information brochure of the Centre d'Etude de la Délinquance Juvénile, Brussels.

44. *Evolution d'une nation: la délinquance juvénile* (Brussels: Centre d'Etude de la Délinquance Juvenile, 1959).

45. Josine Junger-Tas, *Jeunesse scolaire et drogues* [School adolescents and drugs] (Brussels: Centre d'Etude de la Délinquance Juvénile, 1972); idem, *Verborgen yengddelinkwentien gerechtelyke selektie, een onderzok in een stadsmilieu* [Legal selection for prosecution of juvenile delinquents, a study in a city milieu] (Brussels: Studiecentrum voor Jeugmisdadigheit, 1976); Marie-Ange Dechêsne, *La Délinquance juvénile en Belgique de 1971 à 1975* [Juvenile delinquency in Belgium 1971–1975] (Brussels: Centre d'Etude de la Délinquance Juvénile, 1978); Jean-Paul Potvin and Charles Tisseyre, *La Police vue par les juenes* [The police as seen by youths] (Brussels: Centre d'Etude de la Délinquance Juvénile, 1978); Groupe de travail, *Fonction sociale du tribunal de la jeunesse* [Social function of the Youth Tribunal] (Brussels: Centre d'Etude de la Délinquance Juvénile, 1979).

46. Georges Kellens, "Criminologie et politique criminelle" [Criminology and crime policy], *Annales Internationales de Criminologie* (special number) 1973, vol. 12, no. 1–2, pp. 129–134.

47. Report on the stay of Professor Herman Beksert in a crime research center in Belgium. *Przeglad Penitencjarny* 1967, no. 2, p. 79.

48. Georges Kellens, *Banqueroute et banqueroutier* [Bankruptcy and the bankrupt] (Brussels: Dessart et Mardaga, 1974); Economic Crime: Sociological and psychological aspects. Twelfth Conference of Directors of Criminological Research Institutes. Council of Europe, Strasbourg 1976.

49. Shufu Yoshimasu and Sadataka Kogi, "Etudes criminologiques et psychiatriques au Japon" [Criminological and psychiatric research in Japan], *Acta Criminologica* (Montreal: Les Presses de l'Université de Montréal, 1969), vol. 2.

50. Stefan Bauhofer, "Kriminologie in der Schweiz—Stand und Entwicklung" [Criminology in Switzerland—state and development], *Schweizerische Zeitschrift für Strafrecht*, 1980, Brochure 2, vol. 97, pp. 145–174.

51. Société Suisse de Criminologie. *Revue Internationale de Criminologie et de Police Technique*, no. 1, 1979, p. 112.

52. The Australian Institute of Criminology, "A New Venture in Crime Prevention," Canberra, 1975; Third Annual Report 1975, Australian Institute of Criminology; Information Bulletin 1976, vol. 3, no. 2. See also David Biles, *Crime and Justice in Australia* (Canberra: The Australian Institute of Criminology, 1977).

53. José A. Garmendia, *Esquema del delito en Espana* [Scheme of criminality in Spain] (Barcelona: Plaza and Janes, 1973); Alfonso Serrano Gomes and José-Luis Fernandez Dopico, *El delincuente espanol: Factores concurrentes (influentes)* [The Spanish delinquent: Concurrent factors (influencing)] (Valencia: Olvido, 1978).

54. Manuel Lopez-Rey, *Criminologia: Criminalidad y planification de la politica criminal* [Criminology: Criminality and planning crime policy] (Madrid: Aguilar, 1978); Manuel Lopez-Rey, *Crime: An analytical appraisal* (London: Routledge and Kegan Paul, 1970).

55. Alfonso Serrano Gomez, *Delincuencia juvenil en Espana: Estudio criminologico* [Juvenile delinquency in Spain: A criminological study] (Madrid: Editorial Doncel, 1970); Ministerio de la Gobernacion, ed., *Delincuencia juvenil: Estudio de su problematica en Espana* [Juvenile delinquency: Study of the problem in Spain], (Madrid, 1972); Agustin Fernandez Albor, *Delincuencia juvenil* [Juvenile delinquency] (Burgos: Publicaciones de la Universidad de Santiago, 1973); Joaquin Rodriguez Suarez, *Los delincuentes jovenes en las instituciones penitenciarias espanolas (1969–1974)* [Juvenile delinquents in Spanish penitentiary institutions] Madrid: Publicaciones del Instituto de Criminologia, Universidad de Madrid, 1976).

56. Amancio Landin Carrasco, *Estudio criminologico sobre la multureincidencia* [Criminological study of habitual recidivism] (Madrid: Ed. Revista de Derecho Privado, 1975).

57. Sulhi Donmezer, "Turkey," UNESCO Report 1957, pp. 112–115.

58. Comparative studies of criminality in South Africa and other countries were carried out by James Midgley of London. Quoted in *Kriminalistik* 1977, no. 9, p. 422.

8 Integration of Criminological Research in the Scandinavian Countries

Not until after World War II did criminology gain ground in the Scandinavian countries; it really came into its own in the 1950s. The turning point came with the establishment of criminological research institutes in Helsinki, Oslo, Copenhagen, and Stockholm. During the 1960s all the Scandinavian countries except Finland established criminology departments in their universities.

As in many European countries, universities in Scandinavia are the traditional champions of criminological research. Research is divided into "fundamental" and "applied," and it is expected that in-depth and follow-up studies should be carried out by academic institutions. Other research is to a greater or lesser degree linked with the system of state controls. In Denmark, Sweden, and Finland the justice ministries have their own research facilities; they operate as part of the legislative or penitentiary service or, as in the Finnish case, they act independently, though their budget is under the Minister of Justice.

Those countries have different academic and legislative traditions, especially in criminology; it would be erroneous to treat Scandinavian penal legislation as a homogenous unit. However, these states work closely together in many fields, both on official and on informal levels. They have permanent joint institutions, particularly the Nordic Council, and in criminology and penal law, the Scandinavian Research Council for Criminology and the Scandinavian Committee on Penal Law.[1]

The Nordic Council was established in 1952 as the forum for cooperation of the parliaments and governments of the Nordic states; it acts as an initiating and advisory body. One field of council interest is the promotion of cooperation and integration in the field of law. In order to bring greater uniformity to various segments of law, a number of uniform legal acts have been issued, mainly in the field of civil and family law. Implementation of some 150 recommendations made by the Nordic Council allows the Scandinavian countries to attain promising results in the field of cooperation in law.

The Scandinavian Research Council for Criminology was formed in 1962, with headquarters in Stockholm. This council carries out research on criminology and social defense issues. Since 1966 it has been publishing *Scandinavian Studies in Criminology*, collections of essays on criminological research as the effect of common efforts by criminologists and specialists in other penal law disciplines from the various Scandinavian countries.[2] Up to 1977 the council had published five such volumes, representing high standards of scholarship. The Council Secretariat is located in the Institute of Criminological Disciplines, University of Copenhagen.

The council was established primarily for the purpose of coordinating research efforts, as well as informing and educating the public. It has at its disposal certain funds available for research and fellowships.

The first joint research project of the Scandinavian countries is older than the council itself. It concerned crimes committed in the Scandinavian countries, where the offenders have accused themselves. These research findings were published in Norway in 1974. Another topic, promoted by M. Patric Törundd of Finland while he served as science secretary of the council, concerned the chance for supplementing the existing crime statistics with new data concerning the losses and economic consequences of crime. This project led to the publication in Finland of a new statistical series: "Statistics on Losses Caused by Crime." A third important topic sponsored by the council concerned systematic analysis of police operations in Norway. The fourth joint Scandinavian project concerned alternatives to imprisonment, particularly the application of economic sanctions in place of prison sentences.[3]

The council cooperates with criminologists of the socialist countries; for example, the organizing of the First Seminar for Criminologists from Socialist and Scandinavian Countries on "Crime and Industrialization" (Helsinki, August 1974); the proceedings were published in English and Russian.

Scandinavian criminology has many features in common to all the countries involved. This is particularly true for the very close bond, particularly in the past decade, between criminology and empirical sociology, and its reliance on that discipline. Criminal psychology has a lesser influence on Scandinavian criminology. Psychologists and psychiatrists from that region consider crime and deviance from the sociological point of view,[4] although they continue the traditional research and studies on the intellectual capacities and emotional disturbances among criminals in prisons and juvenile institutions.

A second distinguishing feature of Scandinavian criminology is the acceptance of crime as a social problem. The objective of criminological research is to contribute to unraveling this problem and, whenever possible, to indicate a solution.

The third feature, stemming from the second, is the close cooperation between the policymakers and practitioners of penal law on the one hand and criminologists on the other. In the Scandinavian countries it was the criminal justice personnel who took up the initiative to foster modern criminology. Currently all four Scandinavian academic institutes of criminology are headed by professors of penal law.[5]

The effect has been the wide-scale inclusion of criminologists in legislative endeavors connected with criminal justice. This is evident from the criminological research carried out by Knut Sveri for the committee on traffic law reform in Sweden. This also gives rise to some additional problems, considering the limited number of criminologists and the necessity of cutting down certain other research efforts, often more significant from the theoretical point of view.

In all the Scandinavian countries criminological researchers enjoy the broad support of the Ministry of Justice, expressed in appreciation of the significance of such research, financial support, and the provision of various administrative facilities.[6]

Another specific feature of Scandinavian criminology is its' frequently being geared more to the proceedings of authorities than to the behavior of criminals.[7]

Even though the full-scale progress of criminological research in Sweden dates back to the 1950s,[8] as early as the 1930s a book by Olof Kinberg devoted to fundamental issues in criminology was published in Stockholm.[9] For half a century Kinberg was very active in criminological research; as a psychiatrist he concentrated primarily on the psychiatric and biopsychological aspects of crime, attaching great etiological significance to them.

Significant contributions to the advancement of Scandinavian criminology have been made by Thorsten Sellin, who later occupied the sociology chair at the University of Pennsylvania.

In 1959 the University of Stockholm sponsored the organization of an Institute of Criminological Disciplines (Kriminalvetenskapliga Institutet) which is concerned with, among other things, victimological studies and research on violent crimes.[10]

The Faculty of Law at Uppsala University conducts also criminological research, such as a study of self-reported crimes by Nyquist and Strahl (1960), Alvar Nelson's studies of pardons (1953), privileged imprisonment (1954) and the study of drinking habits and criminality, written with other authors (1957).[11]

One example of interesting Swedish research is the 1967 book by the renowned psychiatrist G. Jonsson, *Boy Delinquents: Their Parents and Grandparents*. The study of boys showing maladjustment to social life leads to the conclusion that their difficulties were inherited from their parents, who lived through a similar stage in their adolescence. This leads to the hypothesis of "socially inheritable traits," the transmission of one's own problems to the next generation.[12]

The problem of penalty and its effectiveness occupies a significant spot in Swedish studies and in Scandinavian studies in general. The idea of refraining from punishment was seriously discussed in Sweden at the close of World War II, though the notion of "penalty" was in the end retained in the penal code. A determinist attitude, akin to the one represented by Enrico Ferri, marked the leading Swedish reformer Karl Schlyter, a renowned judge, at one time Minister of Justice and chairman of the codification commission. He believed that one should not present criminals with admonitions and moral indignation; a criminal became what he became due to inborn propensities and the impact of the environment. A consequence of this philosophy is a system of sanctions breaking with the moral indignation assumed in concepts of responsibility, guilt, and punishment.[13]

As early as 1934, Schlyter promulgated the idea of "emptying the prisons." Sentencing to prison was to be a measure of last resort. The first step on the way to limiting the application of prison sentences was the reform of the system of fines as punishment; another measure aimed at the same objective was the introduction of punishment which did not deprive the convict of his liberty. Swedish penal policy aims at maximum differentiation of sanctions, their tailoring to the offender's personality, assuring the offender a chance for productive work. Next to fine or imprisonment, the judge now has at his disposal the following sanctions against adult offenders: suspended sentence, preventive supervision, arrest, placement in a special institution, such as treatment centers for alcoholics and mentally ill patients.[14]

Swedish research on the effectiveness of noninstitutionalized forms of rehabilitation is notable. Borjeson developed a method of forecasting through comparing groups of recidivists and nonrecidivists selected from among the criminals of Gothenburg. He took into account seventy-six factors which could have an influence on recidivism, of which he classified thirty-nine as significant. Analyzing all the significant factors he came up with a numerical "degree of risk" for each offender, qualifying them according to the degree of risk into nine groups.[15]

The Scandinavian Institute of African Studies, established in 1962 at Uppsala, also studies issues of social pathology. It has published a number of valuable monographs, including: R. E. S. Tanner, *Three Studies in East African Criminology* (1970); R. E. S. Tanner, *Homicide in Uganda* (1970); H. F. Morris: *Some Perspectives of East African Legal History* (1970). The findings of certain institute studies have been included in the *Africana in Scandinavian Research Libraries Newsletter*.

The National Council for Crime Prevention (Bröttsförebyggande Radet) was formed in Sweden in 1974 as a government agency under the Minister of Justice. According to its state charter, the council conducts research to determine ways of preventing crime, and to coordinate civic efforts in this field. The council should, therefore, analyze the quantitative and qualitative changes in crime, draw up forecasts in this field, analyze and inspire research into the causes of crime and ways of limiting it, coordinate efforts and supervise the development of criminal policy, taking part in policy shaping through, for instance, conducting policy surveys. Its work is carried out in the following six areas:

1. Trends in crime and changes in society,
2. Juvenile delinquency,
3. Preventive measures,
4. Treatment, resocialization,
5. Alcohol, drugs and criminality,
6. Economic crime.

The council is run by a nineteen-person Board, whose members are nominated from among persons representing the various political parties active in Sweden; the council further includes undersecretaries of state from the departments of justice, social affairs, health and education, representatives of trade unions, and the insurance community. It is headed by O. Reiner, director general of the office having the rank of undersecretary of state. In 1975, preparatory work began on organizing an information bank concerned with the application of crime prevention measures. The council has drafted numerous reports on such subjects as juvenile delinquency and probation.[16]

Svensk Juristtidning, a journal of legal issues, and *Nordisk Kriminalteknisk Tidsskrifft*, a periodical on police technique, also carry articles devoted to criminology.

In Norway, development of criminological research dates back to 1954, the year when that country organized the Institute of Criminology and Penal Law (Institut for Kriminologi of Strafferet) in the University of Oslo, the first one in Scandinavia. Its founder was Johannes Andenaes, an outstanding expert on penal law, renowned particularly for his publications on the preventive significance of penalty. The institute staff also includes two persons well known in the world of criminology, A. Bratholm and N. Christie. Criminological issues are also considered in the sociological research carried out by the Institut for Samfunnsforskning established in Oslo in 1960.

The Norwegian Judges Association (Den Norske Domnierförening), active since 1912, at its annual congresses considers penological issues linked with criminology.[17] Its studies concern the etiology of juvenile delinquency, social welfare for children, legal issues of protecting children, and the functioning of correctional institutions for young people.

The association's most significant research project devoted to juvenile delinquency concerned the comparison of two groups of male adolescents of the same age: a group with convictions for crimes or misdemeanors with a control group having no police record.[18] The findings of this study caused quite a stir, since both groups had very similar traits. In the group having police records there were many young men who were no more nor less criminal than their counterparts in the control group. These and other studies concerning traditional criminality enabled the Scandinavian criminologists to conclude that there are two main types of law violaters: practically the entire male population under the age of twenty and a certain, by no means insignificant, part of the young female population; and a small group, chiefly males, of recidivists, their share in the total number of offenses and misdemeanors not being very high.

Another significant problem taken up by Norwegian criminologists concerns rehabilitation. Researchers, such as J. Galtung, W. Aubert, N. Christie and Thomas Mathiesen have published a number of papers and books on prison populations, questioning the view that prison can improve anyone.[19]

Much attention is devoted to having sociopolitical organizations keep up contacts with imprisoned persons, such as an organization formed in Norway in 1968 for contact with prisoners. Its objective is to reduce the negative effects of imprisonment and to draft concepts of new, nonisolating measures. In 1972 a union of working prisoners was formed in that country, patterned after trade unions.

In 1973, a psychologist, G. H. Vedeler, wrote a book on the ideology of treatment in such "soft institutions" as the therapeutic community. He analyzes the ambivalent role of the personnel in these and other institutions with more or less compulsory treatment.[20]

There has been a marked decriminalization in Norway since 1970 when "drunkenness in a public place" was removed from the penal code as a punishable offense. The same was done with homosexuality. Consideration is also being given to depenalizing abortions, bigamy, and dissemination of pornographic matter. In 1972 Norway, with a population of 3.9 million, had a total of 1,800 prisoners, including persons in temporary detention.[21]

Criminological issues are regularly discussed in print in the *Tidsskrift for Samfunnsforskning*.

In Denmark the earliest criminological studies are connected with S. Hurwitz, professor of penal law, penal procedure, and criminology at the University of Copenhagen. In 1947 he published a textbook on criminology, later translated into English, Italian, and Spanish.

In 1957 the University of Copenhagen established an Institute of Criminal Science (Kriminalistik Institut), engaged in training and research in criminology and social defense.[22] The institute for Prosecution and Criminal Science (Institut for Proces og Kriminalvidenskab) of the Aarhus University also deals with criminology. The research on victimology is conducted by P. Wolf of the Institute of Sociology, University of Copenhagen.

The University Institute of Forensic Medicine, Copenhagen, established in 1910, in addition to its research on forensic medicine, serology, chemistry, and anthropology, is also concerned with selected criminological issues.

An organization for contact with prisoners was formed in Denmark in 1967, studying rehabilitation problems.

Copenhagen has two (specialized) periodicals on criminological issues: *Nordisk Tidsskrift for Kriminalvidenskab*, devoted to Scandinavian criminology, and *Nordisk Tidsskrift for Strafferet*, devoted to Scandinavian penal law.

The problems of heredity and environment are among the most difficult, though fundamental, theoretical issues in criminology. Even though Scandinavian criminology remains under the influence of sociology, it does not negate the significance of hereditary traits in the origin and development of crime. A reflection of this interest was an extensive study of Danish twins. It covered every pair of twins born in the Danish islands in the years 1881–1910, some seven thousand pairs, of whom about half were identical twins. For the identical male twins, the imprisonment correlation amounted to some 35 percent, as opposed to 12 percent for fraternal twins, 50 percent lower than in other studies carried out to date.[23]

In the years 1952–1953, criminologist Karl O. Christiansen and psychologist K. Berntsen have carried out studies of a group of prisoners serving out short-term sentences in Copenhagen prisons, known as "the Danish experiment." The experiment was carried out on two random selected groups of prisoners, of which one was subjected to relatively intensive sociopsychological treatment while the other served as a control group. The study has shown that the convicts subjected to sociopsychological treatment released under certain conditions and those who were assured assistance and treatment after release have a much better record of not repeating offenses than others receiving short-term sentences.

In recent years at the request of the penal law commission a study of recidivism has been carried out for legislative purposes. Is there a difference in the incidence of recidivism between a group released from regular prisons and a group released from institutions of protection in which the sentences have no defined term? The study has shown that the difference in the recidivism rate is insignificant.[24]

The study carried out by B. Kutchinsky concerning the effects of decriminalizing acts consisting of the dissemination of pornography is also interesting.[25]

In Finland an Institute of Criminology was founded in Helsinki in 1963; in 1974 it was incorporated as part of the Research Institute of Legal Policy which, in addition to criminological issues, concerns itself with constitutional and family law. Criminological studies are carried out by the General Research and Criminology Unit which employs lawyers and sociologists.

The Department of Sociology of the University of Helsinki, founded in 1950, also carries out research and training on criminology and social defense.

Studies in Finland center mainly on criminography, crime trends, and evaluations of penal sanction systems. Research on drunken driving, car thefts and violent crimes are also important; certain studies try to establish whether legislative changes have an impact on the magnitude of crime; other studies point to the shortcomings and errors in the system of sanctions, as happened in a study concerned with the parallel application of a general sanction along with withdrawal of the driver's license. One study concerned a draft law on the compensation to be paid by the state to victims of violent crimes, still another was carried out for the government committee charged with the protection of the private lives of citizens.[26]

A few years ago much interest in Finland was concentrated on the issue of probation and conditional release. A reform committee was formed and three economic studies carried out, of which two were experimental and one was concerned with working conditions of former prisoners, with research linked to findings of certain U.S. and Dutch studies. One project was aimed at establishing whether police supervision of people released on probation had an impact on the incidence of recidivism. The last three studies enabled the government commission to obtain a realistic view of the situation and were helpful in making certain radical changes in the laws.[27]

In recent years a draft of an extensive reform of penal legislation has been prepared. One of the studies carried out by sociologist K. Aromaa concerned offenses against work safety; such offenses, particularly the hidden ones, cause numerous problems.

A project, the findings of which were published in 1968 by O. Uusitalo, concerned a comparison between two types of penal institutions: labor colony and prison. In the former the sentence is served without special restrictions; the convicts get full pay for their work, wear civilian clothes, and there are no walls or guards. The study showed that the rate of recidivism after sentences served in both types of establishments was substantially the same. Still, running a labor colony is more profitable to the state than maintaining a prison.[28]

Notes

1. Inkeri Anttila, "La politique scandinave actuelle en matière de criminologie et de contrôle de la délinquance." [Current Scandinavian policy on criminology and crime control] *Revue de droit pénal et de criminologie* 1975, no. 8, pp. 687–689; idem, "Developments in Criminology and Criminal Policy in Scandinavia," *Proceedings of the First Seminar for Criminologists from Socialist and Scandinavian Countries*, Helsinki, August 26–29, 1974, pp. 4–12.

2. Thomas Mathiesen, "Politics in Abolition: Essays in Political Action Theory," *Scandinavian Studies in Criminology*, vol. 4 (Oslo: Oslo Universitets Forlaget, 1974), p. 22.

3. Inkeri Anttila, "La politique scandinave actuelle," pp. 693–694.

4. Ibid., p. 688.

5. Knut Sveri, "Skandinavische Kriminologie" [Scandinavian criminology], *Kriminologische Gegenwartsfragen*, Stuttgart, Ferdinand Enke Verlag, 1970, no. 9, pp. 17–19.

6. Karl O. Christiansen, ed. *Scandinavian Studies in Criminology*, vol. 1. (Oslo: Oslo Universitets Forlaget; London: Tavistock, 1965).

7. Inkeri Anttila, "La politique scandinave actuelle," p. 694.

8. Olof Kinberg, "Sweden," UNESCO Report, 1957, pp. 107–111.

9. In 1935 the English version was published as *Basic Problems of Criminology*; the French version was published in 1960 under the title *Les problemes fondamentaux de la criminologie*.

10. Knut Sveri: "Skandinavische Kriminologie."

11. Acta Universitatis Upsaliensis [Faculty of Law at Uppsala], Uppsala 1976.

12. Inkeri Anttila, "La politique scandinave actuelle," p. 689.

13. Johannes Andenaes, "Przyszłość prawa karnego: Skandynawskie perspektywy" [The Future of Penal Law: Scandinavian Perspectives]. Shortened version of a lecture delivered in Warsaw on May 19, 1973 to the Institute of Penal Sciences of the Polish Academy of Sciences. *Państwo i Prawo*, 1974, no. 1, pp. 42–56.

14. Gerhard Simson, "The Sanctions Against Law Breakers in the New Swedish Criminal Code," *Excerpta Criminologica* 1966, no. 6.

15. Karl O. Christiansen, "Noninstitutional care of offenders in practice: The Danish experience" (Conference at the twentieth International Course in Criminology). *Annales Internationales de Criminologie* 1971, no. 1, pp. 283–309.

16. Summaries of Reports. National Council for Crime Prevention, Stockholm, 1975.

17. Leon Radzinowicz, *In Search of Criminology* (London: Heineman, 1961), pp. 110, 112–113.

18. Knut Sveri, "Skandinavische Kriminologie," p. 22.

19. Inkeri Anttila, "La politique scandinave actuelle," p. 690.

20. Ibid.

21. Johannes Andenaes, "Przyszłość prawa karnego," p. 45.

22. Karl O. Christiansen, "The Institute of Criminal Science, University of Copenhagen," *British Journal of Delinquency* 1969, no. 1.

23. Knut Sveri, "Skandinavische Kriminologie," p. 23.

24. Inkeri Anttila, "La politique scandinave actuelle," p. 690.

25. Ibid., p. 689.

26. Ibid., p. 692.

27. Ibid., pp. 692–693.

28. Knut Sveri, "Skandinavische Kriminologie," p. 28.

9

Development of Criminological Research Institutions in Socialist Countries

Systematic and intensive development of empirical research and theoretical studies on criminological issues in Poland began in earnest in the latter half of the 1950s. Directly after World War II, as research facilities were being rebuilt, criminological projects and studies were undertaken, only to stop after just a few years. An example of this initial activity was the publication in 1945 of the encyclopedic text written by Józef J. Bossowski, designed as an academic textbook.[1] Findings of the earliest empirical studies, concerning mostly postwar criminality and including postwar juvenile delinquency, were presented in legal and other professional publications, indexed in detail by Leon Tyszkiewicz.[2]

During the years of regression (1950–1956) caused by the prevailing dogmatic approach to criminological issues and the definition of criminality as a relic of the capitalist system, there were only a few publications, mostly concerned with crime statistics.[3] The rare publications on other criminological topics included a monograph by Stanisław Batawia on the social consequences of alcoholism[4] and a publication by Halina Spionek on juvenile delinquents ordered by courts to undergo tests in a psychological clinic in Warsaw.[5]

In the latter half of the 1950s the issues connected with combating and preventing crime once again became a topic of wide interest. Scholarly publications appeared, including studies by Paweł Zakrzewski,[6] Anna Pawełczyńska,[7] Tadeusz Cyprian[8] and others, as well as books and articles on legal, sociological, and psychological journals. In 1958 Paweł Horoszowski published a book for the Prison Service Administration Personnel Training Centre.[9]

Criminological research was concentrated initially in the Criminology Division of the Polish Academy of Sciences and the Criminology Division of the University of Warsaw. Later such research was taken up also by the Penitentiary Research Center established in 1961 in the Ministry of Justice (in 1967 renamed the Crime Research Center), and by the Autonomous Section for Research on Crime Problems, formed in 1967 in the Prosecutor General's Office, becoming in 1968 into the Bureau for Crime Problem Studies.

The Ministry of Justice Crime Research Center has carried out numerous studies on such topics as experimental forms and methods of rehabilitating prison convicts, as well as on the roots of crime and its prevention. The center has organized scientific conferences and established contacts with research facilities abroad. Visible evidence of its activities is available in the form of numerous publications on penal law, criminology, and penitentiary training.[10] In 1967 the center established a Psychological-Criminological Advisory Unit, whose tasks consist of assisting courts in issuing psychological-criminological judgments.

The Autonomous Section for Research on Crime Problems, later the Bureau of Studies and next the Bureau of Crime Problem Studies in the Prosecutor General's Office carried out a number of research projects in the years 1962–1974. Its objective was to carry out empirical studies, particularly for the needs of prosecution bodies. The studies concerned such topics as the effectiveness of control operations for detecting economic offenses, the effectiveness of sentence suspensions, currency offenses and smuggling, indictable mismanagement in industry, and the causes of crime. The research unit of the Prosecution Office devoted much attention to coordinating crime research, particularly in setting up and publishing a list of criminological research topics of projects conducted by various research organizations in Poland at the close of 1968.[11]

Leon Tyszkiewicz has emphasized that already during the first few years of renewed interest in criminological research, the achievements of Polish criminology were quite notable, with several topical and methodological issues of special interest: juvenile delinquency; research on adult recidivism, professional crime and the criminal milieux; research on issues connected with methods of sentence execution and reformatory measures; research on economic crime.

A pioneering and unique study was conducted by Witold Swida on the impact of the changed sociopolitical system in Poland on criminality.[12] A detailed comparative analysis of crime in the years 1937 and 1952 was based on very meticulous study of records in the city and district of Kalisz. The study took into account the etiological background of the various types of crime and made a classification of crimes. The study revealed marked differences between crime in the two years, 1937 and 1952. By the same token it discovered a significant impact of the changes in the sociopolitical system on criminality and the directions of change.

Because of the value of the scientific methodology applied in the collection and analysis of data on crime and criminals in Poland one should give special credit to the group of persons connected with the Criminology Division of the State and Law Institute (formerly the Institute of Legal Disciplines) of the Polish Academy of Sciences, headed for many years by Stanisław Batawia. Special mention should go to projects concerned with juveniles (Stanisław Batawia,[13] Helena Kołakowska-Przełomiec,[14] Adam Strzembosz,[15] Paweł Zakrzewski,[16]) juvenile recurrent delinquents (Stanisław Szelhaus)[17], adult recidivism (Zofia Ostrihańska)[18], criminological prognosis (Zofia Ostrihańska)[19], crime statistics, forecasts of criminality and comparative analysis of the frequency of imprisonment (Jerzy Jasiński),[20] impact of industrialization and urbanization processes on crime (Andrzej Mościskier),[21] and homicide (Brunon Hołyst and Halina Janowska).[22] Among the most interesting projects of this group is the recent monograph by Helena Kołakowska-Przełomiec: "Przestępczość i nieprzystosowanie społeczne nieletnich w genezie przestępczości dorosłych" [Juvenile Delinquency and Social Maladjustment in the Genesis of Adult Criminality].[23] The study was carried out on 1,000 randomly selected juvenile delinquents born in 1949. They were criminologically characterized and their later life analyzed. The study made possible several significant conclusions. There was a deeper comparative characterization of young people from rural and urban backgrounds, an analysis was made of the effectiveness of measures applied to juveniles, and a valuable classification of juvenile delinquents was made, establishing the percentage shares of given subgroups in the entire studied population.

Two projects, complementing each other are of high scientific standards; they are described in: Hanna Malewska, Vincent Peyre, and Anna Firkowska-Mankiewicz, "Przestepczość nieletnich" [Juvenile Delinquency][24] and Anna Firkowska-Mankiewicz, "Czynniki biopsychiczne a przestepczość nieletnich" [Bio-Mental Factors and Juvenile Delinquency].[25] Both projects, carried out under international arrangements, studied a rather large group of 606 juvenile delinquents representing the entire country. A considerable number of variables were considered, taking into account biomental, macrosocial and psychosocial factors. The method applied was that of multifactor analysis. The study embodies a comparison of the social situation of juvenile delinquents in Poland and in France. Its positive contribution is the uncovering of the interdependence between the factors influencing delinquency.

Worth noting also are the projects carried out by Zbigniew Bozyczko concerned with pickpockets and burglars.[26] The method of participant observation applied by this author revealed many interesting facts concerning the milieus studied.

An important issue studied by Polish criminologists concerns the recidivism which continues at a high level. Studies have concentrated on a sample of the general recidivist population, young adult recidivists and multiple recidivists.[27] This issue became the topic of special concern for the Polish Academy of Sciences Criminology Department. The Institute of Crime Problems in recent years has also focused its attention on recidivist burglars.

Linked with the recidivism issue is the topic of effectiveness of the penal law measures used for combating crime. This is a relatively new field of interest for Polish criminology. Studies have encompassed every penal measure: the deprivation of liberty penalty,[28] the fine,[29] the limitation of liberty,[30] conditional suspension of penalty execution,[31] conditional early release,[32] conditional discontinuance of penal proceedings,[33] commitment to a medical institution as a preventive measure,[34] protective supervision,[35] supervision of a juvenile by a probation officer,[36] commitment to a re-educational institution,[37] conditional release from reformatory.[38] The normally used criterion of success was lack of recidivism after the application of a given measure.

Another group of studies is concerned with the selection of penal measures for combating crime. There are a number of valuable studies on particular aspects of this issue, relying on various methods of approach. A comprehensive monograph on court sentences is based on a poll conducted among judges in 1966.[39] A very interesting study was devoted to the comparative analysis of the degree of punitivity of penal systems, using statistical data illustrating the frequency of application of various penalties and the number of persons serving prison sentences in Poland and in sixteen other countries.[40] An in-depth statistical analysis has been carried out of the various factors influencing the sentences in cases of public property appropriation.[41] Statistical methods were used for analyzing the link between the average sentence for a variety of offenses in particular provinces and the frequency of such offenses in the same areas.[42]

Polish criminology did not fail to take up the significant problems of criminological prognosis. A theoretical monograph was written on individual prognosis,[43] as well as other studies based on factual data.[44] The latter have led to distinguishing numerous prognostic factors. Such importance was assigned to those factors depending on the discovered correlation between the factors and the ensuing recidivism.

Polish criminological literature concerned with prognosis includes a monograph by Jerzy Jasiński[45] on crime as a mass phenomenon.

Polish criminology has devoted considerable attention to the various aspects of social pathology which are not penalized under provisions of the Penal Code. In this context should be noted particularly the publications concerned with alcohol abuse,[46] prostitution,[47] and drug abuse.[48] Numerous criminological studies treat of the various kinds of offenses; they most frequently rely on the results of polls and inquiries.

A distinct area of criminological research is concerned with psychological and psychopathological issues. Researchers most frequently take up the criminologically significant problem of aggression. A number of monographs have been written on this subject,[49] with due consideration given to the social background of aggression stemming from family circumstances or the subculture of the penal establishments. Two reports are concerned with studies of the mental state of prisoners deprived of liberty.[50] One of the researchers further takes into account the biochemical and physiological-medical tests rare in contemporary criminology. The same research direction is represented by an elaborate monograph of psychopathy.[51]

The Institute of Crime Problems put together and published materials which show that in the years 1970–1974 more than three hundred empirical research projects were carried out in Poland on currently significant issues connected with combating and preventing crime.[52]

In concluding the review of publications one should mention two studies synthesizing the achievements of criminology. The first presents the state of crime and the studies concerning separate categories of criminogenic factors,[53] while the second represents a synthesis of research concerning the incidence and phenomenology of the various types of offenses.[54]

At present the institutional base of criminology in Poland is highly developed compared with the other socialist countries, with the exception of the USSR. Empirical research and theoretical studies in this field are carried out by over twenty institutions, of which the leading are: The State and Law Institute of the Polish Academy of Sciences, the Institute of Crime Problems under the Prosecutor General and the Research Institute on Judicial Law of the Ministry of Justice.

Research and other studies in criminology are further carried out by academic centers: institutes, departments or faculties of penal law, criminology, criminalistics, psychology, psychiatry, sociology, pedagogy, and economics, at nine universities, two medical academies and the Central School of Planning and Statistics. Such studies are also being carried out by the Institute of Judicial Expertises (Cracow), the Academy of Internal Affairs (Warsaw), the Department of Criminalistics of the Civic Police Supreme Headquarters (Warsaw), the State Institute of Special Pedagogy (Warsaw), the Psychoneurological Institute (Warsaw), the Scientific Research Center of the Anti-Alcoholic Committee (Warsaw), the Polish Society of Forensic Medicine and Criminology (Gdańsk), and the Polish Criminalistics Society (Cracow).

One of the tasks of the Polish Academy of Sciences is to coordinate the activity of all scientific institutions in Poland. The Academy carries out this function through special committees appointed for three years tenure. The leading theoreticians and practitioners from various institutions serve on these committees.

For many years the Polish Academy of Sciences has had a Committee of Legal Disciplines, charged with periodic evaluations of the state of Polish legal disciplines[55] and the adoption of program directions for fundamental research in given sections of the law.[56]

The committe organizes periodic scientific meetings dedicated to crucial issues, discussed on an interdisciplinary plane. A number of national sections of international juridical professional associations have been affiliated with this committee.[57]

University law and administration faculties have the largest personnel potential for criminological studies. For the time being the following nine universities have their own departments of law and administration: Warsaw University, Jagiellonian University, Adam Mickiewicz University in Poznań, Wrocław University, Łódź University, Nicholas Copernicus University in Toruń, Maria Curie-Skłodowska University in Lublin, Silesian University in Katowice, and Gdańsk University.

Within the framework of the Polish Academy of Sciences, the Institute of State and Law has been formed for the purpose of carrying out studies in the sphere of legal disciplines.[58] According to its statute, the institute is concerned with research on state and law issues, particularly in the context of the interlinks with other social sciences.

Tasks of the institute cover specifically: implementation of long-term (usually five years) scientific plans, as specified by academy authorities; education and enhancing the qualifications of research personnel; transmitting research findings for practical application; assistance in promoting the knowledge of law; fulfillment of specified other tasks with which it may be charged by academy authorities.

The institute employs 28 professors and assistant professors, 22 lecturers, 18 assistants, and 19 librarians and documentalists. The postgraduate department has 19 fellowships. Altogether, the institute has a staff of 122.

The institute is currently working on a "Polish Juridical Dictionary" and a five-language (Polish-Russian-English-French-German) juridical dictionary with about 10,000 entries.

Regular publication of the Polish Juridical Bibliography, with French translations of the titles of bibliographical entries is another continuing project of the institute.

The Institute of State and Law (formerly the Institute of Legal Disciplines) of the Polish Academy of Sciences and its Criminology Department were formed in 1954. For many years it was the leading criminological research institution in the country. Since 1960 the Criminology Department publishes its findings in *Archiwum Kryminologii* [Archives of Criminology]; so far seven volumes have been published.[59] Most of the published dissertations are concerned with juvenile delinquency, hooliganism, crime in industrialized areas, homicides, robberies, alcoholism, prostitution, court-psychiatric judgments as well as with the general pattern and trends in crime.

The Institute of Crime Problems, established in 1974, implements a comprehensive program of criminological research. The institute is interdepartmental in nature. It is supervised by the Prosecutor General who, in defining the directions of research and ways of utilizing research findings in practice, acts in conjunction with the ministers of justice and internal affairs and with the First President of the Supreme Court.

The prime task of the institute is to conduct multifacet, interdisciplinary studies of problems linked with preventing and combating crime and of other public order violations and to carry out comparative studies of the same phenomena in other countries.

In 1980 the Institute of Crime Problems completed twenty five projects. Most of them were directly geared to practical requirements of prosecution agencies and criminal justice bodies. They concerned such topics as:

effectiveness of combating the most serious criminal, economic and road offenses;

application of certain penal law institutions such as provisional detention, conditional discontinuance of penal proceedings, limitation of liberty and conditional early release;

Other issues of practical interest to prosecution agencies, such as evaluation of the crime statistics system.

Research findings are as a rule accompanied by conclusion addressed to practical operations of prosecution agencies. The findings in certain projects have also been presented at conferences, symposia, and congresses held in Poland and internationally.

Some projects concern issues of interest to other state agencies. This holds particularly true for the whole complex of topics concerning family and juveniles, including the studies on:

family influence on shaping the moral attitudes of children;

factors hindering the enforcement of alimony;

influence of mental handicaps on disrupting social adaptation and on juvenile delinquency;

groups of young people resorting to violence;

juvenile delinquency and young adult offenses.

In addition to research, the institute is also active in the fields of publishing, training, and coordinating criminological endeavors.

The range of publications covers four nonperiodical journals: *Studia Kryminologiczne, Kryminalistyczne i Penitencjarne* [Criminological, criminalistic, and penitentiary studies]—eleven volumes published by 1981; *Patologia Społeczna—Zapobieganie* [Social pathology—prevention]—nine volumes; *Przestępczość na Swiecie* [Criminality in the world]—fourteen issues, and the annual *Bibliografia Wybranych Zagranicznych Publikacji Kryminologicznych, Kryminalistycznych i Penitencjarnych* [Bilbiography of selected foreign criminological, criminalistic, and penitentiary publications]. These journals publish papers and articles by institute employees and by researchers and practitioners from Poland and other countries.

The institute has also published a number of brochures presenting the results of the Fifth United Nations Congress (Geneva 1955) the Ninth International Congress on Social Defense (Caracas 1976) and the state of criminology in the socialist countries. The "Monografie Instytutu Problematyki Przestępczości" [Monographs of the Institute of Crime Problems] series carries the most valuable doctoral and postdoctoral dissertations.

Since 1975 the institute thas conducted a doctoral seminar for a hundred employees of penal prosecution and criminal justice. The Institute of Crime Problems also coordinates endeavors in such forms as preparing the Polish presentation at various criminological congresses, publishing the topics of criminological research projects conducted by various research institutions in the country, suggesting directions of criminological research, and organizing criminological conferences with the participation of delegates from numerous research institutions.

The Research Institute on Judicial law was established in 1973 by the Ministry of Justice Crime Research Center.

The institute is charged with organizing and conducting research on the effectiveness of legal measures applied by the courts and on the proper manner of their application, as well as evolving methods and carrying out studies on: accordance of legal solutions in judicial law with social requirements; rehabilitation activities carried out in penal institutions and in juvenile institutions; preventive undertakings of the courts, their supplementary bodies and organizational units; and functioning of the criminal justice system.

The institute publishes the nonperiodic "Zeszyty Naukowe" [Scientific Fascicles]; by 1981 a total of thirteen volumes were published.

The Crime Research Center, forerunner of the institute, has published a quarterly since 1963, initially called *Przegląd Penitencjarny* [Penitentiary review] and in recent years *Przegląd Penitencjarny i Kryminologiczny* [Penitentiary and criminological review], which devoted much space to criminological issues.

Warsaw University Institute of Social Prevention and Resocialization has a comprehensive training program and the scope of its interests encompasses social attitudes to deviance, the issue of drug addiction, pathology of sexual behavior, the subculture of "git-people" (a Polish phenomenon akin to "punk" groups) among school pupils, and the effectiveness of alcoholic rehabilitation.

Wrocław University Institute of Criminology has organized a number of regional criminological symposia. Their topics concern the criminological aspects of technical progress, issues connected with robbery, road traffic offenses, and recidivism.

The symposia were organized on the initiative of Włodzimierz Gutekunst, institute director. Interesting criminological publication on criminal milieus of pickpockets and burglars were written by the late Zbigniew Bożyczko.

The Academy of Internal Affairs has its Institute of Criminalistics and Criminology. The empirical research carried out there covers such issues as the criminological aspects of organized appropriation of public property, bribery, legal means of securing public order and security, and the sources of economic offenses. The academy publishes a periodical, *Zeszyty Naukowe* [Scientific fascicles], which carries many articles on criminology problems. Sixteen issues had been published by 1978.

The institute of Judicial Expertise in Cracow, with its Psychological-Crimonological Unit has carried through a number of projects concerned with juvenile delinquency. These concerned such issues as the problem of rehabilitating juveniles who fell behind in their schooling, the motives behind delinquent behavior of juveniles, emotional disturbances, offenses in the yes of juveniles, the notion of justice among delinquent and nondelinquent juveniles. The institute publishes the periodical *Z Zagadnień Kryminalistyki* [Criminalistic issues].

Poland's first Criminology Department was organized by the Lódź University. By now all universities have criminological departments or offer lectures on the subject.

In addition to the previously listed publications, criminological issues are also taken up in other periodicals, particularly in *Archiwum Medycyny Sądowej i Kryminologii* [Archives of forensic medicine and criminology], the quarterly of the Polish Forensic Medicine and Criminology society, started in 1951 and appearing until 1968 under the title *Archiwum Medycyny Sądowej, Psychiatrii Sądowej i Kryminalistyki* [Archives of forensic medicine, forensic psychiatry, and criminalistics], as a professional, training, and informative periodical carrying articles on forensic medicine, criminology, and associated disciplines; *Problemy Kryminalistyki* [Criminalistic problems], the publication of the Criminalistics Section of the Civic Police Supreme Headquarters; juridical journals such as *Państwo i Prawo, Nowe Prawo, Gazeta Prawnicza, Prawo i Życie* [State and law, New law, Juristic gazette, Law and life]. Moreover, the Institute of State and Law publishes the following periodicals:

Orzecznictwo Sądów Polskich i Komisji Arbitrazowych [Rulings of Polish courts and arbitration commissions], a monthly magazine giving a selection of recent rulings, along with critical commentaries on these rulings;

Studia Prawnicze [Legal studies], a quarterly carrying elaborate dissertations on various facets of law;

Droit Polonais Contemporain [Contemporary Polish law (in French)], a quarterly carrying articles on current issues in Polish law, reviews of the more significant Polish legal book publications and translations of texts of selected statutes and other normative acts;

Polskoye Sovremennoye Pravo [Contemporary Polish law (in Russian)], a quarterly of similar nature for Russian readers.

Two other publications with long traditions are also worthy of note in this context: *Wojskowy Przegląd Prawniczy* [Military legal review], a quarterly and *Palestra* [The bar], a monthly of the Chief Council of Attorneys.

Regular and irregular periodicals are also published under the sponsorship of academic centers. The most widely circulated are *Ruch Prawniczy, Ekonomiczny i Socjologiczny* [Legal, economic, and sociological movement], a quarterly edited by the Department of Law and Administration, Poznań University, and *Studia Prawnicze* [Legal studies], a publication of the Jagiellonian University, Cracow. Articles and dissertations contributed by their respective law departments have also appeared in the following series: "Acta Universitatis Wratislawiensis" (Wrocław University), "Annales Universitatis Mariae Curie-Skłodowska" (Lublin University), "Prace Naukowe Uniwersytetu Śląskiego" (Katowice University), "Zeszyty Naukowe Uniwersytetu Jagiellońskiego" (Cracow University), "Zeszyty Naukowe Uniwersytetu Łódzkiego" (Łódź University), "Zeszyty Naukowe Uniwersytetu im. M. Kopernika" (Toruń University), "Studia Iuridica" (Warsaw University).

Four textbooks of criminology for the requirements of faculties and research staffs have been published, namely: Paweł Horoszowski, *Kryminologia* [Criminology], Warsaw, State Scientific Publishers, 1956; Leszek Lernell, *Zarys Kryminologii Ogólnej* [Outline of General Criminology], Warsaw, State Scientific Publishers, 1973; Brunon Hołyst, *Kryminologia. Podstawowe Problemy* [Criminology. Fundamental Problems], Warsaw, State Scientific Publishers, 1977 (A second edition, revised and enlarged, appeared in 1979 under the shorter title: *Kryminologia*) Witold Swida, ed., *Kryminologia* [Criminology], Warsaw State Scientific Publishers, 1977.

The beginnings of criminology in the Soviet Union date back to the 1920s. An initiative taken by V. I. Lenin, who stressed the need for studying the causes of negative social phenomena, led to the evolution of a statistical system geared mainly to penal issues. In 1922 a convict's questionnaire was drawn up listing personal data and a description of the circumstances of the crime. Information gathered in this manner was published for some ten years as a statistical series by the Central Statistical Office. The series served as a base for scientific analysis.

In 1925 the People's Commissariat for Domestic Affairs established the State Institute for Studying Criminality and Criminals (Gosudarstvenniy Institut Issledovaniya Prestupnosti y Prestupnika). This institute, gathering together a large number of scholars, became the Soviet Union's first center of criminology. Its research topics covered such issues as: the causes and circumstances of crime; the means and methods of combating crime; penal policy; effectiveness of penitentiary measures.

Criminological research was also carried out by the Section of State and Law (later the Institute of Soviet Construction and Law of the Communist Academy), the Institute of Soviet Law, and various university departments.

Due to misconceptions as to the research directions and methods in criminology, research activities and by the same token the development of criminology gradually ground to a halt, starting in 1929. This situation continued until the twentieth Congress of the Communist Party of the Soviet Union which was followed by criticism of the dogmatic views on the body of penal law issues. The outcome was the establishment in 1957 of the Penal Law Division of the All-Union Institute of Criminalistics in the USSR Prosecution Office and in 1958 of the Civic Police Research Institute, later the All-Union Research Institute on the Protection of Public Order. Consideration was given to the further organization and development of methods for studying crime and criminals. B.S. Utyevski wrote at the time about the necessity of resolving the issue of coordinating and planning the activities of all the ministries, research institutes, and university law departments on the study of crime. He distinguished three main directions of crime study: the state of crime (including its trends of change), the causes of crime, and the personality of offenders.[60]

Due credit for the development of criminology in the Soviet Union should be given to Mikhail N. Gernet (1874–1953), author of numerous dissertations on moral statistics, etiology of crime and suicides, organizer of criminological studies, particularly on the links between crime and alcoholism, including alcohol abuse. As early as 1924 a book, edited by Gernet, was published under the title, *The Criminal World of Moscow*, which presented the findings of large-scale empirical studies carried out with the assistance of students from Moscow University Department of Social Sciences. The same type of study was repeated forty-five years later. The two studies together represent considerable scientific value as they reveal certain rules shaping the state, changes and patterns of crime, point out certain significant changes taking place in the personality of offenders and the causes of crime, and provide a basis for forecasting crime and guiding the processes of its planned suppression in a socialist society.

The Selected Writings of M.N. Gernet was published in Moscow in 1974,[61] a significant addition to criminological literature.

The aforementioned criminological facilities served as the nucleus for creating in 1963 the All-Union Institute for the Study of the Causes and Elaboration of Measures for the Prevention of Crime (Vsesoyuzniy Institut po Izucheniyu Prochin y Razrabotke Mer Preduprezhdeniya Prestupnosti) in Mosow, at present the leading center of criminological studies.

The institute is charged with comprehensive analysis of all issues linked with the suppression and prevention of crime. It coordinates the research on criminology, criminalistics and forensic psychiatry of over three hundred scientific institutions. These include the USSR Academy of Internal Affairs (Academiya Vnutrennikh Del SSSR), the All-Union Research Institute of Court Expertise (Vsesoyuzniy Nauchno-Issledovatelskiy Institut Sudebnikh Expertiz), the Volgograd Higher School of the Ministry of Internal Affairs (Volgogradskoe Vissheye Uchebnoe Zavedeniye Ministerstva Vnutrennikh Del), the Saratov Legal Institute (Saratovskiy Yuridicheskiy Institut), the G.V. Plekhanov Moscow Institute of the National Economy (Moskovskiy Institut Narodnogo Khozaystva imeni G.V. Plekhanova), the Kharkov Legal Institute (Kharkovskiy Yuridicheskiy Institut), the Gorki Higher School of the Ministry of Internal Affairs (Gorkovskoye Vissheye Uchenoe Zavedeniye Ministerstva Vnutrennikh Del).

This last facility was established to train specialized lawyer-economists; it carries out studies aimed at establishing the reasons behind misappropriation of public property and developing measures to prevent such offenses.

The All-Union Institute also offers comments on drafts of legislative acts and on the curricula of various criminological disciplines. The scope of tasks with which the institute is charged indicates that it is the foremost criminological research facility in the Soviet Union; this is also reflected in institute publications: it is responsible for four-fifths of all the publications on criminology and criminalistics and all the publications on forensic psychology appearing on the Soviet market.

The main aims and objectives of the institute cover:

1. studying the causes of criminality and the conditions conducive to various kinds of crime, elaborating measures which would counteract crime;
2. comprehensive treatment of law and the penal process, organization of courts, criminalistic and prosecutors' supervision;
3. studying and drafting generalized conclusions on the operation of investigative bodies, prosecution offices, and courts, for the purpose of improving their mode of activity and assisting criminal justice bodies in their methodology.

The Institute has fourteen organizational units, charged with such issues as: methodology of research; juvenile and young adult delinquency; appropriation of public property; offenses against life, health and public order; psychological problems of the struggle against crime; popularizing the knowledge of law; methodology of investigation; prosecutors' supervision; court law; police science techniques; practical application of research findings; data processing and scientific contacts with other countries.

In addition to the fourteen units, the institute has four laboratories, a publishing section, and a research coordination group.

The institution has undergone considerable change since its inception, best illustrated by numerical data. In 1963 the nine units of the institute (four criminological units, four legal units, and one police science technique unit) had a total scientific staff of 86, including four with postdoctoral degrees and 43 with doctoral degrees. The entire scientific staff of the institute consisted exclusively of lawyers. Ten years later the institute increased its scientific staff to 137 people, representing such disciplines as philosophy, sociology, economy, psychology, mathematics, demography, statistics, and linguistics. Twenty have postdoctoral degrees and 63 have doctoral degrees.

In the ten years of its operation the institute has published thirty six monographs, eight textbooks (including books written jointly with scholars from other institutions), ninety eight scientific-methodological advice brochures for criminal justice personnel, and seventy eight compendia of articles and conference materials. The Scientific Council of the institute promoted 30 post-doctoral and 164 doctoral dissertations (among these 2 post-doctoral and 56 doctoral degrees awarded to practitioners).

In 1966 the institute published *Kriminologia* [Criminology], a textbook written by a team of lawyers and criminologists. This textbook represents a valuable contribution to the literature of socialist criminology, constituting a consistent, uniform presentation of the application of Marxist theory and methodology to studying and suppressing crime.

Other significant publications of the institute include:

Prokurorskiy nadzor v SSSR [Prosecutors' supervision in the USSR] (Moscow: Vsesoyuzniv Institut . . . , Prokuratora SSSR, 1966. Collective monographs with materials from a congress on the subject with the participation of institute staff and lecturers of law schools;

Teoriya dokazatelstv v sovetskom ugolownom processie [Theory of proof in Soviet penal process law] (Moscow: Vsesoyuzniy Institut, 1966;

Igor I. Karpec, *Problema prestupnosti* [Issues of criminality] (Moscow: Yuridicheskaya Literatura, 1969);

Alexey A. Gertzenson, *Vvedeniye v sovetskuyu kriminologiyu* [Introduction to Soviet criminology] (Moscow: Yurdicheskaya Literatura, 1965);

Vladimir K. Zvirbul, *Deyatelnost prokuratury po preduprezhdeniyu prestupnosti* [Prosecution efforts in crime prevention] (Moscow: Yuridicheskaya Literatura, 1971);

Boris S. Nikiforov, ed., *Efektiwnost ugolovno-pravovikh mer borby s prestupnostu* [Effectiveness of penal law measures of criminal prevention] (Moscow, Yurisdicheskaya Literatura, 1968);

Borba s khishcheniyami gosudarstvennogo y obshchestvennogo imushchestva [Suppressing theft of state and public property] (Moscow: Yurisdischeskaya Literatura, 1971) (methodological handbook);

Georgiy A. Zlobin and Boris S. Nikiforov, *Umisel y yevo formy* [Intent and Its Forms] (Moscow: Yurisdicheskaya Literatura, 1972) (monograph).

Criminology, reborn with the inception of the institute, faced scholars with the most difficult problems. It became necessary to redraft all the fundamental sections of criminology, that is, the science of criminality and its rules, the concept of its causes, the concept of the offender's personality, the general theory of crime prevention.

It is an irrefutable success of institute scholars that the resolution of these issues did not take on the form of contemplative considerations and generalized concepts. Efforts were directed at concrete sociological research carried out on the scale of a city, district, enterprise, or industry, in keeping with the given crime or category of offender (such as juvenile delinquents), and later were generalized to the national scale. By the same token the researchers created the empirical foundations for theoretical and practical conclusions.

At present there is a very thorough knowledge of certain overall criminological issues in the Soviet Union. These include, first of all, the general, historical rules of the dynamics, pattern and geography of crime covering the entire time span of Soviet statehood; second, the fundamental description of the offender's personality, with due consideration to the differences manifested with different types of offenses; third, the sociopsychological mechanisms of individual offensive behavior. Considerable achievements were noted in elaborating a general theory of crime prevention.

The most important present task of criminological research is to uncover the deep and complex interlinks between the state, the dynamics, and the pattern of criminality on the one hand and other phenomena and processes occurring in the society, on the other. There is already a clear outline of such links in demographic developments. The same does not hold true of the changes taking place during the period of scientific-technical revolution in the sphere of economics, ideology, and culture. Establishing the fact of the existence and character of such links provides a scientific base for forecasting crime and by the same token allows for scientifically planning crime suppression on a national scale.

It is no less important to draw up a scientific classification (typology) of the offender's personality depending on social and individual-psychological traits, taking into consideration the awareness of law and perception of moral standards. With such typology it is possible to attain a scientific base for individual prevention of crime, to offer useful guidelines to the investigative judges, the sentencing judges and the personnel of reformatory institutions.

The second complex body of issues with which the institute concerns itself is linked with improving the effectiveness of all criminal justice agencies and the entire Soviet system of penal law. The problems of scientifically organizing the operations of criminal justice considered by the institute include: evolving scientific criteria for evaluating the effectiveness of investigative, court, and prosecution endeavors in the field of crime suppression; the external and internal conditions which have to be met for raising this effectiveness.

In this field the institute advised on such matters as establishing data-processing and information sections in prosecution offices and the courts, rationalizing the planning of work for investigative attorneys, judges, and prosecutors; defining the minimum personnel required by criminal justice.

The effectiveness of the penal law system was considered in the context of criminological issues connected with, first of all, planning the crime suppression measures. The exact contribution of the penal law system to the effectiveness of crime suppression was defined. It is contingent mainly on the overall economic, sociopsychological and cultural-educational endeavors of the socialist state. This in turn allows for a more precise definition of the real posibilities inherent in criminal justice, including the ways of improving its effectiveness in resolving the problems which it faces.

Working on the problem of crime prevention as a complex task the institute stresses the need for improving legislative and penal process rules and the practical context of their application. Studies of the penal law and penal process units concern improvements in the system of penal sanctions and their application, more exact delimitation of the penal process function from the administrative and social measures applied to persons violating legal norms, increasing the degree of unavoidability of penal legal norms, increasing the degree of unavoidability of penal repression for violations of Soviet legal norms.

Comparing the research plans of the institute for different years one notes both an extension of the research scope and the interlinking of the various directions of research. Conclusions of one type of study give rise to a new direction of studies, in turn leading to changes in the topics of associated research. It can even lead to the creation of new disciplines and new research teams.

This is particularly noticeable in the field of forensic psychology and shaping the legal awareness of the Soviet people. Criminological studies conducted in the mid-1960s indicated the significance of detailed analysis of the offender's personality. A sociodemographic analysis of the offender's personality did not suffice to explain the causes of individual offensive behavior. It became necessary to resort to the expertise of psychologists. The newly established forensic psychology unit could not at the same time handle the problems of methodology of promoting legal awareness and the issues of offenders' personality. The issue of promoting legal awareness was taken over by a new unit concerned with studying the importance of society participation in crime suppression.

Many projects would not have been possible without, from the outset, applying modern research methods, particularly sociological methods: polling, interviews, observation, document analysis. Much initiative in working out and promoting these methods was shown by N.P. Kosopliechev, A.D. Berenson, W.B. Yastrebov, A.I. Dolgova, W.I. Kaminskaya, W.W. Ustinova, N.G. Yakovleva, and K.F. Skvortsov. Recently the institute added more sophisticated psychological methods to its repertoire, thanks largely to the efforts of A.R. Ratinov and his team. Methods of mathematical statistics have been developed by L.A. Bikov, D.O. Chan-Magomedov, and the crime statistics and data-processing laboratory of D.L. Gladilin.[62]

The plan of institute studies in the second half of the 1970s took into account the fundamental problems of crime suppression. These were taken up in turn, depending on their urgency, on the fundamental practical requirements and also on the possibility of parallel treatment of a body of issues by the available staff.

The analysis of criminality which the institute has carried out for the past fifty five years and the study of its dynamics allow for a detailed definition of the trends of change in crime. The analysis particularly takes into account such factors as: a lack of uniformity in the trend, specific to socialist countries, of a drop in the crime rate (both in the total number of crimes and in specific types of offenses); changes in the criminality levels of various age and social groups, in the countryside and in urban areas; changes in recidivism and group crimes; and changes in prime patterns.

The main objective is to detect the causes behind the most significant changes in criminality. Meeting this objective requires the uncovering of the social phenomena and processes which influence criminality.

The institute has devoted considerable attention to analyzing crime abroad, particularly in the socialist countries. It is also making efforts to achieve closer cooperation with research facilities in the other socialist countries and more exchange of information concerning research findings about the causes of criminality. An important task will be to draw up recommendations enabling the improvement of criminological information services, where shortcomings represent a significant obstacle to studying criminality.

The traditional direction of criminological research, namely studying the causes of crime, covers a very broad range of problems for the institute. It would appear that distinguishing criminology as a discipline should take into account not only the causes of criminality but also all the circumstances—social phenomena and processes—exerting an influence on criminality. This immediately leads to a change in the approach to criminological research which, in the final resort, should permit: (a) definition of all the social phenomena of a criminogenic nature (conducive to criminality or to specific kinds of crime) or of a countercriminogenic nature (conducive to a reduction in crime); and (b) discovery of the feedback between these phenomena and the mechanism of their influence on crime.

This approach became the starting point for defining the scope of studies on the topic: "The impact of social processes on criminality." Acquaintance with the complicated mechanism through which social processes and phenomena influence criminality would be practically impossible without resort to modern research methods and the selection of the most suitable—in this way perfecting the method of multifactor analysis. Institute plans also encompass these objectives. They call for developing the methodology of research on crime in various regions and the various kinds of crime. All such initiatives will facilitate a better acquaintance with criminality.

The comprehensive study of the impact of social phenomena and processes on criminality cannot be achieved exclusively with the assistance of lawyers or through incentives for representatives of other social disciplines to take up these issues. There is a need for organizing complex research on those problems by criminologists, philosophers, sociologists, psychologists, teachers, demographers, economists, and scientists representing other disciplines, as well as for carrying out independent research projects on specific issues falling within their range of interest.

The institute program of research projects takes into account the complex criminological-psychological study of the offenders' personalities.

It is vital to have sociologists, teachers, and other specialists find out about the behavior and personality changes which took place prior to the offense and the mechanisms guiding behavior conflicting with moral norms and antisocial behavior (that is, conflicting with the requirements, not covered by law, of socialist social norms).

One of the leading directions of institute endeavors consists of utilizing scientific-technical progress for working out proposals to improve the effectiveness of crime prevention. The final objective of this direction should be to create a comprehensive, multilevel system of crime prevention.

The precondition for developing such a system, which will function well over a longer span of time, is the application of good methods for forecasting crime. Such forecasts fall within the range of interests of various disciplines. The institute is going to advance research on criminological prognosis and planning the combat against crime.

Plans drawn up through 1985 call for implementing several projects linked with combating crime. Their findings should prove useful in improving the existing forms of preventive activities and in developing new forms. Research will concentrate on early prevention of crime, the educational-preventive role of mass media, and the legal regulation of preventive actions. Research should allow for drafting a system of crime prevention (for employee groups, regions, towns of various size, on a national scale), recommendations concerning improvements in the means for combating the various types of crime and the pathological social phenomena accompanying crime, such as parasitism and alcoholism. There will be research on the causes of juvenile delinquency and ways of counteracting it.

An urgent problem to be solved by Soviet criminologists in the near future concerns the linking into a single system of all the means for counteracting crime. This will be aided through the organization within the institute of a catalogue of projects for improvement of preventive measures.

It is worth noting that a group of institute experts will carry out a complex study of combating unintentional offenses.

Psychological studies connected with the problems of crime prevention will continue, as previously, in three directions: uncovering the causes of criminality and seeking ways of combating it; studying the issue of the inclusion of psychologists as experts in the penal process; and the psychological aspects of detection, prosecution, and adjudication.

Studies conducted between 1976 and 1980 concerned the awareness of law, the internalization of legal norms, and participation of the society in combating crime.

The Penal Law Unit will continue its interests in the issues connected with the application of various types of legal sanctions, the theory and practice of individualizing punishment, and varying criminal responsibility. Plans extend to studying the practice of applying penal law measures for the protection of the natural environment.

The Prosecutors' Supervision Unit, in addition to participating in various complex research projects, also takes up such issues as the effectiveness of actions to implement prosecutors' supervision and supervision of the observance of law in executing sentences.

University law schools and law institutes offer the subject of prosecutors' supervision as an autonomous discipline of law. This term is defined as covering the entirety of prosecutors' operations, namely their tasks, constitution, and operations. The issue of prosecutors' supervision is particularly emphasized in the Soviet Union; studies of this issue are aimed at improving the methods of crime prevention.[63]

Attentions of experts in criminalistics center on improving the existing scientific-technical measures and developing new ones, as well as on their application in detection and court practice, evolving a method of carrying out investigations of various types of offenses.[64]

With institute assistance the Office of the USSR Prosecutor General has drafted and issued recommendations on the organization and methods of improving the training standards of prosecution office staffs. In order to facilitate analytical work and speed up the drafting of statistical reports the institute has developed an information retrieval system for regional prosecution offices. Institute plans call for organization of special courses for investigative personnel. The institute also takes credit for working out a mathematical formula allowing for the calculation of the necessary number of posts of regional (municipal) prosecutors in the Soviet Union for each republic, state, and district.

The institute endeavors to perfect the methods of organization and administration in prosecution bodies, using modern technical aids. The main objective is to create, using computer technologies, an automated system of administering prosecution bodies (OASU–Prokuratura, that is, Organizovannaya Avtomaticheskaya Sistema Upravleniya). In the first half of the 1980s it will be necessary to resolve several issues concerning the development of typical structural links of OASU–Prokuratura on a republican and district scale, securing the system from the information and legal organization standpoint. Projects are being developed for the mathematical background and for the set of technical means which would allow for the establishment and functioning of the Main Information Center and a network of subscribers. It will be important to secure within OGAS (the automated state administration system) the information feedback between OASU–Prokuratura and the automated industrial management systems.

The utilization and promotion of new methods is largely possible through institute efforts in the sphere of research coordination. Institute scientists direct several Coordination Bureaus and the Section of Socialist Law Observance and Combating Crime within the Council for Coordinating Research on State and Law of the USSR Academy of Sciences.

The institute has recently devoted a great deal of attention to the practical application of research findings. Special sessions of the Scientific Council drafted plans for utilizing research results in practice. In order to provide a faster information flow concerning the results attained through research carried out by the institute the two bulletins, *Scientific Information* and *Express Information*, are widely disseminated. A Unit for Checking the Effectiveness of the Utilization of Research Recommendations in the Practice of Crime Prevention was formed in 1971.

Practical application of recommendations by prosecutors, investigators, and courts is facilitated by seminars, fellowships, and conferences devoted to scientific methods. Scientists from the Institute take an active part in such endeavors. Many of them are council members of the Supreme Courts of the USSR and the Russian Federal Socialist Soviet Republic and of the Council on Methods of the USSR Prosecution Office. The scientists regularly participate in drafting legal statutes, in plenary sessions of the USSR Supreme Court and the Supreme Courts of union republics.

The institute has close contacts with similar research facilities in the other socialist countries. Between 1977 and 1980 the institute was visited by eighty seven scientists from the socialist countries. In turn forty five institute scientists visited the various socialist states in Europe and Asia.

Institute personnel takes an active part in international congresses and has contacts with numerous foreign research organizations. This was reflected in the study prepared by renowned Soviet criminologists on the leading issues concerning the pattern, changes, and prevention of crime in the Soviet Union, published in English by the UN Social Defense Research Institute of Rome.[65]

The institute publishes a periodical, *Voprosi borbi s prestupnostu* [Issues of the Struggle against Crime]. Publications on criminological topics also appear in other periodicals, such as *Sovetskoye gosudarstvo y pravo* [Soviet State and Law], *Socyalisticheskaya zakonnost* [Socialist Law Obedience], *Pravovidyeniye* [Knowledge of Law], *Ekonomika* [Economy], *Filosofia* [Philosophy], *Pravo* [Law], *Vestnik Leningradskogo Universiteta* [Leningrad University Journal], *Voprosi preduprezhdeniya prestupnosti* [Issues of Crime Prevention], *Sovetskaya kriminalistika na sluzhbe sledovatela* [Soviet Criminalistics in Investigation Service].

Numerous publications are devoted to the causes of criminality and of the various kinds of crime, as well as to the conditions conducive to crime, that is, the objective circumstances which facilitate the perpetration of crimes.[66]

Comprehensive literature is available on crime prevention, with particular emphasis on the participation of civic organizations in that activity.[67]

The general method of Soviet criminology relies on the application of dialectic and historical materialism. The general method defines and distinguishes the special methods of criminological research, such as the analysis of statistical data, studying court records of penal cases, sociological and psychological studies of offenders' personalities, the conduct of complex criminological research and polling public opinion on crime, its causes, and means of combating it.[68]

There is also considerable emphasis on psychological-criminological studies, as is evident from the increasing number of publications on various aspects of forensic psychology, and attempts to cover this issue in its entirety.[69]

Much attention is devoted to criminological prognosis.[70] In a paper presented at the Seventh International Criminological Congress in Belgrade in 1973, V.N. Kudriavtsev wrote that it is necessary to prepare forecasts of social processes, including the antisocial behavior of citizens, and to plan the activities of criminal justice agencies. Particular advances in this direction have been made in the Soviet Union in recent years.[71]

Soviet criminology has also made considerable strides on the subject of victimology.[72] Along with studying criminality it is thought necessary to study the personality of victims and the circumstances leading to their victimization.[73] There are calls for having criminological and crime statistics publications set aside special chapters devoted to victimization and differentiation of approach to persons who suffered through crime depending on the role of their personality and behavior in a crime-conducive situation; attention is also brought to the need for strengthening the trial guarantees of a "real" victim and for taking the right preventive measures with respect to those victims who acted improperly. Such actions should elevate the formative role of the trial and should contribute to fostering the feeling of man's responsibility for his behavior in various situations.[74]

Soviet literature devotes much space to research and studies on penitentiary theory and practice.

Comprehensive treatment is given to the nature and causes of juvenile delinquency. Complex research projects have been carried out on the subject in the USSR for many years. The studies conducted by the All-Union Institute and by other research facilities concern such problems as the state of and changes in this delinquency, the character and scope of its causes, the personality of juvenile delinquents, the application of penalties and substitute measures, and the principles of combating the individual types of offenses.

This issue is viewed as a component part of the general problem of the nature and causes of criminality, with attention given to such aspects as the unfavorable conditions of upbringing in the family and the closest environment as sources for shaping antisocial views and habits, or the shortcomings in the organization of educational-formative endeavors in schools.[75]

L.N. Anisimov in a monograph presented the historical process of the shaping and development of international law concerned with combating and preventing of drug abuse and also reviewed the narcotics legislation in the United States, the United Kingdom, France, the USSR and the European socialist countries.

Soviet criminology has close links with other social sciences and makes use of their achievements.[76] In the USSR it is defined as a legal discipline, while the majority of criminologists view it as an autonomous discipline, with its own subject and a defined area of the study of social relations.

Numerous publications on penal law also touch upon criminological issues. A.A. Piontkovski (1898–1973), one of the leading Soviet theoreticians of penal law, also concerned himself with criminology.[77]

Criminologists are greatly interested in sociological studies of such social issues as employment, education, and family.[78] Research findings in psychology, particularly social psychology, make it possible to understand the shaping of views and habits in various milieus and to assist in uncovering the causes of the lasting nature of antisocial attitudes of habitual offenders. The links of criminology with pedagogy are particularly noticeable in the case of juvenile delinquency and its prevention. The link between criminology and the economic disciplines manifests itself in part in studying the role and influence of economic laws on the development of social relations and on seeking ways for preventing crime in the various branches of the national economy.

The United States has shown a growing interest in Soviet criminology, as is evident from the fairly large numer of articles and books on the subject.[79] The UN Social Defense Research Institute in Rome also edited a publication in 1974 devoted to the development of Soviet criminology.[80]

Bulgaria is a relative newcomer to criminological research; its first scientific studies of crime data to 1960. The pioneering institutions in this field were the Central Commission for Combating the Anti-Social Acts of Juveniles and the Inter-Ministerial Commission for Studying the Causes of Criminality. This latter institution was in 1968 transformed into the Council for Criminological Studies of the Central Prosecution Office. The same year marked the formation of the Criminology and Criminalistics Institute of the Ministry of Internal Affairs.[81]

The Council for Criminological Studies is an interdepartmental agency operated on behalf of the prosecution office and the ministries of justice and internal affairs, and of the supreme court. The council is presided over by the Chief Prosecutor. The studies carried out by the council serve as a basis for the drafting of suggestions concerning the elimination of crime causes and of crime-conductive conditions. The research staff of the council numbers less than twenty people who draft project premises, coordinate the conduct of research and synthesize the findings. Data collection itself is done by numerous teams which include public prosecutors, judges, legal counselors, local administration personnel, and experts in various fields hired for such projects.

As of the late 1970s the council had the following specialized sections: section one: offenses against the state, economic offenses, offenses against private property and against documents; section two: offenses against life and health, hooliganism (which is treated in Bulgaria as a distinct form of offense), traffic offenses, offenses against work safety rules; section three: juvenile delinquency; section four: activities of prosecution and criminal justice bodies (organization, methods of operation, and effectiveness).

An interesting experiment was the establishment, on the initiative of local authorities, of a regional Criminological Center in Varna. It operates under auspices of the Public Order Commission of the Regional People's Council. The center is staffed, on a completely voluntary basis, by judges, public prosecutors, barristers, legal advisors, and police specialists. The center carries out research on criminology, criminalistics, and forensic psychology, taking part in projects of the Council for Criminological Studies. The center is further charged with promoting better knowledge of law and of other disciplines significant for combating crime.

The main institutional base of criminology in Czechoslovakia is the Research Institute of Criminology of the General Prosecutor's Office (Vyzkumny Ustaw Kryminologicky pri Generalni Prokuratuze). It was established during the 1960s as a departmental facility of the prosecution office and was originally known as the Criminalistics Institute.

The change in designation and scope of operations took place in 1965 by decree of the Czechoslovak Communist Party Central Committee Presidium. In accordance with this decree the institute was to carry out research on the causes and prevention of crime. The projects undertaken in the first few years of institute operation went beyond this narrow field. Particularly notable were the studies on the social and individual factors behind juvenile delinquency which led to the establishment of a Government Commission for Care of Threatened Juveniles.[82]

The findings of an empirical study concerned with juveniles aged fifteen through eighteen were presented in a publication by the institute. The study covered 777 juveniles who were brought before juvenile courts for committing at least their second delinquent act. The control group of non-convicted juveniles included 889 persons, representing 0.1 percent of the entire juvenile population of those ages in Czechoslovakia.[83]

This first stage of institute operations also led to publication of a commemorative volume on the seventieth birthday of Professor Vladimir Solnar, an outstanding scholar, correspondent member of the Czechoslovak Academy of Sciences and former head of the Penal Law Faculty at Prague's Charles University. He guided the education of a generation of Czechoslovak lawyers and made great contributions to the development of penitentiary disciplines. In this volume the penitentiary topics are elaborated upon by Jiri Nezkusil, O. Novotny, G. Prenosil and J. Tolar.[84]

The scope of institute operations was further extended after 1971. Its projects were geared to the needs of prosecution agencies, other state agencies, and civic organizations involved in combating crime. The research activity of the institute concentrated on: the phenomenology and etiology of crime and other social pathology phenomena; means of combating and preventing crime; form and methods of the treatment of offenders, from the point of view of protecting the society and rehabilitating the offenders; the causes of delinquency and other forms of antisocial behavior by juveniles; theoretical issues of Marxist criminology and the fundamental issues and methodology in criminology research; and prosecution methods from the point of view of improving the effectiveness of supervision.

In view of such objectives, the research plans of the institute were directed to studying the problems of legal consciousness, trends and forecasts of crime development, recidivism, juvenile delinquency, and methods of prosecutor's supervison in penal proceedings.

Future plans call for comprehensive studies of the problem of combating crime and extending research; studies are expected to extend to statistical research, the development of criminological research methodology, and penal policy.

The institute has published, among other books, an elaborate study by Oldrich Suchy on recidivism in the socialist and nonsocialist countries, viewed from the criminological and legal points of view, including an analysis of the measures of penal and social reaction to recidivism.[85]

A group of scholars from the criminology division of the Penal Law Faculty of Prague's Charles University has edited a textbook of criminology. It treats with the subject and system of criminology, causes and forms of criminality, crime prevention, the issue of the offender's personality, research methodology, and research methods in criminology. In the chapter devoted to the causes of crime the authors have presented their original etiological concept of the theory of conflict, individual structures, and milieu structures.[86]

In Yugoslavia the University of Belgrade has had a Criminology and Criminalistics Department (Zavod za Kriminologiju i Kryminalistiku) since 1929. In the 1950s criminology institutes were founded in the Law Departments of Ljubljana and Sarajevo Universities.[87]

The Institute of Criminological and Sociological Studies (Institut za Kryminoloska i Socioloska Istrazivanja) of Belgrade is the country's foremost criminological center. For the past two decades it has carried out research in criminology and sociology, publishing monographs and annual reports, and organizing symposia on current problems of crime. The institute has a staff of forty scholars representing various disciplines.

The organizational structure of the institute was changed a few years ago. The structure is flexible; ad hoc research teams are formed for given projects.

Since 1972 the Institute has been publishing the "Zbornik Instituta za Kryminoloska i Socioloska Istrazivanja" [Reports of the Institute of Criminological and Sociological Studies]. In recent years the Institute has published a number of valuable monographs.[88]

Criminological research is further carried out by a number of other institutes and sections, notably the criminology institutes of Belgrade, Ljubljana, and Sarajevo and the Institute of Criminalistic Expertises in Zagreb, and also the university faculties of penal law.[89] Selected criminological issues are also studied by the Institute of Sociological and Political-Legal Studies in Skopje (Institut za Socioloska i Politicko-Pravna Istrazivanja).

The Institute of Comparative Law (Institut za Upredno Pravo) in Belgrade, formed in 1955, is also partly concerned with criminological studies. Some publications of this institute also appear in English and French.[90]

The numerous interesting topics handled by Yugoslav criminology include juvenile delinquency,[91] social pathology,[92] predicting antisocial behavior of the mentally ill, sexual crimes, economic offenses, and homicides.

The extensive range of interests of the Yugoslav criminologists is evident from the following list of topics studied in Belgrade:

minor offenses in Yugoslavia;

impact of economic development on the dynamics and structure of crime;

concentration of social pathology phenomena in urban areas;

causes of the considerable differentiation in convictions by courts of the various republics for the same types of offenses;

suspended sentences and other measures excluding imprisonment in legislation and in practice;

criminological expertise on the offender's personality;

characteristics of road traffic offenses;

the main factors behind traffic offenses;

system of penalties for traffic offenses, specific features of penal policy and traffic safety;

relationship between driver fatigue and the accident rate;

organization and effectiveness of juvenile delinquency prevention;

delinquency of children;

role of supervisory bodies in penal proceedings and implementation of measures to which juvenile delinquents are sentenced;

effectiveness of penal measures applied to juvenile delinquents with special consideration to recidivism;

rehabilitation of juvenile delinquents in Belgrade;

juvenile delinquency in contemporary Europe.[93]

A description of the large-scale activities of the Criminology Institute of the Law Faculty of the University of Ljubljana, including prospects for criminology as a discipline, was presented by Katja Vodopivec, professor at the university and director of the Criminology Institute, on the fifteenth anniversary of the institute in issue 4(1969) of *Revija za Kriminalistiko in Kriminologijo*.

Criminological publications include, among others, *Jugoslovenska Revija za Kriminologiju i Krivicno Pravo*, the journal of the Yugoslav Penal Law and Criminology Society and *Revija za Kryminalistiko in Kriminologijo*, the journal of the Belgrade Institute of Criminological and Sociological Studies. Also, a criminology textbook was published in 1969.[94]

Penologiya is a relatively new journal which has appeared in Belgrade since 1973. In the foreword to the first issue of the journal, clarifying the purpose of publishing a special periodical on this subject, V. Popovic explained that the development of systems of implementing penal sanctions is the center of attention of practitioners and theoreticians. The Yugoslav Association of Penologists has made considerable strides in its efforts to date; the periodical acts as a further aid in obtaining even better results.

The Criminology Institute of the University of Ljubljana Law Department has published a comparative study of certain types of offenses against property in Yugoslavia, Austria, and Poland. The study was divided into four main headings: the problems of international comparative studies of crime; the aim, subject and methodology of research; statistics of offenses in the countries which were studied; and the definition of offenses and classification systems of crime, including a comparison of sentenced groups in the countries under study.[95]

In the German Democratic Republic criminological research is concentrated in four university centers:

The Penal Law Institute, Law Department, Martin Luther University in Halle-Wittenberg; (Institut für Strafrecht der Juristischen Fakultät der Martin-Luther-Universität, Halle-Wittenberg);

Penal Law Institute, Juridical Disciplines Department, Friedrich Schiller University of Jena (Institut für Strafrecht der Rechtswissenschaftlichen Fakultät der Friedrich-Schiller-Universität, Jena);

Penal Law Institute, Law Department, Karl Marx University, Leipzig (Institut für Strafrecht der Juristischen Fakultät der Karl-Marx-Universität, Leipzig);

Penal Law Institute, Law Department, Humboldt University, Berlin (Institut der Strafrecht der Juristischen Fakultät der Humboldt Universität, Berlin).

Criminological research is also carried out by the Walter Ulbricht German Academy of Sciences on State and Law (Deutsche Akademie für

Staats- und Rechtswissenschaft "Walter Ulbricht"), and juvenile delinquency issues are considered by the Criminological Youth Research Society of the Scientific Advisory Committee of the Council of Ministers Youth Office (Forschungemeinschaft Jugendkriminologie beim Wissenschaftlichen Beirat für Jugendforschung des Amtes für Jugendfragen beim Ministerrat der DDR).

The GDR Prosecutor General's Office has a Scientific Center on Crime Research (Abteilung Wissenschaftliche Kriminalitätsforschung) geared mainly to practical actions.

The GDR State Publishers in 1971 brought on the market the second edition of *Sozialistische Kriminologie: Ihre theoretische und methodologische Grundlegung*. The book was written jointly by professors of Berlin's Humboldt University and the German Academy of Sciences on State and Law (Deutsche Akademie für Staats- und Rechtswissenschaft), Potsdam.[96] The elaborate 500-page text is divided into four parts: the theoretical foundations of socialist criminology; the social background of crime in the GDR; the issue of the offender's personality; and the technique and methodology of criminological research.

The authors view the subject of criminology as the study of the causes of crime as a social phenomenon and the development and application of measures to reduce and gradually eliminate criminality as society progresses into a communist society. Writing on the history of socialist criminology the authors refer to the 1845 work by Friedrich Engels, *Circumstances of the Working Class in England*, which among other things listed the causes of crime in a bourgeois society. The GDR authors view this treatise as the beginning og socialist criminology, by the same token disclaiming the views about the lack of traditions or theoretical foundations for such criminology. The authors explain the sources and causes of crime in the GDR as the developmental contradictions of the stage of transformation from capitalism to socialism.

The concluding part of the book is devoted to empirical research issues, with the accent on sociological and statistical research methods. Contrary to the views of most criminologists from the socialist countries, as propounded, for instance, at the Fourth Congress of Criminologists from the European Socialist Countries held in Bulgaria, September 29–October 2, 1975, the authors of the GDR publication give little credit to biopsychological studies of criminals and, by the same token, to individual prognoses.

One of the criminological publications is *Forum der Kriminalistik*, issued by the Ministry of Internal Affairs. Issues connected with the effective elimination of criminal phenomena from social life are also addressed in the literature concerned with the subject and meaning of law.[97]

Development of criminology in Hungary goes back no further than the end of World War II. An Experimental National Criminology Institute was founded following the proclamation of the Hungarian Soviet Republic in 1919, but is was immediately disbanded after the fall of that republic.[98]

The State Criminalistics Institute (Országos Kriminalisztikai Intézet) was established by government decree in 1960 as an interdepartmental facility directly under the Prosecutor General. At the time when the institute was being formed criminology as such was viewed with distrust in Hungary, as a bourgeois discipline. For that reason the word *criminology* was omitted from the designation of the institute. These views changed, and the institute was renamed the State Institute of Criminology and Criminalistics (Országos Kriminologiai es Kriminalisztikai Intézet). Its Scientific Council includes representatives of various ministries and research institutions: the Prosecutor General's Office, the ministries of justice, internal affairs, and health, the Hungarian Academy of Sciences, the Penal Law and Penal Procedure Faculty of the Budapest University and the Administrative Division of the Communist Party Central Committee. The director of the institute is automatically a member of the board in the Prosecutor General's Office.

The institute is organized in four sections: Criminological; Criminalistics; Documentation and Information; and Administration and Finance.

Currently the institute has a staff of forty, including twenty four scientific and research personnel and sixteen administrative workers. The staff includes former prosecutors, judges and employees of the internal affairs sector.

Institute projects are concerned mainly with criminological issues. Studies are carried out in many directions, both in the theoretical aspect and in consideration of the requirements of practical life. For instance, 1969 brought the publication of a book by K. Endre, *Selected Aspects of Victimology*, devoted to the history of this section of criminology, typology of victims, and the prospects for victimological research in Hungary.[99]

Other research projects are concerned with road accidents, recidivism, attempts against life and health, public property theft, female criminality, and unintentional offenses. In recent years a study was concluded on the relation between economic development and the structure and dynamics of criminality.

Research plans, subject to approval by the Scientific Council, provide for undertaking six to seven projects each year. The studies take about two years each, as a rule concluded with a monographic publication on the subject. Every year the institute publishes *Criminological and Criminalistic Studies* which describes the empirical findings and contains articles on criminological theory.

The institute acts as the central facility of criminological research. Programs of university lectures on criminology are coordinated with the institute in Budapest, and institute personnel lecture at universities. Scholars from academic law centers take part in the conferences and symposia organized by the institute. Students interested in criminology attend courses organized in the institute, make use of its library and at times even carry out some of the tasks connected with institute projects.

Research on criminalistics is limited in scope, as studies on police science tactics and techniques are concentrated in the Criminalistics Section of the Hungarian Police Supreme Headquarters. Its personnel conduct tests of such things as car paints, documents, and autopsies. Institute staff participate by going to the scene of the crime.

The State Institute of Criminology and Criminalistics represents Hungarian criminology abroad, having contacts with research institutions of all the socialist countries and of certain other countries, including the United States, Canada, France, Belgium, and the Federal Republic of Germany. The institute is registered in the UN as the official criminological facility of the Hungarian People's Republic. In 1969 the institute became affiliated with the International Society of Criminology in Paris and is a regular recipient of that society's publications and invitations to international congresses and symposia.

Research on crime and its suppression is also carried out by other facilities, and particularly by the State and Law Institute of the Hungarian Academy of Sciences, the penal law and criminalistics faculties of the universities in Budapest, Pecs, Szeged, and the Criminalistics Section of the Ministry of Internal Affairs. These facilities work closely with the institute.

The courts, prosecution offices, police units, and other state agencies are obliged to make available to the institute all materials, documents, and records and to provide assistance in the form of statistical reports and conducting such research as may be requested by the institute.

Research findings are recorded in detail, providing the basis for articles published in law journals, such as *Magyar Jog és Kulfoldi Jogi Szemle, Jogtund omanyi Közlöny, Acta Juridca*, and in its own periodical, *Kriminalisztikai Tanulmanyck*.

Criminological research in Rumania did not start until the 1960s. The earliest efforts in this field were carried out by the Institute of Forensic Medicine in 1963 and 1969 and were concerned mainly with juvenile delinquency.[100]

Criminological studies are carried out currently by three main facilities organized by: the Prosecutor General's Office; the Ministry of Internal Affairs; and the Research Center of the Communist Youth Union Central Committee.

Overall supervision of the endeavors of these three facilities is effected through a coordinating committee, headed by the first deputy of the Prosecutor General. The committee includes representatives of the three facilities listed here, plus representatives of the Ministry of Justice and the University of Bucharest.

Research findings are published as monographs or in law journals, particularly in *Revista Romana Drept* and *Analele Universitatii Bucureşti*. The universities of Bucharest, Jassach, and Cluj offer lectures on criminology.

In the Republic of Cuba criminological research is carried out by the National Institute of Criminology (Instituto Nacional de Criminologia) and a research section in the Prosecutor General's Office. There is also a Cuban Criminological Society.

Mongolia has an Institute for Studying the Causes and Conditions of Crime in Ulan Bator. The institute is subordinate to the Prosecutor General, has a staff of twelve, and is organized in three sections: criminological, economic offenses, and prosecutor's supervision.

This review of criminological research facilities in the socialist countries indicates the existence of certain organizational differences, reflecting the preference for operational forms best suited and most effective under the specific circumstances. This does not prevent frequent contacts in the form of symposia and congresses, exchange of information on research findings and theoretical advances, and even joint research projects.

It is worth noting the international congresses of criminologists from the socialist countries on juvenile delinquency issues. At the congress held at Varna in 1976 the topics concerned juvenile delinquency in large cities. Information given at the congress showed that criminality in many of the socialist countries was diminishing. In regard to etiology, the greatest amount of attention was devoted to the problem of the interrelationship between urbanization coupled with industrialization and juvenile delinquency in the large cities. The view prevailed that these processes do not lead to an increase in juvenile delinquency and, under certain conditions, can even be conducive to reducing such delinquency. It was pointed out that the big city offers particularly wide opportunities for taking up various actions aimed at reducing juvenile delinquency.

The congress also devoted much attention to various organizational problems connected with preventing juvenile delinquency. In most countries the prosecutor or the court acts as the body coordinating such activities. Recently a tendency has appeared to have those functions taken over by educational authorities.

The cooperation between the socialist criminologists and the mutual utilization of theoretical advances and empirical findings is reflected in the publications containing contributions by authors from various countries and providing a representative review of the issues. In Poland the Juridical Publishing House published a book on criminological forecasting, with contributions by various authors.[101] The book contains articles contributed by criminologists from Poland, the Soviet Union, Bulgaria, Yugoslavia, and Hungary. The materials presented in this publication give an insight into the issues of criminological prediction in the countries of the socialist community, including the attempts to use such forecasting as an effective instrument for preventing crime.

A similar type of publication was offered by Poland's Institute of Crime Problems in the form of a collection of selected criminological articles which appeared in periodicals published in the socialist countries. It contained thirty six articles concerning: the main objectives and directions of criminological research; the etiology of crime; the research findings on selected issues in specific criminology; the methodology and state of criminological research; and crime prevention.[102]

Criminological cooperation was further advanced by the Fifth Criminological Congress of the Socialist Countries held in Poland in June 1978, devoted to the significant question of a public participation in crime prevention.

Notes

1. Józef J. Bossowski, *Wiadomości z nauk kryminologicznych* [What we know of criminological disciplines] (Poznań: Księgarnia Akademicka 1946).

2. Leon Tyszkiewicz, "Zarys rozwoju kryminologii w Polsce w latach 1945–1969 [Outline of the development of criminology in Poland 1945–1969], *Ruch Prawniczy, Ekonomiczny i Socjologiczny* 1970, no. 3, pp. 61–72. The author noted the following publications during this period: Maria Żebrowska, "Nieletni przestępcy w Warszawie po wojnie" [Juvenile delinquents in Warsaw after the war], *Psychologia Wychowawcza* 1948, no. 1–2, pp. 34–54; Natalia Han-Ilgiewicz, "Dzieci moralnie zaniedbane przed wojną i obecnie" [Morally deprived children before the war and at present], *Psychologia Wychowawcza* 1948, No. 1–2, pp. 55–62; Stanisław Batawia, "Wpływ ostatniej wojny na przestepczość nieletnich" [Impact of the last war on juvenile delinquency], *Psychologia Wychowawcza* 1948, no. 1–2, pp. 25–33; Stefan Baley *Zagadnienie walki z przestępczością młodocianych na tle współczesnych doświadczeń w Stanach Zjednoczonych Ameryki Północnej* [Issue of combating juvenile delinquency on the basis of modern experience in the United States] (Warsaw: Nasza Księgarnia, 1948); Krzysztof Poklewski-Koziełł, "Działalność sądów doraźnych w 1946 r. w świetle 1021 akt sadowych" [Activity of court martials in 1946 in the light

of 1021 court records], *Demokratyczny Przeglad Prawniczy* 1947, no. 11, pp. 14–28; idem, "Rozbój i sprawy rozboju w 1946 r." [Robbery and robbery cases in 1946], *Demokratyczny Przeglad Prawniczy* 1948, no. 2, pp. 11–16; Zygmunt Sitnicki, "Uwagi ogólne nad statystyka przestepczości w Polsce w 1946 r." [General comments on crime statistics in Poland 1946], *Demokratyczny Przeglad Prawniczy* 1948, no. 2, pp. 9–10; Józef Szczucki, "Rzut oka na statystyke przestepczości za 1947 r." [A look at crime statistics 1947], *Demokratyczny Przeglad Prawniczy* 1949, no. 3, pp. 29–31; Leon Janowski, "Kradzieze w świetle statystyki prezestepczości za rok 1947" [Thefts in 1947 crime statistics], *Demokratyczny Przeglad Prawniczy* 1949, no. 3, pp. 15–20; Wiktor Poznański, "Uszkodzenie ciała i bójki w 1947 r. w świetle akt sadowych" [Bodily injuries and assaults in 1947 in the light of court records], *Demokratyczny Przeglad Prawniczy* 1950, no. 1, pp. 40–50.

3. Paweł Horoszowski, *Statystyka kryminalna* [Crime Statistics] (Warsaw: Państwowe Zakłady Wydawnictw Szkolnych, 1950); idem, "Materiały stastyczno-kryminalne i ich analiza" [Crime statistics data and their analysis], typescript Łódź, 1952); Leszek Kubicki, "Struktura przestepczości w Polsce, w świetle statystyki skazań w latach 1948–1952" [Crime patterns in Poland in the light of convictions statistics, 1948–1952], *Nowe Prawo* 1954, no. 7–8, pp. 39–48; Władysław Hańczakowski, "Wiek sprawcy w świetle statystyki w latach 1946–1952" [Age of offender in statistics 1946–1952], *Nowe Prawo* 1955, no. 6, pp. 32–37.

4. Stanisław Batawia, *Społeczne skutki nałogowego alkoholizmu w świetle badań środowiskowych 100 rodzin nałogowych alkoholików* [Social consequences of habitual alcoholism in the light of a milieu study of 100 families of habitual alcoholics] (Warsaw: Państwowy Zakład Wydawnictw Lekarskich, 1951).

5. Halina Spionek, "Próba nowego ujecia problemów psychologicznych w przestepczości nieletnich" [Attempt at a new approach to psychological problems in juvenile delinquency], *Studia Pedagogiczne* 1954, vol. 1, pp. 246–266.

6. Paweł Zakrzewski, "Współdziałanie w przestepczości dorosłych i nieletnich w świetle badań" [Collaboration in offense of adults and juveniles in the light of studies], *Państwo i Prawo* 1955, no. 6, pp. 910–928.

7. Anna Pawełczyńska, "O niektórych przyczynach chuligaństwa" [On certain causes of hooliganism], in *Chuligaństwo: Studia* [Hooliganism: Studies], ed. J. Sawicki (Warsaw: Wydawnictwo Prawnicze, 1956), pp. 89–127.

8. Tadeusz Cyprian, *Chuligaństwo wśród młodzieży: Problem społeczny i prawny* [Hooliganism among young people: A social and legal problem] (Poznań: Państwowe Wydawnictwo Naukowe, 1956).

9. Paweł Horoszowski, *Kryminologia: Wybrane zagadnienia* [Crim-

inology: selected problems] (Warsaw: Centralny Zarzad Zakładów Karnych, 1958).

10. Jerzy Sliwowski, "Ośrodek Badań Penitencjarnych—nowa placówka naukowa" [Penitentiary Studies Center—new research facility], *Nowe Prawo* 1961, no. 10, pp. 1262–1265; Leon Tyszkiewicz, "Zarys rozwoju kryminologii," p. 66; *Kronika Ośrodka Badań Penitencjarnych* [Chronicle of the Penitentiary Studies Center] 1963, no. 1, pp. 117–120; Hanna Namowicz, "Powstanie i działalność poradni psychologiczno-kryminologicznej w Warszawie [Establishment and Activity of the Psychological-Criminological Advisory Unit in Warsaw], *Przeglad Penitencjarny* 1971, no. 4, pp. 106–107; "List Ministra Sprawiedliwości na dziesieciolecie Ośrodka Badań Przestepczości" [Letter by the Minister of Justice on the tenth anniversary of the Crime Research Center], *Przeglad Penitencjarny* 1971, no. 4, pp. 3, 4.

11. Jerzy Smoleński, "Działalność badawcza w Prokuraturze w latach 1962–1972" [Research activity in prosecution offices 1962–1972], *Studia Kryminologiczne, Kryminalistyczne i Penitencjarne* 1976, vol. 4, pp. 153–171.

12. Witold Swida, *Wpływ zmiany ustroju na przestepczość; (w świetle przestepczości w Kaliszu i powiecie kaliskim)* [The impact of a changed sociopolitical system on criminality; (in the light of criminality in Kalisz city and district)] (Wrocław: Zakład Narodowy im. Ossolińskich), vol. 1 (1960), p. 174; vol. 2 (1962), p. 374.

13 Stanisław Batawia, *Proces społecznego wykolejania sie nieletnich przestepców* [Process of social deviation of juvenile delinquents] (Warsaw: Państwowe Wydawnictwo Naukowe, 1958), p. 337.

14. Helena Kołakowska, "Nieletni recydywiści: Wyniki badań 500 nieletnich recydywistów" [Juvenile recidivists: Findings of a study of 500 juvenile recidivists], *Archiwum Kryminologii* 1960, vol. 1, pp. 55–112; Helena Kołakowska-Przełomiec, "Wyniki badań 432 chłopców nie uczacych sie i nie pracujacych" [Findings of a study of 432 boys "not in school and not working"], *Archiwum Kryminologii* 1972, vol. 5, pp. 32–83.

15. Adam Strzembosz, *Nieletni sprawcy kradzież y w środowisku wielkomiejskim* [Juvenile thieves in a large city environment] (Warsaw: Państwowe Wydawnictwa Naukowe, 1971).

16. Paweł Zakrzewski, *Zjawisko wykolejenia spo*łecznego młodzież y *na terenach uprzemysławianych; wyniki badań w Nowej Hucie* [Phenomenon of social deviation of young adults in industrializing areas; findings of a study in Nowa Huta] (Warsaw: Wydawnictwo Prawnicze, 1969).

17. Stanisław Szelhaus, *Młodociani recydywiści: Społeczne czynniki procesu wykolejenia* [Young adult recidivists: Social factors in the deviation process] (Warsaw: Państwowe Wydawnictwo Naukowe, 1969).

18. Zofia Ostrihańska, "Wielokrotni recydywiści w świetle badań

kryminologicznych i psychologicznych" [Multiple recidivists in the light of criminological and psychological research], *Archiwum Kryminologii* 1976, vol. 7, pp. 7–139.

19. Zofia Ostrihańska, "Prognoza recydywy u nieletnich przestepców oraz wyniki badań prognostycznych 180 recydywistów w wieku 15–16 lat" [Prognosis of recidivism for juvenile delinquents and findings of a prognosis study of 180 recidivists aged 15–16], *Archiwum Kryminologii* 1965, vol. 3, pp. 121–281.

20. Jerzy Jasiński, "Przestepczość nieletnich w Polsce w latach 1961–1967; rozmiary, struktura przestepczości, orzeczone środki" [Juvenile delinquency in Poland, 1961–1967; scope, pattern, measures applied], *Archiwum Kryminologii* 1969, vol. 4, pp. 149–202; idem, "Powrót do przestepstwa i recydywa osób dorosłych w latach 1963–1973" [Return to crime and recidivism of adults, 1963–1973], in *Wybrane zagadnienia patologii społecznej* [Selected issues of social pathology], ed. Maria Jarosz (Warsaw: Główny Urzad Statystyczny, 1975), pp. 123–151; Jerzy Jasiński, "Rozmiary i dynamika przestepczości" [Scope and dynamics of criminality], and "Charakterystyka przestepczości" [Characteristics of criminality], in Jerzy Jasiński et al., *Zagadnienia przestepczości w Polsce* [Issues of criminality in Poland] (Warsaw: Wydawnictwo Prawnicze, 1975), pp. 13–49, 50–90; Jerzy Jasiński, "Zagadnienia przewidywania przyszłego kształtu przestepczości w Polsce" [Questions of predicting the future shape of crime in Poland], *Studia Prawnicze* 1975, no. 43, pp. 3–54.

21. Andrzej Mościskier, "Przestepczość w rejonach uprzemysławianych i zależność dynamiki przestepczości od dynamiki procesów społeczno-gospodarczych; lata 1958–1960 oraz 1964–1966" [Criminality in industrializing regions and the link between crime dynamics and the dynamics of socioeconomic processes; years 1958–1960 and 1964–1966], *Archiwum Kryminologii* 1969, vol. 4, pp. 105–141.

22. Brunon Hołyst, *Zabójstwo: Studium kryminologiczne i kryminalistyczne* [Homicide: Criminological and criminalistics study] (Warsaw: Ministerstwo Spraw Wewnetrznych, 1970); Halina Janowska, *Zabójstwa i ich sprawcy: Analiza Socjologiczna* [Homicides and their perpetrators: Sociological analysis] (Warsaw: Państwowe Wydawnictwo Naukowe, 1974).

23. Helena Kołakowska-Przełomiec, *Przestepczość i nieprzystosowanie społeczne nieletnich w genezie przestepczości dorosłych* [Criminality and social maladjustment of juveniles in the genesis of adult criminality] (Wrocław: Zakład Narodowy im. Ossolińskich, 1977).

24. Hanna Malewska, Vincent Peyré, and Anna Firkowska-Mankiewicz, *Przestepczość nieletnich: Uwarunkowania społeczno-ekonomiczne* [Juvenile delinquency: Socioeconomic conditions] (Warsaw: Państwowe Wydawnictwo Naukowe, 1973), p. 254.

25. Anna Firkowska-Mankiewicz, *Czynniki biopsychiczne a przestepczość nieletnich* [Bio-mental factors and juvenile delinquency] (Warsaw: Państwowe Wydawnictwo Naukowe, 1972), p. 211.

26. Zbigniew Bożyczko, *Kradzież kieszonkowa i jej sprawca* [Pickpocketing and pickpockets] (Warsaw: Wydawnictwo Prawnicze, 1962), p. 199; idem, *Kradzież z włamaniem i jej sprawca* [Burglaries and burglars] (Warsaw: Wydawnictwo Prawnicze, 1970), p. 255; idem, "Z problematyki badań środowisk przestepczych" [On problems of studying the criminal milieu], *Problemy Kryminalistyki* 1969, no. 77, pp. 43–57; idem, "Trzy pokolenia zawodowych złodziei kieszonkowych" [Three generations of professional pickpockets], *Problemy Kryminalistyki* 1975, no. 115–116, pp. 334–345.

27. Other articles on recidivism include: Stanisław Batawia, "Młodociani i młodzi recydiwiści w świetle badań kryminologicznych" [Juvenile and young adult recidivists in the light of criminological studies], *Archiwum Kryminologii* 1965, vol. 3, pp. 9–95; Stanisław Szelhaus, "Wyniki badań recydywistów alkoholików w pierwszym stadium przestepczości po ukończeniu 25 lat" [Findings of studies on recidivists—alcoholics in the first stage of criminality after the age of 25], *Archiwum Kryminologii* 1972, vol. 5, pp. 228–267.

28. Barbara Jarzebowska-Baziak, *Praca wychowawcza w zakładzie karnym dla młodocianych; na tle doświadczeń zakładu w Szczypiornie* [Reeducational efforts in a penal institution for young adult offenders; the example of the Szczypiorno institution] (Warsaw: Wydawnictwo Prawnicze, 1972); Teodor Szymanowski, *Powrotność do przestepstwa po wykonaniu kary pozbawienia wolności* [Recidivism after serving a prison sentence] (Warsaw: Wydawnictwo Prawnicze, 1976).

29. Józef Wasik, "Efektywność środków karnych stosowanych w Polsce mierzona powrotnościa do przestepstwa" [Effectiveness of penal measures applied in Poland, gauged by the rate of recidivism], *Przeglad Penitencjarny i Kryminologiczny* 1972, no. 4, p. 72.

30. Iwona Muszyńska, "Efektywność kary ograniczenia wolności mierzona powrotnościa do przestepstwa" [Effectiveness of limitation of liberty gauged by the rate of recidivism], *Zeszyty Naukowe Instytutu Badania Prawa Sadowego* 1974, no. 1, pp. 68–85.

31. Walenty Moszyński, "Warunkowe skazania" [Conditional conviction], *Nowe Prawo* 1965, no. 2, p. 143; Józef Wasik, "Powrotność do działalności przestepczej po orzeczeniu kar pozbawienia wolności z warunkowym zawieszeniem ich wykonania" [Recidivism after conditional suspension of prison sentences], *Przeglad penitencjarny* 1970, no. 1, p. 47 ff.

32. Andrzej Tobis, *Zasady orzekania w sprawach o warunkowe zwolnienie* [Principles of sentencing in cases for conditional release] (Warsaw: Wydawnictwo Prawnicze, 1972), pp. 146, 147; Józef Wasik,

"Próba oceny efektywności warunkowego zwolnienia na podstawie powrotności do przestepstwa" [Attempt at evaluating the effectiveness of conditional release on the basis of the recidivism rate], *Nowe Prawo* 1970, no. 3, pp. 363 ff.

33. Mikołaj Leonieni and Wojciech Michalski, *Efektywność warunkowego umorzenia postepowania karnego w praktyce sadowej* [Effectiveness of conditional discontinuance of penal proceedings in court practice] (Warsaw: Wydawnictwo Prawnicze, 1975); Andrzej Marek, *Warunkowe umorzenie postepowania karnego w praktyce sadowej* [Effectiveness of conditional discontinuance of penal proceedings in court practice] (Warsaw: Wydawnictwo Prawnicze, 1975); Andrzej: Marek, *Warunkowe umorzenie postepowania w polskim ustawodawstwie karnym* [Conditional discontinuance of proceedings in Polish penal legislation] (Toruń: Wydawnictwo Uniwersytetu Mikołaja Kopernika, 1971).

34. Michał Bereziński, Sylwia Homolicka, and Andrzej Putkowski, *Praktyka stosowania i uchylania środka zabezpieczajacego z art. 99 i 100 k.k.* [Practice of applying and lifting the securing measure specified in Art. 99 and 100 of the penal code] (Lódź: Prokuratura Generalna, Biuro Studiów Problematyki Przestepczości, 1972).

35. Jerzy Sliwowski and Piotr Wierzbicki, "Nadzór ochronny; badania wstepne [Protective supervision; preliminary findings], *Zeszyty Naukowe Instytutu Badania Prawa Sadowego* 1977, no. 6, pp. 125–147.

36. Mieczysław Rudnik, *Badania nad skutecznościa środków wychowawczych i poprawczych* [Studies on the effectiveness of educational and correctional measures], "Zeszyty Naukowe Uniwersytetu Jagielońskiego 318 Prace Prawnicze," script 57: *Przestepczość Nieletnich* [Juvenile delinquency], Cracow, 1973.

37. Józef Wasik, *Próba spojrzenia na efektywność zakładów poprawczych i wychowawczych* [Attempt at evaluating the effectiveness of reformatories and educational institutions], "Zeszyty Naukowe Uniwersytetu Jagiellońskiego 318 Prace Prawnicze," script 57: *Przestepczość Nieletnich* [Juvenile delinquency], Cracow, 1973, pp. 101, 102.

38. Barbara Kowalska-Ehrlich, *Warunkowe zwolnienie nieletnich z zakładów poprawczych* [Conditional release of juveniles from reformatories] (Warsaw: Wydawnictwo Prawnicze, 1973).

39. Tadeusz Kaczmarek, *Sedziowski wymiar kary w Polskiej Rzeczypospolitej Ludowej w świetle badań ankietowych* [Sentencing by judges in the Polish People's Republic in the light of polls] (Wrocław: Zakład Narodowy im. Ossolińskich, 1972).

40. Jerzy Jasiński, "Punitywność systemów karnych: Rozważania nad zakresem, formami i intensywnościa penalizacji" [Punitive degree of penal systems: Considerations on scope, forms and intensity of penalization], *Studia Prawnicze* 1973, no. 35, pp. 61–71.

41. Andrzej Kram, *Sadowy wymiar kary za przestestwa zaboru mienia społecznego w świetle badań prawometrycznych* [Court sentencing for offenses of usurpation of public property in the light of jurimetric studies] (Warsaw: Wydawnictwo Prawnicze, 1977), p. 112.

42. Andrzej Kobus, *Wpływ terenowego zróżnicowania natężenia przestepczości na sadowy wymiar kary w latach 1972 i 1973* [Influence in local differences in crime intensity on the magnitude of court sentences in the years 1972 and 1973] (Warsaw: Ministerstwo Sprawiedliwości, Instytut Badania Prawa Sadowego, 1976), p. 96 and appendix.

43. Paweł Zakrzewski, *Zagadnienie prognozy kryminologicznej* [Question of criminological prognosis] (Warsaw: Wydawnictwo Prawnicze, 1964), p. 224.

44. Hanna Namowicz, *Losy życiowe nieletnich przestepców* [Life fortunes of juvenile delinquents] (Warsaw: Wydawnictwo Prawnicze, 1968), p. 192; Andrzej Tobis, *Zasady orzekania w sprawach o warunkowe zwolnienie* [Principles of adjudicating conditional release cases] (Warsaw: Wydawnictwo Prawnicze, 1972), pp. 7–82; idem, "Z badań empirycznych nad wartościa prognostyczna danych dotyczacych przestepstwa i jego sprawcy" [Findings of empirical studies on the prognostic value of data on the offense and its perpetrator], *Zagadnienia Prawa Karnego* 1977, no. 3, pp. 64–71.

45. Jerzy Jasiński, *Przewidywanie przestepczości jako zjawiska masowego* [Forecasting criminality as a mass phenomenon] (Warsaw: Wydawnictw Prawnicze, 1980).

46. Cited works on alcoholism-linked crime include: Zdzisław Czeszejko-Sochacki, *Przestepstwo rozpijania nieletniego* [The offense of inducing a minor to drink] (Warsaw: Wydawnictwo Prawnicze, 1975); Lech Falandysz, "Problematyka alkoholu jako czynnika wiktymogennego" [The problem of alcohol as a victimogenic factor], *Problemy Alkoholizmu* 1974, no. 5; Tadeusz Kulisiewicz, *Alkohol, alkoholizm i społeczeństwo* [Alcohol, alcoholism and society] (Warsaw: Wiedza Powszechna, 1965); Aleksander Ratajczak, *Stan nietrzeźwości w polskim prawie karnym* [The State of intoxication in Polish penal law] (Poznań: Wydawnictwo Uniwersytetu im. Adama Mickiewicza, 1969).

47. Magdalena Jasińska, *Proces społecznego wykolejenia młodocianych dziewczat* [Process of social deviation of juvenile girls] (Warsaw: Wydawnictwo Prawnicze, 1967); Jadwiga Pabian, "Analiza psychiatryczna i środowiskowa prostytutek krakowskich" [Psychiatric and milieu analysis of Cracow prostitutes], *Archiwum Medycyny Sadowej i Kryminologii* 1973, no. 1, pp. 167–175; idem, "Psycho-socjalne i biologiczne uwarunkowania prostytucji" [Psychosocial and biological conditions of prostitution], *Problemy Kryminalistyki* 1973, no. 105, pp. 542–556.

48. Tadeusz Hanausek and Wiesława Hanausek, *Narkomania* [Drug

addiction] (Warsaw: Wydawnictwo Prawnicze, 1976); Brunon Hołyst, "Narkomania a przestepczość [Drug addiction and criminality], *Farmacja Polska* 1980, no. 4.

49. Danuta Kubacka-Jasiecka, *Funkcjonowanie społeczne osób agresywnych i samoagresywnych* [Social functioning of aggressive and self-aggressive persons] (Wrocław: Zakład Narodowy im. Ossolińskich, 1975); Jan M. Stanik, *Psychologiczne problemy agresji młodocianych w warunkach dyscyplinarnej izolacji* [Psychological problems of juvenile aggression under conditions of disciplinary isolation] (Katowice: Uniwersytet Slaski, 1976); Dobrohna Wójcik, *Srodowisko rodzinne a poziom agresywności przestepczej i nieprzestepczej* [Family environment and the level of delinquent and nondelinquent aggression] (Wrocław: Zakład Narodowy im. Ossolińskich, 1977).

50. Jadwiga Sikora, *Obraz emocjonalności więźniów w świetle badań psychologicznych, biochemicznych i fizyko-lekarskich* [Picture of prisoner emotionality in the light of psychological, biochemical, and physical-medical tests] (Wrocław: Zakład Narodowy im. Ossolińskich, 1973); Bogdan Waligóra, *Funkcjonowanie człowieka w warunkach izolacji wieziennej* [Human functioning under conditions of prison isolation] (Poznań: Uniwersytet im. Adama Mickiewicza, 1974).

51. Jadwiga Kozarska-Dworska, *Psychopatia jako problem kryminologiczny* [Psychopathy as a criminological problem] (Warsaw: Wydawnictwo Prawnicze, 1977).

52. *Tematy empirycznych badań nad przestepczościa w 1978 r.* [Topics of empirical studies on crime] (Warsaw: Instytut Problematyki Przestepczości, 1978).

53. Jerzy Jasiński, ed., *Zagadnienia przestepczości w Polsce* [Issues of criminality in Poland] (Warsaw: Wydawnictwo Prawnicze, 1975).

54. Brunon Hołyst, *Przestepczość w Polsce: Studium Kyminologiczne* [Criminality in Poland: A criminological study] (Warsaw: Wydawnictwo Prawnicze, 1977).

55. An example can be provided by the comprehensive report of the Committee of Legal Disciplines: "O sytuacji w naukach prawnych" [On the situation in legal disciplines], *Państwo i Prawo* 1972, no. 4, pp. 3–24.

56. An example can be provided by: "Program badań podstawowych w zakresie nauk prawnych, opracowany przez KNP" [Program of fundamental studies on legal disciplines, drafted by the Committee of Legal Disciplines], *Państwo i Prawo* 1973, no. 6, pp. 160–162.

57. Leszek Kubicki, "The organization and the main directions of scientific research in the sphere of law in Poland," in: The Polish Lawyers Association, *The Law in Poland: The Chosen Problems* (Warsaw: Wydawnictwo Prawnicze, 1978).

58. Additional information on the Institute of State and Law is available

in: Adam Łopatka, "Wkład Instytutu Państwa i Prawa PAN w rozwój polskiego prawoznawstwa oraz doskonalenie praktyki prawniczej (w 20 rocznice powstania Instytutu)" [The contribution of the Institute of State and Law of the Polish Academy of Sciences to the development of Polish jurisprudence and to the improvement of legal practice (on the twentieth anniversary of the institute], *Państwo i Prawo* 1976, no. 5, pp. 3–11; idem, "Kształcenie i doskonalenie kadr naukowych w INP PAN" [Education and upgrading of research staff in the Institute of Legal Disciplines of the Polish Academy of Sciences], *Państwo i Prawo* 1975, no. 10, pp. 56–60.

59. In 1933 the Criminology Unit of Warsaw University started to publish a periodical entitled *Archiwum Kryminologiczne* [Criminological archives]. A research institution concerned with criminological issues was also operated by the Free Polish University.

60. B. S. Utyevski, "The Issue of Organization and Methods of Studying Criminality and the Offender," *Sovetskoye gosudarstvo y pravo* 1959, no. 11.

61. Mikhail N. Gernet, *Izbranniye proizvyedyenniya* [Selected writings] (Moscow: Yuridicheskaya Literatura, 1974).

62. Vladimir N. Kudriavtsev, "Vsesoyuznomu institutu po izucheniyu prichin y razrabotke mer preduprezhdeniya prestupnosti—10 let" [Ten years of the All-Union Institute for the Study of the Causes and Elaboration of Measures for the Prevention of Crime], *Voprosy borby s prestupnostyu* 1974, no. 20, pp. 3–13.

63. I. V. Zhogin, ed., *Sovershenstvovaniye prokurorskogo nadzora v SSSR* [The practice of prosecutor's supervision in the USSR] (Moscow: Generalna Prokuratura SSSR, Vsesoyuznyi Institut po izucheniyu, 1973).

64. V. V. Klochkov, "Pyerspecteevi nauchnikh issledovaniy" [Prospects of scientific research], *Voprosy borby s prestupnostyu* 1976, no. 24, pp. 3–11.

65. A. A. Gertsenzon, V. N. Kudriavtsev, V. K. Zvirbul, A. B. Sakharov, V. G. Tanaserich, and G. M. Minkovsky, *Recent Contributions to Soviet Criminology* (Rome: U.N. Social Defense Research Institute, 1974), publication no. 8.

66. V. V. Oryekhov, "O prichinakh pryestupnosti v socialisticheskom obshchestvye [On the causes of crime in a socialist society], *Vyestnik Leningradskogo Universiteta* 1972, no. 4; V. K. Zvirbul, "Socialono-istoricheskiy aspiekt issledovaniya prichin prestupnosti" [The social-historical aspect of studying the causes of crime], *Voprosy borby s prestupnostyu* 1969, no. 9; V. N. Kudriavtsev, *Prichinnost v kriminologii: O strukturye individualnogo prestupnogo povedeniya* [Causes in criminology: On the structure of individual offensive behavior] (Moscow: Yuridicheskaya Literatura, 1968).

67. V. V. Panakratov, *Tyeoretischeskiye osnovy ispolsovaniya mye-*

todov socyalnikh nauk pri izuchenyi pruchin prestupnosti [Theoretical background of utilizing social science methods in seeking the causes of criminality], "Myetodologia y myetodika kriminologicheskikh yssledovaniy" (Moscow: Yuridicheskaya Literatura, 1972), pp. 7–13.

68. V. V. Pankratov, ed., *Problemy uchastiya obshchestvennosti v borbye s prestupnostyu* [Problems of social participation in crime suppression] (Moscow: Vsesojuznyi Institut, 1978).

69. Ateist V. Dulov, *Sudyebnaya psichologia* [Forensic psychology] (Mińsk: Yisheyshaya Shkola, 1970).

70. *Sostoyaniye nauchnikh issledovaniy po sudyebnoy psichologyi* (Materiali k I Vsesoyuznoy konferencyi po sudyebnoy psikhologyi) [State of research on forensic psychology (Materials for the first All-Union Conference on Forensic Psychology)] (Moscow: Vsesojuznyi Institut, 1971); B. D. Lyskov, "Aktualniye problyemi sudyebnoy psikhologyi" [Current problems of forensic psychology], *Vyestnik Leningradskogo Universiteta* 1979, no. 5, pp. 76–81.

71. Yu. M. Antonyan, Yu. D. Bluvshtayn, and G. B. Chikoidze, "Prognozirovaniye prestupnogo povyedyeniya y pryedupryzhdyeniye pryestupleyniy" [Forecasting offensive behavior and crime prevention], *Sovetskoye gosudarstvo y pravo* 1977, no. 4, pp. 66–71; G. A. Avanesov, "Sovryemyenniye tryebovaniya, pryedyavlayemiye k metodologyi kriminologicheskogo prognozirovaniya" [Current requirements set for criminological forecasting], *Voprosy borby s prestupnostyu* 1977, no. 26, pp. 15–34; K. F. Skvortsov, "Metodologicheskiye voprosy prognozirovaniya khishcheniy socyalisticheskogo imushchestva" [Methodological issues of forecasting the theft of public property], *Voprosy borby s prestupnostyu* 1976, no. 25, pp. 3–17.

72. S. S. Ostroumov and Z. V. Frank, "O victimologyi y victimnosti" [On victimology and victimization], *Sovetskoye gosudarstvo y pravo* 1976, no. 4.

73. V. S. Minskaya, "Kriminologicheskoye y ugolowno-pravovoye znacheniye povyedyeniya potyerpyevshikh" [Criminological and penal law significance of the behavior of crime victims], *Voprosy borby s prestupnostyu* 1972, no. 16, pp. 9–26; S. B. Soboleva, "Victimologicheskiy aspyekt conflictnikh situatsyi v syemye" [Victimological aspect of conflict situations in the family], *Voprosy borby s prestupnostyu* 1976, no. 25, pp. 37–53; V. Ya. Ribalskaya, "Victimnost kak elemyent structury mekhanizma prestupleniy myescowyerschyennolyetnikh" [Victimization as an element of the structure of the mechanism of delinquent acts committed by juveniles], *Voprosy borby s prestupnostyu* 1978, no. 29, pp. 36–44.

74. L. V. Illina, "Ugolovno-procesualnoye znacheniye victimologi" [Penal trial significance of victimology], *Pravovyedyeniye* 1975, brochure 3.

75. G. M. Minkovsky, "Nyekotoriye prichiny prestupnosti nyesovyer-

schyennolyetnikh v SSSR y myery yeyo pryesupryezhdyeniya" [Some causes of juvenile delinquency in the USSR and means of its suppression], *Sovietskoye gosudarstvo y pravo* 1966, no. 5; E. V. Boldiriev,*Myery pryesupryezhdyeniya pravnarushyenii nyesovyershyennolyetnikh v SSSR* [Means of suppressing law violations by juveniles in the USSR] (Moscow: Izdatelstvo Nauka, 1964); G. M. Minkovsky, "Osnovniye napravleniya y etapy razvitiya issledovaniy problemy borby s prestupnostyu nyesovyershyennolyetnikh" [Basic directions and stages of developing research on problems of struggle against juvenile delinquency], *Voprosy borby s prestupnostyu* 1975, no. 20, pp. 33–48.

76. V. N. Kudriavtsev, "Sociologicheskiy aspect prestupleniya" [Sociological aspect of crime], *Voprosy borby s prestupnostyu* 1973, no. 18, pp. 3–16; V. I. Kaminskaya and L. A. Voloshina, "Kriminologicheskoye znacheniye issledovaniy nravstvyennego y pravovogo soznaniya" [Criminological significance of research on moral norms and legal awareness], *Sovietskoye gosudarstvo y pravo* 1977, no.1, pp. 71–75; A. I. Alexeyev, "Kriminologia y pedagogika" [Criminology and pedagogy], *Sovetskoye gosudarstvo y pravo* 1979, no.10, pp. 89–93; E. B. Urlansis, "O vozmozhnosti ispolzovaniya dyemographicheskikh metodov v kriminologii" [On the possibility of utilizing demographic methods in criminology], *Voprosy borby s prestupnostyu* 1974, no.21, pp.16–28; M. M. Babayev, "Dyemographicheskiye processy y problemy tyerritoryalnikh razlichiy prestupnosti" [Demographic processes and the question of geographic variation of criminality], *Voprosy borby s prestupnostyu* 1974, no. 21, pp.3–15.

77. Andriey A. Piontkovski, *Ucheniye o pryestuplenii po sovetskomu ugolovnomu pravu* [Notion of offense in Soviet penal law] (Moscow: Yuridicheskaya Literatura, 1971).

78. Alexey A. Gertsenzon, "Ugolovnoye pravo y sociologia" [Penal law and sociology] in *Problemy sociologii, ugolovnogo prava y ugolovnoy politiki* [Problems of sociology, penal law and penal policy] (Moscow: Yuridicheskaya Literatura, 1970).

79. Louise Shelley, "Soviet Criminology After the Revolution," *Journal of Criminal Law and Criminology* 70, no. 3, (1979).

80. *Recent Contributions to Soviet Criminology* (Papers Collected by the All-Union Institute for the Study of the Causes and Elaboration of Measures for the Prevention of Crime) (Rome: UNSDRI, 1974), publication no. 8.

81. Georgi Naumov, "On Certain Social Problems of Guiding the Process of Crime Suppression in a Developed Socialist Society," quoted, in Polish translation, in *Kryminologia w krajach socjalistycznych* [Criminology in the socialist countries] (Warsaw: Wydawnictwo Prawnicze, 1976), pp.256 ff.; Veselin Krakashev, *Recidiv y borbata s nyego* [Recidivism and the struggle against it] (Sofia: Nauka i Isskustvo, 1970).

82. Jiri Nezkusil, "O działalności Kryminologicznego Instytutu Badań przy Prokuraturze Generalnej CSRS" [On the activities of the Criminological Research Institute of the Czechoslovak Prosecutor General's Office], *Studia Kryminologiczne, Kryminalistyczne i Penitencjarne* 1975, vol. 2.

83. *Kriminalita Mladeze: Studia o mladistvych delikwentach* [Youth criminality: Studies of juvenile delinquents] (Prague: Vyskumny Ustav Kriminologicky pri Generalni Prokurature CSSR, 1968).

84. *Sbornik praci z trestniho prava* [Collection of writings on penal law], in *K Sedmdesatym Narozeninam prof. dr Vladimira Solnare* [On the seventieth birthday of Professor Vladimir Solnar] (Prague: Panorama, 1969).

85. Oldrich Suchy, *Recidiva: Komparativni Studie*, 2 vols. [Recidivism: Comparative studies] (Prague: Vyzkumny Ustav Kriminologicky pri Generalni Prokurature CSSR, 1971).

86. O. Novotny, ed., *Ceskoslovenska kryminologie: Aktualni problemy* [Czechoslovak criminology: Current issues] (Prague: Panorama, 1971); see also Jiri Nezkusil, ed., *Ceskoslovenska Kriminologie* (Prague: Panorama, 1978).

87. Dragoljub V. Dimitrijevic, "Federal People's Republic of Yugoslavia," UNESCO Report 1957, pp.159–163.

88. These include: Vukasin Pesic, *Ubistva u Jugoslaviji* [Homicides in Yugoslavia] (Belgrade: Institut za Kriminoloska i Socioloska Instrazivanja, 1972); Desanka Lazarevic, *Kratkotrajne Kazne Zatvora* [Short-term prison sentences] (Belgrade: Institut za Kriminoloska i Socioloska Instrazivanja, 1974); Vladan A. Vasilijevic and Dobrivoje M. Radovanovic, *Saobracajni prestupnici* [Habitual offenders] (Belgrade: Institut za kriminoloska i Socioloska Istrazivanja, 1975).

89. Ksenija Korbar, "Kurze Übersicht über neuere kriminologische Untersuchungen in Jugoslavien" [Brief review of the newer criminological research in Yugoslavia], *Kriminologische Gegenwartsfragen* 1970, no.9.

90. Details in *Guide to the Yugoslav Legal System* (Belgrade: The Yugoslav Union for Criminal Law and Criminology, 1977).

91. Aleksandar Todorovic et al., *Prestupnistvo maloletnika u industrijskim naseljima* [Juvenile delinquency in industrialized areas] (Belgrade: Institut za Kriminoloska Istrazivanja, 1966).

92. Ljubo Bavcon et al., *Socjalna patologia* [Social pathology] (Liubljana: u izdanju Pravne Fakultete Univerze v Ljubljani, 1969).

93. *Jugoslavenska Revija za Kryminologiju i krivicno Pravo* [Yugoslav Review of Criminology and Criminal Law] 1971, nos. 1–4.

94. Milan Milutinovic, *Kriminologija: Sa osnovima Kriminalne Politike i Penelogije* [Criminology: Bases of criminal policy and penology] (Belgrade: Prosveta, 1969). 2nd ed. published 1972.

95. Magda Bayer, *Uporedna studija o nekim vrstama imovinakog*

kriminaliteta u Jugoslaviji, Austriji i Poljskoj [A comparative study of some types of property crimes in Yugoslavia, Austria, and Poland] (Ljubljana: Institut za Kriminologijo pri Pravni Fakulteti Publikacija, 1972).

96. Erich Buchholz et al., *Sozialistische Kriminologie: Ihre theoretische und methodologische Grundlegung* [Socialist criminology: Its theoretical and methodological principles] (Berlin: Staatsverlag der DDR, 1971); Gerhard Stiller, *Methoden der sozialistischen kriminologie: Zur Technik und Methodologie der kriminologischen Forschung* [Methods of socialist criminology: The techniques and methodology of criminological research] (Berlin: Staatsverlag der DDR, 1970).

97. Rudolf Arlt and Gerhard Stiller, *Entwicklung der sozialistischen Rechtsordnung in der DDR* [Development of socialist law observance in the GDR] (Berlin: Staatsverlag der DDR, 1973).

98. Antal Bakoczi, [Development of criminological research in Hungary], *Magyar Jog es Kulfoldi Jogi Szemle* 1971, no. 3.

99. József Karoly E. Vigh, [Role and significance of victimology, with special consideration to offenses committed with the use of force], *Acta Facultatis politico-juridicae Universitatis Scientiarum Budapestiensin* 1971, Vol.13.

100. Ch. Basiliade, C. Bulai, and I. Cornescu, [Certain causes of juvenile delinquency in Rumania], *Revista Romana de Drept* 1971, no. 11.

101. *Prognozowanie kryminologiczne: Wybrane zagadnienia* [Criminological forecasting: Selected issues] (Warsaw: Wydawnictwo Prawnicze, 1976).

102. Brunon Hołyst, ed., *Kryminologia w krajach socjalistycznych* [Criminology in the socialist countries] (Warsaw: Wydawnictwo Prawnicze, 1976).

10 Criminological Research in the Developing Countries of Africa, the Middle East, and Southeast Asia

The nearly one hundred states of the so-called Third World of Asia, Africa, and Latin America present some common tendencies and developing perspectives but at the same time they form a mosaic of socioeconomic systems of organizations and cultural, religious, and ethnic traditions.

One can classify the developing countries according to their socioeconomic systems:

1. the most underdeveloped countries of the African Equator, including many countries classified by the UN as "the least developed";
2. the more developed countries of the African Equator and some countries of Southeast Asia;
3. the Arab states, Sri Lanka (Ceylon), and Malaysia; and
4. the Latin American countries, the Philippines, and the island of Réunion.

Although it is not easy to work out the correct typology of these countries, there are several subgroups within the four basic ones.

In the first group, the most underdeveloped countries, are Ethiopia, Niger, Chad, the Upper Volta, Botswana, Ruanda, Burundi, and other countries where traditional methods of production prevail.

In the second group, there are three subgroups: (a) Sudan, Togo, Nigeria; (b) the Ivory Coast, Senegal, and Sierra Leone; also, according to some indicators, Zaire, Liberia, Gabon, Zambia, Dahomey, Cameroon, and Uganda; (c) Pakistan, Thailand, Burma, and India, because of the specific characteristics of this huge land inhabited by 633 million people speaking 255 languages where the population is divided into various groups according to the inherited caste structure.

In the third group—the Middle East, North Africa, Malaysia, and Sri Lanka—exist capitalist enclaves created mostly by the oil extracting industry.

The fourth group, encompassing the remaining countries of Africa, Latin America, the Philippines, and the island of Réunion represent the most developed economic system. It includes three subgroups of countries: the most underdeveloped, the average, and the average developed capitalism, in which hired labor predominates.

This division is by no means complete because only the economic sphere is taken into consideration. In these countries, the processes and social structures are also complicated; they could constitute the premises of another division but our typology corresponds to a large extent to the state of research on criminality and development of criminology in these groups of countries.

In this chapter some problems of the research on criminality in countries classified in the first three groups, that is, countries of the African Equator, the Middle East, North Africa and some countries of Southeast Asia will be discussed.[1]

The nature of criminality existing in these countries is treated only in a very few criminological studies.[2] It stems most of all from the fact that there is a lack of precise statistical data which would reflect all criminal phenomena. The significance of changes resulting from socioeconomic development of many countries has until now been emphasized mostly in sociological and anthropological studies. These studies point to the collapse of the traditional basis of society, to the necessity for individuals as well as whole social groups to adapt to a new style of living and different ways of thinking. The changes have taken place in every sphere of human activity. In a society characterized by primitive agriculture the traditional law and order collapses under the thrust of modern production technology. The old social and family structure disintegrate. Value systems related to religious beliefs lose their sociotechnical power in confrontation with the model of industrial and consumptive society, which is based on permanent changes of techno-logical processes and—as a by-product of these changes—the permanent modification of consumption habits. This leads to a specific macrosocial cognitive discord, to a specific opposition of underdevelopment and progress. Thus, for these countries a reevaluation of a considerable part of their cultural heritage becomes the necessary condition of accelerated develop-ment. The constantly growing rate and scope of the process of new cultural adaptation leads to the appearance of anomie. Many conflicts in the sphere of norms and values become inevitable, at least in transitional phases. Conflicts of this type frequently constitute the genesis of psychosocial maladjustment and related deviant and criminal behavior.

Studies on criminality in developing countries are usually conducted in the context of a lack of demographical equilibrium in these countries, social changes, and maladjustment to new conditions.

The greater availability of hygienic products and medical preventive care and the prevention of famine has greatly increased the probability of survival in the period of infancy, leading to a high rate of population growth. The increase in population is accompanied by considerable modifications in he demographical structure of the society. The consequence of a changing age pyramid are the distinct transforming conditions of social equilibrium within the tribal communities. These tribal arrangements, relatively stable until now, as well as custom norms based on prohibitions and taboos, were the guarantees of order and a historically tested indicator of social relations defined, among other factors, by sex and age. In the cultural heritage based on oral transmission all the major social roles in the spheres of politics, religion, economy, education, and sanctions until recently belonged almost exclusively to the tribe's elders, the genuine and only depository of traditions and customs. Now, in the developing countries, individuals who are not over the age of twenty make up more than half the population. In this new shape of the demographical structure, the growing importance of the young causes greater and greater cracks and flaws in the existing community of power of the tribe's elders as well as in the national economy and the system of values.

The information barrier which existed through the ages is being removed in the face of fast development of mass media. The selective picture of a "welfare society" is in itself a specific advertisement where only the most spectacular features are exposed. The young generation which is most susceptible to the influence of "the effect of demonstration." A higher level of education allows a more complete reception of information about he new ideological trends and different consumptive models coming from the industrial countries. New aspirations are being born, the implementation of which becomes impossible under the patronage of old tribal leaders. Thus, the old personal authority as well as a considerable part of the culture imposed by it is being rejected.

The rapid growth of population, especially in the most economically neglected regions, has also created serious economic problems. The classical cultivation-oriented type of rural economy still retains its self-sufficient character, based on production. The still-primitive agricultural technology makes it impossible to increase productivity and to adjust the production of food to the ever-increasing demand.

Lack of prospects compels a considerable part of the population to leave the rural community in search of a means of living. The migration movement runs in the direction of great plantations, mines, and towns. In the years 1920–1950 the urban population of the Third World increased almost threefold, and in recent years it has been increasing on the average by 5–8 percent annually, that is, it doubles every 10–15 years. The growing migration contains mostly young individuals, the most rebellious and dynamic. This process causes far-reaching social disintegration in the rural areas and disrupts community life in towns, industrial regions, and plantations.

The countryside is to a large extent being left without active and highly efficient people. A secondary postmigratory disruption of demographical equilibrium takes place. In the rural community there is a relative increase in the participation of women and the elderly. On the one hand, the social sex relations begin to take on pathological forms, on the other, the tribe's elders who keep law and order lose their prestige to the migrants who have greater income. Thus, the traditional system of community control is disintegrating.

The wave of migrants finds the ground unprepared as far as jobs and living conditions are concerned. This increase of urban population which cannot find jobs leads to the creation of social marginality not only from among the unemployed but also from among people employed occasionally. The unnatural change of the sex ratio caused by a considerable increase of the number of men in a given area leads to a rapid growth of prostitution and related forms of crime.

People from the country are faced with an unfamiliar way of living. Separated from the clan, uprooted from a narrow family circle, devoid of structures which guarantee them moral and emotional balance, they must live in a highly differentiated community. In such a community various customs and traditions of different ethnic groups take on the form of obligation which functions in highly industrialized countries. This causes frequent conflicts among different system of values, a symptom of a new source of psychological and social maladjustment and creating the feeling of complete loneliness in migrants and "criminogenic ground."

The fundamental social problem facing the developing countries today is a relatively harmonious transition from the heritage of the past to modern progress. The acceptance of spontaneous economic development brings about a great risk of weakening the effectiveness of many institutions necessary to guide social life. The increased growth of urban population only to some extent stems from natural growth; it is related primarily to increased emigration from the rural areas. Thus, in developing countries, the extensive development of towns is simply incidental to factors which draw newcomers to towns by their attractiveness and also to marasmus and lack of prospects in the rural areas. The country is not able to withstand the demographic pressure. For many members of the tribal community, escape to town is the only way of freeing oneself from the regime of tribal customs and conditions, for instance, women looked down upon by fellow tribesmen because they are sterile or divorced, young people angry with their parents or those who do not agree to the marriage partner chosen by elders.

In the developing countries the town has become the symbol of modern times and a new way of living. For some people it is only a transitional stage, an attempt at a new life which would enable them, after returning to the village, to have greater prestige in the hierarchy of the old community. Others move only with a strictly defined, utilitarian aim, which could be, for instance, to obtain means to pay for a first wife or to pay back family debts. However, for the majority of migrants, the basic motives of moving to the metropolitan area are the social aspects of town life, like public services, public utilities, the possibilities of learning, and attractively spent leisure. All these factors have become the causes of great internal migrations and even international population moves. These migrations in the direction of towns give rise to numerous social problems. The growth of population is faster than the growth of economic potential, development of industry, development of the public services sector, and especially an adequate housing industry. The signs of this type of "urbanization" are unemployment and new areas of poverty located around towns.

Besides these obvious pathological aspects, moving to town also prompts the transformation of traditional family relations. It weakens many social pressures and creates in the individual a state of apparent freedom. The newcomer loses himself quickly in unfamiliar moral categories and new socioeconomic conditions. Different surroundings necessitate the coexistence of many differentiated elements, and this situation gives rise to many conflicts among individuals and among different cultural groups. This state, characteristic of every society in the phase of fast changes, leads to the emergence of new and multiplication of old forms of criminal behavior. This happens both among adults and young people; the study of this type of phenomena enables one to estimate the level of social degradation.[3]

The economic conditions and the character of city living favor the change from the model of extended family to the nuclear family. This change leads to a distinct weakening of the family. Divorces, separations, and informal arrangements become more frequent. Children become the first victims of these social changes. The disappearance of prohibitions on which upbringing was based and the destruction of the classical model of the extended family, guaranteeing strong emotional ties, causes children to be left without proper educational care and deprived of proper emotional atmosphere. This is conducive to juvenile delinquency.

If economic development takes place in a spontaneous and sudden way, without consideration of the nature of the so-called backward social structures, then it is real "cultural genocide" accompanied by many phenomena of social pathology. Violent increase of criminality is one of the most obvious symptoms.[4]

The structure of the national economy of the countries of the Middle East and North Africa and also Malaysia and Sri Lanka is, compared to countries of the African Equator, more developed. In these countries, however, considerable social differences exist, with heterogeneity of social classes and castes, politics, and systems. These are, above all, the heritage of the past. The urbanization and demographical processes take place in a similar way as in the countries of the African Equator, but different legal systems and cultural traditions cause the research in the field of combating crime to be more developed here. Law in these states has always been to a large extent of a religious character.

The estimation of the extent of crime in the developing countries is very difficult. The statistics, frequently erroneous and incomplete, because they cover only cities, allow for just an outline of antisocial behaviors.

Urbanization, industrialization, universalization of teaching, improvement of health conditions, increase in the standard of living—all these are factors of progress, but if they are introduced too hastily they disrupt the equilibrium and stability of traditional social communities. The clash of two cultures, "western" and "primitive," releases many criminogenic factors. Some criminologists are of the opinion that criminal behaviors in the developing countries are intensifying.

The specific nature of criminality in the developing countries can be seen on the one hand, in some traditional behavior, and on the other, in offenses characteristic of industrialized societies.

On the first level, various types of offenses clearly overlap. Offenses related to magic rites or quackery, poisonings, casting spells, trade in blood or in human bones, homicides of witches, ritual rapes are some examples of this type of crime. They exist mostly in rural communities.

Criminality related to situations which bring about conflicts among different value systems is on the rise. Frauds, stealing public property, cashing uncovered checks, and corruption are types of offenses which result from a conflict of values and cultural habits and characteristics of city life different from the community life. Individuals who work in town have many obligations towards the members of their clan. If they cannot fulfill them, they have a strong urge to meet these needs in an illegal way. Thus the modern forms of crime arise: robbery, organized criminal activity, and the trade in narcotics become more frequent.

On the second level, outlined by penal law, two forms of crime also overlap: one form is defined by modern codified penal legislature, the other by a set of behaviors defined as criminal by the old customary law. As a result of the introduction of a penal code many acts which until now were not looked upon as criminal have become penalized—for instance, polygamy, witchcraft in various forms, provoking miscarriage, and infanticide.

M. A. Boni, President of the Supreme Court of the Ivory Coast, made the following outline of criminality in Africa on the basis of research conducted in Abidjan:

African delinquency, occurring mostly in the backward African milieus, where witchcraft, quackery, and magic rites play the dominant role;

circumstantial delinquency—the result of the need to possess an object in a specific moment;

utilitarian delinquency—for example, fraud;

the so-called criminalité de perversion, a new phenomenon in African relations—for example burglaries done by organized groups, and robberies.

Although this division is not clear-cut, it gives a picture of criminality in developing countries. However, at the Fifth International Symposium of Comparative Criminology, held in Santa Margerita, Italy, May 16–18, 1973, M. Ette, director of the Institute of Criminology at the University of Abidjan, expressed the opinion that is is difficult to talk about the "characteristic African" criminality, because the offenses perpetrated in this region are similar to offenses perpetrated in the rest of the world, except that the structure of criminality presents itself differently.

B. Leunmi holds the opinion that there are few African countries conducting independent studies on criminality which take into account local conditions in the strict sense of the word and that Africa does not have its own "criminological school." Empirical studies are infrequent and fragmentary. This is connected with the state of development of administration in a given country and the lack of professional staffs in the field of social sciences. It is also related to the political problems of these states where the sociopolitical life is still in the making. In spite of this in many developing countries of Africa and Asia there exist scientific centers which study problems of crime, its combating and prevention.

In Thailand research and teaching in the field of criminology has been conducted since 1959 by the Research Division, Department of Corrections in the Ministry of Internal Affairs. Research is conducted by specialists in the field of criminology, sociology, state administration, statistics, and social problems. The monographs published by the division have concerned, among other topics, recidivism, disciplinary measures applied in penitentiary institutions, and escapes from prisons.

In Zaire, the Center of Criminology and Social Pathology has existed at the National University in Kinshasa since 1969. Research conducted so far concerns, among other subjects, corruption, traditional methods of treatment of the mentally ill, the costs of crime, and the training of personnel for correctional institutions.

Uganda, until 1974, did not have a specialized center of criminological studies. The research in this field was conducted, among others, by the Law Development Center, the Makerere Institute of Social Research, and the Nsamizi Training Institute. Among the publications the only known periodical is the *Uganda Law Focus* published by the Law Development Center.

In Bangladesh, the Institute of Social Welfare and Research at the University of Dacca was founded in 1959. It studies, among others, the problems of crime, especially juvenile delinquency. The institute has published the following monographs: *Social Factors of Juvenile Delinquency in East Pakistan* (1962) and *Studies on Crimes and Misdemeanors of Juveniles in East Pakistan* (1966).

In India there are several institutions which conduct scientific research and teaching in the field of criminology, the oldest, the All-India Crime Prevention Society having been founded in 1950. Its research has so far concerned juvenile delinquency, suicides, sexual offenses, and the personality of children of former offenders. The society publishes an information bulletin and has edited several monographs, among them studies on juvenile delinquency and the anthropological aspects of delinquency.

The Institute of Criminology and Forensic Sciences, founded in 1971, conducts research and teaching with the participation of psychologists, sociologists, criminologists, and specialists in forensic sciences.

The Bureau of Police Research and Development conducts research in criminology, statistics, police administration, and other matters. The Bureau publishes the following periodicals: *Criminality in India, Death Accidents and Suicides in India,* and *Reports on the Development and Research of Police."* It has published various monographic works concerning among other things, homicides, bank security, prevention of crime, the society's attitude towards police in detecting offenses, and police organization.

The National Institute of Social Defense, Department of Social Welfare in the Ministry of Social Welfare also studies the problems of criminology and social defense. The institute has published a periodical *Social Defense*; its monographic works dealt with, among other topics, the moral and social threat to women and girls, child beggary, and juvenile delinquency.

The Institute of Advanced Studies in Sociology, founded in 1963, and the National Institute of Research and Training in Public Cooperation and Child Development, founded in 1966, deal with the problems of criminology as a secondary field.

In the capital of the Ivory Coast, the Institute of Criminology at the University of Abidjan was created in 1969.[5] The research conducted on this country shows that as a result of the process of urbanization, industrialization, and migration (two-thirds of the perpetrators of all crimes come from other African countries) the number of traditional offenses decreases, especially the ones which result from family and clan solidarity and from the cult of the dead spirits, whereas—mostly in the cities—the number of frauds, thefts, and embezzlement of public funds is on the increase.

More frequent become such phenomena as drug traffic (Indian hemp) manslaughter, bodily injury, or the activity of organized criminal groups.[6]

In Indonesia, the Institute of Criminology was founded at the University in Djakarta; it conducts research and teaching in the field of criminology and social defense, and employs specialists not only in law and criminology but also in other fields of science, such as medicine and forensic chemistry. The subjects of research are, among others, problems of prostitution and juvenile delinquency.

In Iraq, there are two institutions dealing with the problems of criminology and social defense. One is the International Arab Bureau for Prevention of Crime founded in 1960 in Baghdad under the auspices of the League of Arab States. Besides conducting scientific research the Bureau edits the periodical *Criminal Statistics in Arab Countries*. Numerous monographs have been published, concerning, for example, juvenile delinquency in Iraq, correctional institutions in Arab states, the policy of crime prevention, and procedural aspects of individualization of sentences.

The National Center For Social and Criminological Research in Iraq with headquarters in Baghdad was founded in 1970. The center conducts research and training activities; its also publishes the periodical *The Review of Social and Criminal Research*. Numerous monographs concern among other topics, the problems of prostitution, vagrancy of youth, robberies, the rights of women related to work and social securities, the realization of the principles of the declaration on the development and social progress in Iraq, the organization of penitentiary institutions in Iraq, and the relationship between alcoholism and crime.

Tunisia does not have a special center for criminological research. The Center of Study and Social and Economic Research at the University of Tunis deals with criminology as a secondary field. It has published monographs on the subjects of economic classes and cultural identity in Tunisia and juvenile delinquency. The center publishes the periodical *Revue Tunisienne des Sciences Sociales* [The Tunisian Review of Social Sciences].

In Egypt, the first program of criminological research was elaborated in 1956 in the National Institute of Criminological Research.[7] Three years later, the Institute's name was changed to the National Center for Social and Criminological Research with headquarters in Cairo. The center also deals with criminalistic research; its main objectives are: the improvement of the state of education and culture of the Egyptian and Arab societies, with the view of contributing to the development of these societies and the progress of the social sciences; the conducting of studies on social problems and the granting of consultations serving the creation of a rational basis for a social defense policy; and the training of personnel for the needs of counseling related to the effective implementation of the principles of social policy.

The center has at its disposal nine research units conducting studies on the problems of industrialization, development of rural areas, public opinion, family, psychology and education, criminal behavior, youth, penitentiary institutions, and criminalistics. The center has a statistical workshop and a criminalistics laboratory. Among the most important research topics are the following: migration of population, control of population growth, drug addiction, social effects of court cases, evaluation of television programs, slums, divorces, prostitution, vendettas, homicides, the effectiveness of short-term deprivation of liberty sentences, and forgeries of documents.

The same center, besides research activity, organizes various conferences, seminars, and training courses—regional and international—on crime prevention, the treatment of offenders, social attitudes of citizens, and criminalistics. For example, two conferences on the problems of prevention took place in 1961 and 1963 and criminalistics symposia in 1963 and 1965.

The results of empirical research and the theoretical aspects of criminology are published in two periodicals: the *National Review of Criminal Sciences*, which has appeared three times a year since 1957 and the *National Review of Social Sciences*, which has appeared three times a year since 1964. The periodicals are published in Arabic and include summaries of publications in English and French.

Moreover, in Cairo, the Arab Organization for Social Defense against Crime was founded in 1960 by the League of Arab States. The periodical *Arab Review of Social Defense Problems* appears in Arabic. The monographs concern the results of research on the problems of economic offenses, prevention, the minimum rules of the UN on the treatment of offenders, drug abuse, and other topics.

In 1967 the Egyptian Society of Political Economy, Statistics, and Legislation (Société Egyptienne d'Economie Politique de Statistique et de Legislation) organized the Arab Center of Study on Social Defense. Articles on criminology are published in the periodical *L'Egypte Contemporaine*.

The participation of the developing countries at the Fifth UN Congress on the Prevention of Crime and Treatment of Offenders which took place in Geneva, September 1–12, 1975 gives one an idea about the state of research on criminality in these countries.

In the Kingdom of Saudi Arabia, criminological research is conducted by the Crime Prevention Research Center, Ministry of Interior.

In recent years, there has been much discussion of the influence of Islamic legislation on the prevention of crime. Some of the problems considered have been: definition of crime according to Islamic legislation and the sources of the Islamic legislation, means of evidence in Islamic law, effect of religion on crime, effect of the Koran teaching "to enjoin the good and refrain from evil deeds" on crime prevention, and the influence of Islamic education on crime prevention.

The 1976 Riyadh symposia materials were published as *The Effect of Islamic Leglislation on Crime Prevention in Saudi Arabia*.[8]

This book—as stated in the preface—is the product of a serious undertaking unique of its kind, for it contains a number of specialized scholarly papers that treat the relationship between the Islamic legislation as it was revealed to the Holy Prophet around fourteen centuries ago and the pragmatic implementation of this legislation in the Kingdom of Saudi Arabia.

The work asserts the stability and low crime rates throughout the Kingdom of Saudi Arabia. This is clearly illustrated by the comparative statistics which the reader will find there. These statistics demonstrate that between 1386–1395 A.H. corresponding to the Gregorian years1966–1975, crime rates were far lower in the kingdom than in other countries.

Notes

1. William Clifford, *An Introduction to African Criminology: Eastern Africa* (Nairobi: Oxford University Press, 1974); Frank Ferrier et al., *Développement et Société: Compte rendu des seminaires sur l'Afrique Occidentale* [Development and society: Report on West Africa seminars] (Montreal: Centre International de Criminologie Comparée, 1972). See especially Jean-Claude Muller, "Droit coutumier et structures judiciares nouvelles: Quelques considerations" [Customary law and new judicial structures: Some considerations], pp. 370–378; Pierre M. Lagier, "Criminalité et justice en Afrique Occidentale" [Criminality and justice in West Africa], pp. 380–431; Mustapha El Augi et al., "L'Afrique du Nord et l'Asie de l'Quest." *Développement et Société. Compte rendu des seminaires sur l'Afrique du Nord et l'Asie de l'Ouest* [Development and society: Report on North Africa and Western Asia seminars] (Montreal: Centre International de Criminologie Comparée, 1975). See especially Mustapha El Augi, "Le phénomène de la criminalité au Moyen-Orient [The crime phenomenon in the Middle East], pp. 212–246; Adrien Bassitche, "Changement social et criminalité au Moyen-Orient" [Social changes and criminality in the Middle East] pp. 249–271; Mustapha El Augi, "La réaction sociale dans ses formes institutionnalisées et noninstitutionnalisées au Moyen-Orient" [Social reaction in its institutionalized and noninstitutionalized forms] pp. 275–294.

2. Yves Brillon et al., *Les besoins et les perspectives en matière de prevention du crime et de traitement des délinquants en Afrique Occidentale: Compte rendu du Premier Colloque de Criminologie Comparée d'Afrique Occidentale* [Needs and perspectives in the matter of crime prevention and the treatment of delinquents in West Africa: Report of the First West Africa Conference in Comparative Criminology] (Abidjan: Centre International de Criminologie Comparée, 1972). Yves Brillon et al., *Prevention du crime et planification en Afrique Occidentale: Compte rendu du Quatrième Colloque de Criminologie Comparée d'Afrique Occidentale* [Crime prevention and planning: Report of the Fourth West African Conference in Comparative Criminology] (Abidjan: Centre International de Criminologie Comparée, 1974).

3. Georges Balandier, "Le contexte socio-culturel et le coût social du progrès" [Sociocultural context and the social costs of progress], *Tiers Monde* 1956, p. 302.

4. Yves Brillon, "Développement économique et criminalité en Afrique Occidentale" [Economic development and criminality in West Africa], *Revue Internationale de Criminologie et de Police Technique*, 1973, no.1.

5. Yves Brillon, see note 4.

6. Jean Pinatel, "La criminalité dans le monde" [Criminality in the world], *Revue de Science Criminelle et de Droit Pénal Comparé* 1971, no.2.

7. Mahmoud M. Mostafa, *Principes de droit pénal des pays arabes* [Principles of penal law in Arab countries] (Paris: Librairie générale de droit et de jurisprudence, 1972).

8. *The Effect of Islamic Legislation on Crime Prevention in Saudi Arabia*. Proceedings of the symposium held in Riyadh, 16–21 Shawal 1396 A.H. (October 9–13, 1976). (Rome: Ministry of Interior, Kingdom of Saudi Arabia, Crime Prevention Research Center, 1980).

11 The State of Criminology in Latin American Countries

The group of Latin American countries, plus the Philippines and Réunion Island, is divided into three subgroups, depending on the structure of their national economies.[1]

The first subgroup, the most backward countries, includes Guatemala, Honduras, Nicaragua, Paraguay, and the Dominican Republic. In those countries agriculture accounts for 60 to 90 percent of all employment, while industry is limited largely to cottage enterprises for processing farm produce.

The second, halfway developed, subgroup includes El Salvador, Ecuador, Bolivia, Peru, and Panama; their economies are also dominated by agriculture, but a larger number of farms employ hired labor.

The third subgroup includes Argentina, Brazil, Colombia, Costa Rica, Mexico, Venezuela, Uruguay, and Chile; here the vast majority of the working-age population works for wages and the manufacturing industries are capitalist-dominated. Among all the developing countries these represent the highest level of capitalist development and at the same time have the largest concentrations of the urban marginal population.

The phenomenon of social marginality in these countries is the result of the centuries of colonial subjugation by Spain or Portugal and later by English, French, and North American capitalism, which established a peripheral, neocolonial structure serving its own economy. This economic dominance decided the directions of economic development in particular countries.

Rafael Garcia Garza has expressed the view that the phenomenon of social marginality represents a historical reflection of colonialism and national subjugation, with its causes deeply rooted in the international economic system which leads to injustice and the appearance of differences due to the preponderance of the industrialized countries and their domination over the undeveloped countries.[2]

The phenomenon of the urban social marginality arose from the migration of people from nonurban environments in search of better living conditions. The lack of housing or the lack of funds to obtain housing led the migrants to build primitive tin and cardboard shanties; the hopelessness of all efforts to obtain jobs gradually led to life in ever-deepening poverty, with no medical care and no opportunity to send children to school. The populations of shantytowns are known under a variety of names: *favelas* in Rio de Janeiro, *villas miserias* in Buenos Aires, *ciudades peridas* in Mexico, *callumpas* in

Chile, *limonades* in Guatemala, and *ranchos* in Caracas. Caracas alone has some 200,000 tin and cardboard shacks, each inhabited by an average of seven people.

The outskirts of the big cities are the seats of poverty. Children in particular are undernourished. In the years 1960–1965, 30–45 percent of the entire South American population was illiterate. Men and women usually live in nonformalized unions (60 percent in Venezuela); broken or incomplete families, often demoralized, are more the rule than the exception.

Latin America represents some 16–17 percent of the entire Third World population. This geopolitical area is also responsible for some one-third of all exports and one-half of the entire manufactured production of the developing countries.

This factor causes the degree of urbanization in Latin America to be much higher than the Third World average. In Africa no more than 8 percent of the people live in cities of over 100,000 population; in Asia the proportion is slightly higher, some 12 percent; for Latin America the figure is 24 percent. By 1985 it is expected that the big-city inhabitants will account for nearly 40 percent of the entire Latin American population.

The per capita national income in the individual Latin American countries is highly varied. In Venezuela, Argentina, Mexico, Uruguay, and Panama it amounts to more than $600 per year, while Haiti is at the other extreme, $85 per capita annual income. Yet even in countries with a relatively high national income there are tremendous inequalities in the distribution of incomes. Venezuela can serve as an example: the oil industry, the main source of national wealth, employs only an insignificant number of job seekers. The cities attract thousand who are unable to find decent living conditions; in effect the cities are ringed with shantytowns populated by people in dire poverty. The existence of such environments cannot but reflect on the level of crime in this geopolitical area. Further, the Latin American countryside is dominated by various superstitions, representing a potpourri of Indian and Negro beliefs, particularly witchcraft, superimposed on Christianity and in effect breeding all types of criminals.

In contrast to many developed societies, where the system of law is based on the principle of legality, power in many of the Caribbean countries is held by minorities who achieved their position by illegal means. There is no way of knowing the degree to which the population identifies with the law systems of those countries, or the means of intervention or the determinants of social reactions to the application of law. There is also no knowledge of whether the acts viewed as offenses by the political system of those countries are accepted as such by the population.

Badly interpreted, unjustly applied, wrong law, directed by regimes of dubious legality, could become a significant factor conducive to crime. In the

Caribbean countries the situation which evolved through the abuse of penal law is often marked by: (a). identification of law with the political regime which in turn identifies itself with the sole political party in power or even the individual in power; (b). the objective of penal law which is to eliminate opposition, antagonism, and resistance to the political regime; (c). severe, often brutal, penal law, frequently contained in regulations using muddled terminology, conducive to its abuse; (d). the lack of civic guarantees and protection; (e). the formation of military tribunals and the servility of certain judges to the regime.

The consequences of such abuse of law include destruction of the value of the legal system which is linked with the idea of state security, in this case, laws are subordinate to the security of the political party or the regime of the rulers and a hegemony situation.

There is a deformation of the legal structures, contents, and interpretations, with respect to betrayal, sabotage, propaganda against the regime, and similar matters.

The legislative systems of penal law in the Caribbean area are modeled on Spanish, French, Belgian, Italian, German, and English systems and represent a variety of doctrines of law.

Most codes in this region have been developed "per analogiam," which rarely corresponds to national reality and in no case refers to studies of their own societies. The most recent codes rely mainly on the dogmatic Italian— German model. For instance, the 1960 penal code of Guatemala is a faithful copy of the Argentine draft of the same year and fails to take account of the considerable differences between those two countries. The penal code of El Salvador was drafted by Professor Ruiz de Funes who has no knowledge of the El Salvador society.

Creation of penal law, treated technically, often leads to situations where the codes are an assembly of pieces from different jigsaw puzzles, with fragments stemming from various foreign texts viewed as best serving the purposes of the regime in force, without concern for harmonizing the whole or for having it adequately reflect the realities of the country. In this way the penal code adopted in Costa Rica in 1941 was a mélange of the penal codes of Spain, Colombia, Cuba, Italy, Mexico, Panama, Switzerland, Uruguay, Venezuela, and Brazil.

For the past fifteen years attempts have been made to unify Latin American penal legislation and to draft a typical penal code. Does it make sense to have such a code on a continent with such a high proportion of native, autochtonic populations? Should not the effort go in the opposite direction, so that in countries with a high percentage of native population with traditions dating far into the past there will be a system of dual legislation, one for the white and another for the native populations?

The legal system of the Caribbean area remains considerably influenced by the United States Constitution; it is marked by a repressive character, with frequent abuse of imprisonment.[3]

Latin America is marked by much political violence, as is evident from the political crimes—82 murders of national rulers between 1806 and 1967, terrorism and guerrilla activities, raids on banks and gambling casinos, attacks on army and police installations, temporary occupation of towns or buildings, bombings, armed assaults on prisons, mass murders, kidnapping and imprisonment of hostages and 328 plane hijackings in the years 1958 through 1971.[4]

Penal courts are highly repressive, all too often applying and abusing imprisonment.[5] This occurs both in regular and in juvenile courts. The number of prisoners has been steadily increasing.

Criminology in those countries concerns itself also with a variety of socioeconomic phenomena linked with criminality, such as the breakdown of family and social bonds, development of privileged classes and the growth of bureaucracy, with the inherent rise in white-collar crime.[6] There is a large-scale illegal traffic in marijuana between Mexico and the United States. In 1970 four clandestine cocaine-extruding laboratories were uncovered: two in Chile, one each in Peru and Bolivia. Interpol has formed a special Committee on Currency Counterfeiting which includes thirty-six members, mostly from the developing countries, where currency counterfeiting is on the rise, such as Guatemala. In 1972 the Argentine police detected a gang trading in narcotics and trafficking in works of art stolen from French and Italian museums. The developing countries have also noted an increase in female crime.

The crime which is beginning to menace Latin American societies has become a factor inspiring criminological research. The people responsible for the socioeconomic development of Latin America are faced with a choice as to whether to multiply the existing models of industrial development and the development of large cities or whether to seek new solutions. At the same time the specific nature of the socioeconomic conditions compels criminologists to consider the aptness of past findings of this discipline for combating and preventing local types of crime.

Criminologists in Latin America aim to formulate their own criminological ideas which would reflect the economic, social, and cultural conditions of this area. At the international course on criminology held at Mendoza, Argentina, the Venezuelan representatives proposed formation of an inter-American society of criminological research, aimed at coordinating the efforts of academic centers and other research institutions.

Criminological research in Latin America began before World War II, although not until the latter half of the 1970s did new research facilities proliferate, which advanced the studies of crime.

The First Congress of Latin American Criminologists was held in 1938 in Buenos Aires and the second in 1941 in Santiago de Chile. Buenos Aires was the site of the First Congress of Pan-American Criminology in 1947. Later international congresses of Latin American criminologists (1969, Mendoza; 1971, São Paulo; 1973, Maracaibo; 1975, Guayaquil) were concerned mainly with the advancement of scientific research and studies in this economically, culturally, politically, and anthropologically highly varied region, though united by a common language, Spanish, used in all countries (with the exception of Portuguese, used in Brazil). In order to advance such studies an International Center of Biological Criminology and Forensic Medicine was formed in São Paulo.

Latin America has world-renowned criminologists, authors of criminological textbooks, such as H. V. de Carvalho (Brazil), A. Peixoto, L. Ribeiro (Chile), G. Uribe Cualla (Colombia), J. Morales Coello (Cuba), C. B. Quiros (Mexico), R. Elias y Aparicio (Peru) and J. R. Mendoza (Venezuela).

The situation in Latin American criminology was comprehensively presented by Roberto Bergalli in *Criminologia en America Latina, Cambio social: Normatividad y comportamientos desviados*, (Buenos Aires: Ediciones Pannedille, 1972). The author particularly emphasizes the economic and political context in explaining the causes of criminality on the South American continent. An important role in interpreting the etiology of crime is played by ethnic and cultural factors.

A particularly high level of criminological research has been achieved in Venezuela, Argentina, Mexico, and Colombia; each of these countries has a number of criminological research facilities. Research institutes have also been formed in Uruguay, Chile, Brazil, Ecuador, and Costa Rica. Latin America has a total of some thirty institutes and associations carrying out criminological studies. Altogether they publish about sixteen journals.

In Venezuela criminological research is conducted on a wide scale; at present, it is dominated by applied research and an interdisciplinary approach, the application of quantifying methods, using control groups, and priority treatment of juvenile delinquency.[7]

The oldest facility of this type is the Institute of Penal Sciences and Criminology in Caracas, established in 1948. This is part of Venezuela's Central University, employing researchers with such specialities as law, sociology, criminology, and psychology. The institute focuses primarily on crime in Venezuela, conducting studies on the general theory of indictable acts, publishing two periodicals, *Anuario del Instituto de Ciencias Penales y Criminologicas* and *Boletin del Instituto de Ciencias Penales y Criminologicas*. Between 1970 and 1976 institute staff has published thirteen monographs.

The Criminological Research Center of the Zulia University Law Department (Centro de Investigationes Criminologicas, Universidad del Zulia), Maracaibo, was organized in 1964. The center employs researchers in psychology, sociology, and statistics. It conducts research on the legal and social aspects of the criminalization process, criminality in the Zulia Province, further studying the problems connected with the use of marijuana by the Maracaibo population. The center publishes two periodicals, *Capitulo Criminologico* and *Boletin Informativo*.

Since 1970 Caracas has had a Crime Prevention Center at the Ministry of Justice (Direccion de Prevencion del Delito). This institution has researchers with such specialities as law, sociology, psychology, criminology, pedagogy, and statistics. Studies are devoted to crime prevention, the etiology of drug abuse, prostitution, and the customs of offenders. There are also studies on the crisis of criminal justice.

Venezuela has a Society of Penal Law and Criminology (Sociedad Venezolana de Derecho Penal y Criminologia). This institution is concerned principally with forensic medicine in Venezuelan law, penal law and penal procedure in the Constitution of Venezuela, bank robberies, and drafting a lexicon of Venezuelan penal law.

Since the 1960s Venezuela has published numerous items on criminology, notably the textbook of criminology by Elio Gomez Grillo. Primarily an introduction, the author accepts criminology as an interdisciplinary science encompassing such fields as anthropology, biology, psychology, and sociology. He also presents the methods of crime study according to the principle of "criminal geography".[8]

Arnoldo Garcia Iturbe is the author of another book which represents an introduction to criminology.[9] He has given broad consideration to the statistics of crime in Venezuela and in certain other countries, also taking up comparative criminology. Limitation of its bibliography solely to Spanish-language publications is a definite drawback.

Lola Aniyar de Castro takes up the issue of criminology and social reaction. She presents the main theoretical directions in criminology and from this draws conclusions as to the further development of this discipline in Venezuela.[10]

The theoretical aspects of the new stream of critical criminology have been taken up by Jorge Sosa Chacin. He approaches criminology as a "supplementary discipline" having the main aim of studying the causes of crime and supplying data for penal law reform.[11]

A reconnaissance trip to the socialist countries made by Elio Gomez Grillo led to a book presenting certain aspects of crime and the system of penalties. The material is excessively synthetic to permit drawing more general conclusions.[12]

Gomez Grillo also devoted a study to crime in Caracas, a city which registers more than half of all the crime committed in Venezuela, even though it has only 20 percent of the country's population. He devoted much attention to the issue of juvenile delinquency, a typical phenomenon in greater Caracas.[13]

The earliest criminological research in Argentina is connected with the Instituto de Clasificacion of the Federal Penitentiary Service in Buenos Aires, organized in 1907. It employs specialists in criminology, medicine, sociology, psychology, social work, and penal law. Its projects have been concerned with such issues as the ecology of crime in the Argentine capital. A regular publication is the *Revista Penal y Penitenciaria*.

In 1950 this institute formed an Institute of Criminological Research and Training, with the aim of studying offenders serving sentences in the Buenos Aires area, assisting those under care of the Society for Assistance to Prisoners, former prisoners on probation, teaching criminology, and studying crime as a social phenomenon.[14]

Research on offenders is the task of a social workers' team trained in the Institute of Criminological Research and Training. Whenever possible, a milieu report is drawn up. The social worker prepares it on the basis of interviews conducted at the offender's place of residence, in his neighborhood, at his job, and in the police precinct. Tests are used wherever possible. On the basis of these data physicians, psychiatrists, and lawyers study and examine the prisoner and then prepare a so-called criminological study of the given prisoner, containing a criminological diagnosis and prognosis, classification of prisoner adaptation, recommendations as to prisoner placement in a given penitentiary institution, the type of work, training and discipline, and the duration of the basic penalty.

Following the conditional release of the prisoner, supervision is taken over by the Society for Assistance to Prisoners, directly subordinate to the institute. The society has branches in various parts of the Buenos Aires district and tries to rely in its operations on social workers trained in criminology.

The institute offered the first training in 1950; regular lectures on criminology have been offered since then. The student must be over eighteen, have a secondary school certificate or sufficient vocational qualifications; most of the students are women. This training is intermediate between secondary and university levels, and research is concentrated on case studies in such fields as homicide, female crime, and juvenile delinquency.

A criminological institute (Instituto de Investigacion y Ciencia Criminologica) was established by an Argentine government decree of 1958, under the General Directorate of Prisons. It carries out research and training in criminal anthropology, criminal sociology, penology, and penitentiaristics.

A number of academic criminological centers were organized by Argentine universities following World War II.

The Institute of Criminological Research and Comparative Penal Law (Instituto de Investigacion Criminologica y Derecho Penal Comparado) was established in 1969 in Buenos Aires to consider the criminological issues of bank robberies, counterfeiting, the costs of crime and crime prevention, crisis of criminal justice, and similar problems.

The Institute of Penal Law and Criminology (Instituto de Ciencia Penal y Criminologia) in Santa Fe, established in 1955, concerns itself, among other things, with studies of white-collar crime. It has an exceptionally elaborate publishing record, with numerous monographs on penal law and criminology.

The Mendoza Center of Criminological Research (Centro de Estudios Criminologicos de la Provincia de Mendoza), organized in 1966, specializes in research and organizing training courses for prison personnel and police officials. It has published research findings on the social disintegration of criminals, prostitution, suicides, and police procedures with juvenile delinquents. The center publishes the *Revista del Centro de Estudios Criminologicos de Mendoza.*

The Penal Law Institute (Instituto de Derecho Penal) at the National University of Cordoba, formed in 1956, includes criminology in its field of interests. The institute publishes the *Cuadernos de los Institutos.*

The Forensic Medicine and Criminalistics Institute (Instituto de Medicina Legal y Criminalistica), organized at Tucuman in 1962, also conducts studies of selected criminological issues connected with road accidents, victimology, and suicides. It publishes the *Revista del Instituto de Medicina Legal y Criminalistica.*

The Argentine Criminological Association (Sociedad Argentina de Criminologia), founded in 1933, conducts studies on crime prevention policy and the etiology of crime, with particular emphasis on the influence of environmental factors and the physiopsychological personality of a "dangerous" person, and individual therapy for better rehabilitation effects.

The Criminological Association of Rosario (Sociedad de Criminologia de Rosario), founded in 1966 as an academic institution, conducts interdisciplinary research on penal law, forensic medicine, criminology, and psychology.

The Association of Crime Sciences and Forensic Medicine of Tucuman (Sociedad de Ciencias Criminales y Medicina Legal de Tucuman), founded in 1952, carries out research and large-scale training, particularly in the fields of forensic medicine, criminalistics, and criminology. It publishes the *Revista de Medicina Legal y Criminalistica de Policia de Tucuman.*

The first criminological monographs in Argentina date back to the 1940s; a monograph on the psychoanalysis of crime was published in 1947.[15]

There are also notable studies on juvenile delinquency.[16] In explaining the causes of juvenile delinquency, researchers used the subculture concept. The studies covered the large urban agglomerations of Argentina, where in the slum areas conditions exist which are conducive to the development of subcultures.

In a book devoted to the psychological and sociological aspects of juvenile delinquency, Pedro R. David formulated the demand for establishing a "new criminology" for the Latin American countries which would stop the process of criminalization and dehumanization, thus becoming a tool of social equality.[17]

There are also psychological studies of certain types of crime (homicides, fraud, sexual crimes), but they are casuistic in nature, failing to result in more significant scientific analysis.[18]

Since 1930 the capital of Mexico has had the Institute of Social Studies (Instituto de Investigaciones Sociales) with a staff of fifty-five scholars conducting research on sociocultural issues, including the problems of criminality. Since 1939 the institute has been regularly publishing the *Revista Mexicana de Sociologia*.

The Penitentiary Center of the State of Mexico (Centro Penitenciario del Estado de Mexico) has been active since 1966. It employs a staff of twenty-eight scientists conducting research and teaching (lawyers, economists, psychiatrists, educators, and physicians). Its projects concern recidivism, victimology, criminal factors, and preparation of a training manual for prison staff.

The National Institute of Penal Sciences (Instituto Nacional de Ciencias Penales) was founded in 1976; it conducts research and teaching in penology.

Mexico City is also the seat of the Mexican Criminological Society (Sociedad Mexicana de Criminologia).

Colombia in 1969 founded the Institute of Penal and Criminological Sciences (Instituto de Ciencias Penales y Criminologicas) as part of the Law Department of the Colombian Externado University.

In 1937 the Institute of Penal and Penitentiary Sciences (Instituto de Ciencias Penales y Penitentiarias) of the University of Bogotá Law Department was founded; it has a staff of twenty-one specialists on law, medicine, and psychology. It publishes the periodical *Revista del Instituto de Ciencias Penales y Penitenciarias*.

Studies on prostitution and criminality are also carried out at the Institute of Penal Law and Criminology (Instituto de Derecho Penal y Criminologia) of the University of Medellin. Formed in 1963, it currently has a staff of seven specialists on penal law and criminology.

Since 1961 Bogotá also has had a Section for Socio-Juridical and Crime Prevention Research in the Ministry of Justice (Oficina de Investigaciones Socio-Juridicas y de Prevencion del Delito). Its research focuses on juridical system, the etiology of crime, and crime prevention. It publishes the periodical *Boletin de Informaciones Socio-Juridicas*.

The Forensic Medicine Institute (Instituto de Medicina Legal) has been active in Colombia since 1914 doing research and training. It has a staff of 187 specialists and publishes the periodical *Revista Instituto Nacional de Medicina Legal de Colombia*.

The first edition of the criminological textbook by E. Alfonso Reyes appeared in 1968.[19] It emphasized the objectives and tasks of criminology, which include studying criminal behavior, formulating the principles of penal policy, and presenting recommendations regarding prevention. The book represents a systematic summary of the fundamental issues of criminology.

An interesting attempt to interpret crime in Colombia was made by Fernando H. Rojas. He applied the Marxist theory of class conflict to explain the causes of increases in crime.[20] (In the years 1945–1970 crime increased five times.) The author was not successful, however, in establishing a link between the social origin of the offender and the fact of his conviction. For a foreign reader this publication is informative, as it allows for an orientation in the tendencies in the trends and structure of crime.

One should also note the criminological lexicon put together by Alvaro O. Perez Pinzon, the latest publication of the criminological literature of Colombia. The lexicon was designed as an introduction to the fundamental issues of criminology.[21]

Chile established the Institute of Penal Sciences (Instituto de Ciencias Penales de Chile) in 1937, as a research and training facility employing specialists on law, sociology, and medicine. The institute publishes a periodical, the *Revista de Ciencias Penales*.

Since 1936 Chile has a Criminology Institute (Instituto de Criminologia de Gendarmeria de Chile) with a staff of thirteen specialists on psychology, psychometry, electroencephalography, law, endocrinology, and other disciplines. Institute studies are dominated by penitentiary issues. It publishes a periodical, the *Revista Chilena de Ciencia Peniteciaria y de Derecho Penal*.

Costa Rica also has an institution charged with criminological research. It was established in 1971 in San Jose as the State Criminological Institute (Instituto Nacional de Criminologia, Direccion de Adaptation Social). The institute has specialists on law, sociology, social work, penal administration, psychology, psychiatry, statistics, architecture, and engineering.

Moreover, San Jose is the seat of the United Nations Latin American Institute for the Prevention of Crime and the Treatment of Offenders, founded in 1975.

The Criminology Institute (Instituto de Criminologia) of the University of

Quito, Ecuador, was founded in 1936. It employs specialists in such fields as medicine, law, penal law, neuropsychiatry, sociology, anthropology, and statistics, and carries out research on the implementation of penal measures, rehabilitation, and crime prevention. The institute publishes the *Archivos de Criminologia, Neuropsiquiatria y Disciplinas Conexas.*

Uruguay has two institutions concerned with criminological research. In 1943 the Institute of Criminology (Instituto de Criminologia) was founded in Montevideo. It carries out research on clinical criminology. The staff consists of specialists on law, psychology, medicine, and social work; it publishes the periodical *Revista de Criminologia.*

The Inter-American Institute of Juvenile Affairs (Instituto Interamericano del Niño) was organized in Montevideo in 1927. It employs specialists on law and social sciences and concentrates in its research on juvenile delinquency issues. It publishes the periodical *Boletin del Instituto Interamericano del Niño.* Operations of this institute are financed by the Organization of American States.

Brazil in 1964 founded the National Institute of Criminalistics, serving research and training functions. It has a staff of fifty, which conducts various criminalistics analyses. It also devotes a certain amount of attention to criminological issues.

The Institute of Criminology of the Guanabara University has since 1962 published a periodical devoted to criminology and penal law in Brazil, under the title *Revista Brasileira de Criminologia e Diretto Penal.* Since 1968 a periodical has been published on crime sociology: *Sociologia Criminal.*

The Institute of Social Medicine and Criminology (Instituto de Medicina Social e de Criminologia), founded in 1970 in São Paulo, conducts research and teaching; it employs sociologists, psychologists, physicians, lawyers, and social workers. Its research concerns drug dependence problems, recidivism, maximum and medium security prisons, and similar matters; its periodical is *IMESP.*

Peru has no traditions in criminological research; the first monograph on criminology was published in 1970.[22] It represents an introduction to criminological problems, but due to its character does not include any research findings. As is evident from the second volume of this book, Peru has great expectations for psychoanalysis and individual psychology and also for psychopathy as defined by Kurt Schneider. Another publication is the study of the influence which political processes have on shaping the picture of crime. An attempt was made at a comparative treatment of crime in Poland, France, the United Kingdom, the Soviet Union and Peru in the context of their political systems. There seems to be considerable methodological errors in the study, since the scope of comparative analysis is limited only to the political systems, with no consideration of the economic, cultural, ethnic, religious, or other factors.

Notes

1. Frank Ferrier et al., *Développement et Société: Compte rendu des seminaires sur l'Amerique Latine* [Development and society: Report on Latin America seminars] (Montreal: Centre Internationale de Criminologie Comparée, 1973).

2. Rafael Garcia Garza, "Issue of the Margin in Latin American Countries: Causes, Effects, Proposals for Resolution" (Paper presented tto the Ninth Congress of Social Defense in Caracas, August 3–7, 1976.) The congress was devoted to the issue of the social margin.

3. José M. Rico, "Crime et justice pénale dans les Caraibes" [Crime and penal justice in the Caribbean], part 2, *Revue Internationale de Criminologie et de Police Technique* 33, no. 4 (1980), pp. 371–378.

4. Lola Aniyar de Castro and José M. Rico, *La violence en Amerique Latine* [Violence in Latin America] (Montreal: Centre International de Criminologie Comparée, 1980).

5. Angel Pino, "Criminalité en Amerique Latine" [Criminality in Latin America], in Frank Ferrier, et al., *Développement et Société*, pp. 406–423.

6. Franco Ferracuti and Roberto Bergalli, *Tendencias y necesidades de la investigacion criminologica en America Latina* [Tendencies and necessities of criminological research in Latin America] (Rome: United Nations Social Defence Research Institute, 1969).

7. This is the conclusion of, among others, F. Canestri Francisco, in "Venezuela—une criminologie Latino-Americaine?" [Venezuela—Latin American criminology?], *Annales Internationales de Criminologie* 1973, no. 1–2.

8. Elio Gomez Grillo, *Introduccion a la criminologia, con especial referencia al medio venezolano* [Introduction to criminology, with special reference to Venezuela], 2nd ed. (Caracas: Publicaciones de la Facultad de Derecho, Univeresidad Central de Venezuela, 1966).

9. Arnoldo Garcia Iturbe, *La delincuencia y el delincuente* [Delinquency and the delinquent] (Caracas: Monte Avila Editores, 1972).

10. Lola Aniyar de Castro, *Criminologia de la reaccion social* [Criminology of social reaction] (Maracaibo: Instituto de Criminologia de la Universidad del Zulia, 1976).

11. Jorge Sosa Chacin, *Criminologia critica* [Critical criminology]

(Caracas: Publicaciones del Departamento de Ciencias Penales Criminologicas, 1978).

12. Elio Gomez Grillo, *Los Delitos y las penas en los paises socialistas* [Crime and punishment in the socialist countries] (Caracas: Editorial Afaneo de Caracas, 1980).

13. Elio Gomez Grillo, *La delincuencia en Caracas* [Delinquency in Caracas] (Caracas: Sintesis Dosmil, 1972).

14. Oscar Blarduni, "The Institute of Criminological Research and Training, Province of Buenos Aires, Argentina," *International Review of Criminal Policy* 1964, no. 22, pp. 77–80.

15. Luis Jimenez de Asua, *Psicoanalisis criminal* [Psychoanalysis of crime], 5th ed. (Buenos Aires: Ediciones Rosada, 1959). First edition published 1947.

16. Carlos Alberto de Pierris, *Delincuencia juvenil* [Juvenile delinquency] (Buenos Aires: Bibliografica Omeba, 1963); see also Lois B. Defleur, *Delinquency in Argentina: A study of Cordoba's youth* (Seattle: University of Washington Press, 1970).

17. Pedro R. David, *Sociologia criminal juvenil* [Juvenile criminal sociology] 5th ed. (Buenos Aires: Ediciones de Palma, 1979). First edition published 1968.

18. Hilda Marchiori, *Psicologia de la conducta delectiva: Observaciones sobre un casuistica* [Psychology of offensive behavior: Casuistic observations] (Buenos Aires: Ediciones Pannedille, 1973).

19. E. Alfonso Reyes, *Criminologia* [Criminology], 2nd ed. (Universidad Externado de Colombia, n.p., 1975).

20. Fernando H. Rojas, *Criminalidad y constituyente* [Criminality and its determinants] (Bogota: C.I.N.E.P., 1977).

21. Alvaro Orlando Perez Pinzon, *Diccionario de criminologia* [Lexicon of criminology] (Universidad Externado de Colombia, 1979); see also Hans-Jörg Albrecht, "Literaturbericht: Kriminologie und Kriminalsoziologie des romanischen Sprachbereichs" [Literature report: Criminology and crime sociology of the Romance Language Group], *Zeitschrift für die gesamte Strafrechtswissenschaft* 92 no. 3 (1980), p. 839.

22. Guillermo Olivera Diaz, *Criminologia Peruana* [Peruvian criminology], 2nd ed. (Lima: Tipografica y Offset Peruana, vol. 1, 1973; vol. 2, 1978).

12

The Role of the United Nations in Combating and Preventing Criminality

Combating and preventing crime in the modern world, with its great variety of economic, political, social, and cultural systems, is a complex process which involves the undertaking of many-sided activities.

Crime, in its character and intensity, is different in the developed countries than it is in those countries which have just liberated themselves from colonialism or in the socialist countries. Varied also are the causes and circumstances of crimes although these countries have numerous interests in common. They are linked, most of all, by the needs of commerce. The development of technology, facilitation of transport and communication, greater ease in crossing the borders for reasons of tourism, jobs, or recreation, long-distance communication and the migration of population—all this leads to a situation in which a large portion of the world's population is constantly on the move, transferring to other countries good as well as bad behavior patterns. Under these circumstances the issues of combating and preventing crime cease to be the exclusive domain of domestic interest.

In past ages—in the periods of slavery and feudalism—international cooperation in this field concerned the extradition of fugitives.[1] To this end agreements were signed by rulers or governments of states. It was only in the nineteenth century that international governmental organizations were founded to guarantee a permanent institutional cooperation between states. In addition, nongovernmental international organizations reflecting arrangements between persons, institutions, or associations from many countries were set up. In 1972 there were 2,750 such international organizations, including 2,470 nongovernmental.

The aim of the latter is mainly the organization of congresses, conferences, and the conduct and presentation of scientific research. The activity of nongovernmental international organizations is not based on international agreements but has great significance for the development of international cooperation.

The first international organization encompassing all international cooperation, including prevention of crime, was the League of Nations in 1919. Currently League objectives are promoted by the United Nations, founded on the basis of an agreement known as "the United Nations Charter," concluded in San Francisco on June 26, 1945.

In modern times, two fundamental forms of international cooperation in the field of crime prevention evolved: bilateral or multilateral international agreements; and the activities of intergovernmental and nongovernmental international organizations.

In the second part of the nineteenth century and the first thirty years of the twentieth, before World War II, this cooperation resulted in many conferences on criminology, international agreements on the extradition of criminals, and other forms of legal reciprocal aid of states, and also in the unification of legal responsibility for some offenses irrespective of regulations enforced in the place where they were committed and irrespective of the citizenship of the offenders (delicta iuris gentium). These offenses were: piracy, slave trade, white slave traffic, forgery of money and securites, drug traffic, and distribution of obscene publications. The resolutions of the international agreements signed on the principle of so-called world-wide criminal repression as regards crimes representing public menace found their expression in the criminal law of those states which ratified such agreements. Some of such agreements concerning, for example, the prohibition on white slave traffic (1921) and slavery (1926), were signed on the initiative of the League of Nations, which formally continued in existence until April 18, 1946, though ceasing practical functioning at the beginning of 1940.

In the last decades, especially after World War II, several specific kinds of crimes have appeared with greater intensity and have been reclassified. This is due to modern development of socioeconomic relations, which, in their scope and dynamism, have gone beyond the existing forms of rational, legal, and social control. Modern times are characterized, among other things, by the passing from simple, uncomplicated criminal forms to more sophisticated and sinister forms.[2] "International crime" has been defined as a crime: committed or having its effect on the territory of more than one state; which is a result of arrangements between the offenders, who remain in different countries; committed by individuals or organized gangs (mafias) on the territory of countries foreign to them.

The United Nations early realized the danger which is brought about by international crime.[3] In 1950 the General Assembly of the United Nations agreed to take over the functions of the International Penal and Penitentiary Commission by establishing the International Penal and Penitentiary Foundation (resolution No. 415 [V] December 1, 1950). All issues concerning crime are dealt with by the bodies of Social and Economic Council and the UN Secretariat.

The Economic and Social Council, one of the six main organs of the UN, consisting of fifty-four members (eighteen persons elected for three years) conducts research on socioeconomic problems. The following commissions, committees, and organizations are related to work on the prevention and combating of crime:

Commissions

Commission for Social Development

Commission on Human Rights with Subcommission on Prevention of Discrimination of Minorities

Commission on Narcotic Drugs

Committees

Council Committee on Non-Governmental Organizations

Committee on Crime Prevention and Control

Organizations

World Health Organization (WHO)

United Nations Educational Social and Cultural Organization (UNESCO)

International Narcotics Control Board (INCB)

International Labour Organization (ILO).

The UN Secretariat, because of its administrative and coordinating functions, deals with the issues of prevention and struggle against crime through the Crime Prevention and Criminal Justice Branch, headed by G. O. W. Mueller. This branch is one unit of the Social and Economic Affairs Department.

It aids other institutions and coordinates the work of four scientific and research institutes of the UN—in Cairo, Rome, Costa Rica, and Tokyo—and also acts as a consultant to UN members.

The UN Secretariat has carried out the World Survey of crime trends and patterns for the years 1970–1975. In the years 1982–1983 the UN Secretariat is scheduled to prepare a second World Survey covering the years 1976–1980.

On the initiative of Professor Mueller a conference was held on October 5–8, 1981 at the Rutgers State University in Newark (School of Criminal Justice). It was devoted to the discussion of monitoring methods of world trends in criminality and of the strategies of prevention.[4]

Participating in the conference were sixteen scientific workers representing UN regional institutes, universities, and other scientific centers. In the course of discussions views were exchanged concerning the questionnaire which was the basis of the first World Survey and many changes were introduced aiming at perfecting the methods of collection and analysis of statistical data.

It was also pointed out that there is a need to limit the number of statistical reports for the UN to the most serious offenses. The problem of alternate sources of information, other than governmental, was also considered. It is a very complicated issue. On many occasions the representatives of UN member-states stressed that the problems of criminality are the internal affairs of each country and that any intervention in this field could be seen as a violation of the sovereignty of a particular state.

The conference also agreed that the World Survey should be conducted and elaborated mainly on a regional scale. This will render the statistical data more comparable.

A group of experts deemed it necessary to prepare a very clear and detailed definition for each term used in the questionnaire. For example, the very obvious and simple term of "unintentional homicide" may refer to different criminal behaviors in different countries.

A decision was made to create a working group to prepare a draft questionnaire, which will then be reviewed by experts. It was also pointed out that the questionnaire needs to include questions concerning the organizational structure of courts and private police, as well as the existing state police.

Considerable discussion centered around the problem of the selection of social and economic development factors in relation to criminality. It was decided to broaden the catalogue of these variables by considering new elements such as the gross national product, the distribution of income, the level of migration, age and other demographic characteristics of the population. Problems related to the strategy of crime prevention were also considered at the conference.

It should be said, however, that surveys of world criminality do not give any basis for comparability of statistical data. They to some extent give an orientation as to the situation in particular regions of the world and particular states. Another fact must also be kept in mind, that is, statistics for "export" are by no means faultless, because they tend to "improve" the existing state of affairs.

Congresses organized by the UN are an international forum where the methods of combating crime are discussed and programmed.

The First Congress convened August 22–September 3, 1955, in Geneva, with 512 participants, including 51 government delegations. The most important outcome of the congress was the so-called "Minimum Rules of the

Treatment of Prisoners" and suggestions concerning the selection and training of prison staffs. "Minimum Rules," approved by the Economic and Social Council and recommended to UN member states, prohibit the use of corporal punishment, confining prisoners in dark places, and the application of inhuman or debasing methods in the treatment of prisoners.

The Second Congress was held August 8–20, 1960, in London, with 1,131 participants, including the representatives of 70 government delegations, among them the delegations of socialist countries, including Poland. The following issues were taken up: new forms of juvenile delinquency, its causes and prevention, in particular the role of social police forces in the prevention of juvenile delinquency and the treatment of juvenile offenders; the prevention of crime related to social and economic changes in the developing countries; the problem of punishment by short term deprivation of liberty; and the treatment of prisoners during their prison terms; protection of the released prisoners; prisoners' work for the national economy, and the problem of prisoners' remuneration for their work.

The Third Congress convened August 9–18, 1965, in Stockholm, with the participation of 1,083 persons, including 74 government delegations.[5] The main subject of debate, held in six sections, was the prevention of crime. The Polish delegation presented six papers which concerned the following problems: social changes and counteracting crime; the role of society, family, education, and job environment in the prevention of crime; a social program concerning the prevention of juvenile delinquency; prevention of relapse into crime; measures applied to offenders, other than prison terms; special preventive measures and the treatment of juvenile delinquents.

The Fourth Congress took place in Kyoto, Japan, August 17–26, 1970, with the participation of 1,014 persons, incuding 388 members of official government delegations. The main subject discussed during the sessions was the problem of crime and development. The following issues were discussed in the four sections: social protection policy related to planned development; prevention of crime, especially juvenile delinquency, in the context of national development; minimum UN rules concerning the treatment of prisoners, taking into account the changes in the field of rehabilitation.

At the Fifth United Nations Congress on the Prevention of Crime and the Treatment of Offenders, held in Geneva, September 1–12, 1975, apart from the representatives of 91 states (members and non-members of the UN) the delegates of the following bodies were also present: two international organizations—the Council of Europe and the Arab League; three international specialized organizations: the World Health Organization, the United Nations Educational, Scientific, and Cultural Organization and the International Narcotics Control Board; twenty-eight international nongovernmental organizations.

The congress was preceded by several regional meetings in Tokyo,

Brasilia, Budapest, and Lusaka. Sessions of the congress were held in five sections, and the following problems were discussed:

Section 1: new forms and evolutions of crime on a nationwide scale, crime as business, corruption, seizure of art works, abuse of alcohol and narcotics, violent crime (kidnapping, hijacking, violent bank robberies, terrorist acts), road traffic offenses;

Section 2: problems concerning criminal legislation, principles of court proceedings and other forms of social control in the field of crime prevention, decriminalization, depenalization (participants postulated the decriminalization and depenalization of family conflicts, juvenile delinquency, breaking the road traffic laws, shoplifting and avoiding alimony payments);

Section 3: the functions and scope of police activity (recruiting and training of policemen, the role of police in fighting against new forms of crime, the relations of police with the society);

Section 4: treatment of offenders in custody and prisons, treatment of former prisoners by the society, forms and methods of rehabilitation of criminals;

Section 5: the economic and social costs of crime.

The Sixth United Nations Congress on the Prevention of Crime and the Treatment of Offenders convened in Caracas, August 25–September 5, 1980. Official delegations of 95 states, representatives of 56 governmental and nongovernmental organizations, special UN agencies and national liberation movements participated in the Congress. In all, 900 persons were present.

The main topic discussed was the quality of life, prevention and the struggle against crime in the context of social and economic development. These aspects were especially stressed in the UN Secretary General's message. In it, Kurt Waldheim said that the prevention of crime and criminal justice should be regarded not solely from a technical or legal point of view: law and its application must agree with the economic reality of the member states, must reach further and function as a catalyst of change and progress.

The congress convened in two committees, where the following subjects were discussed: crime trends and crime prevention strategies, juvenile justice, crime and the abuse of power: offenses and offenders beyond the reach of law, deinstitutionalization of corrections and its implications for the residual prisoners, UN guidelines and norms in criminal justice—from standard-setting to implementation, new perspectives in crime prevention and criminal justice and development, international cooperation, and the issue of capital punishment.

In the last two decades the increase of crime in many regions of the world and the appearance of new, more menacing, forms of crime have created very serious and difficult problems for the state organizations and societies of many countries. The UN reports and discussions point out that this increase concerned mostly violent crimes, offenses against property, a group of acts described as white-collar crimes. There is also a relatively new phenomenon of various types of "computer abuse."

During the discussion on the treatment of juvenile delinquents, the social forms of prevention were mentioned. The role of the family and the system of education was especially stressed. Moreover, the experiences stemming from the functioning of separate courts for juveniles were discussed.

During the Fifth Congress (Geneva, 1975) the subject of offenders and offenses beyond the reach of the law had been discussed. This matter was further elaborated at the Sixth Congress by introducing the notion of the so-called golden crime which encompasses acts performed by persons toward whom the organs of prosecution and criminal justice are helpless due to their high political or economic status. Examples of such acts are, among others, bribery, corruption, tax evasion, credit and customs fraud, embezzlement of social funds, breach of foreign currency regulations, real estate speculation, smuggling, offenses against the environment, overpricing of bills, exploitation of laborers (especially immigrants), export and import of low-quality or dangerous products, as well as other offenses, which often infringe upon human rights (for example, apartheid and other forms of oppression or discrimination). The abuse of political and social power brings about serious damage in the quality of life and the well-being of citizens. This was strongly stressed, together with examples of colonialism, neocolonialism, occupation, discrimination, and the oppression of the weak and helpless.

Lack of accurate data concerning the relation of crime to the abuse of power makes the rational prosecution of such acts impossible. Representatives of many states suggested forming additional mechanisms on a national scale so that such acts and offenders could be brought to light. It was recommended to start with, among other things, a systematic gathering and exchange of information concerning various aspects of power abuse, to introduce changes in criminal law assuring an appropriate scope of penalization of such acts and to develop international cooperation in the field of minimum standards in international trade transactions.

At present, general opinion is that methods of work in penitentiary systems should be based on respect for human dignity. However, conditions in the prisons of many countries, the prolonged term of confinement in arrests during criminal procedure, and the high social cost of keeping many condemned persons in prisons expressed in moral as well as material terms, point to serious discrepancies between universal ideals and the reality. The number of prisoners must undoubtedly be reduced. It is therefore necessary to introduce alternative solutions. To achieve better results from penitentiary practice the offenders should keep in touch with their social environment.

The various ways of keeping and renewing such relations should be studied through a closer cooperation of penitentiary institutions with the representatives of social services. Important factors of effective propagation and realization of UN norms and guidelines in the field of criminal justice are, among others, society's cooperation, founding of national human rights committees, establishment of procedures on settling disputes, ratification of international humanitarian agreements and their strict obeyance, and the enacting of standard regulations (based on the "Minimum Rules") in the field of criminal justice.

Only half of the member states guarantee decent living conditions for their prisoners.

For many years the issue of capital punishment has been seriously considered in many UN papers. Opinions on that subject, as is well known, are divided, a fact amply reflected in law and practice. Up to August 1980 among the 153 member states of the UN, only 39 states had abolished capital punishment, 21 of them completely, 14 for common offenses, 2 did not apply it by custom, and 2 federal countries abolished it in some of their states. The Sixth Congress did not pass a resolution presented by Austria and Sweden (in spite of its compromise formula) on the necessity of abolishing capital punishment. Every state stuck to its own opinion. It was agreed, however, that it is a unique punishment and should be applied in specified rare cases only, taking into consideration the possibility of its complete abolition. The obligatory application of capital punishment for some offenses was criticized.

A measure of UN interest in the problems concerning new perspectives on crime prevention was the establishment of a special working group concerned with these problems (see chapter 18).

During the seventh session of the UN Committee on Crime Prevention and Control, held in Vienna, March 15–24, 1982, preparations were made for the Seventh United Nations Congress on the Prevention of Crime and the Treatment of Offenders in 1985. The Committee proposed the following five topics to be taken up by the Seventh Congress.

1. *New dimensions of crime prevention and criminal justice in the context of development.* This topic will serve as a vehicle for identifying and strengthening international cooperation in crime prevention, and for defining new guiding principles for the future course of action on crime prevention and criminal justice.

2. *The criminal-justice system and changing socioeconomic conditions.* This topic will focus attention on the overall criminal-justice system, especially on its potential to adapt to social changes.
3. *Youth, crime, and justice.* This topic will be considered in the broader perspective of International Youth Year, which also falls in 1985, and with respect to the development of standard minimum rules for the administration of juvenile justice.
4. *Victims and victimizers: abuse of power, justice, and redress.* This topic will cover such aspects as the prevention of discrimination in criminal justice and the compensations of victims, especially victims of the abuse of power.
5. *Formulation and applications of UN standards and norms: the protection of human rights in criminal-justice administration.*

The effectiveness of these congresses is viewed critically by some scientists. They object that the implementation of motions and recommendations of congresses by some state governments is slow. The Minimum Rules of treatment of prisoners and suggestions concerning prison staffs (adopted at the Geneva Conference in 1955, and then in 1957 recommended to governments by the Economic and Social Council) are applied without reservations by only a few states. The neglect of governments in this field was pointed out in the report of the UN Secretary General, prepared in 1973 for the experts of the working group on issues of Minimum Rules.[6] In spite of these and other reservations, one should not minimize the congresses' significant although slow influence in the struggle against crime.

The Crime Prevention and Criminal Justice Branch, one of the units of the Department for Social Affairs of the UN Secretariat, coordinates the activity of four scientific and research institutes.

The first one—the United Nations Asia and Far East Institute for the Prevention of Crime and Treatment of Offenders (UNAFEI) was founded in 1962 in Tokyo on the basis of an agreement with the Japanese government.[7] The tasks of this institute are: the training of judges, penitentiary administration and other appropriate institutions, and conducting research on the prevention of crime in this region of the world and on methods of treating prisoners. These tasks are fulfilled by the institute through:

1. The implementation of an educational program which has as its aim acquanting its participants with basic theories of criminology, the phenomena of crime, penology, and other scientific fields of study (law, sociology, psychology, psychiatry). Up to April 1977, the institute had organized forty-seven training courses for 1,200 participants.

The main topics of these courses were the following: criminal policy in developing countries in Asia and the Far East; the development of open rehabilitation institutions; problems connected with short-term confinement;

prevention of juvenile delinquency; systems of probation, conditional release, after-care, social rehabilitation; the role of women in rehabilitation institutions; the planning of research on the prevention of crime, with special attention paid to the influence of urbanization and industrialization on crime.

2. The keeping of contacts with state governments and appropriate institutions of this region by supplying them with the necessary information and cooperation in organizing and undertaking preventive measures;

3. Conducting research of a comparative and interdisciplinary character;

4. Publication of the results of scientific projects, monographs, and other data in "UNAFEI Series," "UNAFEI Newsletter" (the institute's activities, training programs, and the like), and "Resources Material Series" (monographs, reports from sessions and meetings of working groups).[8]

The institute has a well-stocked library and its Materials and Information Section serves as a regional center of documentation concerning, among other matters, the structure and organization of penitentiary institutions.

Until 1970, the institute was subordinate financially and administratively to the UN and the Japanese government. In 1970, the office of director of the institute was taken over from the UN by Japan, which provides nearly all the financing of this institution. This does not mean, however, that the institute is solely a Japanese endeavor.

The second institute—the United Nations Social Defense Research Institute (UNSDRI), with headquarters in Rome, was established in 1967 and its activity is manifested through:

1. The promotion, coordination, and conduct of research on crime and its prevention on an international, regional, and national scale. The research encompasses the following problems: discrepancies in notions of deviations, the participation of society in the criminal process, influence of migration on crime, etiology of juvenile delinquency, organization and administration of penitentiary institutions, organization of the administration of justice toward juveniles, fights against drug and narcotics abuse, corrective treatment, prisoners' rights, prison atmosphere, fears and disturbances, thefts and forgeries of art works and objects of archeological value.

2. The development of comparative research and exchange of experience through the coordination of research enquiries in different countries, with special attention paid to the developing countries.

3. The conduct of research in selected countries together with appropriate national organizations or experts from these countries.

4. The promotion of research methods and research results on an international scale, and facilitation of the exchange of information.

5. The supply of technical assistance and organization of educational activities to appropriate institutions.

6. Cooperation with international nongovernmental organizations.

7. The organization of symposia on the subject of, for example, the influence of economic crises on criminality.

8. The publication of manuals, studies, and reports on the institute's activities.[9]

The third organization—the Institute for Social Defense, was established in Cairo in 1972, on the basis of an agreement between the UN and the Egyptian government within the framework of the National Centre for Social and Criminological Research. The institute's activities cover the African countries and the Middle East countries (Arabic-speaking countries).

The institute's task is to conduct scientific research in the field of criminology and to organize courses for policemen, judges, social workers, and administration employees and other interested persons or social groups. In accordance with the agreement between the Egyptian government and the UN, this institute:

1. Conducts and supervises research on trends in social and economic development in relation to the control and prevention of crime and the treatment of offenders.

2. Organizes training courses in English, French, and Arabic.

3. Supplies the governments of this region, on their request, with information and provides consultation.

The institute organized: an international research course in the field of social defense (April–June 1972); training courses on social defense for Arab states (March–June 1973); UN training courses on human rights for employees of criminal justice (June–July 1973); a conference on the evaluation of social defense problems in Africa. Also, the institute hosted a meeting of a group of experts summoned by the UN Committee on the Prevention of Crime with the aim of working out an international plan of crime prevention action.[10]

The fourth and latest is the United Nations Latin American Institute for the Prevention of Crime and the Treatment of Offenders, which was created in 1975, with headquarters in San José (Costa Rica). The institute's tasks are set forth in an agreement signed by the UN and the Costa Rican government. They are as follows:

1. The organization of training courses—including theoretical as well as practical problems—for persons responsible for the policy of crime prevention and the treatment of offenders.

2. The conduct of lectures and seminars on selected research topics.

3. Collection and dissemination of information.

4. Conduct and support of interdisciplinary research, concerning crime problems in this region of the world (especially such issues as violence, drug addiction, corruption), the social and economic costs of crime, methods of crime prevention on a regional and national scale.

5. The facilitation of exhange of the experiences of different countries.

6. The undertaking of efforts to apply the UN guidelines and recommendations by the states, and also participation in the development and realization of programs on crime prevention.

7. The support of international cooperation in this region in the field of prevention and struggle against crime.[11]

A permanent periodical publication of the Crime Prevention and Criminal Justice Branch, an institution which coordinates the work of those four institutes, is the *International Review of Criminal Policy*. At first it appeared semiannually and since 1963 annually in three languages: English, French, and Spanish. Articles concerning UN activity in the field of crime prevention and the treatment of offenders, reports, communiqués, information on international meetings, and a bibliography are part of each issue.

Also, the *International Journal of Criminology and Penology* has been appearing since 1972.

Notes

1. The literature mentions as one of the oldest international treaties the agreement signed in the thirteenth century B.C. by the Pharaoh of Egypt, Ramses II, and the ruler of the Hittites, Hattusilish III, which stated, among other things, that if a person should flee from Egypt to the state of the Hittites, the ruler of the Hittites would not keep him but send him back to the state of Ramses.

2. Brunon Hołyst, *Przestepczość drugiej połowy XX wieku* [Criminality in the second half of the twentieth century] (Warsaw: Wiedza Powszechna, 1975), p. 9 ff.

3. The periodical *International Review of Criminal Policy* 1952, no. 2, includes basic information on international organizations in the field of crime prevention and the treatment of offenders.

4. Ad hoc meeting of experts in the implementation of the second United Nations survey of world crime trends and crime prevention strategies. Rutgers, State University of New Jersey, October 5–8, 1981. A Working Paper prepared by the Secretariat.

5. "Troisième Congrès des Nations Unies pour la Prévention du Crime et le Traitment des Délinquants," *Nations Unies*, (New York, 1967), pp. 1 and 65.

6. Manuel Lopez-Rey, "The Role of the United Nations Congresses on the Prevention of Crime and the Treatment of Offenders," *Federal Probation Quarterly*, September 1973.

7. *International Review of Criminal Policy* 1976, no. 32.

8. In March 1977 a report on activities in 1976 was published. See:

United Nations Asia and Far East Institute Report for 1976 and Resource Material Series No. 13, Tokyo.

9. *International Review of Criminal Policy* 1976, no. 32; The Institute Information Folder, Misc. No. 6, Rome, July 1975.

10. *International Review of Criminal Policy* 1976, no. 32.

11. *International Review of Criminal Policy* 1977, no. 33, p. 65.

13 The International Society of Criminology

The International Society of Criminology was founded in Rome in 1937; it now has its headquarters in Paris. The purpose of the society is to develop criminological research and coordinate initiatives and international undertakings concerning the prevention and counteraction of crime. To this aim the society organizes international congresses every five years, conducts criminological courses, edits publications, collects scientific documentation, and prepares staff training programs. Article 3 of the Statute of the society describes it in the following manner: The Society shall seek to attain its aim by: congresses and publications; the establishment of an institute designed to be an international center of study, research and criminological documentation; all other means, such as the exchange of professors and students, the creation of scholarships and prizes, and the organization of lectures and courses, considered appropriate by the Society or its Boards of Directors.

The highest body of the society is the General Assembly which is convened at least once every five years. Between the assembly's sessions, the board of directors manages the society's work. The board consists of twenty-four members elected for five years by the assembly; furthermore, the board can appoint a maximum of five additional members. The board elects from among its members an executive committee which directs everyday work. The executive committee is assisted by a scientific committee consisting of fifteen members.

The society organized eight international congresses devoted to various problems of criminology:

First Congress (Rome, 1938) on the etiology and diagnosis of juvenile delinquency and the role of the judge in combating crime;

Second Congress (Paris, 1950) on the personality of the offender, comparative criminology, and problems of criminal statistics;

Third Congress (London, 1955) devoted to the traits differentiating the offenders among themselves and other persons (the so-called differentiative criminology) and recidivism;

Fourth Congress (The Hague, 1960) on the psychological aspects of the behavior of offenders;

Fifth Congress (Montreal, 1965) on penitentiary problems;

Sixth Congress (Madrid, 1970) on the results of scientific studies concerning the person of the offender.

The Seventh Congress took place in Belgrade in 1973. Its sessions were concerned with the principal tendencies in modern criminology—the sociological and clinical orientation as well as the criminal-political. Discussions were held in three sections on the following topics: the stereotype of offender labeling; criminal personality and typology of offenders; evolution in the field of criminal policy. All these problems were analyzed from the point of view of the aforementioned orientations existing in modern criminology.

The Eighth Congress convened in Lisbon in September 1978. The representatives of sixty countries participated. The main discussions were held in eight sections.

Section 1. The problems of crime genesis. Distinct tendencies in the direction of clinical criminology were observed. In spite of the fact that a dominant role was assigned to the social determinants of criminality, it was stated that pathology of biophysical traits may influence criminal behavior of particular persons. It is difficult, however, to explain crime as a mass phenomenon by the pathology of biophysical traits.

Section 2. Criminal justice. The planning of criminal justice, costs, diversion, and the scale of penal means, were discussed. The activities of criminal justice are very costly, thus there is more emphasis on the "economization of criminal justice."

Section 3. The problems of the treatment of offenders. Recently, in many countries there has been a gradual limitation of sentencing to liberty deprivation as being too costly in relation to the results achieved by rehabilitation. Liberty deprivation is being substituted by other forms of punishment, for instance, a fine or restricted liberty. A wisely applied system of fines can in many cases successfully substitute for the punishment of deprivation of liberty. This is effective especially in those countries which have a relatively high standard of living. Research results show that punishment by a fine can be equally as painful and deterrant as a short-term punishment by deprivation of liberty, and does not cause the negative consequences of the latter.

In the evaluation of the punishment of liberty deprivation, reformist and abolitionist tendencies can be discerned. However, demands to do away with the punishment of deprivation of liberty are at present still unrealistic.

Section 4. Juvenile delinquency. In many countries the phenomenon of social maladjustment of minors has become a grave social problem. This section also, instead of defining the socioeconomic conditions, devoted considerable attention to the clinical approach to the analysis of juvenile delinquency. The concept of a "criminal personality" of juveniles is being revived.

Section 5. Victimology. For the first time a congress on criminology devoted much attention to this problem. Issues concerning the methodology of victimological examinations were discussed, as were indemnity to victims and aid to victims of sexual offenses, family disputes, and other offenses. In 1979 the Third World Symposium on Victimology took place in Münster, which serves to show the importance of these problems.

Section 6. Crime prevention. Every epoch, social system, and culture creates a different sort of maladjustment problems, dysfunction, and crime. In solving these problems one should frequently seek new means supported by a detailed diagnostical analysis of the pathological phenomena. In modern criminology it is extremely important to identify the areas threatened by crime or showing an increase in crime, the more so considering that the development of modern societies is characterized by great changes in quality as well as in quantity, unlike other historical periods of considerable socioeconomic and cultural stability. During the sessions it was said that the prevention of crime based on the diagnosis of circumstances can take on various, characteristically different forms.

1. Prevention of detrimental phenomena at their conception.
2. The creation in the frame of every institutional or spacio-objective system the means to allow for immediate liquidation of existing detrimental effects, in the time which does not allow for the consolidation of these effects.
3. The creation of neutralization systems of negative effects for the person or group which participate or exist in an institutional or spacio-objective arrangement.
4. The creation of specialized, autonomous forms of prevention on a global scale, best carried out by the system of education and socialization.
5. The creation of specialized institutional forms of diagnosis of circumstances, prevention and therapy of effects as well as the propagation of behavior and situations conducive to social progress.

The activation of social forces for the cause of crime prevention becomes the order of our times. The participation of society, when it is adequately directed, can become a great preventive force of undesirable situations from the individual as well as the social point of view and at the same time it can create situations which have positive values—promotive for individuals, groups or the social macrostructure.

The optimizing of preventive methods requires a detailed analysis concerning the problem of the effectiveness of preventive actions. The study of effectiveness is one of the most difficult methodological tasks; there are relatively few studies and research papers in this field. It seems particularly important to formulate methodological guidelines for the measurement of effectiveness which would guarantee validity as well as comparability of data on an international scale.

Section 7. Epistemology and history of criminology. Increasingly, criminology has become a multidisciplinary science in its subject as well as its research methods.

Section 8. The deontology of criminological research. Recently, attention has been turned to the necessity of elaborating the moral principles of criminological research, which take the man as its subject. It concerns, among others, allowing experiments to be performed on prisoners, the objectivity of studies, the publication of research results (guarantee of private rights). This concerns also the adequate selection of the research team.

The Ninth Congress will take place in Vienna in 1983. The topic will be the relation of criminology to social policy.

Since 1952, the International Society of Criminology has organized courses in various countries:

Paris 1952: the medical, psychological and social examination of offenders;

Paris 1953: the problem of the dangerous state;

Stockholm 1954: society and crime;

London 1954: achievements in the field of study and treatment of offenders;

Rome 1955: crime and personality;

Lausanne 1956: prevention of crime;

Vienna 1957: criminology and accidents in communication;

Brussels 1958: prevention of unintentional offenses;

Copenhagen 1959: treatment of offenders in Denmark;

Fribourg 1960: criminology, the penitentiary system, and teaching;

Madrid 1961: mentally abnormal offenders;

Jerusalem 1962: criminality in the developing countries;

Cairo 1963: economic development and problems of social behavior;

Lyons 1964: the equipment of criminology;

Rome 1965: treatment of adult offenders;

Abidjan 1966: criminology in the French-speaking African countries;

Montreal 1967: criminology in action;

Belgrade 1968: the problems of recidivism in its various aspects;

Mendoza 1969: the function of criminology in penal law, criminal trials, execution of sentences, and in the treatment of offenders, study and teaching;

Lagos 1970: noninstitutional treatment of offenders;

San Paulo 1972: general and special criminology;

San Paulo 1973: criminological problems in Brazil;

Maracaibo 1974: criminology and violence;

Teheran 1974: drugs and crime;

Guayaquil 1975: criminalization and decriminalization;

Pau-Bayonne/St. Sebastien 1976: research in juvenile maladjustment and delinquency;

Wuppertal 1977: conflict of youth with institutions;

Montreal 1980: police, justice, and the community;

Pamplona 1980: the role of criminology in the new democracies;

New York 1981: new dimensions of criminality;

Aix-en-Provence 1981: the latest developments in the knowledge of criminality.

National criminological societies also organize congresses and seminars. Every five years the International Society of Criminology grants the Denis Carroll prize for the most outstanding achievements in the field of criminology.

The society takes part in the activities of the United Nations, the Council of Europe, and UNESCO. Since 1962 the society has published the "International Annals of Criminology" (formerly the "Bulletin"), and publishes, with UNESCO, a "Selected Documentation on Criminology."

Since 1969 the society has undertaken organizational efforts which aim at conducting interdisciplinary studies on an international scale. Two international centers have so far been established: the International Center for Comparative Criminology, at the University of Montreal in 1969; and the International Center of Clinical Criminology at the University of Genoa in 1975.

14

The Role of the Council of Europe in Combating and Preventing Crime

The Council of Europe represents twenty-one member states: Austria, Belgium, Cyprus, Denmark, France, the Federal Republic of Germany, Greece, Ireland, Iceland, Italy, Liechtenstein, Luxembourg, Malta, The Netherlands, Norway, Portugal, Spain, Sweden, Switzerland, Turkey, and the United Kingdom.

The objectives of the Council of Europe in the penal and criminological fields are:

1. to help to adapt preventive and repressive crime policy to contemporary social needs while taking account of both the need to protect the fundamental values and structures of human society and the principles of the preeminence of law and the respect for human rights;
2. to foster international cooperation in the prevention and punishment of crime and the treatment of offenders;
3. to encourage, where appropriate, the harmonizing of individual national efforts to work out comprehensive policies to control crime and defend the community; encourage the critical examination and development of such policies through the exchange of information and research findings.

The realization of this program has been entrusted to the European Committee on Crime Problems (CDPC). The committee consists of specialists in the legal, penological, and criminological sciences; it is assisted in its work by the Criminological Scientific Council comprising seven eminent criminologists who submit technical opinions, compile information, and submit the proposals concerning the committee's work. At its plenary session each year the committee examines the various aspects of crime policy and decides on ways and means of implementing it.

The CDPC program is implemented by a number of select committees and working groups, through organizing seminars and colloquia, criminological research conferences, and criminological research fellowships, as well as through cooperation with other international organizations.

Committees

The CDPC established several committees of experts working on specific crime problems:

1. *Extradition and mutual assistance.* This committee has been set up to examine the practical application of the European Convention on Extradition and the European Convention on Mutual Assistance in Criminal Matters.
2. *Relations between conventions in the penal field* (other than extradition and mutual assistance conventions). The committee's aim is to determine how these conventions are applied in practice and to ensure that they are not mutually incompatible. The resolutions elaborated by this committee in 1979 concern the European conventions on the transfer of proceedings in criminal matters, the international validity of criminal judgments, the supervision of conditionally sentenced or conditionally released offenders and the punishment of road traffic offenses.
3. *A European Convention on the Suppression of Terrorism.* The convention was opened for signature in January 1977.
4. *Problems raised by certain new forms of concerted acts of violence.* The committee will propose measures likely to improve international cooperation.
5. *European standards on custody pending trial.* On the basis of the European Convention on Human Rights this committee prepared a set of European standards to be applied to persons awaiting trial.
6. *The punishment of road traffic offenses.* Among other things, the committee has drawn up and adopted the "Guidelines for Offenses to Be Included in a European Highway Code."
7. *Harmonization of national legislation and practice regarding the control of the acquisition and possession of firearms by individuals.* The European Convention on the Control of the Acquisition and Possession of Firearms by Individuals was opened for signature in 1978.
8. *Theft and destruction of works of art.* This committee has been working since 1978 on the definition of offenses against the cultural heritage, international cooperation in preventing such offenses, the settlement of problems inherent in the concept of "bona fide owner," transnational restitution and statutory limitation, and the preparation of a draft European Convention on the Suppression of Offenses against Cultural Property.
9. *Methods of state compensation for victims of crime.* These are to be based on principles for standards to be applied internationally. This

committee drew up the resolution adopted in 1977 by the Committee of Ministers of the Council of Europe.

10. *The role of criminal law in the protection of the environment.* The committee completed its work in 1977, submitting the report and recommendations to member governments.

11. *The relationship between the public and crime policy.* The committee focuses on public participation in policy for alternatives to imprisonment, protecting victims, and crime prevention. It is studying both legislation and practice in member states and criminological research on the subject.

12. *Cooperation between the public and the police in the prevention of crime.* The committee has prepared the program covering: the police structure best suited to cooperation with the public, population groups causing the problems, forms of cooperation between the public and police and the difficulties, and ways of securing public cooperation.

13. *Decriminalization* problems. The committee has made a comparative study of trends and criteria concerning all forms of decriminalization used in Council of Europe member states.

14. *Economic (business) crime.* The committee studies the factors affecting business crime (economic, psychosocial and legal) as well as the legislation and practices of the member states concerning prevention and criminal penalties.

15. *Violence.* Examples of the committee's studies are the transfer and safekeeping of funds of criminal origin and kidnappings followed by ransom demands.

16. *Juvenile delinquency.* In the 1960s a CDPC select committee conducted a study into postwar juvenile delinquency in Europe. In 1978 a new select committee published a report summarizing the facts and trends over the last twenty years and describing the various legal systems for the prevention and treatment of social maladjustment among young people.

17. *Dangerous prisoners.* Since 1978 the committee has worked on: the definition of dangerous prisoners and of dangerousness, the various categories of dangerous prisoners, individual treatment of dangerous prisoners, technical problems, isolation of dangerous prisoners, prison staff, and similar matters.

18. *Foreign nationals in prisons.* Among other problems, the committee has studied legal standards providing for a simple procedure for the transfer of foreign prisoners to their state of origin, and ways and means of alleviating the particular difficulties faced by foreign nationals in prisons.

19. *"The Standard Minimum Rules for the Treatment of Prisoners."* The resolutions of this document presented at the fourth Conference of

Directors of Prison Administrations in 1979 recommended establishing the committee to review the whole of these rules in Council of Europe member states and to draw up a revised version as well as setting up a standing committee to foster improvements in prison affairs.

20. *Prison regimes and legal foundation with practical operation of the prison leave systems.*

The CDPC organized four conferences of Directors of Prison Administrations which dealt with the problems studied by the committees listed, as well as with recidivism, prison work, and the role of voluntary workers in the treatment of offenders.

Seminars

The CDPC organizes seminars and study tours for personnel of prisons and other persons who deal with penitentiary problems. Since 1975, the seminars have included such topics as: electronic data-processing in prison administration, social rehabilitation of delinquents, the procedure of prisoner selection and the differentiation of the forms of penal treatment, management in prison at all levels, present forms of juvenile delinquency and possible remedial measures, the importance of prison labor in a modern prison structure, the preparation of prisoners for release, organizing a probation service in a large city, cooperation between local authorities and prison probation administrations, treatment of postadolescents and young adults, execution of sentence in small prisons, and the limitations and possibilities of individual treatment.

The CDPC also organized seminars for juvenile court judges and for judges and members of prosecutors' departments dealing with business crime.

Criminological Research

The CDPC organizes Criminological Research Conferences alternatively with the Criminological Colloquia, criminological research fellowships, publishes a bulletin on current criminological research in Council of Europe member states, and conducted the survey of criminological research coordination agencies and application of the results to crime policy. The findings of this survey were published in a 1979 report by the Council of Europe.

The objectives of the Criminological Research Conferencs are: to review and assess criminological research into a specific subject; to make suggestions concerning any aspects of the subject requiring further study; to provide information for the guidance of Council of Europe member states in devising their criminal policy and planning Council of Europe activities in the sphere of crime problems.

The previous two conferences of the directors of Criminological Research Institutes (1976 and 1979) were devoted, respectively, to the criminological aspects of economic crime and to public opinion in relation to crime and criminal justice.

The criminological colloquia dealt with the following issues: means of improving information on crime, police and the prevention of crime, and criminological aspects of the ill-treatment of children in the family.

The Council of Europe awards individual fellowships and organizes coordinated criminological research fellowships enabling a team of four research workes to conduct a criminological study of common European interest, such as: prosecuting practive governed by the expediency principle, the criminality of women, and prison management.

The Council of Europe regularly publishes a bulletin on current criminological research in Council of Europe member states.

The European Committee on Crime Problems cooperates with the United Nations, Interpol, the International Association of Penal Law, the International Penal and Penitentiary Foundation, the International Society of Social Defense, and the International Society of Criminology.

Since 1978 the Council of Europe has published the *Bulletin d'information sur les activités juridiques au sein du Conseil de l'Europe et dans les états membres*, which aids in comparative studies of the direction of current crime policy in the various European countries.

This chapter is based on the report of the Council of Europe, "Council of Europe Activities in the Field of Crime Problems," published in Strasbourg in 1980.

15 The International Society of Social Defense

The beginnings of doctrines and of the movement of social defense are found in the works of F. Gramatica and the creation of the Center of Studies on Social Defense in Genoa in 1945 (Centro de Investigatione di Difesa Sociale). Criticizing the classical penal law, Gramatica put forward a "subjective" theory founded on the analysis of human nature seen as natural existence and on the analysis of the relations between individual and the society. Opposing the right of the state to punish, Gramatica acknowledged the right of defense against antisocial behavior. He argued that the state is obliged to socialize people by measures necessary to protect the individual against himself and to defend the society, that is, to guarantee order. He demanded, instead of penal law, social defense law. In the latter "offenses" ae indicators of subjective antisocial behavior of the individual and measures of social defense are undertaken instead of punishment.

Only two years later, after elaborating a program defining the principles and objectives of the movement of social defense with the participation of other scientists, the Center in Genoa became the International Center of Studies of Social Defense (Centro Internazionale de Studi di Difesa Sociale). The objectives of this center were: to point out the unjustness of the opinion claiming the right of society to punish; to bring together representatives of various sciences—law, philosophy, pedagogy, medicine—interested in social defense with the aim of carrying out the necessary reform of the penal system; to study measures which are more adequate to the new system of criminal justice and new penal proceedings; to define antisocial behaviors and their subjective elements, to outline adequate criteria for distinguishing them and for the evaluation of possibilities of guiding them.

The center publishes the periodical *Revista di Difesa Sociale.*

The first international congress of scientists who joined the movement held in San Remo (Italy), November 8–10, 1947. This congress passed a resolution which transformed the center into the International Institute of Studies on Social Defense (Istituto Internazionale per gli Studi di Difesa Sociale). During sessions, differences of opinion came to light between the Italian and the French scientists, especially Marc Ancel. According to a later work by this author,[1] the new social defense does not strive to substitute social defense law for penal law, but only aims to include this movement in the binding penal law, excepting only capital punishment and life imprisonment.

In spite of differences of opinion the San Remo congress unanimously passed the final resolution and six detailed resolutions concerning: the introduction in political parties' programs of a clause assuring special privileges for political offenders; the introduction of forensic medicine in law departments; the teaching of other auxiliary sciences at these departments; the introduction on a wide scale of the moral education of society; the specialization of judges, limitation of publications of information about scandalous events; the abolition of capital punishment.

The Second International Congress took place in Liège and Spa, October 3–8, 1949. The subject was the human personality from the point of view of the rights of society in relation to the rights of man.

Also at this congress doctrinal differences came to light, in spite of which several resolutions were passed unanimously, among them the resolution concerning the state's obligation to create the necessary conditions for the betterment and development of human personality, and another concerning the application of preventive measures.

The congress, by majority vote, opposed eugenic sterilization—even with the consent of the person concerned—preventive sterilization of offenders, castration, and the use of drug analysis in penal proceedings.

The congress passed a resolution concerning the creation of an international society under the name of the International Society of Social Defense (SIDS) (Société Internationale de Défense Sociale). In article 2 of the approved statute the society's objective was thus described: "The Society intends—coordinating its activity with the activity of already existing special societies—to study the best means of combating crime, profiting in a specific way from the results of scientific studies concerning man, so as to rethink again the basis of the relation between human personality and the society." The interim headquarters of the society were located in the Institute in Genoa.

Before the third Congress two preparatory meetings were held: in San Marino and in Caracas. At the Pan-American meeting in Caracas the Inter-American Institute of Social Defense was established.

The third Congress convened in April 1954 in Antwerp. Shortly before, the Economic and Social Council of the United Nations granted the society a consultative status of B category. The problems discussed at the congress concerned the individualization of punishment in the process of sentencing and of execution of penalty. The final resolution drew attention to the necessity of examining the offenders. The congress moved its headquarters to Paris, an expression of the already prevailing French influence.

Six months later, the advisory board of the SIDS accepted the so-called minimum program, elaborated by Marc Ancel, H. Hurwitz and I. Strahl. The program defined the essential goals of the movement, the basic principles of penal law, its theory, and a program of penal law development. In one part of the program defining the basic principles of the movement, it was stated that the struggle against crime must be looked upon as one of the most crucial tasks facing society. Any measures used to this end must be seen as having as their objective not only the defense of society against offenders but also the protection of members of society against the risk of committing an offense. Thus, society acting in these two fields introduces what may justly be called social defense. The movement of social defense trying to ensure the protection of a group through the protection of its members, desires to give the human personality a dominant role in all aspects of the social organization. Penal law should be seen as one means of decreasing criminality.

The Fourth Congress was held in Milan, April 2–5, 1956, where the headquarters of the society's branch, called the Center of Prevention and Social Defense (Centro Nazionale di Prevenzione e Difesa Sociale) were located. The congress's theme was the prevention of crimes against life and man's bodily inviolability. The final resolution concerned, among others, the question of unintentional offenses, not only from the point of view of repression but also from the point of view of prevention. Moreover, the society's statute was changed. Article 1, which describes the aims of the society, stated that the International Society of Social Defense is a nonprofit organization, which intends to study the problems of criminality, relating them to the system of crime prevention, including the rehabilitation of the offender and the protection of individuals from the danger of attempting to commit or to relapse into crime.

The Fifth Congress convened in Stockholm, August 25–30, 1958, and the problems discussed at its sessions focused on the question of administrative and court interventions in relation to children and socially maladjusted young people. The following issues were discussed: the stages of development of socially maladjusted youth; the social institutions created to protect juveniles; the selection of means and criteria applied to juveniles.

The subjects of the Sixth Congress, held in Belgrade and Opava, May 22–28, 1961, were the problems concerning juvenile delinquents and their treatment. The final resolution stressed the specific problem of young-adult delinquency, that is, persons who are over the age of minority but under 25 years of age. A postulate was put forward to introduce special regulations authorizing the magistrates to apply or not to apply sanctions and also to make changes during the execution of punishment.

At that time, four major international organizations engaged in penal law and criminology: the International Association of Penal Law, the International Penal and Penitentiary Foundation, the International Society of Criminology, and the International Society of Social Defense signed an agreement stipulating that each organization would alternatively, every five years, be the organizer of a congress, and once every five years they would organize a joint meeting. The first such joint meeting (colloque) took place in April 1963 at Bellagio, Italy—its topic was the problem of mentally ill offenders. Successive meetings, organized in the same city, concerned the elaboration of penal sentences (1968) and decriminalization (1973).

The Seventh Congress took place in Lecce, Italy, November 19–24, 1966, on the subject of interdiction of practising the profession and other kinds of activities. It was pointed out that sometimes such bans exceed the needs of social defense. At this congress F. Grammatica resigned as president of the society and on his motion Marc Ancel was elected president.

The Eighth Congress convened in 1971 in Paris, to consider the techniques of judicial individualization.

The Ninth Congress was organized in August 1976 in Caracas.[2] The issues concerned the problems of social marginality and justice. In the course of analysis, sociological, anthropological, cultural, psychological, and legal aspects were taken into consideration. In most countries the problem of social marginality has grown to become one of the most serious social, economic, and even political problems. Such milieus are dominated by a specific criminal subculture characterized, among others, by hedonism, where values like social uselessness and negativism are esteemed. The movement of Social Defense, whose objective is the humanization of penal law and the elaboration of a new method of reacting to criminal acts, puts forward a postulate of getting the support of the widest social circles for the limitation of social marginality. During the sessions much attention was focused on the problem of social maladjustment of the young.

The Tenth Congress was held at Salonika, September 28–October 2, 1981; its subject was cities and criminality. The reports and discussions focused on criminological, sociological and juridical aspects, such as distribution of offenses within the city, distribution of juvenile delinquency within the city and in the social class structure, the city and recidivism, types of offenders in different environments, criminogenic social processes in city life, violence and the city, urban social control, the socioecological system, characteristics of the slums, city areas where foreign-born people live, urbanization and marginality, industrialization and juvenile delinquency, urbanization and its influence on penal legislation and on criminal law and procedure, and legal measures to improve urban social control.

Among other activities of the social defense movement there was the establishment, in 1953 in Paris, of the Commission for the Study of Social Defense Problems. At the commission's first session, Marc Ancel, in defining the scope of its work, used the term "new social defense," the principles of which are explained in the reference in note 1. The commission then became the Center of Studies of Social Defense. Beginning in 1953, these institutions annually organized French congresses under the name

"Days of Social Defense"; some were held with the participation of representatives of other neighboring countries, such as England, The Netherlands, Belgium, and their territories.

The society's official periodical was the *Bulletin de la Sociètè Internationale de Défense Sociale*, formerly the *Revista de Difesa Sociale*, now it is the *Cahiers de Défense Sociale*.

The International Society of Social Defense has consultative status with the Economic and Social Council of the United Nations.

In 1960 the Leage of Arab States created the Pan-Arab Organization for Social Defense which organized meetings and seminars devoted to problems of criminality in Afro-Asiatic countries.

Notes

1. Marc Ancel, *La Défense sociale nouvelle: Un mouvement de politique criminelle humaniste* (Paris: Editions Cujas, 1954).

2. For the Ninth Congress the Institute of Crime Problems prepared a special publication. See Brunon Hołyst, ed., *Some Problems of Crime Prevention in Poland: The Ninth International Congress of Social Defense in Latin America* (Warsaw: Polish Scientific Publishers, 1976).

16 Activity of the International Criminal Police Organization in the Field of Criminology

The results of criminological research play an ever-increasing role in police work. These results are used not only in the process of crime detection but also in the prevention of negative social phenomena.

Detailed discussion of this matter will be preceded by a short summary of the organizational structure and history of Interpol.

In 1893, on the initiative of William S. Seavy, the International Association of Chiefs of Police was organized—members were police chiefs in the United States. Issues concerned with the struggle against criminality were discussed at a Chicago congress. At present, the association has over two thousand members, police from the United States, Canada, and fifteen other countries.[1] In October 1897, the National Police Bureau of Identification was set up in Chicago; in 1902 it was transferred to Washington. In 1924, it was incorporated into the Federal Bureau of Investigation.

The phenomenon of rising crime at the beginning of the twentieth century prompted the idea of establishing international cooperation among the police organizations of various countries.

In 1913, Scotland Yard decided to enter into cooperation with European and American police. To this end, photographs of all known criminals were sent to many countries with a request for mutual help and the exchange of evidence material.[2]

At the first International Police Congress in Monaco, in 1914, a proposal was put forward concerning the setting up of an international criminal police organization. A German delegate, Robert Heindl, also pointed to the necessity of cooperation in the field of crime prevention. World War I hindered the realization of these postulates.

In discussing the development of international cooperation in the field of combating crime one should mention the efforts of a captain of the Royal Danish navy and commissioner of police, Jorge van Houten, who, in 1919, as a private person—with the approval of the Danish government—proposed to the police of many countries the establishment of an International Criminal Police Organization under the auspices of the League of Nations. Its tasks were to be: research in crime in every country; preparing motions concerning international agreements on combating crime for the League of Nations; acting as consultant to organs of the League of Nations in cases which do not directly concern the police but are in some way connected with it; collecting "mug shots" of international criminals and "wanted" letters; helping to capture criminals who fled to another country; informing countries about the present situation in the field of combating crime.

Moreover, van Houten proposed to publish a periodical which would include information on international offenders.[3]

Some years later, van Houten, referring to the Convention Internationale relative à la Répression de la Traite des Blanches signed on May 18, 1904, in Paris by plenipotentiaries of various countries and to the Protocole de Clôture, signed in Paris on May 4, 1910, suggested that the international organization concerned with the fight against the white slave trade broaden its scope of activity to other crimes. Such an organization was to exist outside the League of Nations since not all countries were League members.

Van Houten's proposal was not considered because its author spoke as a private person. Moreover, the first years after the war were not favorable for carrying out such concepts. Governments, occupied with liquidating the effects of the war, did not show much interest in establishing an international organization to combat crime.

It is not a coincidence that many concepts aiming at organizing the combat against international crime were taken up by the Vienna police. After the fall of the Austro-Hungarian monarchy, the Vienna police had at its disposal a large number of materials concerning criminal offenses committed in Austria, Czechoslovakia, Yugoslavia, Poland, Rumania, and Hungary. Due to historical conditions Vienna, for nearly twenty years, was the seat of international criminal police organization.

In 1923, the president of the Vienna police and former chancellor of Austria, J. Schober, convened in Vienna an international police congress. It was the first international congress, in the true meaning of the word, because members from every continent except Australia participated in it.[4] At this congress, various concepts of the forms of international cooperation were put forward.

Serbia's representative, J. Bankovitsch, suggested accrediting police attachés in police headquarters of particular countries. Their duty would be to develop cooperation with a given country in the field of combating criminal offenses. The Danish representative, Broekhoff, pointed to the existence in many places—Belgium, Czechoslovakia, The Netherlands, Poland, and Hungary—of special offices for combating counterfeiters and underlined the necessity to organize such offices in every other country with the aim of establishing mutual cooperation.

After the discussion, it was resolved to establish the International Criminal Police Commission (ICPC). Austria's representative, Schulz, presented the main tasks of this organization: collecting materials on international offenders, their punishability, "wanted" letters published in search gazettes of individual countries, establishing records of individual offenders according to their methods of activity, collection of "mug shots" and fingerprints and the dissemination of information concerning individual offenders, publication of an international review of criminal police problems, as well as statistics and annual reports.

The aim of this organization was to ensure mutual far-reaching cooperation within the limits of each nation's binding legal norms, among the organs of the criminal police of every country and the recommendation of the most adequate ways of combating crime. Vienna was chosen as the headquarters of the General Secretariat, for an unlimited period, that is to say, until the participants should decide to transfer it to another city.

Representatives of every nation were members of the commission (theoreticians and practitioners of criminalistics could also become members). The executive committee was made up of the president, vice-president, five clerks, and the general secretary. The secretary and two clerks had to be representatives of the president's nation. Once a year a plenary session of the members of the commission was held. At least half of its members had to be present and a majority of votes be cast in order to pass a resolution.

The first session of the International Criminal Police Commission was held on May 19, 1924, in Vienna, and in 1925 the periodical *International Public Safety* was published.

Every year the number of member-states of the commission increased. In the Vienna congress, the representatives of twenty states participated and in 1926 at the Berlin congress twenty-eight states were represented. By 1938, thirty-four states were cooperating with the International Criminal Police Commission.

One of the major issues with which the commission concerned itself in the period between the world wars was counterfeiting, as well as the forgery of checks and other securities.

In 1922, Adler organized in Vienna an office, under the Association of Austrian Banks and Bankers, the aim of which was the prevention of forgery of all forms of money and other documents. The bureau had at its disposal a large number of exhibits. In 1923 the first number of the periodical *Counterfeits and Forgeries* appeared in two languages. A few months later, it became an organ of the commission, and Adler was nominated chief expert in forgeries. After the annexation of Austria, in 1938, the Viennese bureau was taken over by the Gestapo. At that time, Adler organized a new bureau in Holland, which continued the same activity. Not only banks but other credit institutions of Europe cooperated with the bureau; the number rose from 29 in 1924 to 155 in 1935.

The problem of forgeries was discussed during many plenary sessions of the commission. Since the time of the commission's establishment this issue has been in the center of criminal police attention in every country. It was widely discussed during the fifth session, which took place November 10–12, 1928, in Berlin.

Other problems with which the commission was concerned were the white slave and narcotics trades and juvenile delinquency.

After the end of World War II the alarming increase of crime influenced the development of cooperation among police of the various states.

In 1945, after an agreement was reached with Scotland Yard, the International Criminal Investigation Office was established in the Hague.

On the initiative of the Belgian government, representatives of seventeen states met in Brussels June 3–5, 1946 with the aim of reactivating the International Criminal Police Commission. In this field, the general inspector of Belgian police, long-term president of the commission, and honorary president of the ICPC, P.E. Louwage, was a major figure. At the twenty-fifth session, which took place in Vienna, in 1956, a new name was adopted: International Criminal Police Organization (ICPO), and new statutes were enacted.

The bodies of this organization are: General Assembly, Executive Committee, General Secretariat, National Bureaus, Consultants.

Delegates meet once a year at the General Assembly, which is the highest body of this organization. Ordinary members are delegates of their governments, extraordinary members are elected at the session, by a two-thirds majority vote, from among those persons whose knowledge in the field of science and technology may be useful in the work of the organization. The names of the candidates for extraordinary members must be submitted two months before the opening of the General Assembly. The General Assembly elects the executive committee which is composed of the president, two vice-presidents, and six delegates. The president is elected for a term of five years, and vice-presidents for a term of two years. After their term in office expires they can be reelected. On Dec. 31, 1980, there were representatives of 127 states in Interpol.

The tasks of the International Criminal Police Organization are clearly stated in the 1946 statutes. Interpol's aim is to develop the cooperation among the police of the various countries, within the limits of each state's legislation.

Interpol, because of its scope of activity, serves three basic functions: coordination of activities, keeping documentation, dissemination of information about the forms and development of international crime.[5]

Interpol coordinates—in the broad sense of the word—the activities of individual states. Once a year, during plenary sessions the delegates of governments define the organization's policy, and discuss methods of international cooperation and the more important issues of crime prevention and repression. The plenary sessions also appoint special subcommissions which then elaborate concrete issues. Generally, in every member-state there is a National Central Bureau (NCB) of Interpol. This bureau is a kind of intermediary in all issues between the authorities of its country and similar bureaus in other states and the General Secretariat, which works out recommendations concerning the forms and methods of crime repression.

Report No. 5 entittled "The I.C.P.O.—Interpol National Central Bureaus: Policy," adopted by the General Assembly at its session in 1965 and appended to the General Regulations, is to be the basis for the organization and orientation of the work of all NCBs.

This report states, among other things, that the NCB should work with all departments in the country including local police branches, customs and immigration offices, and the treasury department. All the branches of a country's police should support the international police action, working with the NCB.[6]

A coordinating role is also played by international seminars organized by Interpol and devoted to selected problems.

Interpol keeps documentation concerning international crimes and criminals, a dactyloscopic archive, a photographic card index and an index of the modus operandi of perpetrators.

In 1970 the Interpol General Secretariat handled 10,875 international cases. By 1974 this figure had increased to 25,679, and by 1979 to 43,437. The increase was particularly marked in drug cases, thefts, frauds, and counterfeits and forgeries.[7]

Interpol's statutes do not allow cooperation in cases treating criminal activity of a political, religious, military, or racial character.

A radio network transmitting from Paris is used for the informative and instructive activities of Interpol. Moreover, since 1946 the General Secretariat has been publishing a bulletin which includes a list of articles published in criminalistics and criminological journals.

The following will illustrate the Interpol General Secretariat's activity in the period between sessions. During the period October 1978–August 1979 there were three regional conferences (Eighth European Conference, February 1979, Third Caribbean Interpol Conference, May 1979 and the Fifth Asian Regional Conference, August 1979). The General Secretariat transmitted the descriptions of 509 international criminals, information concerning 153 cases of theft, and 17,361 items of information to National Central Bureaus.[8]

Interpol concerns itself with many problems, such as juvenile delin-quency,counterfeit of money, the illegal narcotics trade, acts of terror and violence (with special attention to hijacking).

The problem of the prevention of juvenile delinquency deserves much attention. This activity often includes the joint elements of criminalistic and criminological prevention.

Over the past years juvenile delinquency has posed a serious problem in the work of the police departments in almost every country.[9] Nowadays, preventive action on a large scale predominate among the means of crime repression, such as the creation of special police units whose task is to combat juvenile delinquency. Some years ago, the General Secretariat of ICPO prepared an exhaustive report on this subject.[10]

Interpol has long been concerned with juvenile delinquency. Back in 1926, at the third session of the General Assembly, which took place in Berlin September 27–30, the significance of this problem was given much attention with connection with a debate on the participation of women in police work.

At the fourth session of the General Assembly, July 6–8, 1928, for the first time resolutions were passed concerning "female police force" and "police departments for juveniles." In the unanimously passed resolution it was stated that women are effectively able to protect children in danger and that women's work in this field would surely bring positive results.

After World War II the serious increase of crime among juveniles caused Interpol to undertake new initiatives. At the seventeenth session of the General Assembly of Interpol in Prague, September 6–10, 1948, a resolution was passed which obliged the organization to concentrate its efforts on the problem of juvenile delinquency. At this session, a special committee of experts was established, composed of the representatives of nine countries: Australia, Austria, Belgium, Czechoslovakia, Egypt, France, Norway, Venezuela, and Italy. At the same time, a suggestion was made that a favorable move would be to select a specialized criminal police section to better combat juvenile delinquency.

Since 1949 in Interpol reports special attention has been devoted to the social functions of police organs. This in a way influenced the twenty-first session of the General Assembly, in Stockholm, June 2–12, 1952, in that it passed a resolution calling for the creation in police departments of special sections for crime prevention, especially prevention of juvenile delinquency.

The preventive aspects of police activity, with special attention to juvenile delinquency, were discussed also from a psychiatric point of view in 1953 and 1954 (the twenty-second session in Oslo, June 24–29, 1953, and the twenty-third session in Rome, October 9–14, 1954).

In 1955, after detailed research, the General Secretariat published an exhaustive study on youth police clubs in fourteen countries.[11] The report from the twenty-fourth session of the General Assembly, in Istanbul, September 5–9, 1955, stressed the necessity of maintaining contacts between police, parents, and teachers, and between police and children.

In 1956, new important steps in this direction were undertaken. At the twenty-fifth session of the General Assembly, in Vienna June 7–13, 1956, the General Secretariat submitted to members of Interpol a project for a training program for policemen working with juveniles.[12] In the introductory remarks to this program it was pointed out that the personnel working with juvenile delinquents should be carefully selected. The chosen persons should have suitably high intellectual and moral qualities, and should show an interest in working with juveniles. Results of a scientific selection carried out with the aid of psychological tests decide whether the candidate is admitted to entrance examinations for a special course.

Courses for beginners encompass such subjects as child psychology, the causes and forms of juvenile delinquency, principles of legal responsibility of juveniles, cooperation among parents, educators, social workers, and police, and contacts between police and juveniles. Three months of specialized training was taken as the minimum for those policemen who will concern themselves with the problem of juvenile delinquency.

A special supplementary program for those policemen who occupy a high post in the organizational structure of police for juveniles was also envisaged. These policemen, according to the Interpol General Secretariat's recommendations, should obtain additional training in the field of management, criminal law, and criminology.

Also, in June 1957, at the twenty-sixth session of the General Assembly, in Lisbon, a report concerning the employment of women in police forces for work with juveniles was approved. This report suggested that "women be employed in departments, the aim being to reduce juvenile delinquency."[13] At the thirty-second session of the General Assembly, in Helsinki, August 28, 1963, attention was also paid to the issue of prevention, especially juvenile delinquency. In 1979 Report No. 11 was published, devoted to the evolution of juvenile delinquency in the years 1974–1977.

The issue of currency counterfeiting has been the center of attention of police organs for over fifty years, and now has gained the status of a serious problem.[14]

The first international congress devoted to the research and prevention of forgeries of coins took place in Paris, June 3–6, 1965. This congress was convened by the International Association of Professional Numismatists.[15] During the debates it was said that the interest of collectors should be protected by international law.

There were, in one particular year, 46 million counterfeit U.S. banknotes in circulation, both within the United States and abroad. This figure is negligible when it is compared with the 2.6 trillion genuine U.S. banknotes in circulation all over the world.

The number of different types of counterfeits have been listed very carefully since 1946, and on July 1, 1976 there were 4,382 types of counterfeit U.S. banknotes in circulation; the figure for the various types of counterfeits of currency issued by all countries was 7,247.

In order to make it possible to pursue counterfeiters across national borders, a number of countries signed an international convention on April 20, 1929, under the auspices of the League of Nations. So far, conferences have been held in Geneva (1930), Copenhagen (1935), The Hague (1950), Copenhagen (1961), Mexico City (1969) and Madrid (1977).[16]

In October 1970, the Brussels General Assembly included in its Program of Activities a series of courses designed to train police officers to combat currency counterfeiting. The first course, conducted in French, was held in Saint-Cloud in November 1972 and was attended by fifteen participants. The training program was organized at three levels: theoretical, technical, and practical.[17]

Special seminars are organized with the aim of exchanging information on currency counterfeiting. For example, a seminar entitled "Developments and trends in currency counterfeiting offenses and law enforcement methods" was held at the Police Academy in Hiltrup, September 1–5, 1975. It was designed for police officers and magistrates responsible for enforcing currency laws in West Germany, but experts from Switzerland, the United States and the ICPO-Interpol General Secretariat also attended. Papers on the following topics, among others, were submitted and discussed: international illicit traffic in counterfeit gold coins (links with other forms of crime; cases handled by the C.I.D. and the Public Prosecutor's Office); international crime and currency counterfeiting as seen by the ICPO-Interpol General Secretariat/.[18]

The fact that it is now possible in many countries to cash or otherwise use checks and travelers checks with little or no difficulty or delay has led to the appearance of new types of swindlers, now operating internationally. In 1978, the General Secretariat received 392 reports of cases involving the fraudulent use of stolen or counterfeit checks or travelers checks; total losses amounted to U.S. $15,000,000.[19]

The illegal narcotics trade and its effect—drug abuse—is now looked upon as a worldwide social problem. The increasing amounts of narcotics found in various social groups, not only medical, but also in schools, universities and other places, are proof that the phenomenon of narcotics abuse is spreading constantly. Objective circumstances, such as easier access to drugs, profitability (for producers and dealers), development of tourism and other forms of international contacts—all this favors the spread of narcotics abuse. There are also subjective reasons, such as fashion, snobbery, or simple curiosity.

Interpol's reports on the illegal narcotics trade in the world do not adequately illustrate the present situation. Even according to optimistic estimations, detectability in the field of narcotics trade reaches only 10 percent. Moreover, Interpol has at its disposal only the information concerning those countries which signed the 1961 unified convention on intoxicating drugs. In spite of these reservations, the cited statistics enable us to say that the illegal narcotics trade has become a problem for the whole world.

In 1979, an international center of information on means of illegal drug traffic was set up in Interpol. It noted an increase of cases connected with narcotics from 21,088 in 1978 to 24,424 in 1979. A special bulletin in four languages was published concerning the most serious problems in the field of the illegal narcotics trade. In January 1979 a special conference was held in Interpol's headquarters with the participation of heads of European special task forces who combat the illegal narcotics trade.

In 1970, the General Secretariat of ICPO conducted research in fifty-five countries on drug abuse among people twenty-five years of age and younger. The results showed an increase of such cases in almost every country with the exception of Japan and Thailand. The greatest number of young drug abusers was found, in 1969, in the United States, then respectively, in Brazil, the Federal Republic of Germany, Hong Kong, Australia, France, Israel, and Turkey. The most widespread narcotic was found to be marijuana (97 percent), amphetamines (35 percent) and heroin (20 percent).

On the American continent minors try drugs for the first time when they are thirteen to fifteen years of age, in Europe, generally when they are eighteen years of age (except for Finland and Norway). The percentage of girls among drug abusers reaches 22 percent in Europe, in America on the average 15 percent (in the United States 18 percent, in Brazil 40 percent).

The money necessary to pay for narcotics comes from various sources: usually it is pocket money received from parents, money from prostitution (Japan), beggary (South Korea) from selling drugs (Norway, Austria, Sweden) and from criminal activities (Finland, Sweden, the United States, New Zealand). The report shows that in the majority of countries young drug abusers do not want to undergo voluntary treatment. At the same time, police agencies do not have the necessary means to effectively combat the spread of narcotics abuse among the youth.[20]

In the face of rising narcotics costs the young look for substitute means, for example, sniffing various gaseous chemicals or solvents, which often lead to acute poisoning or even death.[21] Drug abusers, especially the young ones, show great inventiveness; for example, in 1970 in Frankfurt am Main, young people were found to be using pain-killer tablets.[22] Obviously, police officers who work in this field of criminality, must, in addition to their traditional training, have a good knowledge of pharmacology. The problem of adequate police training for the combating of drug addiction was the topic of Interpol plenary session's discussion in 1969 in Mexico and in 1970 in Brussels.

The thirty-eighth session of the ICPO General Asembly in Mexico in October 1969 refused to deal with the problem of prosecution of hijacked civil airplanes, considering that such acts are performed, as a principle, from political motives.[23] However, in October 1970, in Brussels, ICPO passed a resolution obliging the General Secretariat to cooperate fully with international aviation organizations (ICAO, IATA) in the field of prevention and combating of air piracy acts. It also recommended that periodical analyses be made in particular countries.[24]

Now, in every case of airplane hijacking Interpol will, above all, look at the criminal aspect of this offense. The resolution passed at the thirty-ninth session is, therefore, an important step forward in combating the threats to security in air communication.

In 1971, the Interpol General Secretariat published a report, "Security in International Civil Aviation."[25] It was written on the basis of information submitted by thirty-nine countries and territories. Among the European countries which sent information materials were Austria, Belgium, Denmark, France, Greece, Spain, Norway, Portugal, Switzerland, Sweden, and Italy.

Preventive measures applied in international air communication concern various fields of security.

The first group encompasses the protection of airplanes on the ground (airports) and the protection of installations and ground service. In the majority of international airports there is a physical barrier (walls, chain and rope fences, wire fences, plate glass) separating the traffic area from areas with public access. The core areas of international airports are guarded in thirty-eight countries. In cases where the areas of traffic and land installations are linked with external areas underground by tunnels and canals, which is the case in fifteen countries, access to these passages is secured by adequate means. Entrance to the areas where baggage and mail are stored is controlled in 36 countries. In the majority of countries which have submitted information to Interpol, airplanes left in the traffice area are guarded. This supervision is especially strict in cases where the airplanes belong to endangered aviation associations. In thirty-four countries airplanes are searched before the passengers are let on board.

The second group concerns the search of passengers, crew, and baggage. The passengers generally know that transport of firearms is prohibited and that controls performed in most countries have as their aim the detection of arms. Unidentified baggage is not loaded into the plane; passengers' movements between control points and airplanes is under observation. In periods of increased danger additional safety measures are applied: very strict identification control of passengers between entrance gates and the airplane (twenty-four countries), counting of passengers after they board the plane, in order to make sure that their number agrees with the number taken during control (thirty-seven countries), taking passengers off during stops in travel and careful search of the plane (twenty-seven countries), search of the hand baggage of passengers and crew (twenty-eight countries).

The third group concerns the control of larger baggage and airmail parcels, performed by customs staff, police, or employees of airlines. The most frequent control devices are decompression cabins, magnetometers, and X-ray apparatus. For example, in the United States, by February 1, 1973, 1091 magnetometers had been installed at airports.[26]

The protection of works of art has also been given much attention by Interpol. The First International Symposium on Thefts of Works of Art and Cultural Property was held at Interpol headquarters in June 1977. The General Secretariat submitted a report on the meeting to the General Assembly and this report was also studied by the committee.

It had been noted that in most countries there were no special files or idexes for thefts of works of art. The symposium has stressed the importance of good cooperation at the national level among police forces, customs services, public institutions, and professional art circles.[27]

Interpol cooperates with the United Nations; Interpol's representatives took part in United Nations congresses on the prevention of crime and the treatment of offenders; one section of the Fifth Congress discussed the role of police forces with regard to changing needs and ensuring a minimal level of effectiveness of work. The session's motions expressed the opinion that international cooperation among police forces in the face of rising crime should be broadened.

New ideas concerning international cooperation in the field of the prevention and combating of crime are being put forward, for example, international computer (or bilateral) police agreements. According to Jean Nepote it is perfectly possible to store in a computer's memory a list of persons implicated in international crime cases, a list of persons wanted to serve sentences or to help the police with their enquiries, or a list of stolen cars and firearms.[28]

Interpol also cooperates with other international organizations, such as the International Civil Aviation Organization, the Council of Europe, and the International Council for Narcotics Control.

Interpol's organ is the periodical *International Criminal Police Review*, published in English, French, and Spanish versions. This review has been published without interruption since September 1946. In a periodical entitled *Contrefaçons et Falsifications*, published in The Hague, notices concerning banknote and passport forgeries are published as well as samples of original currency; they are received by the police, banks, and other institutions.

Interpol has carried out the analysis of many issues concerning aspects of criminology as well as aspects of criminalistics. Problems concerning drug addiction, juvenile delinquency, the treatment of offenders, criminal geography, the participation of society in the prevention of crime, corruption, violent crimes, victimology, illegal traffic in works of art, road accidents, suicides, and prostitution can serve as examples. In 1979, Report No. 13 discussed the problems of environmental protection, with special regard to the role of police in this field.

More and more now Interpol's review publishes articles devoted exclusively to problems of criminology.

Many symposia also discuss criminological problems. In the years 1959, 1964, and 1970 symposia on road offenses were organized at Interpol's headquarters; in the years 1962 and 1971 the problems of organized crime were discussed, and in 1969 the main topic of an international conference was the prevention of crime. Also at other symposia (in the years 1965, 1969, and 1971) among other discussions devoted to the application of electronic machines in police organs, the issue of the lack of data for the needs of criminological analyses was not overlooked.

Interpol undertook efforts to elaborate a system of international criminal statistics. It was published for the first time in 1954, and concerned offenses recorded in the period between 1950 and 1952 in thirty-two countries. Its role was mainly to present trends in crime development, and not to give accurate gauges of its intensity.

Interpol's representatives take an active part in every international conference which concerns itself with the various aspects of criminality. Thus, the scope of interest of ICPO has been broadened by the problems of criminology, because the achievements of this science are being increasingly applied in the prevention and combating of crime.

Notes

1. See Harry Soderman and John O'Connel, *Modern Criminal Investigation*, 5th ed. (New York: Funk and Wagnalls, 1952), p. 25.

2. See John Thomson, "Ein internationales Polizeibureau," *Archiv für Kriminologie* 1923, vol. 75, part 2.

3. See Jorge van Houten, "Internationale Zusammenarbeit auf kriminalpolizeilichem Gebiet," *Archiv für Kriminologie* 1923, vol. 75, part 1.

4. See Robert Heindl, "Der internationale Polizeikongres in Wien," *Archiv für Kriminologie* 1924, vol. 75, part 1.

5. *International Criminal Police Review* 1973, no. 268.

6. Jean Nepote, "Reflections on the Work of Interpol National Central Bureaus," *International Criminal Police Review* 1975, no. 287, p. 97.

7. André Bossard, "Review of International Crime Trends," *International Criminal Police Review* 1976, no. 296, p. 58.

8. "Rapport d'activité," *Revue Internationale de Police Criminelle* 1979, no. 333, pp. 279–280.

9. Only in a few countries, such as Spain, Jordan, and Laos, does juvenile delinquency not pose a serious social problem.

10. Special Police Departments for the Prevention of Juvenile Delinquency, Paris 1960.

11. Detailed information on the subject of these clubs' activities was published in Interpol's periodical (special issues). *International Criminal Police Review* 1955, no. 90; 1956, no. 95 (appendix).

12. "The Training of Police in Matters Connected with Juvenile Delinquency," Report submitted by the General Secretariat of ICPO to the twenty-fifth session of the General Assembly, Vienna, June 7, 1956.

13. "Juveniles Police," Report submitted by the General Secretariat of ICPO to the twenty-sixth session of the General Assembly, Lisbon, June 17–22, 1957.

14. The biggest money counterfeit affair in the world, known as "the Bernhard action" dates back to World War II. Starting in 1941, on Himmler's order, and under B. Kruger's direction £75 million in counterfeit money was produced in the Sachsenhausen concentration camp. The aim of this action was to cause a crisis in the British economy. See Walter Hagen, Unternehmen Bernhard. Ein historischer Tatsachenbericht über die grösste Geldfälschungsaktion aller Zeiten, (Hamburg Kriminalistik Verlag, 1955).

15. See "News and Notes: France," *International Criminal Police Review* 1966, no. 194, p. 26.

16. Jean Nepote, "Currency Counterfeiting," *International Criminal Police Review* 1980, no 341, pp. 213, 217; see also Jean C. Bellour, "The Counterfeit Currency Group at the I.C.P.O.-Interpol General Secretariat," *International Criminal Police Review* 1976, no. 295, pp. 46–48.

17. Serge Langlais, "Training Courses on Counterfeit Currency," *International Criminal Police Review* 1974, no. 280, p. 194.

18. Serge Langlais, "Seminar on Currency Counterfeiting Problems," *International Criminal Police Review* 1975, no. 292, p. 261.

19. Jean C. Bellour, "International Fraud," *International Criminal Police Review* 1980, no. 338, p. 139.

20. "Etude sur l'usage des stupéfians et des psychotropes pare la jeunesse," *Revue Internationale de Police Criminelle* 1971, no. 248.

21. Such cases were observed in Poland between 1969 and 1972.

22. Peter Loos, "Rauschgiftzubereitung," *Kriminalistik* 1970, no. 7.

23. "Generalversammlung der Interpol 1969," *Kriminalistik* 1970, no. 4.

24. "39 Generalversammlung der Interpol," *Öffentliche Sicherheit* 1970, no. 11.

25. "Security in International Civil Aviation," *International Criminal Police Review* 1971, no. 253.

26. Robert Adam, "Der Kampf der USA gegen die Luftpiraterie," *Öffentliche Sicherheit* 1973, no. 1.

27. "General Assembly, 1st to 8th September 1977, 46th Session, Stockholm, Sweden," *International Criminal Police Review* 1977, no. 313, p. 316.

28. Jean Nepote, "The Future of International Police Cooperation: A project of an idea," *International Criminal Police Review* 1975, no. 290, p. 183.

17 Other International Organizations Dealing with Problems of Criminality

The first organization which specialized in international exchange of opinions and research findings on crime was the International Penal and Penitentiary Commission, founded in 1872 in London. The materials concerning the commission's work were published in the periodical *Recueil de documents en matière pénale et pénitentiaire* [Collection of criminal and penitentiary materials], published in Bern. Besides conducting research the commission also organized international congresses; in all, under the auspices of the commission twelve congresses were held, devoted to penitentiary, criminological, preventive, and legal problems. These congresses took place in London (1872), Stockholm (1878), Rome (1885), Saint Petersburg (1890), Paris (1895), Brussels (1900), Budapest (1905), Washington (1910), London (1925), Prague (1930), Berlin (1935) and The Hague (1950).

The congresses' materials were published in "Actes des Congrès Pénitentiaries Internationaux" [Documents of international penitenriary congesses].[1]

The commission ended its work in 1951, and its functions were taken over by the International Penal and Penitentiary Foundation (Foundation Internationale Pénale et Pénitentiaire) and other UN agencies. The foundation's headquarters are in Brussels, and its main objectives are the promotion of studies on combating crime and the treatment of offenders, as well as publications dealing with these issues. The foundation has a consultative status at the UN and cooperates with other organizations, in particular with the International Society for Criminology, the International Society of Social Defense and the International Association of Penal Law. These associations organize seminars every five years with the aim of discussing a particular problem, such as the three seminars organized in Belagio, Italy, on the following topics: mentally ill offenders (1963), preparation of a sentence (1968), problems of decriminalization (1973).

In 1888, on the initiative of Franz von Liszt, A. Prins and G. van Hamel, the Union International de Droit Pénal (International Union of Penal Law) was founded. Its tasks were to search for the causes of crime and to work out rational methods of prosecution. In several countries, national branches were established. With the cooperation of lawyers, physicians, and psychologists, between 1894 and 1899 valuable work on the analysis of

341

criminal law was published: *Die Strafgesetzbuch der Gegenwart in rechtsvergleichender Darstellung* [Modern criminal law in a comparative review].

The activity of most national branches, and the union's itself, was stopped by World War I, but the work was continued in the Association International de Droit Pénal (AIDP) (International Assoication of Penal Law) founded in Paris in 1924. Its objectives are the study of penal law problems as well as criminology. Close contact with the League of Nations served to broaden the research in the field of criminal policy. A specially organized bureau under the name of Bureau International pour l'Unification du Droit Pénal conducted studies on the possibility of unifying penal law. The association was granted consultative status at the UN and national branches exist in many nations.

Before World War II four congresses of the AIDP took place: in Brussels (1926), Bucharest (1929), Palermo (1933) and Paris (1937) and seven congresses convened after the war: Geneva (1947), Rome (1953), Athens (1957), Lisbon (1961), The Hague (1964), Rome (1969) and Budapest (1974). The following issues were the subject of the Budapest Congress: the evolution of the means and methods of penal law; abuse and trade of narcotics; compensation to the victims of offenses; punishment for hijacking airplanes.

The twelfth congress took place in September 1979 in Hamburg. In 1978 the Polish section of the association organized an international seminar on legal and penal problems of environmental protection.

In its scientific activities the AIDP allows its members to hold views of different schools or theories of penal law. The organization is governed by the statute approved in 1969, at the Rome Congress. Article 2 of the statute has the following meaning:

1. The IDP believes that crime, its prevention and repression should be regarded from the point of view of scientific research on crime and offender as well as from the point of view of legal guarantees of the society and the offender.
2. The AIDP conducts the research in all the main legal systems of substantive and adjective law, written law as well as common law, also problems of international penal law.
3. In its work the AIDP—an international nongovernmental organization with UN consultative status—is based on the principles of the UN Charter and the General Declaration of Human Rights. In 1972, AIDP created the Institut International Superieur de Sciences Criminelles (International Higher Institute of Criminal Sciences) with headquarters at Syracuse, Sicily. The institute conducts postgraduate courses with the aim of training specialists in the field of penal sciences. Moreover, it has

organized three international symposia, during which the following problems were discussed: road traffic homicide and psychopathology, the role of the judge in a modern society, and terrorism and political crimes. AIDP's periodical is the *Revue International de Droit Pénal*, published in Paris.

On the initiative of A. Lenz, in 1937 in Vienna, Die Kriminalbiologische Gesellschaft (Association of Criminal Biology) was founded. At present, this association is called the Association of General Criminology (Gesellschaft für die gesamte Kriminologie). Its members are the representative of Austria and Italy, and it carries out research on every aspect of criminality, especially the social and psychological ones. Much attention is also devoted to the problems of juvenile delinquency, road traffic accidents, alcoholism as a criminogenic factor and the cooperation between the judge and expert in studying the personality of the offender. The association's periodical is the *Monatschrift für Kriminologie und Strafrechtsreform*, and the reports of the association's meetings have been published since 1952 in *Kriminalbiologischen Gegenwartsfragen*.

The International Association of Juvenile and Family Court Magistrates in Brussels has contributed considerably to the propagation of new ideas in combating juvenile delinquency and maladjustment of youth. The association began in Paris in 1928 as the International Association of Children's Judges and that name was adopted from its foundation in Brussels in 1930. In 1958 its name was changed to the International Association of Youth Magistrates and the present name was adopted at its tenth congress in 1978. The objectives of the association are:[2]

1. To establish links between judges, magistrates, and specialists from all over the world who are attached to a judicial authority of whatever nature concerned with the protection of youth or the family.
2. To study, at the international level, all problems raised by the functioning judicial authorities and bodies for the protection of youth and the family: to ensure the continuance of the principle governing those authorities and to make them more widely known.
3. To examine legislation designed for the protection of youth and the family and the various systems existing for the protection of the maladjusted young or young people in social or moral danger with a view to improving such system both nationally and internationally.
4. To assist collaboration between nations and competent authorities with regard to foreign minors, especially with a view to their repatriation or treatment.
5. To encourage research into the causes of the criminal behavior or maladjustment of youth, to combat their effects and to seek their

permanent prevention and rehabilitation program; to concern itself with the moral and material improvement of the young people's destiny and, in particular, with the future of youth in moral and social danger.

6. To collaborate with international associations which are concerned with the protection of youth and the family.

The association represents about forty countries, with over 500 members. It has consultative status within the United Nations and UNESCO and cooperates with the Council of Europe, the International Labor Organization, Interpol and many nongovernmental organizations. After World War II, the association organized congresses in 1950, 1954, 1958, 1962, 1966, 1970, 1974 and 1978. The last two congresses, the ninth in Oxford, the tenth in Montreal, were devoted to "Justice for Juveniles in a Changing World" and "The Magistrates in the Face of Environmental Pressure on Youth and the Family," respectively. The association has branches in many countries. The association publishes "News of the Association" in the quarterly *International Child Welfare Review*; besides, the congresses' reports are edited after each congress.

In 1956, in Paris, the International Association of Crime Prevention (SIPC) was founded (Société Internationale de Prophylaxie Criminelle) at first under the name of the International Association of Social Prevention.

The aim of the association is to study individual and social causes of crime and means of combating them. SIPC organized two international congresses: in 1959 in Brussels on the subject of "Technological Civilization and Crime" and in 1967 on "Prevention of Crimes against Humanity." The association's periodical is the *Etudes Internationales de Psycho-Sociologie Criminelle*.

The International Academy of Forensic and Social Medicine was organized in Paris in 1937. At the fifth congress, which took place in 1961 in Vienna, the word "social" was dropped from the academy's name, the reasoning being the notion of "social medicine" is too general and encompasses too many fields. The present name is the International Academy of Forensic Medicine.

The academy's first congress took place in Bonn in 1938 in accordance with a resolution passed at the twenty-first Congress of Social and Forensic Medicine of French-Speaking Countries, which convened in paris in 1937. At the beginning the academy's periodical was the Italian *Zacchia—Rivista de Medicina Legale e della Assicurazioni*. Since 1948 the official periodical has been *Acta Medicinae Legalis e Socialis*. The academy unites scientists from more than a dozen states, Poland among them, and cooperates closely with the World Health Organization.

The World Society of Victimology was founded as an outcome of the Third International Symposium on Victimology (Münster, September, 1979; previous symposia were held in Jerusalem in 1973, and in Boston in 1976). One of the society's initiators, Hans J. Schneider, is chairman of its executive committee. The aims of the society are: to develop victimological theory and comparative victimization research; to prepare legislative motions and preventive methods, social and individual; to develop international cooperation; and to create a forum for exchange in the field of various sciences and cultural and ideological solutions.

In 1976 the international journal *Victimology* was founded, headed by E. Viano. The society expects to edit an *International Review of Victimology*, beginning in 1982. The world's first Institute of Victimology was created in Japan in 1969. The countries which have the most developed research in the field of victimology are the United States, the USSR, the Federal Republic of Germany, and Japan. From the beginning of the existence of victimology, much research effort has focused on the problem of the typology of victims. The classical typologies in this field are Hans von Hentig's and Beniamin Mendelsohn's; later works were by E. A. Fattah, Thorsten Sellin, M. E. Wolfgang and A. A. Silverman.

The International Center for Comparative Criminology was organized in 1969 on the initiative of Denis Szabo in the University of Montreal. The center was founded as the result of an agreement between the university and the International Society for Criminology. The aim of this center is to develop international cooperation in the field of training and conducting of criminological comparative studies. The Center cooperates with many criminological institutes all over the world. It contributed greatly to the development of criminological research in the developing countries. The centre has organized international symposia in various countries. The first international symposium on the methods of research and priority topics in comparative criminology took place in 1969 in Montreal.[3]

In June 1972 in Abidjan, the first conference of comparative criminology of West African states was organized. This conference laid down the direction of crime prevention and the treatment of offenders.[4] The International Center for Comparative Criminology often organizes regional seminars devoted to current criminological problems; for example, in 1974 in Teheran a seminar was held on the subject of "Narcotics and Crime: Etiology and Prevention."[5] Also in socialist countries (Poland and Czechoslovakia) symposia for countries of Central Europe were organized.

The World Health Organization, with headquarters in Geneva, is one of the specialized UN agencies which continues the activity of the International Bureau of Public Health, founded in 1907 in Paris, and the Health Organization of the League of Nations, founded in 1923 in Geneva. The first session of the General Assembly of the WHO took place in 1948 in Geneva.[6]

The WHO's activities are many-sided and diverse; among others, they are concerned with combating and preventing crime connected with alcoholism, drug abuse, or veneral illnesses. The results of the WHO's activities are published in a periodical, *Official Records of the World Health Organization*. The Union Internationale de Protection de l'Enfance (International Union for the Protection of Children), with headquarters in Geneva, devotes its attention to some aspects of criminology. The union publishes the periodicals *Revue Internationale de L'Enfant, International Child Welfare Review*, and *Revista International del Nino*, as well as monographs. The present name was adopted in 1946, after the union of an organization, founded in 1920 under the name of Union Internationale de Secours aux Enfants with an associattion, founded in 1921 in Brussels called Association pour la Protection de L'Enfance. The union has consultative status with the Economic and Social Council (ECOSOC), UNESCO, WHO, FAO and with the Council of Europe. The organization's aim is to propagate the principles of the Declaration of Children's Rights, to help children in misfortune, such as natural disasters, to upgrade the standard of child care, and to contribute to the moral and physical development of children and young people. Moreover, the union grants help to national organizations in establishing more advanced legal norms for the protection of children, conducts comparative studies, sets up committees of consultants, and organizes conferences of experts, training programs, world congresses and the World Child Day.

The International Center for Family Studies (Centro Internazionale di Studi della Famiglia) was established in 1973 for the purpose of study, documentation, and promotional services in support of the family. The Center cooperates with various international organizations (United Nations, Council of Europe, International Bureau of the Child, and others). The Center also organizes international meetings on the family. The meeting in 1978 on "Love Fruitful and Responsible" was opened by Cardinal Karol Wojtyla, three months before his election as Pope; the next, in 1979 on "The Family, the Natural Environment of the Child" and in 1980 on "Family Policy in Europe" and the most recent international congress on "Mass Media and the Family."

The International Commission of Jurists was founded in 1952 in Geneva. It has thirty national sections and consultative status with UN Economic and Social Council, UNESCO and the Council of Europe. This organization conducts activities aimed at abiding by the principles of law. The commission studies, among other things, living conditions in prisons and the problem of capital punishment and informs the public about violations of human rights. For instance, in 1969 the commission focused world attention on the living conditions in South African prisons. The commission puts forward proposals suggesting that countries publish accurate statistics on the numbers of prisoners, categories of offenders, regimes applied in penal institutions, and the like. Considerable attention is paid to political prisoners.

The International Commission of Jurists cooperates with the United Nations in the field of the implementation of "Minimum Rules" and the protection of human rights. ICJ also pays attention to the growing problem of violence in the modern world, which leads to the erosion of moral standards.

Since 1969, documents and scientific studies have been published in the quarterly *International Commission of Jurists Review*, which combined two publications: the *Bulletin* and the *Journal*. Special studies published have been, for example, "Law and Order and Human Rights" (1966), "The Erosion of Law and Order in South Africa" (1968), and "Events in East Pakistan" (1971).

The International Council on Problems of Alcholism and Addictions (Counseil International sur les Problèmes de l'Alcoolisme et de Toxicomanie), with headquarters in Lausanne, was founded in 1907 in Stockholm, under the name of Bureau International Contre l'Alcoolisme; the present name was adopted in 1968. The council has consultative status with the UN Economic and Social Council and the World Health Organization. Its task is to develop international cooperation in the field of prevention and treatment of alcoholism and other addictions, and the collection and dissemination of information on all aspects of this problem—medical, legal, sociological. The council publishes reports, pamphlets, and monographs on its activities and organizes international congresses. Its members are associations, national committees, ministries, and private persons from different countries, including Poland.

The International Federation of Senior Police Officers, with headquarters in Essen was founded in 1950 in Metz, under the name Fédération Internationale Amicale et Indépendante des Fonctionnaires Superieurs de Police; the present name has existed since 1957. The federations' main aims are participation in every kind of research connected with police training and the prevention of crime; efforts to improve the organization and efficacy of police work; and abiding, on an international scale, by the principles of police ethics. To achieve these aims the federation conducts studies of problems of traffic police, preventive and social action of the police, police and human rights; the international code of police deontology; protection of police officers in times of war and occupation. The federation organizes international congresses and seminars, publishes, every two months, "Chroniques Internationales de Police" and "International Police Information." Studies of the following problems have been published: "Police and the Mental Health of Children," "Road Safety," "The Preventive and Educational Role of Police." The federation has consultative status with the UN Economic and Social Council, UNESCO, and the Council of Europe. Its members represent more than a dozen countries, including Poland.

The International Prisoners Aid Association was founded in 1950 in Milwaukee. The aim of the association is to give postpenitentiary care and to undertake activities which should prevent crime, especially recurring crime. Considerable attention is paid to the rehabilitation of prisoners. Some of the topics of studies are problems concerning conditional release and suspension of sentences. The association's representatives take an active part in UN congresses on the prevention of crime and the treatment of offenders. The association's newsletter appears every four months.

The International Humanist and Ethical Union was founded in 1952 in Amsterdam at the first International Congress of Humanist and Ethical Culture, and its headquarters are in Utrecht, Holland.

The union's objective is the unification of associations, groups and individuals from every country, interested in the propagation of the principles of ethical and scientific humanism which are seen as care for the improving of human life through the protection and development of human values and the inculcation of democratic convictions in every social system. The union cooperates with international institutions and outstanding persons who strive to improve the human condition, and in particular those who offer help in formulating educational and cultural programs, UNESCO and ECOSOC among them. It organizes congresses and conferences and has created the HIVOS foundation (Institut Humaniste pour la Cooperation au Développement). The unions' periodical is the quarterly *International Humanism*; it also publishes reports from congresses in the *Bibliography of Humanism*.

The World Medical Association was founded in 1947, in Paris. Its present headquarters are in New York. The association works toward raising the educational level of medical studies as well as developing medicine, enhancing ethics, and improving the quality of medical services all over the world. Cooperating with ECOSOC, it conducts studies of medical hospital service, social insurance, industrial medicine, and work medicine. In addition, the association organizes world conferences on the subject of teaching medicine, stores central archives for medical documents, and elaborates guidelines for researchers in clinical medicine. The general assembly of the association convenes once a year. The association's periodical is the bimonthly *World Medical Journal* and *International News Items*; other publications are monographs and reports on the assembly's conferences. In 1974, sixty-two national organizations were members of the association.[7]

The International Association of Forensic Sciences was founded in 1957, during the International Meeting of Forensic Pathology in Brussels and Ghent. The present name was adopted at the fifth meeting in Toronto. The associations' headquarters are in Wichita, Kansas (USA). The basic aim of the association is the development of forensic sciences through organization of meetings (every three years) devoted to the exchange of experience in these sciences. The first one took place in 1957 in Brussels; others have been in New York, London, Copenhagen, Toronto, Edinburgh and Zurich. In 1978 at the Wichita meeting the subject was "Violence in the World," and experts on anthropology, biology, criminalistics, pathology, psychiatry, toxicology, law, medicine, and other sciences participated in the working sessions.

The International Reference Organization in Forensic Medicine and Sciences (INFORM) was established in 1966 during a meeting in Copenhagen. Its headquarters are in Wichita. The organization's aim is supporting the development of forensic sciences in the world throught he exchange of experience and fostering of scientific research. INFORM's activity takes the following forms: publishing an *Annual Quarterly Newsletter* and *International Bibliography of Forensic Sciences*; publishing compilations of international literature and periodicals concerned with forensic issues; organizing conferences on the problems of civil and criminal law for Western countries; setting up and conducting an international information service on forensic problems, institutes and associations, publications and the training of staff, and legal systems; acquainting the members of the organization with world literature on those subjects; writing manuals on forensic problems; developing research in the field of forensic medicine for particular nations and ethnic groups; the preparation of training programs for scientists of forensic sciences.

The International Academy of Forensic Psychology has existed since 1968. It headquarters are in Dallas. The academy is an international association of psychologists, psychiatrists, judges, and prosecutors dealing with problems of forensic psychology. It publishes the *Journal of Forensic Psyhology*.

The International Center for Clinical Criminology was organized in 1967 at the University of Rome. The aim of clinical criminology is to study the person of the offender in order to give a diagnosis and prognosis and to adjust methods of penitentiary treatment.[8] The group of specialists who conduct clinical criminological research comprises physicians, psychologists, and educators. Research most often concerns special penitentiary institutions. In some countries, among others Italy, France, Japan, Denmark, and The Netherlands, and in certain South American countries these studies are advanced. *Quaderni di Criminologia Clinica* is published in Italy. Institutes of clinical criminology have also been founded in Toronto, Montreal, Lyon, and Herstedvester.

The literature points out the danger of confusion the notions of "illness" and "offense" because of the term *clinical criminology*.[9] The French criminologist Jean Pinatel distinguishes general criminology from clinical. Complete separating of clinical criminology is very difficult, but in spite of this some authors want to broaden the scope of the notion of clinical criminology even further by including in it homicides, thefts, and recidivism.

The International Association of Chiefs of Police has existed since 1893. Its headquarters are in Gettysburg, Pennsylvania (USA). The association organizes training courses on the subjects of criminalistics and criminology and conducts sttudies in the methods of combating terrorism and means of reaction to organized forms of violence. Under the auspices of the association research on the causes and social results of the increase of crime in schools and the phenomenon of drug abuse is conducted. The association publishes *The Police Chief, Journal of Police Science and Administration,* and *The Police Yearbook.*

These international organizations, which concern themselves exclusively or to a large extent with criminological studies do not exhaust the list of organizations whose activity is connected with these problems and is the objective of organized international cooperation.

Participating in various international conferences on criminology are also representatives of many other organizations, among them: Amnesty International, Catholic International Union for Social Service, International Alliance of Women—Equal Rights, Equal Responsibilities, International Catholic Child Bureau, Lutheran World Federation, International Committee of the Red Cross, International Union for Child Welfare, Pax Romana, Salvation Army, Young Men's Christian Association, World Young Women's Christian Association, National Indian Brotherhood, and the International League of Security Companies.

Notes

1. Negly K. Teeters, *Deliberations of the International Penal and Penitentiary Congresses 1872–1935,* (Phildelphia: 1949) University of Pennsylvania Press.

2. Article 2 of the Statute of the International Association of Juvenile and Family Court Magistrates.

3. Denis Szabo, et al., "Priorités et Méthodologie en Criminologie Comparée," Actes du Premier Symposium International de Criminologie Comparée. Montréal 1969.

4. International Center for Comparative Criminology and The Abidjan Institute of Criminology: First West African Conference in Comparative Criminology, *Needs and Perspectives in the Matter of Crime Prevention and the Treatment of Delinquents in West Africa* (Montréal: Université de Montréal, 1972).

5. Centre International de Criminologie Comparée du Moyen Orient. *Drogue et criminalitée: Etiologie et prevention* (Montréal: Université de Montréal, 1974).

6. World Health Organization, *The First Ten Years of the WHO* (Geneva, 1958); *Handbook of Resolutions and Decisions of the World Health Organization and the Executive Board 1948–1967* (Geneva, 1967).

7. Union des Associations Internationales, *Annuaire des Organisations Internationales,* 15th ed., publication no. 227 (Brussels, 1974).

8. *Jean Pinatel, Criminologie* (Paris: Spes, 1963); 'Benigno Di Tullio, *Principes de criminologie clinique* (Paris: PUF, 1967); idem, *Horizons in Clinical Criminology* (Hackensack, N.J.: National Council on Crime and Delinquency 1969). See also Christian Debuyst et al., *Criminologie clinique* (Brussels: Ch. Dessart, 1968).

9. Hans Göppinger, *Kriminologie*, 3rd ed. (Munich: Verlag C.H. Beck, 1976), p. 31.

18 New Perspectives in Crime Prevention

Problems of crime prevention have for years been a subject of intense concern to the governments in many countries, irrespective of their political system, and to the public at large; there are also numerous scholarly studies of the issue. For more than twenty-five years the United Nations has also devoted special attention to problems of crime prevention. Among the member states from every region there is increasing awareness that criminality is becoming an ever more important obstacle to progress toward attaining a higher quality of life for everyone.

The crime rate which has been growing for the past two decades in many countries and the appearance of new, sinister forms of criminality have faced state and civic bodies with very serious and difficult issues.

The prime social problem faced by the developing countries is to achieve a relatively harmonious shift from the heritage of the past to progress in its modern sense. Acceptance of unchecked economic growth brings in its wake the grave danger of undermining the efficient functioning of numerous institutions required for guiding social activity. Urbanization, industrialization, universal schooling, improved health care, higher living standards—all these spell progress, but their excessively rapid introduction throws out of joint the equilibrium and stability of traditional social communities. The clash of two cultures—the "western" and the "primitive"—unleashes a whole chain of crime-conducive factors. The specific character of criminality in the developing countries is manifested, on the one hand, by the necessity of penalizing certain traditional behaviors and, on the other hand, by reacting to crime of the type prevailing in industrial societies. Criminality in these countries is often politically tainted in that many of the criminal acts are committed on one side by persons holding political power and on the other side by individuals or groups protesting against the existing political and social set-up.

The general situation is aggravated by the fact that women and adolescents represent a large share of the general increase of criminality.[1]

Available data indicate that in many countries the incidence of female criminality has in recent times increased faster than the incidence of male criminality. For instance, in the United States between 1960 and 1972 female criminality grew three times faster than male criminality, with gain as the main motive for committing crimes. In Japan between 1962 and 1972 female criminality went up 13.6 percent, in the Federal Republic of Germany the female share in all crimes came to 15.4 percent—in 1970 this went up to

17.1 percent. In Poland the share of crimes committed by females oscillates around 12 percent. Further studies are needed on the link between socioeconomic advances, female integration in national progress, and female criminality.

Reports show that in most countries there are increases in three types of crimes: violent crimes, committed in an organized manner, with premeditation, for the purpose of considerable material gain or due to political motives; crimes against property; white-collar crimes covering fraud, embezzlement, corruption, black market operation, and computer crimes.[2]

Reviews of criminality by region can be found in various UN publications and special literature.[3]

In the socialist countries, as is evident from UN reports, the prevalent forms include crimes against property, particularly public property, and offenses linked to the abuse of alcohol, as well as economic crimes.

In the search for the etiology of the growing criminality, attention is increasingly focused on socioeconomic factors, particularly those linked with industrialization, urban growth, migration, and unemployment. Upbringing, education, and culture are also significant factors.

The preventive measures used in the past have turned out to be useless and at times even crime-conducive, which points to the urgent need to change these methods on a social, economic, and political scale.

Preventing criminality goes beyond the penal legislation notion of general and specific prevention, linked with the size of the sentence. The notion of preventing criminality now extends to a complex of measures which can have an impact, even indirectly and as a side effect, on removing the causes and conditions for committing crime as well as on uncovering other manifestations of social pathology. These measures encompass such things as economic moves, better schooling, shaping civic awareness, and many others.

Prevention of criminality is a complex notion covering a wide body of social and political issues, penal policy, penal law, and criminalistics. This in itself shows that, taking into account the differences in the level of development of societies, in their political systems, social welfare, educational and similar institutions, it is not possible to have uniform views as to the measures and methods of crime prevention, not only on a global or regional scale, but frequently even on the scale of one entire country.

The overall body of issues linked with prevention of criminality could be defined as criminal policy.

Considering premises, aims, and methods, it is possible to classify preventive activities in several categories: criminalistic prevention, criminological prevention, penal policy, and penitentiary prevention.

Criminalistic prevention means a complex of methods and measures aimed at preventing or hindering a crime from being committed. The methods of criminalistic prevention are dominated by objective elements—in the main, this comes down to physical counteraction of the intention to commit a criminal offense. Examples of this are: the securing of premises against break-ins, protecting banknotes and other securities against counterfeiting, observation of suspects, more frequent patrols after dark, and similar measures. Criminalistic prevention encompasses direct action by law enforcement bodies, state and civic institutions, and individuals, with the aim of preventing a given, specific crime. Proper securing of premises is as much a manifestation of criminalistic prevention as the apprehension, after observation, of an offender preparing to commit an offense or in the course of committing an offense.

Penal policy is aimed at adapting the penalty to the type and circumstances of an offense and the offender's personality in such a way as to contribute to its objective of protecting society, at the same time guaranteeing, whenever possible, the return of the offender to life in society.

The range of penal prevention should be extended to the issue of prosecution efficiency. A high proportion of detected offenders becomes an important factor preventing potential offenders from taking up crime. As rightly pointed out by Jeremy Bentham, British lawyer, philosopher, and economist (1748–1832) "unavoidability of punishment is more effective than its severity." Effective operation of penal prosecution bodies becomes an element influencing those who are considering the risk of taking up an offensive activity.

Penitentiary prevention, coming down to the very execution of sentence, is solely aimed at shaping the conditions under which the sentenced penalty is served in such a way as to achieve an optimum degree of convict rehabilitation.

Criminological prevention, dealing mainly with issues of crime genesis and etiology and relying largely on methods falling within the scope of psychology and social formation, is aimed at guiding human activity in a positive direction and at changing negative attitudes and tendencies. Among all sections of criminology it is outstanding in special practical value, though clearly enough it remains closely linked with research on the causes of crime. After all, this research provides the basis for developing crime prevention measures and methods (phenomenological and etiological studies).

Preventive measures can be directed at a larger, numerically unspecified body of persons or at a single individual; depending on whether one refers to prevention on a social or an individual scale.

Preventive activities can also be classified according to other criteria, such as prevention of recurrent offenses, of economic crimes, of juvenile delinquency, or of traffic offenses. The need to apply manifold methods of prevention stemming from various disciplines is due, among other things, to the variety of the causes of crime.[4]

The final aims of criminology define the directions of search for preventive methods, particularly in situations where the applied systems of penal repression are insufficient for effective general and specific prevention. This is evident certainly from the phenomenon of recurrent offenders, on the average oscillating around 30 percent of the total. Concerning certain offenders, such as drug addicts and sexual criminals, there is talk of the need for therapeutic methods, since in many cases the causes for offensive behavior stem from various types of perturbations in given spheres of mental processes.

Every stage of society's development has its implications in the field of criminality. Changes in sociopolitical systems influence the structure and rate of social pathology phenomena. Growing criminality calls for thorough etiological and symptomatological analysis before formulating the conclusion to be used for preventive purposes.

Two bodies of problems particularly should increase the intensity of criminological research and the programming of preventive actions: recurrent offenders and juvenile offenders. Many countries have evolved special programs for preventing such crimes.[5] These are exceptionally important fields for study, as they constitute an important factor shaping criminality and the effects of struggle against it. A particularly serious criminological phenomenon is recidivism by juveniles.

The scientific and technical revolution presents new problems for criminology and penal law. Car traffic growth combined with lack of care by drivers leads to increasing traffic offenses and accidents. New machinery and increasing automation with insufficient personnel training or disregard for safety rules is behind the large number of work accidents. The man–machine relationship requires reevaluation.

The social aspect of preventive issues must also extend to the moral field of responsibility. This means that everything should be viewed from an overall perspective, allowing for the possibility of giving up some of one's own aims and opportunities to achieve those aims for the good of a higher order.[6]

Contemporary technical civilization requires a general reorientation of moral doctrines, transforming the traditional individualistic morality into a social ethic. These changes could reduce the negative effects of technical advances.

The effects of human activity in the modern world, because the mechanism of various feedbacks have a multiplier effect, can reveal themselves far beyond the direct horizon of the person who triggers the effect. This means that contemporary man has to have sufficient self-discipline to allow him the right moral evaluation of the forseen effects of his actions.

General approval of crime-preventive activities has led to having them reflected in legal norms. Statutory provision of the obligation to take up such actions concerns mainly the bodies charged with detecting and prosecuting crime and with justice administration.

Such norms constitute the foundations and define the institutional framework for activities of prosecution and justice administration bodies in the field of prevention. At the same time they provide an opportunity for civic and economic organizations and institutions to join in the process. After all, the effectiveness of criminological prevention methods depends fully on coordination of state bodies with civic institutions and individuals. This coordination strengthens and links with reality the system of *criminological* prevention.

One should particularly emphasize the issue of developmental psychology. Programs in the field of crime prevention should be founded in a thorough knowledge of the laws governing man's psychosomatic development. For instance, identifying irregularities in a child's development can frequently contribute to preventing the emergence of antisocial behavior.

Functioning of the state and social system of crime prevention requires continuous analysis; two kinds of problems in this area are discussed later in this chapter. The rehabilitative function of a prison sentence constitutes a separate issue. Certain negative effects of this penalty have been skimmed over in previous publications.[7]

Planning in the field of crime prevention requires an information base which should reflect the changes taking place in the intensity and pattern of crimes. There is increasing criticism of the reporting system within penal prosecution and justice administration bodies and its functioning.

Official criminal statistics should be extended to include data held by health, education, and welfare administrative bodies, insurance companies, economic analysis units, and the like. Socioeconomic data would allow for evaluations of the quality of life touched by criminality.

Our knowledge concerning the scope of criminality has been extended considerably through development of penal victimology. Inteviews with victims provide a valuable source of information concerning crime trends.

Another popular technique is the method of self-reports; a selected group of persons is asked to provide answers concerning their violations of the law. Data shows that the number of offensive acts committed by the respondents is quite high, though the offenses are not of a serious nature. These methods have thrown some light on the well-known criminological issue of the dark number.

In order to program preventive action it is necessary to forecast trends in criminality. The methods and techniques of forecasting criminality in the aggregate, as a mass phenomenon, are still being evolved. Forecasting tendencies in criminality and its control cannot be treated separately from forecasts of general economic and social trends.

Criminological forecasts are drawn up using a large variety of methods, techniques, and research tools. In the most general terms all these procedures are connected either with extrapolation or with expert evaluation or finally with models. At the fifth United Nations Congress (Geneva, 1975) it was pointed out that extrapolation cannot be valid for periods of more than three years and that extrapolation is not possible on the basis of past experience, considering that quantitative changes could be accompanied by qualitative changes.

In contrast to the use of the complicated methodology of statistical studies, there is the possibility of drafting forecasts by the Delphic method of using expert opinion.

Any evaluation of criminality prevention programs has to take account of strategy effectiveness, that is, the degree to which set objectives are achieved, and its results, that is, the changes it brings about. Social and financial costs should also be taken into account.

It is pointed out in UN reports that, up to now, better results have been obtained in primary prevention than in secondary or third degree prevention.

The structure of an offense consists of three main elements: perpetrator—act—victim. Rational prevention, therefore, has to consider preventive actions with respect to these elements.

Human formation is a long-term process; thus the question arises of providing a positive direction to human activity and of exerting an influence in the direction of changing negative attittudes and tendencies. This aim is served by the system of state and social education. The positive influences exerted by the closest environment, namely the family, peer groups, and coworkers, are also important.

Many countries have sophisticated industries producing security equipment; there is always the possibility that the companies producing such equipment could be a source of information for professional criminals. This brings up the problem of state control of such companies.

Offenses permeate contemporary life as a mass phenomenon, violating numerous sectors of public and individual interest. Thus, counteracting this phenomenon should be the concern of society as a whole and should not be limited to official bodies established for the purpose. In particular, every person should show proper concern for his own life, health, and property. This also means that an antivictimization policy is important.

Prevention of criminality as a separate sector of theory and practice appeared during the time when criminality had become a social phenomenon, when its wide-ranging consequences began to be felt.

Taking into account the intensity of criminality, it becomes particularly valuable to have a systematic approach to preventive issues. One example could be prevention of criminality by restructuring the environment. Formation of so-called defensible space in architecture and town planning yields very positive effects in improving the degree of inhabitants' security.

This also lessens the feeling of isolation and anonymity in contemporary urban life.

Expanded planning of criminality prevention on the scale of a given environment, with the leading role of state institutions, constitutes one of the most noticeable changes in many countries over the past few years.

In planning preventive activities it is extremely important to identify the features of criminality differentiation in space and time. This purpose is served by, among other things, criminality atlases.

Administrative divisions can be used to a greater extent than they have been so far as an element facilitating a reduction in the phenomena of so-called social pathology, including criminality. Administrative divisions are shaped by socioeconomic, geographic, geophysical, transport, and ethnographic factors and historical traditions, which together constitute a body of considerations through which the administrative division at the same time reflects the differentiation in space of the incidence of criminality. Every criminological atlas allows for a general description of the territorial differentiation in criminality within a given country, containing information which can be used in drafting a long-range plan of struggle against criminality in its space aspect. Individual maps illustrating the types of offenses provide a source for an hypothesis explaining how the character of a given region, its history, its current local socioeconomic issues, developmental prospects, and links with other regions shape the structure and rate of the crime taking place there. Therefore, they can inspire defined scientific studies. The maps also serve an informative function for local administration in promulgating a long-range regional policy of combating and preventing criminality.

A gauge of the current requirements and interest of the United Nations in problems of new perspectives in crime prevention was the creation of a special working group of Committee 1 during the sixth UN Congress on the Prevention of Crime and the Treatment of Offenders.

1. A working group of Committee 1 was established in accordance with the Economic and Social Council decision 1980/106 of February 6, 1980, to consider agenda item 8 entitled: "New perspectives in crime prevention and criminal justice and development: the role of international cooperation." Sergio Garcia Ramirez (Mexico) was elected chairman of the working group; Brunon Hołyst (Poland) and M. Kara (Libyan Arab Jamahiriya) were elected as vice-chairmen. Brunon Hołyst also served as the Rapporteur.[8]

2. In view of the importance of crime prevention and criminal justice in the context of economic growth and social progress and the need to strengthen international cooperation in this field, the Economic and Social Council, at its 1980 organizational session, decided to include this additional item in the provisional agenda for the sixth congress. A

working paper of the secretariat on the subject was considered by the
working group. It was the general view of the working group that the
working paper provided a constructive framework for its discussions and
contained several useful recommendations. Discussions were based on
the fact that cooperation in the struggle against crime can be promoted
only under conditions of ensuring one of the main goals of the United
Nations, that is, maintaining international peace and security and
international cooperation.

3. The attention of the working group was directed to resolution 43 adopted
   by the World Conference of the United Nations Decade for Women:
   Equality, Development, and Peace, entitled "Exploitation of the prostitution of others and traffic in persons," in which it, invited the sixth
   United Nations Congress on the Prevention of Crime and the Treatment
   of Offenders to make concrete recommendations in regard to the
   relationship between development and the exploitation of and traffic in
   persons.

4. It was recognized that crime prevention and criminal justice are integral
   to efforts to promote development. UN General Assembly resolutions
   on the establishment of a new international economic order and on the
   new international development strategy have emphasized that the ultimate aim of development is the constant increase in the well-being of the
   entire population through its full participation in the development
   process and in ensuring a life worthy of human dignity. Efforts to
   minimize, if not to eliminate, crime and promote criminal justice are of
   immediate and direct relevance to securing these objectives. Crime
   prevention and criminal justice should therefore be viewed within a
   developmental context and in their interrelationships with economic
   growth and social change.

5. Crime is a complex phenomenon which results from the action of a
   broad range of social, economic, cultural, historical, and political
   factors. The development process is even more complex at the con-
   ceptual than at the operational level. The interplay between crime and
   development is readily perceived but difficult to define with precision.
   Both at the national and international level, some progress has been
   made in understanding the interaction between certain aspects of
   development in fields such as urbanization, industrialization, employment, and migration, and the incidence and types of criminality. The fact
   that assessing the impact and interrelationship of crime and development
   is complicated and difficult should not diminish the need to make these
   assessments objectively and systematically. It was recalled that the fifth
   congress had identified costs associated with criminal activity within
   four broad categories. It was suggested that these should be constantly
   reviewed and updated.

6. Much more work is necessary to better comprehend the interactions between crime and development with a view to evolving appropriate policy options for development planning. It was felt that development per se was not responsible for the increase in crime. Crime, with its attendant costs to society, was seen not only as a hindrance to development but also, in some cases, as a consequence of the latter, particularly of unplanned or inadequately planned economic growth and social imbalance. A cautionary view was also expressed to the effect that it is difficult, if not impossible, to establish universally applicable definitions and policies in regard to crime and to development, Both these factors are inseparably related to the economic, social, political, and cultural conditions of each country. Each country has the right and responsibility to deal with these problems in the light of its own priorities and requirements. The view was expressed that policies, norms, and guidelines for international cooperation in crime prevention and criminal justice and development should take into account the economic and social realities of developing countries, and that indigenous capacities and capabilities should be strengthened. At the same time, however, there is considerable need and scope to promote cooperation among countries through, in particular, judicial assistance, exchange of information, experiences, knowledge, and skills in dealing with these problems. This is even more true at the regional and subregional levels, given the comparability of problems and potential solutions of the UN member countries.

7. It was recognized that the participation of the public and individuals in crime prevention and criminal justice is essential. Considerable emphasis was placed on the importance of crime prevention in the context of the development of the human potential. References were made to the close linkages between prevention of crime and social justice. The view was expressed that crime prevention and criminal justice must be viewed from the perspective of human rights which includes the right to development, which was considered a human right by the General Assembly of the United Nations.

8. It was the view of the working group that there is a need to involve all relevant disciplines in dealing with the problem of criminality, a multidisciplinary subject. Crime prevention should be viewed as a component, but not necessarily a dominant one, in intersectoral planning, given the wide spectrum of priorities needed for development. However, it was emphasized that systematic efforts have to be made to incorporate crime prevention and control in national development planning and to ensure a more comprehensive and multisectoral approach to the reduction, if not elimination, of crime.

9. The view was expressed that criminality and development should be

considered not only within a national context. The impact of international economic relations on this problem is considerable. There is a need to give attention to a variety of international issues, including those relating to the functioning of transnational corporations and to the cooperation among countries in investigating the prosecuting transnational organizations that have engaged in criminal offenses. Such efforts may, while adding a further dimension to the understanding of the phenomenon of criminality, and while facilitating international efforts to combat such criminality, also suggest the need for improvements in international economic relations which will help to reduce crime.

10. While recognizing the need for more research and analysis of various issues relating to crime and development, it was generally felt that these should be accompanied by action-oriented measures, particularly in the provision of technical assistance to member countries, as required, and the strengthening of operational activities. The need was noted for not ónly intensifying scientific research but also for applying their results in the practice of organs of criminal justice. In particular, it was proposed that this problem be considered in a comprehensive manner at the meetings of the committee and the congress. Several representatives emphasized the need to strengthen appropriately the activities of the United Nations system in the field of crime prevention and criminal justice, particularly those of the Crime Prevention and Criminal Justice Branch. The pivotal role and work of the Committee on Crime Prevention and Control was recognized and it was generally felt that these should be further reinforced and adequate arrangements made for preparations of important issues between sessions of the committee.

11. Adequate attention should be given to the treatment of offenders. With the acceptance of the principle that the ultimate object of a correctional system is the reformation and rehabilitation of offenders, institutional methods are undergoing basic changes. In this area also there is considerable scope for exchange of experiences and information between countries. The view was expressed that attention should also be given to the problems of the victims of crime and the need for them and their next of kin to be adequately compensated and, in this connection, for work in the area of penal victimology.

12. References were made to the important role of the United Nations in the advancement of international cooperation for crime prevention and criminal justice, including that of the Congresses, the Committee on Crime Prevention and Control, the Crime Prevention and Criminal Justice Branch, the United Nations Social Defense Research Institute, regional research and training institutes, the network of national correspondents, intergovernmental and nongovernmental organizations and scientific institutions and other mechanisms and bodies. In this

connection, the potential role of regional commissions was also fully recognized. The need to strengthen support for the United Nations Social Defense Trust Fund was also pointed out. Speakers also stressed the importance of considering the availability of resources in settling United Nations priorities in the crime field.

13. At the same time, a number of statements emphasized the importance of having the organs of the United Nations consider only the most important issues relating to international cooperation in the struggle against criminality. Also, concern was expressed over the fact that the agenda for the sessions of the Committee on Crime Prevention and the agenda of the United Nations Congresses were overloaded in a number of instances; this does not promote thorough and in-depth consideration of the items.

14. In the context of these overall considerations, the working group was in general agreement with the following recommendations:

a. To develop a precise definition of the scope and sphere of activities of United Nations organs in the field of crime prevention and criminal justice in connection with social and economic development.

b. To initiate and develop further research and analysis on the interrelationship between crime and specific socioeconomic issues, for example, employment, migration, urbanization, and industrialization, and sociocultural issues such as the role of the family and schools in education, taking into account diversities in national situations and drawing upon national and regional experiences.

c. To reinforce and strengthen, on a national level, data collection and work on social indicators to provide a sound empirical basis for such research and analysis.

d. The need to study in particular the emergence of new types of criminal activity in the context of changing socioeconomic structures, including international structures and relationships.

e. To request the Secretary General of the United Nations to carry out, after close consultation with the member states, an in-depth study on crime prevention and the treatment of offenders within the framework of the establishment of the new international economic order, particularly bearing in mind the needs of underdeveloped countries.

f. To initiate and develop systematic exchange of information as an important component of an international plan of action for crime prevention and control. Also, to elaborate sociocriminological studies in collaboration with countries which so request, in order to provide an opportunity for assistance in the efforts to control crime. The United Nations should provide information on world trends in crime and criminal policies on a regular basis and in close and continuing cooperation with member countries and relevant bodies. This will require that the capacity of the United Nations to collect, analyze, and disseminate information in the form most useful to member countries be strengthened. To that end, the United Nations should study the possibility of establishing unified statistical plans which would serve as a guide for member states and as a way of collecting, analyzing, and disseminating information.

g. To initiate and develop at the national and local levels wherever they do not exist, planning and coordination between experts in the field of crime prevention and criminal justice and representatives of other development sectors, and to encourage participation in crime prevention measures by members of the community. Assistance should be provided to strengthen national institutions. Efforts should also be made by the United Nations to utilize such institutions, including universities and scientific institutes, in research and operational activities and also to promote training and exchange of technical expertise among member countries.

h. To promote international cooperation through, in particular, judicial assistance, exchange of information, and experience in regard to the treatment of offenders and the problems relating to the victims of crime.

i. To reinforce the capacities and capabilities of the United Nations Social Defense Research Institute and the regional institutes, such as the United Nations affiliated Asia and Far East Institute for the Prevention of Crime and the Treatment of Offenders and the Latin American Institute for the Prevention of Crime and the Treatment of Offenders, as well as the establishment, as soon as possible, of the African Institute of the United Nations for the prevention of crime and the treatment of offenders, for research and analysis and to initiate work in this field in the regional commissions. In this connection, there is also need to maintain a close link between the Committee on Crime Prevention and Control and the United Nations Social Defense Research Institute and regional institutes, and a need for close cooperation between the United Nations and its regional institutes in the field of crime prevention and criminal justice and national institutions established by member states in several countries. The national correspondents in the field of crime prevention and the treatment of offenders should be involved more actively in research into the analysis of crime trends and crime prevention strategies in their respective countries.

j. To increase on a bilateral and a regional basis and also through the United Nations, the provision of technical assistance to member countries, upon request, in relation to the development process through, inter alia, the establishment of interregional and regional advisory services and the maintainance of a roster of experts whose services can be made available when required.

k. To reinforce, in particular, considering the available resources, training facilities by organizing, within and outside the United Nations, training courses and seminars, group study tours, and provision of fellowships.

l. The need for the United Nations to act as a catalyst in promoting cooperation among developing countries, particularly technical cooperation, in dealing with problems in this area. This should be primarily done at the regional and subregional levels through, inter alia, the convening of seminars, symposia, and pooling of knowledge and resources.

m. The need for the Committee on Crime Prevention and Control to give specific and continuing attention to the problems of crime and development, in close collaboration with other relevant United Nations bodies, particularly those at the regional level, in order to make effective policy recommendations.

n. The need in particular for the Committee on Crime Prevention and Control to give specific attention to the relationship between development and the exploitation and traffic in persons in response to the invitation contained in resolution 43 adopted by the World Conference of the United Nations Decade for Women: Equality, Development, and Peace.

o. To promote closer relations between the committee within its competence and the work of other relevant bodies concerned with crime and related problems, such as transnational violence, economic criminality, human rights, and drug trafficking.

p. The need for future congresses to keep the subject of crime and development under review in the context of changing socioeconomic situations, taking into account the results of scientific research.

q. The United Nations Social Defense Trust Fund should be utilized in consultation with member states. Funds available in the United Nations for crime prevention and criminal justice should be utilized to the maximum extent possible as seed money for the promotion of appropriate activities at the national level.

r. To reinforce and strengthen appropriately the capacities of the United Nations system, particularly that of the Crime Prevention and Criminal Justice Branch, in order to provide substantive and effective services to the Committee on Crime Prevention and Control, the United Nations Congresses and to the various organizations, including the United Nations Social Defense Research Institute, the regional institutes and intergovernmental and nongovernmental organizations concerned with the subject.

From the point of view of rational prevention a considerable role falls to legal education of the society. This problem has been of late particularly emphasized in the United States. Special crime prevention programs have been instituted, designed to improve the legal consciousness of the society.[9]

Legal education should be approached as an integral component of civic formation. The current state of public legal awareness must be recognized as a weak link in general civic education. These are the fundamental premises behind the proposal to introduce, on a wider scale than previously, elements of criminological knowledge, treated as part of obligatory education.

The point is to obtain action over a number of educations system channels. This is one of the significant tasks for the departments of education, justice, police, and the mass media.

What should be the scope of factual information provided in the field of criminology and penal victimology? One could suggest: general legislative principles, the main groups of penalized acts and behaviors, criminality patterns and changes, means and methods of offensive actions, civic protection against crime, fundamental principles of civic cooperation with bodies professionally geared to prevention and crime detection.

There are also problems of differentiating information, such as: the level of knowledge disseminated to everyone and exacted according to the requirements of the given educational institution; the level of knowledge disseminated to a given occupational group and exacted; the level of knowledge disseminated generally or selectively to age and occupational groups in extracurricular forms and not exacted in the form of tests or exams.

The mass media should shape antivictimization attitudes, thereby certainly contributing to a drop in victimization.

Notes

1. Freda Adler, *The Incidence of Female Criminality in the Contemporary World* (New York: New York University Press, 1980).

2. U.S. Department of Justice, National Criminal Justice Information and Statistics Service, Law Enforcement Assistance Administration, *Computer Crime: Criminal Justice Resource Manual* (Washington, 1979).

3. Sixth United Nations Congress on the Prevention of Crime and the Treatment of Offenders, *Crime Trends and Crime Prevention Strategies* (Caracas, August 25 to September 5, 1980, pp. 15–22; *International Review of Criminal Policy* 1980, no. 35, 1979, pp. 13, 24, 38, 44, 55, 67, 71; William Clifford, *An Introduction to African Criminology* (Nairobi: Oxford University Press, 1974); Marshall B. Clinard and Daniel J. Abbott,

Crime in Developing Countries: A Comparative Approach (New York: John Wiley, 1973).

4. Hartmut Schellhoss, "Necessity and Function of Interdisciplinary Criminology," in *Criminological Research Trends in Western Germany: German Reports to the Sixth International Congress on Criminology in Madrid 1970*, ed. Günter Kaiser and Thomas Würtenberger (Berlin: Springer Verlag, 1972), pp. 101–110.

5. U.S. Department of Justice, Law Enforcement Assistance Administration, Office of Juvenile Justice and Delinquency Prevention, *Delinquency Prevention* (Washington, 1979); Michael C. Dixon and William E. Wright, *Juvenile Delinquency Prevention Program* (Nashville: Peabody College for Teachers, 1975); Daniel Glaser, "Coping With Sociocultural Causes of Youth Employment and Crime," in *Crime and Employment Issues* (Washington, D.C.: American University Law School, Institute for Advanced Studies in Justice, 1978), pp. 53–65; Eleanor Glueck and Sheldon Glueck, *Family Environment and Delinquency* (Boston: Houghton Mifflin, 1962); *New Roles for Youth in School and the Community* (New York, National Commission on Resources for Youth, 1974; Ivan F. Nye, *Family Reationships and Delinquent Behavior* (New York: Wiley, 1958); Office of Juvenile Justice and Delinquency Prevention, *City Life and Delinquency: Victimization, Fear of Crime, and Gang Membership* (Washington, 1977); Paul A. Strasburg, *Violent Delinquents: A Report to the Ford Foundation from the Vera Institute of Justice* (New York: Monarch, 1978); Victor L. Streib, "Juvenile Courts Should Not Mandate Parental Involvement in Court-Ordered Treatment Programs," *Juvenile and Family Court Journal* 1978, no. 2, pp. 49–56.

6. Alfred Stümper, "Kriminalpolitik," *Kriminalistik* 1971, no. 6.

7. Penal institutions all over the world have recently been marked by rampant violence. See, for instance, Centro Internazionale di Richerche e Studi Sociologici, Penali, e Penitenziari, *La violenza nelle sue implicatione penitenziare* [Violence and its penitentiary implications]. A study seminar at Messina, Dec. 12–17, 1977. (Messina-Catania, 1978); Raymond Screvens, Bruno Bulthe, and André Renard, *La violence dans les prisons* [Violence in prisons] (Centre National de Criminologie, Brussels: Bruylant, 1978), publication no. 6.

8. Sixth United Nations Congress on the Prevention of Crime and the Treatment of Offenders, *New Perspectives in Crime Prevention and Criminal Justice and Development: The Role of International Co-operation,* Caracas, September 1980.

9. See, for instance, U.S. Department of Justice, Office of Juvenile Justice and Delinquency Prevention, *Prevention of Delinquency Through Alternative Education* (Washington, 1980); Robert F. Arnove and Toby

Strout, *Alternative Schools for Disruptive Youth* (Bloomington: Indiana University School of Education, 1978); Ralph E. Bailey and John C. Kackley, *Positive Alternatives to Student Suspensions: An Overview* (St. Petersburg, Fla.: Pupil Personnel Services Demonstration Project at Children's Hospital, n.d.); Birch Bayh, *Challenge for the Third Century: Education in a Safe Environment—Final Report on the Nature and Prevention of School Violence and Vandalism* (Washington: U.S. Government Printing Office, 1977); Richard G. Boehm, *An Evaluation of the Berrien Country School-Based Delinquency Prevention/Diversion Program: Peer Group Counseling* (Berrien County, Michigan: Probate and Juvenile Court Services, 1977); Albert P. Cardarelli, *Neighborhood Strategies to Prevent Delinquency and Enhance Positive Youth Development through Interagency Coordination* (Boston: Boston University, 1977); John R. Clark, *An Evaluation of the City of Rochester: "Rochester Alternative School"* (New Hampshire: Governor's Commission on Crime and Delinquency, 1978); Delbert S. Elliott and Harwin L. Voss, *Delinquency and Dropout* (Lexington, Mass.: D.C. Heath, 1974); Joyce L. Epstein and J. M. McPartland, *The Effects of Open School Organization on Student Outcomes* (Baltimore: Center for Social Organization of Schools, John Hopkins University, 1975), report No. 194; Arthur D. Little, Inc., *Alternative Education Options* (Washington: U.S. Department of Justice, Law Enforcement Assistance Administration, Office of Juvenile Justice and Delinquency Prevention, 1979); Richard J. Lundman and Frank R. Scarpitti "Delinquency Prevention: A Recommendation for Future Projects," *Crime and Delinquency* April 1978, pp. 207–220.

19

The Teaching of Criminology

There is a close connection between the system of teaching of criminology and the character of this science, which according to Thorsten Sellin is a synthesis as well as interaction with other sciences which contribute to its principal notions.[1]

The specific and autonomous character of criminology stems from its tendency to achieve a specific aim: the explaining of criminal behavior and finding preventive measures against it. Criminology unites four basic disciplines: psychopathology and psychiatry, sociology of crime, geography or ecology of crime, and crime statistics.[2] It also profits from the achievements of many other fields of knowledge, especially criminalistics, penology, criminal law, forensic psychiatry, forensic medicine, forensic chemistry, and criminal policy. Thus, the scope of knowledge included in criminological studies is particularly extensive. The development of this science, many-sided and spontaneous to a large extent—depending on what disciplines are given priority—has been uneven.

As far as criminology is related to other sciences one can distinguish two basic systems: the European, with a strong connection between criminology, law, and medicine, and the North American, dominated by sociology. Elements from other branches of sciences have been added to both systems as auxiliary disciplines. There is also a new radical interdisciplinary approach which does away with the differentiation between the dominating science and the auxiliary ones and leads to the acknowledgment of criminology as an independent science, and the dealing with it as a new, distinct profession.[3]

Apart from strictly criminological institutes which conduct research and implement training programs, other scientific institutes which are concerned mostly with law, sociology, sometimes psychology, medical sciences, anthropology, or political economy do similar work.

Strictly criminological institutes are, for example, the Center of Criminology of the University of Toronto, Ecole de Criminologie of the University of Ghent, Institute für Kriminologie of Frankfurt am Main and Heidelberg Universities, Institut de Criminologie of the University of Nancy, and the Institute of Criminology of Cambridge University.

These institutes, however, are not concerned exclusively with criminology; for example, the Institute of Criminology at the University of Nancy also conducts research in the field of forensic medicine, forensic psychiatry, and corrections.

369

On the other hand, not all scientific institutes of criminology study all aspects of this science; some of them purposely limit their activities to the study of some of its aspects or problems. For instance, Centre d'Etude de la Délinquance Juvénile in Brussels studies only the problem of juvenile delinquency; the same is true of the Kriminologisches Institut at the University of the Saar, the Kriminoloski Institut Pravnogo Fakulteta at the University of Sarajevo. There are other institutes with even greater specialization such as the Department of Criminology at the University of Melbourne which studies alcohol offenses.

Sometimes the name of an institute indicates its scientific interest in other penal sciences, especially in criminal law. This is the case, for instance, of the Institute of Penal Law and Criminology of the Law and Political Sciences Department (Instituto de Derecho Penal y Criminologia de la Facultad de Derecho y Ciencias Sociales) of the University of Buenos Aires, the Institute of Criminal Sciences (Institut für Kriminalwissenschaften) at Münster, and the Institute of Penal Law (Institut für Strafrecht der Juristichen Fakultät) at the universities of Berlin, Halle, and Lipsk. At these, especially, the study of criminology gives way to law, the main object of scientific interest.

In Europe the teaching of criminology has developed not only in university law departments but also now in most university scientific institutes, chairs, and seminars, which study at least some aspects of criminology.

Italy is the exception, where criminology is taught mainly at the Faculty of Medicine as criminal anthropology; for example, at the Institute of Criminal Anthropology (Istituto di Antropologia Criminale) of the University of Rome and chairs of criminal anthropology at the Departments of Medicine in the universities of Genoa, Naples, and Turin.

In many countries psychological, medical, and other institutes are also sometimes concerned with problems of criminology; for example, the Center of Research in Human Relations (Centre de Recherches en Relations Humaines) in Montréal, the Institute of Psychology (Institut de Psychologie) at the University of Montréal, the Burden Neurological Institute in Bristol, the Institute of Psychiatry at the University of London, the University Institute of Forensic Medicine and Clinical Criminology (Institut Universitaire de Médicine Légale et de Criminologie Clinique) in Lyon, and the Institute of Social Research (Institut for Samfunnsforsking) in Oslo.

Since 1935 criminology has been taught at the college of law, sociology, and economics in the London School of Economics and Political Science.

In Switzerland there is no chair of criminology and at only one, the University of Lausanne in the academic year 1979–80, did A. Mergen from Mainz have a cycle of lectures. At the University of Zurich, in 1977 a criminological seminar was held. Only rarely are seminars and lectures held and they are conducted usually by professors of penal law, while specialists in the field of psychiatry, psychology, and criminology are seldom invited. An exception here, is the University in Basel, where for some time Günther Kaiser of the Federal Republic of Germany has been introducing students to the study of criminology.

In the United States criminology has been developed by sociologists. Under the influence of pragmatism, which is very characteristc of the social sciences in the United States, criminology tends in the direction of applied penology and social work; this fact explains the important role which is attached to schools of social work. The increasing demand for professional workers in criminology led to the introduction of criminology in the curricula of social service schools and at the departments of sociology in universities. Most of the social workers in the United States who work with adult and juvenile delinquents and children in moral danger are graduates of schools of social work and departments of sociology.

In the United States, the following institutes conduct the research and educational work in the field of criminology:

The American Academy For Professional Law Enforcement, founded in 1973; the academy is involved in education and development programs in the field of law enforcement; its aim is to maintain professional and ethical standards.

The American Academy of Judicial Education provides educational programs and services to state court judges, organizes in-state judicial education seminars and conferences.

The Academy of Criminal Justice Sciences, founded in 1963 as a department of the University of Nebraska, carries on research and educational activities. It also publishes a bulletin.

The American Humane Association, founded in 1876; its aim is, among other things, to provide training on child abuse and animal abuse and to promote better services for each.

The Association of Trial Lawyers of America, founded in 1946; the association engages in promoting the education of practicing lawyers.

The Cornell Institute on Organized Crime, founded in 1975; its main objective is organizing training seminars on the investigation and prosecution of organized crime and on the development of techniques and strategies for its control.

The Institute of Contemporary Corrections and the Behavioral Sciences, founded in 1965; it is an educational agency serving institutions of higher learning and the practitioners responsible for the administration of criminal and juvenile justice.

The Joint Commission on Criminology and Criminal Justice Education and Standards, founded in 1977; the commission is involved in developing and publishing minimum standards for postsecondary education programs in criminology and criminal justice.

The National College of Criminal Defense Lawyers and Public Defenders (University of Houston), founded in 1973; the college develops and provides training programs for criminal defense attorneys.

The National College of District Attorneys (University of Houston), founded in 1969; the college provides postgraduate education for public prosecutors at all governmental levels.

The National College of Juvenile Justice, founded in 1937, provides training for judges and other juvenile justice personnel.

The National Crime Prevention Institute (University of Louisville), founded in 1971; the institute is involved in training and educating officers in anticipating, recognizing, and appraising crime risk and ways of removing or reducing it.

The Social Committee on Youth Education for Citizenship, founded in 1971; the committee engages in integrating law-related studies and curriculum in schools for grades kindergarten through 12.

The Texas Crime Prevention Institute, founded in 1974; the institute organizes training and technical assistance in crime prevention.

National criminological institutes sometimes have the character of national research centers, for example, the National Center of Criminology (Centre National de Criminologie) in Brussels, the National Institute of Criminology (Instituto Nacional de Criminologia) in Havana, and the National Center of Social and Criminological Research in Cairo.

In some socialist countries institutes involved in the study of criminology exist at Academies of Sciences; for example, the Institute of State Law at the Hungarian Academy of Sciences and the Institute of State Law of the Polish Academy of Sciences.

Most departmental institutes or other organizations engaged in the study of criminology are situated within the Ministries of Justice—for example, the Institute of Education and Research (Homosogokenkyusho) in Tokyo and the Institute of Research on Penitentiaristics (Centraal Opleidingsinstitut van het Gevangeniswezen) in The Hague—or within the prosecutor's office, as in the USSR, CSSR, GDR, and in Poland. Sometimes research is conducted by police bureaus; such work is conducted by the Federal Criminal Bureau (Bundeskriminalamt) in Wiesbaden.

Among institutes of international organizations are the UN Latin

American Criminological Institute (Instituto Latinoamericano de Criminologia) in Sao Paulo and the Institute of Social Defense in Luxemburg.

Criminology is taught mostly at higher schools. In higher-degree education of lawyers, psychologists, sociologists, and teachers criminology is only one of the curriculum subjects. However, the Institute of Criminology at Cambridge University organizes annual courses, the programs of which include all aspects of criminology. Some institutes and schools, especially in the U.S., confine themselves to training persons who, as psychologists, sociologists, social workers, or criminologists, are employed in the administration of justice or social work offices sensu largo.

A special educational program preparing someone for the profession of criminologist with the possibility of getting a diploma or a doctorate is yet to be developed. For example, the Department of Criminology (Département de la Criminologie), at the Faculty of Social Sciences in Montréal, prepares graduates with the degree of Master of Arts in Criminology. The department initially directed its teaching program to persons with a master's degree in other disciplines, then proceeded to establish its own doctoral program and has since increasingly moved into the teaching of undergraduate courses. A scientific degree (Graduado en Ciencias Criminologicas) is also granted to graduates of courses taught at the Institute of Criminology (Instituto de Criminologia) at the Law Department of the University of Madrid. In the United States the degree of Master of Arts in Criminology is granted to the graduates of the Graduate School of Arts and Sciences at the University of Pennsylvania, and the degree of Master of Arts in Sociology with Specialization in Criminology to the graduates of the Department of Sociology and Anthropology of Boston University. Postgraduate studies, among others, in the field of criminology are held in the Institute of Penal Law and Criminological Sciences (Instituto de Derecho Penal y Ciencias Criminologicas) at the University of Bilbao. Higher schools conduct doctoral seminars on criminology.

Unlike the higher schools, extramural institutes conduct mostly research work, and pay less attention to teaching. The latter concerns mostly the preparation of personnel for achieving scientific degrees. This involves the staff of an institute as well as, for instance, the personnel of a department in which a given institute works. Such a doctoral program on criminology in Poland is conducted by the Institute of Crime Problems.

In Poland criminology is taught mostly in nine university institutes. Moreover, the Institute of State and Law of the Polish Academy of Sciences, the Academy of Internal Affairs, the Research Institute on Judicial Law of the Ministry of Justice, and the Institute of Crime Problems are also involved in teaching.

The training program in the field of criminology, based on the International Standard Classification of Education, usually requires that a person have secondary education. At the end of one's studies one receives the degree of Master of Arts or Master of Sciences and a doctorate or equivalents of these degrees. The program includes sessions or seminars, and in order to obtain higher degrees an original research study in the form of a doctor's thesis or a graduate thesis is required. The topics of courses organized for students who are not interested in scientific degrees usually include introduction to criminology, the principles of investigating offenders, psychopathology and psychodynamics of crime, characteristics of normal and abnormal personality, methods of measuring personality and clinical diagnosis, social origin and characteristics of crime, sociology of legal institutions, the history of crime and treatment (methods) of offenders, scientific methodology, the policy of applying law, penal law, and field work in criminology. Auxiliary studies include lectures on economies, history, law, social sciences, and behavioral sciences. Courses aimed at achieving scientific degrees in their lectures and research projects concern the following topics: the history of crime and treatment of offenders, organized crime and the professional offender, the penitentiary community, alcoholic and drug abusers, perpetrators of sexual crimes, characterological deviations, white-collar crimes, nonconformist cultures, group psychotherapy in correctional institutions, and other topics. These courses also include lectures on mathematics, statistics and natural sciences.[4]

Particular attention is paid to the teaching of criminology in the United States. Most persons working professionally in the field of criminology were educated in schools of social work or at university departments of sociology. Some of the sixty schools of social service, which grant scientific degrees after two years of graduate studies, train practitioners for social service. However, the prevailing opinion is that due to the inadequacies of our knowledge about the validity of various reeducational and rehabilitation methods, a general education in social sciences—with particular attention to deviant behaviors— would be more useful for future specialists than the education overestimating the technical or "professional" aspects of this service. There is talk about the conflict between conservatives and innovators, the latter being in favor of the introduction of radical changes aimed at elaborating special interdisciplinary educational programs for criminologists.[5]

I will conclude by saying a few words about the teaching of criminology on the international scale. Here a rather important role is played by congresses and conferences organized by the United Nations, the International Society for Criminology, the International Association of Penal Law, and the International Association of Social Defense. However, only training programs organized by the International Society for Criminology can be regarded as having a truly international character of teaching.

In regional activities, one should mention the work of the Section of Social

Defense of the Arab League and the Scandinavian Criminological Scientific Board.

Beginning in 1969, the International Society for Criminology has under-taken the initiative of organizing the teaching and interdisciplinary studies through the creation of international centers in the regions having particular importance for criminological activity. Such posts are: the International Center for Comparative Criminology at the University of Montreal (1969), and the International Center for Clinical Criminology related to the Faculty of Medicine at the University of Genoa (1975). The United Nations, on the other hand, organized the Research Institute of Social Defense in Rome (1968) and regional institutes of staff training in the field of the administration of justice in Japan (1959), in Egypt (1974), and Costa Rica (1975).

The proper level of teaching in the field of criminology will contribute to the propagating of criminological research and to a better understanding of its significance, especially by practitioners.

Notes

1. Leonard J. Hippchen, "The Teaching of Comparative and World Criminology in Graduate Schools of Sociology and Criminal Justice," *Intenational Journal of Comparative and Applied Criminal Justice* 1977, no. 1.

2. Denis Szabo, *Criminology in the World* (Montreal: International Center for Comparative Criminology, 1977).

3. Denis Szabo, "The Teaching of Criminology in Universities: A Contribution to the Sociology of Innovation," *International Review of Criminal Policy* 1964, no. 22.

4. Szabo, *Criminology in the World.*

5. Szabo, "The Teaching of Criminology."

Bibliography

Abstracts on Criminology and Penology (formerly *Excerpta* Criminologica). Published since 1961 by the University of Leiden, The Netherlands.

Bibliografia wybranych zagranicznych publikacji kryminologicznych [Bibliography of selected foregin criminological publications]. Yearbooks of the Institute of Crime Problems, Warsaw, published since 1975.

Crime and Delinquency Literature. Hackensack, New Jersey: National Council on Crime and Delinquency, 1970–.

International Annals of Criminology. Paris: Société Internationale de Criminologie, 1962–.

International Bibliography on Crime and Delinquency. New York: National Research and Information Center on Crime and Delinquency, 1963–.

International Review of Criminal Policy. New York: United Nations, 1952–.

Pinatel, Jean. "Select Bibliography." *International Social Science Journal.* Paris: 1966, no. 18.

Radzinowicz, Leon, and Hood, Roger. *Criminology and the Administration of Criminal Justice.* London: Mansell, 1976.

Selected Documentation of Criminology. Paris: UNESCO, 1961.

Criminologie Canadienne: Bibliographie Commentée. Solliciteur Général Canada, 1977.

Sellin, Thorsten, and Savitz, Leonard D. *A Bibliographic Manual for the Student of Criminology.* New York: National Council of Crime and Delinquency, 1965.

Smith, Ollie L.; Caplan, Marc H.; and Boston, Guy D. *Directory of Criminal Justice Information Sources.* 2nd ed. National Institute of Law Enforcement and Criminal Justice, L.E.A.A., U.S. Department of Justice, September 1978.

Wright, Martin. *Use of Criminology Literature.* London: Hamden, Butterworth, 1974.

Wolfgang, Marvin E.; Figlio, Robert M.; and Thornberry, Terence P. *Criminology Index, Research and Theory in Criminology in the United States 1945–1972.* New York: Elsevier, 1975.

Textbooks

Gercenzon, A. A.; Karpiec, I. I.; and Kudriawcew, V. N., eds. *Kriminologiya. Uczebnik.* 3rd ed. Moscow: Juridiczeskaja Literatura, 1976.

Gibbons, Don C. *Society, Crime and Criminal Careers: An Introduction to Criminology*. 2nd ed. New York: Prentice-Hall, 1973.

Glaser, Daniel, *Handbook of Criminology*. Chicago: Rand McNally College Publishing Company, 1974.

Göppinger, Hans E. *Kriminologie*. 3rd ed. Munich: C.H. Beck, 1976.

Haesler, Walter T., ed. *Neue Perspektiven in der Kriminologie. Nouvelles Perspectives en Criminologie* [New Perspectives in Criminology] Sonderband der Reihe "Asozialität and Psyche", (Zürich: Verlag der Fachvereine an den Schweizerischen Hochschulen und Techniken, 1975).

Hołyst, Brunon. *Kryminologia*. 2nd. ed. Warsaw: Państwowe Wydawnictwo Naukowe, 1979.

Hood, Roger, and Sparks, Richard. *Key Issues in Criminology*. New York: McGraw-Hill, 1970.

López-Rey, Manuel. *Crime: An Analytical Appraisal*. London: Routledge and Kegan Paul, 1970.

Mannheim, Hermann, ed. *Pioneers in Criminology*. London: Stevens, 1960.

Mannheim, Herman. Vergleichende Kriminologie. 2 vols. Stuttgart: Ferdinand Enke Verlag, 1974.

Pinatel, Jean. *La Criminologie*. Paris: Spes, 1960.

Radzinowicz, Leon. *In Search of Criminology*. London: Heinemann, 1961.

Radzinowicz, Leon, and Wolfgang, Marvin E., eds. *Crime and Justice*, vols. 1–3. New York: Basic Books, 1977. Volume 1: *The Criminal in Society*. Volume 2: *The Criminal in the Arms of Law*. Volume 3: *The Criminal Under Restraint*.

Reckless, Walter C. *American Criminology: New Directions*. New York: Appleton-Century-Crofts, 1973.

Schafer, Stephen. *Theories in Criminology: Past and Present Philosophies of the Crime Problem*. New York: Random House, 1969.

Sutherland, Edwin H. and Cressey, Donald R. *Criminology*. 9th ed. Philadelphia: Lippincott, 1970.

Periodicals

Acta Criminologica, Montréal.

Australian and New Zealand Journal of Criminology, Melbourne.

Archiwum Kryminologii, Polish Academy of Sciences, Institute of Law Sciences, Criminology Faculty, Warsaw.

British Journal of Criminology, London.

Canadian Journal of Criminology and Corrections, Ottawa.

Crime and Delinquency, Hackensack, N.J.

Criminology, Berverly Hills, Calif.

International Annals of Criminology, Paris.
International Criminal Police Review, Paris.
International Journal of Offender Therapy and Comparative Criminology, London.
International Journal of Criminology and Penology, New York.
International Review of Criminal Policy, New York.
Issues in Criminology, Berkeley, Calif.
Journal of Criminal Justice, Toronto.
Journal of Criminal Law, Criminology, and Police Science, Baltimore, Md.
Journal of Research in Crime and Delinquency, S. Hackensack, N.J.
Kriminalistik und Forensische Wissenschaften, Berlin.
National Review of Criminal Sciences, Cairo.
Nederlands Tijdschrift voor Criminologie, Meppel.
De Nordiska Kriminalist Foreningarnas Arsbok, Stockholm.
Patologia Społeczna: Zapobieganie, Institute of Crime Problems, Warsaw.
Przestepczość na świecie, Institute of Crime Problems, Warsaw.
Revue de Droit Pénal et de Criminologie, Brussels.
Revue de Science Criminelle et de Droit Pénal Comparé, Paris.
Revue Internationale de Criminologie et de Police Technique, Geneva.
Revue Internationale de Droit Pénal, Paris.
Socyalisticheskaya Zakonnost, Moscow.
Sovetskoye Gosudarstvo i Pravo, Moscow.
Studia Kryminologiczne, Kryminalistyczne i Penitencjarne, Institute of Crime Problems, Warsaw.
Voporosi Borbi s Prestupnostu, Moscow.
Zeszyty Naukowe, Research Institute on Court Law, Warsaw.

Encyclopedias and Dictionaries

Adler, Johann A., ed. *Elsevier's Dictionary of Criminal Science in Eight Languages*. London: Elsevier Science Publishers, 1960.
Branham, Vernon C., and Kutash, Samuel B., eds. *Encyclopedia of Criminology*. New York: Philosophical Library, 1949.
Kaiser, Günther; Sack, Fritz; and Schellhoss, Hartmut. *Kleines Kriminologisches Wörterbuch*. Freiburg: Herder, 1974.
Schneider, Hans J., ed *Die Psychologie des 20. Jahrhunderts. Bd. 14 Auswirkungen auf die Kriminologie*. Zurich: Kindler Verlag, 1981.
Sieverts, Rudolf, Schneider, Hans J. *Handwörterbuch der Kriminologie*. Berlin: Walter de Gruter, 1966–1977.
Yamerollos, Elie-Jean, and Kellens, Georges. *Le crime et la criminologie*. Paris: Marabout Université, nos. 196–197, 1970.
Another valuable source is *A World Directory of Criminological Institutes*

2nd ed., published 1978 by the United Nations Social Defense Research Institute in Rome. Information on teaching criminology, though somewhat outdated, is available in the UNESCO Report: *The university teaching of social sciences. Criminology*, Paris 1957; this report is cited in the text as the UNESCO Report.

Index of Names

Index of Subjects

Index of Institutions
and Organizations

About the Author

Brunon Hołyst is a director of the Institute of Crime Problems in Warsaw, Poland, and head of the Department of Criminalistics at the University of Łódź. His research works cover the field of criminology, forensic psychology, and criminalistics. He has created numerous scientific concepts, among others, penal victimology, the syndrome and potential of criminality, the essence of the motivational process, the essence of the concept of criminology, and factors favorable to the effectiveness of investigation. He is the author of sixteen books and more than 150 articles published in Poland and abroad, as well as being editor-in-chief of twenty-two books and a few periodicals devoted to criminology and criminalistics, among others, *Criminological, Criminalistic, and Penitentiary Studies; Social Pathology—Prevention,* and *Criminality in the World.*

Professor Dr. Hołyst is vice-chairman of the Scientific Commission of the International Society for Criminology, a member of the Scientific Commission of the World Society of Victimology and of the editorial committee of the "International Revue of Victimology," and correspondent of the Canadian International Academy of Humanities and Social Sciences and of the Canadian Inter-American Research Institute. He is vice-chairman of the Polish Society of Forensic Medicine and Criminology, founder and vice-chairman of the Polish Criminalistics Society, and a member of the scientific board of several Polish institutes. He has taken an active part in a number of international congresses, conferences, and symposia, having been one of the Conference Patrons of the international conference to commemorate the bicentenary of John Howard's "The State of the Prisons," at Canterbury in 1977; scientific director of the Prevention Section, eighth International Congress on Criminology, Lisbon, 1978; chairman of Section 1, third International Symposium on Victimology, Münster, 1979, and a member of its advisory board; vice-chairman of the Working-Group, Committee 1, sixth UN Congress on the Prevention of Crime and the Treatment of Offenders, Caracas, 1980; vice-chairman of the ad hoc meeting on the implementation of the Second United Nations Survey of World Crime Trends and Crime Prevention Strategies, Rutgers—The State University of New Jersey, 1981.